Prison Librarianship
Policy and Practice

# Prison Librarianship Policy and Practice

SUZANNA CONRAD

McFarland & Company, Inc., Publishers
*Jefferson, North Carolina*

ISBN (print) 978-1-4766-6633-4
ISBN (ebook) 978-1-4766-2702-1

LIBRARY OF CONGRESS CATALOGUING DATA ARE AVAILABLE

BRITISH LIBRARY CATALOGUING DATA ARE AVAILABLE

Front cover image of library © 2017 Izabela Habur/iStock;
*background* prison fence © 2017 Elerium/iStock

Printed in the United States of America

*McFarland & Company, Inc., Publishers
Box 611, Jefferson, North Carolina 28640
www.mcfarlandpub.com*

# Acknowledgments

First, I would like to thank the practitioners who helped document the practices within their correctional institutions by participating in a national survey and in individual interviews. Both the survey results and the interviews show that these librarians and library staff are at times overwhelmed and understaffed. I appreciate the time that they took to contribute to my research, especially the 11 interview participants who spent anywhere from 30 to 90 minutes to discuss their work.

I would also like to thank Cal Poly Pomona University Library and the institution in general for providing support for this project. This includes the Institutional Review Board whose staff and chair provided timely and helpful feedback on approaching my research. The financial support from various grants was also extremely helpful in completing this research in a timely manner. Thank you to the Research Office for providing funding for time to complete the book through the Research, Scholarship, and Creative Activity (RSCA) program. Thank you to Faculty Affairs for providing assigned time under the Teacher-Scholar Program. Also, thank you to the Faculty Center for providing a Faculty Mini-Grant, which was used to administer the mailed portion of the national survey and to purchase materials.

Thank you to the confidential peer reviewers who provided excellent feedback on the draft of the book.

I'd also like to thank the state prison's warden and correctional officers who allowed me to tour their facility including their libraries and education department.

Thank you to Alison De Almeida who served as a student research assistant on the project. Her attention to detail has been an enormous help in delivering a cleaner manuscript. I am sure she will blossom into an excellent editor!

Lastly, I'd like to thank my husband Oliver Conrad and the Yaukey family for cheering me along the way. Writing a book is a multi-year endeavor and both my husband and family encouraged me to stay on track and finish.

# Table of Contents

# Preface

This book is an exploration comparing policy to practice within prison libraries. National and state policies, scholarly and trade literature, and relevant court cases on prisoners' rights to library and legal materials services are all discussed and presented. Later parts of the book address the neglected nature of the prison librarian profession and detail partnerships between public and prison libraries, and present research from a national survey and from eleven interviews with practicing prison librarians. The results of this research are tied back to national and state policies, showing disconnects between outdated policies and current practice.

Not enough is written about prison librarianship, nor is the profession well served with national and state policies. My experience inside a prison library is limited to a tour of a state prison facility; otherwise I do not encounter the day-to-day challenges that active prison librarians must face; all of the representations in this book are therefore from the approach of an outside researcher. As a non-practitioner, my interest in the topic is curiosity and an interest in ethics in librarianship; prisoners stand to benefit heavily from good library services, but are often not afforded access because of heavily controlled environments.

Most of the research in this book covers policy and practice in state and federal prisons. Topics that frequently emerge when discussing prison librarianship include the purpose of the prison library, administration, general library services, library needs assessment, collection development, intellectual freedom, prisoners' rights, privacy, and access to legal materials whether through law libraries or other means. Research from chapters 8 and 9 focuses on practices within U.S. penal institutions.

Other important recently published works on this topic include *The Prison Library Primer: A Program for the Twenty-First Century* by Brenda Vogel, *Library Services to the Incarcerated: Applying the Public Library Model in Correctional Facility Libraries* by Sheila Clark and Erica MacCreaigh, and *Reading Is My Window: Books and the Art of Reading in Women's Prisons* by Megan Sweeney. Vogel has written a wealth of literature on the topic of prison librarianship and her work continues to remain relevant. Additionally, contributions from Larry E. Sullivan, Vibeke Lehmann, Glennor Shirley, and Rhea Joyce Rubin incorporate additional perspectives from both practitioners and researchers. Most publications on prison librarianship are practical guides or experiences, little scholarly research is being published in book form on this topic.

Unfortunately, scholarship on the topic has waned in the last decade; this decline started in the 1980s. The field needs a new leader, one who is a practitioner, to step forward and encourage national policies to be re-written and encourage more documentation and scholarship on the topic of prison librarianship.

# Introduction

There are more people incarcerated in the United States than ever before with numbers growing at an alarming rate. According to the American Correctional Association's *2013 Directory Adult and Juvenile Correctional Departments, Institutions, Agencies, and Probation and Parole Authorities* there are 1,369 adult state and private prisons in the United States.[1] It is difficult to determine the exact number of individuals incarcerated in these prisons in the United States currently, since no national census body has consistent reporting across different forms of incarceration. The Sentencing Project, an organization dedicated to reform in prison sentencing policy, claims that the United States has the most incarcerated persons in the world with 2.2 million prisoners. The Sentencing Project details the increase in incarcerated individuals by 500 percent over the last three decades, which has led to "prison overcrowding and state governments being overwhelmed by the burden of funding a rapidly expanding penal system."[2] Steven Raphael and Michael Stoll, in their 2013 book *Why Are So Many Americans in Prison?*, reference a higher number of incarcerated individuals than the Sentencing Project with an estimated total of 2.3 million at the end of 2009. In this book and in their previous book *Do Prisons Make Us Safer?*, Raphael and Stoll also discuss the rapid increase of prison populations over the last few decades, mentioning such reasons as increases in sentencing for illegal drug trade, the "deinstitutionalization of the mentally ill," less opportunities for work for low-skilled trades, and a progressively more punitive prison system.[3]

With this ever-increasing number of prisoners entering correctional institutions yearly, the prison library has frequently been mentioned as a means of providing escape from the day-to-day harshness of incarceration. But this is not a population easily assisted with services library patrons might encounter in public libraries, schools, or institutions of higher education. Inherent restrictions centered on the need to maintain security prevent many standard public library services from being offered and may also necessitate prison administration censorship of certain types of materials. Regardless, many agree that prisoners maintain certain constitutional rights while incarcerated, which can be fulfilled and maintained through the use of a prison library or prison law library.

Many state and national library associations speak out against inequities especially when related to the freedom to read. The American Library Association continues to update its *Intellectual Freedom Manual*, a vehicle for espousing the association's stance on the library's role in facilitating intellectual freedom. Prisoners, however, appear to be in a grey area, rarely explicitly included in general policies by national associations. While the American Library Association does acknowledge prisoner constitutional rights with the "Prisoners' Right to Read," few similar policies have been published or established and even that policy includes mandates for censorship of certain materials. Other policies from state associations, state department(s) of corrections, and similar bodies are likewise vague, ambiguous, or non-existent when it comes to policy on prison librarianship. This includes collection development policies and what rights prisoners maintain while incarcerated, which might be affected by the adequacy and appropriateness of a prison library collection. In practice, even more ambiguities appear to exist; authors frequently cite the contradictions of maintaining security and providing access to materials.

Brenda Vogel, a well-published former prison librarian, who won the *Library Journal* Librarian of the Year award in 1989 for raising awareness of her field, mentions the dilemma of this neglected patron group, stating: "It is pleasing and puzzling to find that correctional library programs have continued to hang on and in a few cases thrive even without credible research to awaken the public or the policy maker to their contribution, in spite of being without an active constituency, organized advocates, or national and local correctional association recognition."[4]

This book, *Prison Librarianship Policy and Practice*, was authored to further investigate discrepancies between policy and practice. The book discusses the reasons and implications for lack of research and scholarship in this field from researchers or practitioners with valuable contributions to share.

The explorations presented in this book are important because prison libraries are drifting in many states. Some states have de-professionalized or even eliminated the librarian positions that used to be required by national correctional and library policies. Prison libraries fight for non-existent budgets and face challenges providing relevant programming to prison patrons. The peril of many of these libraries affects the librarian profession since positions that used to be available to skilled librarians at reasonable pay rates are no longer offered in some states. Libraries are easy targets for correctional administration, often absorbed by or taken over by other units. This is easily something that could, and has, happened in other areas of librarianship.

The consequences of the drifting and in some cases shrinking prison library does not just affect professional librarians; library services, which have frequently been viewed as rehabilitative, are slowly reduced or impacted. Prisoners have limited resources to assist them with re-entering the community and have less to do in idle time. While there are no studies correlating the effects of the prison library on community safety or ex-prisoner outcomes, the effects of illiteracy certainly impact the level of success a prisoner can achieve once released.

There are certain ideals that attract individuals to the career of librarianship. As a practicing academic librarian and former public librarian who believes in intellectual freedom, I sincerely believe that individuals should have the right to make decisions about what they read and what they think. While completing my Master of Library and Information Science (MLIS), I came across an article about the Steven Hayes trial. Hayes was on trial for a host of horrible crimes against the Petit family in Connecticut. Because Hayes had previously been incarcerated, the prosecution was requesting that his prior reading lists be included as evidence, since many of the books he had read depicted violent crime. The media postulated that this list included the award-winning true crime work *In Cold Blood* by Truman Capote.

I was in the midst of completing an ethics course when I read about Hayes and the prosecution's attempt to include his reading lists as part of his trial. As a student with ethics and privacy issues fresh in my mind, I had two fundamental questions about this attempt—why were the records retained in the first place, and second, was it acceptable to categorically deny prisoners the right to certain award-winning reading materials? This was troubling to me; while I do understand that providing materials on bomb-making, lock-picking, and certain other materials may indeed threaten the security of the institution, the line between protecting security and heavily violating rights to intellectual freedom could quickly become a slippery slope. Throughout this book, the challenge of finding a balance between policy and practice continues to emerge; prison librarians have to weigh administrative constraints against their instincts as trained librarians.

The ambiguities between policy and practice spawned my interest in writing this book as many of the practices within correctional institutions seem to, sometimes out of necessity, deviate from the basic principles and ethics of librarianship. How can administrators and librarians find compromises in an environment where the patronage could heavily benefit from the educational and rehabilitative opportunities of a library, especially one run like a public library? This book will address this question through literature, policy, and case law review followed by qualitative research on the prison library experience in practice.

While some state and national policies dictate that a prison library be modeled after a public library focused to serve its constituents, practice often deviates from this ideal, especially when considering the security needs of the institution. Partnerships with public libraries are described throughout this book, with a particular emphasis in chapter 7; these partnerships include such services as interlibrary loan, materials donations, partnerships for family and early literacy, and reentry programs that increase prisoner awareness of public library support after incarceration.

According to the Association of Specialized and Cooperative Library Agencies' guidelines, the term correctional institution refers to "prisons, penitentiaries, classification and reception centers, correctional institutions, treatment centers, prerelease units, work camps, boot camps and shock incarceration centers" and the guidelines only apply to institutions with more than 300 prisoners.[5] Vibeke Lehmann and Joanne Locke's guidelines apply to institutions with more than 50 incarcerated individuals and they define a correctional institution as the following: "All facilities where individuals are held in incarceration. These facilities may be referred to as prisons, jails, remand centers, detention centers, forensic hospitals, or other types of institutions administered by the prison authorities."[6]

For the purposes of this book, all qualitative research will focus on federal and state adult correctional institutions with at least 50 incarcerated prisoners. Jails and detention centers are mentioned in some of the literature and in court cases, but often have less stringent requirements for provision of library service or access to legal materials due to the shorter sentences of prisoners incarcerated in those institutions. Federal and state institutions are subject to federal or state-wide policies, which are more accessible to the public than individual jail policies created by counties. According to the American Correctional Association (ACA), the average prison sentence is 33.40 months and most convicted criminals serve 67.94 percent of their sentencing time.[7] Because of longer sentences in prisons and this accountability to national and state bodies, this book and the corresponding research have been focused to look at state and federal institutions. This focus is not intended to be a devaluation of the services offered in jails; many jail library programs are well led and flourishing.

## History of Prison Libraries

Rhea Joyce Rubin claims that the first prison in the United States was established in Nantucket in 1676. The first jail, and also the first institution to offer religious book service to prisoners through the Prison Society, was the Walnut Street Jail in Pennsylvania, which was built in 1773.[8] The Walnut Street Jail was an example to other institutions; many of the early prison libraries and outreach programs were similarly stocked with Bibles and religious literature. *The Oxford History of the Prison: the Practice of Punishment in Western Society* refers to the late nineteenth century educational programs in prisons as "rudimentary educational programs, prison libraries, and the intercessions of official chaplains" and states that they "affected only an insignificant portion of the prison population."[9] Adam Hirsch describes the approach of solitude as a means of correcting behavior and preventing "moral contagion" with the intervention of the church and Bible.[10] Megan Sweeney also cites the importance of religious reading works in early U.S. prisons, which were provided with the goal of initiating moral change.[11] Larry Sullivan and Brenda Vogel reference the historic role of the prison library and mention that institutions have "attempted to improve character through reading since the inception of the penitentiary in the late eighteenth century."[12]

Administration of early U.S. prisons was commonly influenced by two debating approaches to imprisonment: labor and solitude. Hirsch discusses these two views of criminal incarceration. Redirecting criminally minded prisoners to keep busy was an idea influenced by sixteen century English politics; Hirsch cites a critique in 1596 from Edward Hext as one of the first to encourage more workhouses and hard labor for incarcerated individuals.[13] The concept of seclusion as a rehabilitative force also began to emerge; philanthropists in the mid to late eighteenth century began to discuss the role of solitude in allowing criminals to reflect upon past crimes.[14] This conflict between the prison as the workhouse and as a place for solitary reflection was occurring in the decades prior to the establishment of Castle Island in Massachusetts, the first state prison established in the United States in 1785. With the establishment of the Eastern State Penitentiary 50 years later in 1829, this idea of solitary confinement as a means of penitence persisted. Per historical descriptions from the Eastern State Penitentiary website, "proponents of the system believed strongly that criminals, exposed, in silence, to thoughts of their behavior and the ugliness of their crimes, would become genuinely penitent."[15] Meanwhile, the state of New York established the Auburn Prison in the early 1820s, with a focus on labor over solitary confinement.[16]

As the concepts of labor and solitude were debated and implemented in various constellations in new institutions, such as Auburn and Eastern, prison libraries, if they existed, were primarily restricted to religious reading materials.[17] Other institutions gradually began to add secular reading materials in the early nineteenth century. Multiple authors mention the instigation of an in-house prison library in 1802 in Kentucky State Penitentiary, which included non-religious works in its collection. Heiress Linda Gilbert, as part of her "Gilbert Library and Prisoners' Aid Society," initiated a number of prison libraries in the 1800s.[18] In New York's Sing Sing prison in 1844, secular materials also began to be offered to prisoners; newly appointed matron Eliza Farnham began encouraging prisoners to read materials that were not explicitly religious in nature, evoking controversy and criticism from prison administration.[19] Farnham's efforts were part of a campaign for phrenology, a new approach at the time to combat, diagnose, and cure criminal behavior. The Walnut Street Jail, the first to offer religious reading materials to prisoners as early as 1773, also started stocking non-religious books in 1853.[20]

In these decades prior to the Civil War, a few instances similar to Farnham's approach of diagnosing and curing through scientific method began emerging in the North and continued after the war resolved. Kathrina Litchfield cites the instigation of the National Prison Congress in establishing the basic principles of "rehabilitation over retribution, criminal classification, probation, and education" as future focuses for reform.[21]

Even though books, including secular works, were more accessible to prison populations, the prison library or some form of recreational reading was not necessarily guaranteed to prisoners prior to the Civil War. In the decades following the Civil War, Northern states continued to be at the forefront of providing prison library service. According to Jonathan Abel, by 1873 all Northern states had libraries in prisons.[22] The New York Prison Association established what may be viewed as the first prison library policy in 1877 with the publication of *Catalogue and Rules for Prison Libraries to Aid in the Suitable Selection and Economical Maintenance of Reading Matter in the Prisons and Jails.*[23] Nevertheless, often these services were deemed to be inadequate. In 1909, Miriam E. Carey of the ALA Committee on Hospital and Institution Libraries conducted a survey documenting the insufficiency of prison library collections.[24] Other education policies were developed that affected the prison library; in 1931, *The Education of Adult Prisoners* was published, which included passages on the effects of reading.[25] Studies from the American Library Association were published about prison libraries in the early 1930s. Around the same time, the American Correctional Association published the first prison library manual.[26]

During the 1950s, the approach of prison administration continued to change to be more rehabilitative in nature. This was most evident in the 1954 renaming of the American Prison Association's title to the American Correctional Association.[27] Bibliotherapy also became a more prevalent discussion in the 1950s in California prison libraries through the work and recommendations of Herman Spector, Dr. C.V. Morrison, and James A. Quinn.[28]

In 1966, Congress passed the Library Services and Construction Act (LSCA), which provided matching funds for institutional libraries in states, thereby vastly improving the condition of prison libraries, services, and talent employed in the libraries.[29] Lehmann discusses the benefits of this act, especially for the funding allocated to library services in correctional institutions. According to Lehmann, minimum funding levels were established, which initiated many otherwise non-existent library services as well as created librarian positions.[30] This act would have been passed at the height of the rehabilitative movement within prison administration; research on bibliotherapy had also gained traction in the prior decade. Additionally, prisoner voices were reaching the public; in 1954, Caryl Chessman's bestselling book *Cell 2455 Death Row* was published, which detailed his experiences as a death row prisoner in a California prison.[31] Subsequent publications from California prisoners included books from authors Eldridge Cleaver, Bobby Seale, George Jackson, and Huey Newton.[32] As the Civil Rights Movement progressed during this same period, prisoners' voices began to be heard by the nation. The combination of the gradual move to a rehabilitative approach in prisons, bibliotherapy initiatives, and the Civil Rights Movement seem to all be factors in the inclusion of institutional library services in the LSCA Act from

1966. Gervase Brinkman lauded the effects of the LSCA Act in an *American Libraries* article from 1970, stating that the LSCA "contributed significantly to the improvement of library services for the forgotten Americans in state institutions" and that "state institutions should begin to experience the real value of good library service as an instrument of healing and rehabilitation."[33] Unfortunately, when the Library Services and Technology Act passed in 1997, these designated funds from the LSCA evaporated, which was likely a strong influence on the steady decline of the prison library and especially the move to eliminate professional prison librarian positions that persists today.

Multiple authors mention the hands-off doctrine that existed prior to the Civil Rights Movement. According to Michael Mushlin, the hands-off doctrine was the federal courts' refusal to intervene in prisoners' rights issues. He states: "The Constitution did not breach prison walls for over 170 years. Indeed, during most of the history of this country, there was some question as to whether prisoners had any constitutional rights at all."[34] Both Vogel and *The Oxford History of the Prison* reassert Mushlin's theory that the Civil Rights Movement encouraged the loosening and disappearance of the hands-off doctrine. Court cases involving prisoners' rights became more frequent with groundbreaking lawsuits such as *Bounds v. Smith* in 1977 establishing prisoners' rights to access legal materials in libraries. *The Oxford History of the Prison* states: "the recognition of the needs of inmates for successful integration into society … paved the way for the recognition of their rights."[35] The prison library served the purpose of providing services pursuant to prisoners' rights. Abel mentions the evolution of the prison library to the prison law library, stating: "In fact, prison law libraries emerged from a larger tradition of general-interest prison libraries whose goals were to provide religious and secular education, to rehabilitate prisoners psychologically and socially, and to distract prisoners from the monotony of institutional life."[36]

Other authors present the role of the prison library in fulfilling legal requirements to provide access to the courts. Mushlin defines the right of access to the courts as "the most basic of the rights possessed by inmates; certainly it is the foundation for every other right an inmate has." He further stresses the importance of this right, because "without access, inmates have no way of vindicating their rights through judicial action."[37] Mushlin details the requirements for satisfying the meaningful access mandate in his four-volume book *Rights of Prisoners*. He discusses the history of the right including relevant court cases and resolutions. He also describes a number of different ways to fulfill meaningful access, one of which is the provision of a law library. Mushlin provides information on the recommendations from court case *Bounds v. Smith* and also mentions a publication from the American Association of Law Libraries (AALL) Special Interest Section on Contemporary Social Problems, both of which provide a basic list of what to collect in a prison law library.[38] There may be recommended texts for provision of law library services, but there are not currently any comprehensive standards besides recommendation lists from the AALL. Individual state authorities and sometimes policies in individual institutions seem to guide these selections, if legal library materials are provided at all.

In the 1980s, the previously fruitful partnership between the ALA and the ACA began to deteriorate. This was primarily influenced by the 1982 ALA publication of the "Resolution on Prisoners' Right to Read." Multiple interviewees from chapter 9 discuss the dissolution of this partnership and the effects that the lack of central corrections policy has had on the role and importance of the prison library within their institutions. At the same time, increased convictions from the War on Drugs in the 1980s led to the not so gradual increase in incarcerated populations, which ultimately have caused current overpopulation in prisons.

Even the prison law library, despite the 1977 *Bounds v. Smith* ruling, has not always maintained its necessity as a core prison library service. This is mostly a result of the landmark case *Lewis v. Casey* and the passing of the Prison Litigation Reform Act in 1996. *Lewis v. Casey* required that actual injury be shown by prisoners claiming violations of their constitutional rights to meaningful access to the courts, thereby limiting the number of cases involving inadequate legal collections in prison libraries. As a result, a number of states closed their prison law libraries and began offering alternative legal assistance instead. The Prison Litigation Reform Act (PLRA) was passed by Congress to control what was seen as excessive prisoner litigation in federal courts. A number of organizations lobbying for prisoners' rights, including the group Human Rights Watch, have objected to some of the restrictive clauses of the PLRA. This group specifically states that the PLRA "undermines both the public interest and US human rights obligations."[39] Regardless of those who contest the legislation in the PLRA, it still remains in effect for the purposes of reducing excessive and frivolous prisoner litigation.

## The Role of Education in Prisons

In many prison systems the general prison library is offered as a service of the education department or unit. This linkage is not always as intuitive or helpful as might be presumed; often prison libraries report to the education department but may not be prioritized as much as other services within that department. Regardless, the roles and connections to education departments in prisons are still worthy of investigation.

Researchers have frequently shown that prisoners have been educationally disadvantaged prior to incarceration, especially when compared to the general public. Caroline Wolf Harlow, for instance, collected statistics in 1997 about the number of prisoners in federal and state prisons that had a high school diploma or the equivalent and found that about 41 percent had not completed high school.[40] She states that "correctional populations report lower educational attainment than do those in the general population."[41]

The presumed role of education in reducing recidivism is also frequently discussed in literature on education in prison. The ACA reports that the average rate of recidivism in 2013 was 42.6 percent across genders.[42] In a study published by Laura Winterfield, Mark Coggeshall, Michelle Burke-Storer, Vanessa Correa, and Simon Tidd in 2009, education was deemed to have a role in reducing recidivism: "Increasing educational proficiency has shown promise as one strategy for assisting inmates in finding gainful employment after release and ending their involvement with the criminal justice system."[43] Within this study the authors investigate the effects of post-secondary education (PSE) on the rates of recidivism in three states. While they only find that PSE showed "promise" as a strategy for reducing repeat offenses due to questionable results and statistical significance of the findings, the authors did find that "involvement in PSE affects inmate behavior and creates a safer prison environment."[44] Similarly, Gerald Gaes reviews a number of studies on prison education and brings attention to some of the poor research design in many studies. Nevertheless, he finds that the general results from most studies report that education assists with successful reintegration in the community.[45] Furthermore, he states that "strong observational studies support a conclusion that correctional education reduces recidivism and enhances employment outcomes."[46] The educational priorities of the institution may positively or adversely affect the success of the prison library depending on how important prison library service is to administration when compared to other potential educational priorities. As will be shown in subsequent chapters with detailed surveys and interviews, the inclusion of the library under educational programs often leads to a lower prioritization of library services.

## The Role of the Prison Library

In her well-known and comprehensive text *Prison Library Primer*, Brenda Vogel mentions the prison libraries' role in providing reentry materials among countless other library services.[47] Vogel, with her history as a prison librarian and prolific writer, provides many insights on the purpose and role of the prison library. In a *Library Journal* article from 1997, Vogel discusses the importance of the library and similar programs for encouraging successful reentry so that the prisoner, upon release, is not "unprepared to function crime-free after confinement."[48] Furthermore, she asserts that there has to be some balance between punishment and protection and that "the denial of reading and libraries furthers punishment."[49] Vogel also mentions that there are no laws, court decisions, or constitutional rights that ensure access to a prison library.[50]

Vibeke Lehmann, a seasoned prison librarian who previously worked at a correctional institution in Wisconsin, has frequently published on the topic of prison librarianship. In an article from 2000, she states: "One can safely say that incarcerated persons have a large number of unmet needs, which translate into a high demand for information, learning materials, and self-improvement resources; the library, in cooperation with other prison programs, can play a vital role in meeting these needs. Inmates who want to use their time constructively are likely to become avid library users."[51]

Other practitioners mention the role of the prison library as a respite from daily prison life and a means for the incarcerated to understand and maintain their health and wellness, develop academic, vocational, or social skills, and seek guidance or tools for overcoming difficult times in their lives.[52] Julia Schneider and Ron Chepesiuk write of the difference that prison libraries can make if supported by administrators and librarians.[53] In an article from Jenna Scafuri in *Corrections Today*, she claims 92 percent of prisoners use the general interest reading libraries in prisons in Colorado.[54] Few seem to dispute the place and purpose for the prison library, but as will be seen in some of the policies, the prison library often is not given the administrative power that might allow services to be offered that parallel those available to the greater public. Based on the research from the later chapters of this book, the success of an individual prison library program appears to be linked to the current administration in that particular institution. With a new warden, policies may be interpreted differently and the role of the prison library may gain or lose importance as a fundamental service for prisoners.

## Controversies Surrounding Prison Libraries

There is frequent debate between delivering punishment to convicted criminals and offering respite through books, libraries, and other educational programs. Public opinion often encourages retribution without much consideration of the realities of incarceration. Many might believe that prisoners, once convicted, have foregone many of the rights they might enjoy in the world outside prison. Certainly, many rights of prisoners are necessarily restricted when incarcerated whether for purposes of security or retribution. Few, however, argue that prisoners should not have the right to read.

Occasionally, prisoners' reading habits make the news. As mentioned earlier in this chapter, in 2010 there were a handful of articles surrounding Steven Hayes' trial in Connecticut and the exclusion of some of his reading lists from evidence. Hayes was convicted of a combination of crimes including murder, rape, robbery, and arson in a gruesome case where the Petit family mother and two daughters were brutally murdered. According to an article in the *New York Times*, prosecutors believed that Hayes had read true crime novels during a previous incarceration and that these novels may have provided guidance in his eventual crimes against the Petit family.[55] The author of this article surmised that Hayes might have read *In Cold Blood* by Truman Capote, or *The Girl with the Dragon Tattoo*, both of which include explicit scenes. Ultimately the defense attorneys were able to have the reading lists excluded since the inclusion of these materials was considered prejudicial to Hayes.[56]

The Hayes trial and discussion around his prior prison reading lists led to a larger inquiry from Connecticut Senator John Kissel, who contacted the Department of Corrections and prison officials to determine what kinds of materials were available to prisoners. Kissel encouraged a policy change that would prevent prisoners from reading any materials including violent scenes.[57] Exactly how many works or what kinds of works would be excluded were not clear from Kissel's comments, however, he did mention that if works were not currently excluded in Connecticut prison library policies, he would pursue legislation to have these works excluded.[58]

This inquiry by Kissel expanded to an Associated Press investigation in which they reviewed policies in Connecticut correctional institutions and determined that a number of books were in circulation in prisons that depicted violent activities including such works as Capote's *In Cold Blood*, Ann Rule's *If You Really Loved Me*, and *Along Came a Spider* by James Patterson. According to the Associated Press, "inmates in Connecticut prisons have access to true crime books and works of fiction that depict murder and graphic violence, with no apparent restrictions based on a reader's criminal history."[59] The Associated Press investigation also notes that other policies and directives in effect in Connecticut prisons were far more detailed than those concerning libraries.[60]

A number of institutions, including the American Civil Liberties Union of Connecticut and the American Library Association, issued responses to Kissel and the Associated Press report. The ACLU released statements that they would protest bans such as the ones Kissel proposed.[61] Deborah Caldwell-Stone, the Deputy Director of the American Library Association, points out that there was no correlation or evidence linking reading and crime and that blanket removal of violent works was therefore unwarranted.[62] Beverly Goldberg, writing for *American Libraries*, mentions that Kissel and prison administration intended to revise policy based on the policies established by federal prison libraries to determine "how those policies balance prison security against the threat of First Amendment lawsuits."[63]

News coverage of this case waned after 2010, but Kissel's attempts and successes at reform were mentioned in the Connecticut Department of Correction 2010 Annual Report. Specifically, a development of a new "Sexually Explicit Materials Ban" is mentioned that is, according to the report, a result of a study of similar policies across the United States. The annual report also mentions a new library policy that may have been developed as a result of the Hayes trial controversy; this policy was authored by the Division's Standards and Policies Office after review of the Federal Bureau of Prisons' similar policy.[64] The two policies discussed in this report appear to be two administrative directives: "Inmate Communications" (10.7) and a new directive "Library Services" (10.16).

The "Inmate Communications" administrative directive closely follows the Department of Corrections, Title 18, Sections 18–81–28 through 18–81–51. The obvious additions in the directive include the reliance on a "Media Review Board" to review questionable or objectionable materials and more detailed descriptions of the kinds of materials that should be excluded.[65] In the Title 18 sections, the Media Review Board is not referenced, rather the Unit Administrator appeared to have the purview to make review decisions.[66] This review board was not initiated by administrative directive 10.7; a "Publication Review Board" or "Media Review Board" is mentioned in all annual reports found on the Connecticut Department of Correction's website. Annual reports dating back to 2007 were found. It is, nevertheless, interesting to note that the amount of items being reviewed increased drastically in most of the last few years since the Hayes controversy. In 2011, reviews of materials were up by 35 percent (from 2,007 to 2,716 items reviewed). In 2012, only a 17 percent increase was seen (from 2,716 to 3,181), but in 2013, a 41 percent increase happened (from 3,181 to 4,493 items reviewed). If 2013 is compared to 2007, the first date an annual report was found, a 223 percent increase is shown.[67] It seems likely that Kissel's campaign to increase review of explicit material was effective. Yet, this policy appears to also be the policy that received negative press in August 2013.

According to an article in the *Hartford Courant*, the Media Review Board had banned a Wally Lamb novel on the basis of some sexually explicit passages. Complaints led the book to be reinstated and called for a revision of the policy. The Media Review Board, as of August 2013, consisted of 17 department employees including one prison librarian.[68] Other journalists also commented on the new review processes as excessive; a *National Journal* article from Matt Berman, also from August 2013, criticizes some of the choices of the Media Review Board including banning some parts of the *Game of Thrones* series. Berman also links to documents listing the banned books from an August 2013 meeting.[69]

The second directive on library services that appeared to be a result of Kissel's initiatives also included a "Library Materials Review Committee." This committee should, according to the directive, consist of three members appointed by the Unit Administrator. Members should include library staff, security staff, and a representative of the Unit Administrator. The library staff does have some discretion to review materials within this directive, but must forward questionable materials to the review committee.[70] The language in this directive, like Directive 10.7, is very similar to the language included in the Title 18 Sections.

The Hayes trial received much coverage in the press, especially due to the discussion of the defendant's prior reading choices potentially spurring his later criminal actions. But this is not the first time that controversies about prison reading materials have made the news. In 1995, an article in *American Libraries* mentioned the censoring of Holloway House and Jackie Collins books from South Carolina prisons. The Director of Library Services Dick Coolidge states: "most prison libraries buy them. They're probably the most frequently read books we have." In this case, the media had been alerted to the books' presence in the prisons from a former corrections department employee. The subsequent media coverage fueled the decision to remove the books from South Carolina libraries. Within this article, the innovative nature of the program in South Carolina is also mentioned; Coolidge specifically, discusses some of the additional programs they have to keep prisoners occupied such as pet therapy, arts and crafts, and discussion groups. These programs are geared toward illiterate prisoners.[71] Less than six months later, this innovative program was eliminated. Many prison library programs in South Carolina were closed or repurposed; many attributed these changes to the new governor's stance that the public wanted to see more punishment in prisons. A pet therapy program was eliminated as well as a trustee program for seventeen prisoners.[72] Included in these reforms was also a new review process for book purchasing, which was deemed to be especially "cumbersome," requiring multiphase approval from various stakeholders.[73] Sources felt that the library was demoted to only being able to provide reading materials to prisoners, not to make additional impact on illiterate populations.

Other journalists draw attention to prisoner inequities generally in the news. In Colin Dayan's *Boston Review* article from 2007, he discusses inherent human rights violations caused by restricting access to certain newspapers and magazines from prisoners involved in the *Beard v. Banks* case.[74] Dayan argues that prisoners are already subject to the "highly abnormal condition" of incarceration and that prisoners should still maintain certain rights to read what they want.[75]

## Summary

Even in this brief introduction, the disparities between attitudes about prison library service amongst legislators, prison administration, prison librarians, and the public leave one confused about policy and practice. As an outsider to the field it is easy to make statements about what seems ethical as a practicing librarian. This is especially natural to do when considering core principles of librarianship such as intellectual freedom as espoused by the American Library Association. But this is, of course, not that clear cut. Prisoners have lost certain rights by losing their freedom and some measures must be taken to ensure the security of the institution. Each institution will also have its own administration, which may or may not see the educational, recreational, and rehabilitative value of a prison library. Since many individual prison library policies are admittedly vague, interpretations may change from one administrator to the next.

Throughout my investigations, I have been continually impressed by the practicing prison librarians who have participated in my surveys and interviews. I am not a practitioner; all correspondence with the participants in my survey and interviews were aware of my affiliation. Instead of being met with judgment by practitioners viewing me as an outsider, I was greeted by those who were excited that someone was interested in telling and representing their stories. I have hopes that non-practitioner works such as mine could inspire these individuals to share their own experiences more broadly.

Many of the interviewees from chapter 9, who were all practicing prison librarians or recently retired prison librarians, talked about general roles of the prison library. Respondent Heather described her experiences working with the prison library population as more rewarding than her previous public library experience because of the ability to make a difference in reaching underserved populations:

> I know in the public library sector they talked a lot about reaching the underserved portions of the country, the underserved neighborhoods, the underserved people.... If you really want to work with an underserved population that would definitely be the inmate population. Their reading levels are low—if they've got a ninth grade reading level, you know that's good. You know most of them don't read that well. A lot of them have learning disabilities. They're not developmentally disabled necessarily, but they've always had trouble in school let's say. So they're very appreciative of you—well most of the time they are—about you taking the time to talk to them about whatever it is that is on their mind. They have a very convoluted idea about the administrative justice system. They tend to be very narrowly focused. Everything's always about them. You can tell that they're people who have never really engaged with their community other than in a criminal way. They don't really have a broad area of contact with the culture like most library users do out in the world. So it's really a challenge to work with them and it's really interesting to see because as you know there's a huge percentage of the population that's incarcerated.

Interviewee Jennifer talked of the role that a prison librarian can play in giving people second chances. She told one story about a prisoner she gave a second chance:

> I had this one guy that never had any money so you had to give him a certain amount of stuff because he was there in court. You have to constantly give him envelopes or stamps or whatever it is. And I finally was just like, "I'm tired of this person, I'm going to hire him." And he was, this forty-five-year old guy! So I hired him and he really couldn't do anything, so one of his jobs was like cutting up scrap paper. But it was the first job that he had ever had in his entire life and all of the sudden he had coworkers—my other clerks—because they kind of hang together and talk and chit chat. So he had some friends that weren't the same as the people in the units and then he had enough money and he bought himself a radio. And watching him change from so angry to all of the sudden, you know, "I could pay off these debts. You know I don't have to be this nasty old man" ... you have to be willing to step up and talk to prisoners and think about your whole job. Your job is the Department of Corrections, we're helping them become better people ... some of them do.... I read a statistic or a prisoner book or whatever and what keeps people out of prison instead of coming back is that they don't want to disappoint somebody who believed in them while they were in prison. Somebody has to be able to talk to them and give them that kind of encouragement.

Policy details the role of the prison library, but the interviews presented in chapter 9 bring a human element to the role of the prison librarian. These interviews, while they speak to practice in prison libraries, also highlight what the experience is like as a prison librarian.

Within this book, I review and analyze existing policies on prison librarianship, present and discuss literature on the topic, and provide information about a number of court cases disputing prisoners' rights to library service, meaningful access to the courts, or other debates about prisoners' right to read. In some cases, the literature on prison librarianship is rather lean both for widely published policies and for scholarship on the topic. My approach in this book is as an outside researcher, so it was necessary to gain some sort of perspective about what is actually happening inside some of the correctional institutions across the United States. This was accomplished through qualitative research conducted with actual practitioners. This method allows me to present more information about day-to-day practices in prison libraries, so that this can be compared to relevant policy. Much of the existing literature on prison librarianship details the profession and how to successfully manage a prison library. Since I am not a prison librarian, providing how-to advice is not sensible. My contribution is instead an attempt to look at a professional field of librarianship without bias and try to determine reasons for the ambiguities between policy and practice.

This book consists of nine chapters in three parts. The first part, "The Prison Library in Context: Current and Historic Purposes and Policies of Prison Libraries," includes a review of prison library policies and literature. This part is broken into three chapters. The first chapter reviews current and historic prison library policies in the United States that are national in scope. The second chapter analyzes state prison library policies and these policies' adherence to national standards. The third chapter presents recent literature on key issues in prison librarianship. These chapters provide some background including current policies in place nationally and at the state level.

The second part of this book, "Neglect and Disadvantage: The Prison Library as the Forgotten Field of Librarianship," consists of four chapters. Chapters 4 and 5 present a discussion of court cases related to constitutional rights violations such as the right to read and the right to meaningful access to the courts. Additionally, these chapters include detailed bibliographies of court cases that touch upon these constitutional rights issues. Finding literature on prison librarianship is also no small feat nor are the curricula in library science particularly focused on this field; in chapter 6, I discuss the lack of national policies when compared to other fields of librarianship, assess and analyze the frequency of scholarly publications on prison librarianship in the last few decades, and review the curricula from current graduate schools offering library and information science degrees to determine if prison librarianship is promoted as a career alternative for new graduates. Chapter 7 includes a discussion of the public library model for prison library service and also presents some examples of current partnerships between public organizations and prison libraries.

Part three of this book, "Research and Discovery," includes two chapters with qualitative research. Chapter 8 includes results and discussion from a national survey of prison librarians, which was developed as an expansion of my previous exploratory research on prison librarianship published in *The Library Quarterly* in 2012. This survey, even though it is not comprehensive enough to be generalizable, certainly highlights the ambiguities of policymaking in prison libraries while also showing the challenges that many of these librarians may face. Chapter 9 takes this research a step further by presenting results from in-depth interviews with 11 prison librarians working in various states. Lastly, the conclusion summarizes the results from the preceding chapters including how my qualitative research relates to the policies and literature on the topic of prison librarianship.

I hope that this work can serve as a resource for those studying prison librarianship by providing a discussion of policies and literature from the last few decades. While I have amassed a lot of literature and data, along with qualitative research from surveys and interviews, this work still feels exploratory. Absolute comprehensiveness seems to be impossible without the backing of a major correctional body such as the American Correctional Association or the Association of Specialized and Cooperative Library Agencies.

I hope that this book can be a resource for active practitioners to understand what others in similar institutions may be doing to tackle challenges in the profession.

Many of the librarians I spoke to in the last chapter felt disconnected from other prison librarians and even other librarians in general. I hope that this work can help them gain perspective about how their institution's policies and practices compare to other institutions. Lastly, I hope that this research can incite more scholarly and professional interest in a field that has the potential of impacting not only the institution and its patrons, but also the broader community—a community that many of these patrons will eventually re-enter.

# List of Abbreviations

**AALL**—American Association of Law Libraries
**AASL**—American Association of School Librarians
**ABA**—American Bar Association
**ACA**—American Correctional Association
**ACLU**—American Civil Liberties Union
**ACRL**—Association of College and Research Libraries
**ALA**—American Library Association
**ALCTS**—Association for Library Collections and Technical Services
**ALSC**—Association of Library Service to Children
**ASCLA**—Association of Specialized and Cooperative Library Agencies
**BCC**—Blind Carbon Copy
**DOC**—Department of Corrections
**GED**—General Education Development
**IFLA**—International Federation of Library Associations and Institutions
**LAN**—Local Area Network
**LCSA**—Library Services and Construction Act
**LIS**—Library and Information Science
**LITA**—Library and Information Technology Association
**LLAMA**—Library Leadership and Management Association
**LMS**—Library Media Specialist
**LSTA**—Library Services and Technology Act
**MLIS**—Master of Library and Information Science
**MLS**—Master of Library Science
**PLA**—Public Library Association
**PLN**—Prison Legal News
**PLRA**—Prison Litigation Reform Act
**PSE**—Post-Secondary Education
**RUSA**—Reference and User Services Association
**SLA**—Special Libraries Association
**TASC**—Test Assessing Secondary Completion
**WAN**—Wide Area Network
**YALSA**—Young Adult Library Services Association

1

# Current and Historic
# National Policy

*They've just taken the browsing library, turning it into something else, a room that
they need, and distribute the books any which way to the units. So they're just books
on shelves. And the potential for the library to be an instrument or a support to the
programs is not considered. The potential of the library to help with vocabulary
because the vocabulary of any book is greater than the vocabulary on any television
show. And to be connected with the outside world through reading instead of just getting sound bites on the television. And so I'm trying to save the general library ...
and I don't have the support.*

—Linda, Interviewee from Chapter 9

*So now we're run by a completely different agency and in my opinion none of whom
are educators, or have ever been educators, never will be educators, so it's a very different environment for that in terms of bureaucracy and leadership and vision.... 
We've been, as a sub, sub agency, largely dismantled. The master's level of library science or information science or any of these—a master's is not required for these jobs
now. Anytime someone leaves, retires, whatever, the position is rewritten to require
a bachelor's of I think just about any field and no experience. So accordingly salaries
were notched down so it's different ... we used to have a headquarters of some sort
that gave us a centralized voice and also an organizing ordering place and that has
all been dismantled and defunded and the positions have been moved. So we're literally a whole bunch of lost fish in a foreign pond with no money.*

—Jack, Interviewee from Chapter 9

U.S. national policies on prison librarianship in adult correctional institutions have
been notably lacking in the last twenty years since the Association of Specialized and Cooperative Library Agencies (ASCLA) published the policy *Library Standards for Adult Correctional Institutions* in 1992. In the foreword to these standards, previous editions of library
standards for correctional institutions are discussed including the "Objectives and Standards
for Libraries in Adult Prisons and Reformatories" jointly published in 1944 by the American
Prison Association (now the American Correctional Association) and the American Library
Association (ALA). Additional editions from 1962 and 1966 are also mentioned, as well as
the previous *Library Standards for Adult Correctional Institutions* from 1981, all of which
involved some sort of joint effort from ALA and the ACA.

The ACA stopped authoring joint policies with the ALA after the 1982 publication of the "Resolution on Prisoners' Right to Read," which the ACA refused to adopt.[1] This means that the 1981 edition of these standards is the last policy regarding adult correctional institutions accepted by both the corrections community and the library community. Since the 1992 ASCLA standards were published, most standards for prison libraries have either been carried over from that publication, taken from the much less comprehensive ACA standards, or inferred from prisoner litigation related to library issues. In a previous article, I called for a revisiting of this policy in order to establish the current state of affairs in prison libraries.[2] Certainly the revision of this policy is long overdue and has been, according to some of the interview participants from chapter 9 and discussions on the ALA prison list-serv,[3] under discussion within ASCLA committees.

In this chapter, I will present and discuss policies and standards currently in place in many prison libraries, including these very outdated national policies, the most recent of which were only accepted by the library community and not the corrections community. This chapter should provide some background as to how policy has developed over the years and how a prison library might interpret these national policies.

## Purpose of the Prison Library According to Policy

In Section 2–4022 of the ACA's 1981 edition of *Standards for Correctional Institutions*, the library is viewed as one of a few minimally required "constructive programs" that should be made available in a correctional institution.[4] Vibeke Lehmann and Joanne Locke also reference the constructive nature of the prison library and give credit to the prison library as a place where prisoners can maintain a certain sense of normalcy while developing literacy, following personal interests, and pursuing lifelong learning, which may ultimately assist with combating recidivism.[5] William J. Coyle lists a number of supposed purposes for the prison library, some of which he refutes as ineffective, including rehabilitation and reentry assistance, bibliotherapy, and recreational reading facilities.[6] Coyle, who was writing under a different landscape in the 1980s, has generally discouraged the public library model that most other prison librarianship authors espoused. Additionally, he questions the role that the library plays in rehabilitation, claiming that no empirical evidence exists to support this claim. Most prison librarianship scholars, including practitioners like Daniel Suvak, disparage his work.

Others consider accessing library services and materials to be one positive use of a prisoner's time; one which administrators should acknowledge as beneficial, particularly for improving conduct in the institution, public relations, budget increases, and for staff opportunities.[7] In the American Bar Association's Standards for Criminal Justice's *Treatment of Prisoners*, library access is intended for the purposes of accessing recreational reading as well as educational materials, newspapers, or other informative periodicals and can assist with the reduction of recidivism when the programs are particularly educational or rehabilitative.[8] According to Mary Bosworth, the prison library offers "the opportunity for self-development and relaxation in a period of time that will inevitably be unpleasant and stressful."[9]

Naturally though, many administrators express concern over the security risks associated with library materials including concealing contraband, spreading inflammatory ideas that might incite violence, or presenting ideas that might cause harm to one or more of the prisoners. Many policies, standards, and general literature on prison librarianship acknowledge the trepid nature of the ideals of providing open access to library and reading materials compared to the security necessities of incarceration. Linda Bayley, Leni Green-field, and Flynn Nogueira acknowledge a conflict between the goal of confining prisoners and the principles of librarianship, nevertheless assert that these two purposes can work in tandem.[10] Per John Palmer's *Constitutional Rights of Prisoners*, jailhouse administration may justify restricting access to books and similar materials due to "clear and present danger" that would possibly occur if the prisoners were able to access to the materials.[11] In the ALA's policy "Prisoners' Right to Read," the idea of acceptable censorship for items that present an obvious danger is presented, especially if the work describes the manufacture of weapons, explosives, or other topics that might aid an escape attempt. Bayley et al. confirm that in practice, prison administration is hesitant to allow materials that create legitimate penological concern such as materials on "lock-picking or gunsmithing, sexually explicit or ethnic materials."[12]

The conflict between the prison administration's goal of maintaining security in the institution and the library's goal of avoiding censorship is not one that will disappear. There are, as the ALA has acknowledged, requirements to maintain security that could be threatened by certain types of materials. This therefore appears to be a perpetual challenge for the prison librarian; walking the fine line between professional ideals and appeasing prison administration.

## Administration

The ASCLA standards are specific about the space requirements for a library including restrictions and recommendations for general locks for the entire facility, proper lighting, acoustics, climate control, load bearing, electricity, visual layout, secure storage spaces, management offices, telecommunication services, emergency communication equipment, and accessible spaces. Throughout their standards, they outline the square footage requirements for housing materials, seating the user population (with at least seven percent coverage of the entire population), for staff workstations, group meeting space, and work rooms for staff.[13] Lehmann and Locke define similar requirements for the usage and size of spaces in the library with a lower threshold of at least five percent for user seating.[14] Bayley et al. are less specific, perhaps because their guidelines were authored at least ten years prior to the ASCLA guidelines. They recommend a dedicated library space as the best alternative for service, however, permit bookmobile or book cart services when a space is not available.[15]

Most policy documents also include sections recommending the level, education, and comprehensiveness of non-prisoner staff for the prison library. The ASCLA recommends that a professional librarian with a master's degree in library science (MLS) or equivalent manage the library; the standards are more specific about the layers of librarians at institutions based on their size including at least a statewide coordinator, director, and assistant librarian with MLS degrees. Staff should include library techs and clerks with the appropriate associate's degree or high school diploma.[16] The need for a higher-level coordinator is established by the Department of Justice in the *Federal Standards for Prisons and Jails* as well, as is a non-prisoner staff member onsite and any other personnel deemed necessary as part of a needs assessment.[17] In the ACA 2003 *Standards for Adult Correctional Institutions*, the need for a library supervisor, preferably with the appropriate MLS degree is mentioned, as is the importance of a needs assessment to determine prisoner and general staffing needs necessary for providing continued service to prisoners.[18] Lehmann and Locke similarly define basic requirements for number of staff and those who are considered professional librarians.[19]

While many policy documents acknowledge the need for professionally trained staff with appropriate education or experience, the position and required education of the librarian within the institution is less clear. Bayley et al. highlight this issue well: "One difficulty for professional librarians is often that the jail library is so different from what it *should* be."[20] The role of the librarian as cross-communicator between prison administration, staff, and prisoners can be challenging. Linda Schexnaydre and Kaylyn Robbins encourage jail library training that includes administrators and not just library staff since co-planning library services creates the best communicative relationship.[21] The ASCLA recommend that a library director have hierarchical equality to other departments managed by a director; similar to other departments, the library director should have the ability to write strategic plans, procedural documentations, policies, and request audits.[22] Coyle focuses on the role conflict of a prison librarian: the need to balance legal and ethical correctional issues with the ethical principles of librarianship.[23]

Both the ASCLA and Lehmann and Locke recommend that the library hold a line item in the prison budget, that funding for books be calculated by the population size, and that a sizeable budget be made available for the library to begin operations.[24] The ASCLA guidelines have more specificity regarding budgets allocated based on usage, space and equipment costs, budget for professional development activities for librarians and staff, and a budget to fund vendors, interlibrary loan, systems, cataloging supplies, and databases.[25] Bosworth states that most prison libraries are funded through the education department.[26] The ACA's *2013 Directory Adult and Juvenile Correctional Departments, Institutions, Agencies, and Probation and Parole Authorities* clearly lists budgets per different expense categories for a total U.S. prison budget of $42 billion per year, yet education and in particular libraries are not accounted for as clear line items in the budget. Categories defined by the ACA 2013 directory include salaries/benefits, administration, custody/security, operations/maintenance, treatment programs, offender health care, food services, and an "other" category.[27] It is likely that education and/or library services are compressed into another category; the rationale behind various categories is not broken down within the reported ACA budgets.

## Library Services

The Department of Justice describes minimum library services, stating that they should include the acquisition of materials suitable to the prison population, provide an organized collection for easy use, maintain circulation policies that are appropriate for the prisoners' needs, offer readers' advisory service, ensure that services are marketed well to the institution, and staff a well-lit, acoustically pleasant, climate controlled, and inviting environment.[28] The ASCLA standards encourage an annual needs assessment of prisoners so that library service can be focused to meet these needs, and state that the collection should be logically organized for the most efficient use and circulation.[29] Prisoners, according to the ASCLA, should be able to use the library for a number of purposes including getting information on the institution; maintaining interaction with the outside world; to obtain job skills; to enhance educational pursuits; to enable rehabilitation; to read for purposes of learning or personal pleasure; or to obtain information on life after parole.[30] Additionally, both the ASCLA and Lehmann and Locke state the importance of user services such as reader services, library instruction, interlibrary loan, other advisory services, reference services, and services for people with disabilities.[31]

In an earlier publication, the ACA also stresses the significance of an atmosphere where patrons can enjoy the library. The ACA suggests reference materials should be collected that would assist with issues of reintegration, help with survival while incarcerated, and provide information on developing job and educational skills.[32] The purpose of assisting with reentry, can, according to Bayley et al., encourage prisoners to "return successfully to the community if, during their incarceration, they are provided services and materials that help them prepare for reentry."[33] Bayley et al. give additional examples of programming that might support these goals including help completing GEDs or getting high school diplomas; "learner's advisory service"; programs assisting with college-level examinations; correspondence courses; seminars or classes on reentry; special interest topics or programs; referrals to legal services; and general information and referral services.[34]

The Department of Justice mentions the possibilities of collaboration with public or community libraries to acquire and circulate materials, and encourages the usage of interlibrary loan services.[35] The ACA also mentions the correlation to the public library model and recommends filling in the gaps with interlibrary loan.[36] Lehmann and Locke state that "an incarcerated person has not relinquished the right to learn and to access information," and suggest the public library as a model to emulate.[37] The public library model, per Sheila Clark and Erica MacCreaigh, adheres to the ALA core values of modern librarianship, which are in place in public libraries. The most challenging of these to include in a prison library is the "access and intellectual freedom, privacy and confidentiality, and social responsibility."[38] Many scholars and practitioners acknowledge the challenge in this model, as well-stated by Bayley et al.: "the services provided to jail inmates should duplicate, as closely as possible, the services offered to the general public, although this may not always be possible."[39] Coyle is perhaps the biggest opponent of the public library model, and he questions the idealism of library services to support prisoner rehabilitation.[40] The public library model in prisons is often mentioned in trade and scholarly literature and will be further discussed in chapter 7.

Technology is an issue that most certainly needs to be updated within national standards. The ASCLA includes technology equipment guidelines in their standards, however, mostly reference obsolete technology such as typewriters.[41] Lehmann and Locke expand upon these requirements to include public access computers and photocopiers, and encourage technology use when it does not threaten security, such as automated card catalog systems, multimedia access, Internet and email for staff, and where possible, Internet access for prisoners.[42] The "Prisoners' Right to Read" includes a section encouraging prisoner access to public computers and the Internet.[43] The concept that the banning of or restricting of technology might have detrimental effects has been frequently mentioned in more recent literature on prison librarianship[44]; this topic will be discussed in more detail in chapter 3. It seems only natural that technology standards would need to be revisited by authoritative bodies, if only to bring the standards to the twenty-first century and to better prepare prisoners for reentry in an increasingly digital world.

## Needs Assessment

Prisoner needs for library services will vary vastly from prisoner to prisoner due to the diversity of incarcerated populations. Reading levels and prior educational differences amongst the prisoners necessitate a broad collection that appeases the whole spectrum of prisoners' educational backgrounds. Needs assessment in the context of this book is defined as collecting information about the library's patrons and potential prisoner users to determine what kinds of services or materials they would benefit from; this book will not encompass correctional practices of classifying prisoners to establish security levels or treatment. Some organizations creating library policies call for systematic needs assessments in a general manner,[45] while other authors provide more information on administering successful needs assessments through information interaction with prisoners and staff, examination of intake forms or data, and questionnaires.[46] These assessments should include demographic information, special interests and hobbies of the patrons, reading habits, and patron recommendations. Other authors recommend ongoing user satisfaction surveys to create communication about the collection between the library staff and prisoners.[47] Multiple authors suggest that needs assessment can be a means to improving communication between prison administration and the prison library whether through sharing of assessment results[48] or through the creation of a library advisory board, which includes prison library staff, general institution staff, and prisoners.[49]

## Collection Development

Material selection is often a contentious topic in the policies and literature surrounding prison librarianship. While policy dictates that a similar service to the public library model should be provided to prisoners, in practice the security of the institution often prevents such an open approach to providing materials to prisoners. This conflict between intellectual freedom and maintaining a secure correctional institution is an ongoing challenge for both prison librarians and prison authorities.

Often the challenges implicit in providing prisoner access to materials and maintaining a secure institution can be reduced by clear collection development policies. The ASCLA acknowledge the importance of a collection development policy that clarifies the target audience, includes materials that are useful for life after parole, provides guidelines for reference services to patrons, defines processes for acquiring new materials and removing materials, acknowledges necessary policies to ensure the institution's security, and documents weeding procedures.[50] In the ACA guidelines from 2003, this need for a written policy is also addressed including the processes for material selection and for library management.[51] Lehmann and Locke assert that written policies can support administrative decisions and should include demographics of the readership; reentry materials; reference materials and materials supporting other prison programs; recommendation processes and processes for challenging the inclusion of certain items; weeding procedures; and policies on donations.[52] Bayley et al. provide guidelines for creating a collection development policy including a justification of what the collection will include, the goals of the library service, the patron base, gift policy, selection criteria, and formats carried.[53]

Lehmann and Locke outline a number of selection criteria that should be used to select materials, which adhere to the institution's established collection development policy and are broad so as to appease diverse interests. Specifically, for each item the librarian should consider the appropriateness of the subject, the appeal to the readers, critical acclaim or reception by the general public, significance of the work, accuracy, appropriateness for library use, relevance to the existing collection, and the cost.[54] According to the ASCLA, "library materials shall be selected to meet the informational, cultural, educational, vocational, and recreational needs of the inmate population and of the correctional institution."[55] The ACA's 2003 standards similarly stress the importance of selecting materials to meet the population's needs, stating that access to a reference collection must be provided "containing general and specialized materials, and planned and continuous acquisition of materials to meet the needs of the institutional staff and inmates."[56] Lehmann and Locke emphasize that the collection should emulate those offered in a public library or school setting and should "meet the informational, educational, cultural, recreational, and rehabilitative needs of the prison population."[57] Bayley et al. stress the importance of selecting materials that meet the specific needs of that institution's prisoners and staff including materials that accommodate various reading levels or account for special circumstances in the institution.[58] Many of the ALA "Library Bill of Rights" tenets echo these sentiments regarding selecting materials of interest to the specific population. For instance, a common idea is that material should be selected based on patron interest and that materials should represent multiple viewpoints or "should not be proscribed or removed because of partisan or doctrinal disapproval."[59]

The policies and standards also detail the types of materials that a prison library should carry. Materials include the typical types of materials one might find available to the general public including books, newspapers, magazines, audiovisual materials, and technology.[60] Lehmann and Locke encourage the inclusion of diverse types of content such as reference materials, fiction, biographies, non-fiction, legal materials, poetry, graphic novels, comics, self-study aids, easy-to-read books and materials, large-print, audiobooks, audiovisual materials, information about the community, literacy materials, puzzles or games, magazines, and newspapers.[61] Bayley et al.'s list of materials is similarly comprehensive and includes reference materials, legal materials, fiction, non-fiction, educational materials, materials promoting reentry, materials addressing specific populations, materials written by offenders and ex-offenders, and any materials helpful or useful for correctional staff.[62] Additional material types that the "Prisoners' Right to Read" mentions include literature written in a foreign language, bilingual literature, and tools for learning languages.[63] The ABA maintains that the institution should allow and provide access to a library that has both recreational reading and educational materials, as well as newspapers and other periodicals that allow prisoners to stay connected to the outside world—including broadcast media.[64] The ASCLA encourage resource sharing and consortial arrangements to provide materials and services not available in the institution.[65] Interlibrary loan is consistently mentioned as a means of gaining access to additional materials at lower costs.[66]

It is impossible to discuss collection development policies in prison libraries without addressing the underlying issues with censorship. Even the ALA's most recent version of the "Prisoners' Right to Read" acknowledges that some materials will not be possible to include in the collection because of security concerns.[67] This is in direct conflict with the ALA "Library Bill of Rights" idea that all censorship should be challenged.[68] The restrictions on collection, which could often be interpreted as censorship by the prison librarian, are, according to Bayley et al., ongoing discussions that will need to occur between the librarian and administration with evaluations on a case-by-case basis.[69] In John Palmer's *Constitutional Rights of Prisoners*, censorship controlled by the prison administration is frowned upon; prison administration should, according to Palmer, not be given too much freedom in defining "clear and present danger," especially if used to restrict access.[70] In theory, this is a noble approach; in practice it appears to be implemented depending on interpretations by the local institutions.

## Intellectual Freedom

In the United Nations' *Universal Declaration of Human Rights*, "everyone has the right to freedom of opinion and expression; this right includes freedom to hold opinions without interference and to seek, receive and impart information and ideas through any media and regardless of frontiers."[71] Prisoners automatically lose most freedoms when they are convicted of a crime and incarcerated. In the ALA's "Prisoners' Right to Read," these rights, as defined by the UN, are referenced as basic human rights that are implicit to prisoners as well.[72] It is interesting to note that the ALA includes this statement on prisoners' rights in the *Intellectual Freedom Manual*, implying that the ideals of intellectual freedom apply to prisoners as well.

In the *Intellectual Freedom* manual, certain tenets of librarianship and intellectual freedom are established. According to the ALA, "libraries have always been a forum for ideas, even those that may be unorthodox, unpopular, or offensive."[73] This freedom to cultivate ideas is not, according to the ALA, limited to a selective few, but rather to everyone. In the manual, the ALA asserts that intellectual freedom serves as the foundation for freedom with the most frequently infringed upon right being the freedom to read, especially in the form of censorship in libraries and restriction of the general public's access to materials. However, "libraries preserve those freedoms guaranteed by the First Amendment."[74] In the ALA "Library Bill of Rights," policy dictates that attempts should be made to avoid infringement of free expression and access to information should be unencumbered.[75] The library is virtually the only place in the prison where a prisoner can make his or her own choices according to Lehmann and Locke,[76] serving as a vital means for retaining intellectual freedom.

Historically, intellectual freedom has been a recurring theme in court cases and literature on prisoners' rights. According to Rabun Sanders, Hazel Kerper, George Killinger, and John Watkins, courts began siding in the favor of the right of expression as early as the 1960s, especially when prison security is not threatened. Sanders et al. state: "courts will no longer tolerate the complete deprivation of such a basic right as freedom of speech."[77]

The literature suggests that basic rights exist even for incarcerated prisoners. These basic rights seem to include freedom of expression and speech. The applicability of other constitutionally protected rights, however, is unclear from current policies. Many of these rights have been the subject of litigation; more information on some of these cases will be presented in chapters 4 and 5.

## Prisoners' Rights

The 1992 standards from ASCLA define a number of rights implicit to prisoners and clearly reference corresponding documents from the ALA pertaining to these rights. Specifically, prisoners should maintain the right to read and have access to information free of cost. Specific policies from the ALA, which are recommended as policies for prison libraries, include the "Library Bill of Rights," "Resolution on Prisoners' Right to Read," "Policy on Confidentiality of Library Records," "Freedom to Read," and the "Freedom to View."[78] Some of these policies have been updated since the 1992 publication of the ASCLA standards; the policies mentioned above refer to the version of the ASCLA standards approved at the time of the policy's publication. A prisoner, however, is also entitled to refuse services. In this regard, multiple policies state that prisoners are not required to participate in any programs or activities, or use library services.[79]

Coyle, whose book brought a barrage of criticism[80] for his views on the falsity of the prison library as a rehabilitative force, states: "Many of a new generation of service-oriented librarians have taken note of the attention that has been given to the rights of prison inmates and have suggested that library services are one of the things to which inmates have a right, independent of correctional goals."[81] It is not apparent whether Coyle agrees with the idea of the prisoners' rights to read, but his stance on the library as an influence on rehabilitation is clear: from his perspective there is no empirical evidence to support the prison library as a rehabilitative force.

Regardless of Coyle's perspective on the role or success of the prison library, many policies attest to the existence of the prisoners' right to read. Perhaps the most poignant policy presented is the "Prisoners' Right to Read" from the American Library Association. The policy presents the following key concepts regarding the prisoners' right to read:

- Prisoners cannot be sequestered intellectually; obtaining access to information from the outside world is necessary in order to transition to eventual release and freedom.
- An individual, in particular a prisoner, has to be afforded the knowledge to learn how to be free.
- Suppressing ideas makes it difficult for a prisoner to transition to living in a democratic society.[82]

The "Prisoners' Right to Read" further states that prisoners have the "right to seek, receive, hold and disseminate information from all points of view, without restriction including those ideas that might be highly controversial or offensive to others."[83] Similar views are presented in the ALA "Resolution on Guantanamo and the Rights of Prisoners to Read," with the insistence that the incarcerated in Cuba be "afforded the right to read and supplied with materials enabling them to do so by the United States Department of Defense and its libraries."[84] According to Bayley et al. "inmates have the right to read, and quality jail library service can help them exercise this right,"[85] and "from the librarian's point of view, the jail population is simply another segment of the public that demands and deserves service."[86]

The rights referenced by various policies and authors above are not limited to those in the general population of the prison. According to many sources, prisoners in other units of the prison such as solitary confinement should also be given access to library resources. The U.S. Department of Justice states that library services should be accessible by all incarcerated patrons including "a full range of legal, reference, and reading materials for education and recreational purposes."[87] Restricting access to library services is only permitted in certain cases with documentation. For instance, the ASCLA only recommends restricted access to library services when the prisoner has specifically abused library privileges in a documented manner.[88] Lehmann and Locke confirm that prisoners in all security classifications should be permitted library privileges; library services should be available at times that do not conflict with other educational or work programs.[89] These standards imply that prisoners cannot lose library privileges for other infringements in the institution.

Many policies and guidelines recommend the minimum number of hours that a prison library should be open for prisoner visits. In section 18.05 of the *Federal Standards for Prisons and Jails*, the facility or access to materials must be made available at least five days a week in a long-term institution.[90] The ASCLA includes a provision that prisoners have a right to access the library for at least five hours weekly.[91] Most of these policies require that these services should be available to prisoners regardless of sentence or location in the institution. This specifically refers to prisoners not housed in the general population in the prison.[92] The ASCLA recommends that prisoners in solitary confinement or units outside the general prison population have access to the library either in off hours, via a collection in their unit, via a book cart with a rotating selection, or via request, i.e., prisoners are allowed to select from a list of materials. In addition, these prisoners should have access to circulation services, interlibrary loan, reference, be permitted to suggest materials for purchase, and should be considered when doing annual needs assessments.[93]

Historically, access to library services in prison has been the topic of multiple court cases, many of which will be presented in chapters 4 and 5. In 1996, the Prison Litigation Reform Act was passed to prevent prisoners from overwhelming the judicial system with frivolous lawsuits. Specifically, this law required "exhaustion of administrative remedies"; in essence the prisoner had to have submitted grievances to prison authorities that had been ignored before the case could be heard at trial.[94]

## Privacy

Privacy and confidentiality of transactions and interactions in the library are national issues that have, in light of recent legislation, often come into question. According to the Federal Trade Commission's "Fair Information Practice Principles," anyone from whom information is collected should be given proper notice of the collection, be offered the possibility to consent, and be able to personally review the data collected.[95] The USA PATRIOT Act stands in conflict with many of these principles, in particular the ability of the FBI to collect information from Internet service providers without judicial review or explicit consent from the individual. Section 215 of the USA PATRIOT Act gives the FBI the right to request library records with a warrant or justification.[96] The ALA responded to the USA PATRIOT Act in 2005 demanding that the privacy rights of library users be restored through renewed legislation: "The American Library Association opposes any further initiatives on the part of the United States government to constrain the free expression of ideas or to inhibit the use of libraries as represented in the USA PATRIOT Act expansion bill marked-up in secret by the Senate Select Intelligence Committee."[97]

Even with many of the provisions of the PATRIOT Act reaching their sunset date in June 2015, library provisions were renewed through 2020, initiating a stern response from ALA: "Nothing is more basic to democracy and librarianship than intellectual freedom. And, nothing is more hostile to that freedom than the knowledge that the government can compel a library—without a traditional judicial search warrant—to report on the reading and Internet records of library patrons, students, researchers and entrepreneurs."[98] It is not surprising that the confidentiality of prisoners' records would be questioned in a time when even the public's library records are no longer truly confidential. There are, nevertheless, still standards and policies regarding the retention of prisoners' records and library records. The ABA Standards for Criminal Justice specifically mention that maintaining prisoners' records is a right maintained by the prison administration; however, that confidentiality should be maintained for these prisoner records with few exceptions.[99] These standards make no explicit mention about maintaining library records.

Furthermore, none of the ALA's policies regarding confidentiality of library records address policies for privacy in correctional institutions. According to the "Policy on Confidentiality of Library Records," circulation records are to be held confidential and this confidentiality should only be breached in cases when these records are subpoenaed by a court of law.[100] Due to the nature of circulation requiring individual patron accountability, it is impossible not to collect some personal identifiers about the library patrons, even in prison. The ALA acknowledges the necessity of collecting personally identifiable information for managing a library's collection but encourages libraries to be cautious about what information they are collecting. The ALA recommends only collecting the basic information needed to maintain operations, making sure records are kept secure, and disposing of records when they are no longer needed.[101] In the ALA's "Policy Concerning Confidentiality of Personally Identifiable Information about Library Users," records to be held confidential include "database search records, reference interviews, circulation records, interlibrary loan records and other personally identifiable uses of library materials, facilities or services."[102] Bayley et al. recommend to "keep only the records that are really useful"[103] including a card catalog or shelf list, subscription records for databases, checkout records,[104] results from library services and materials needs assessment, frequent request lists, usage statistics for the number of visitors or percentage of prison population that frequent the library, reference questions, number of visits if using a cart or bookmobile, total number of checkouts, material usage, records from interlibrary loan, and evaluation results.[105]

In the "Code of Ethics of the American Library Association," the ALA states: "we protect each library user's right to privacy and confidentiality with respect to information sought or received and resources consulted, borrowed, acquired or transmitted."[106] In an interpretation of the "Library Bill of Rights" by the ALA, "confidentiality exists when a library is in possession of personally identifiable information about users and keeps that information private on their behalf."[107] Within this interpretation, the ALA also maintains that privacy in a library allows a patron to ask questions without those questions being scrutinized or their uses of the library being profiled. The ALA further expounds upon the ideals of impartiality in the "Policy Concerning Confidentiality of Personally Identifiable Information about Library Users," stating: "Libraries are impartial resources providing information on all points of view, available to all persons regardless of origin, age, background, or views. The role of libraries as such a resource must not be compromised by an erosion of the privacy rights of library users."[108] None of these policies provide clarity on whether the confidentiality and privacy offered to a patron in the outside world is applicable to the prison library patron. The only national policy from the ALA that specifically addresses prisoners' rights is the "Prisoners' Right to Read." Due to the inclusion of that policy in the *Intellectual Freedom Manual*, however, certain applicability of other policies may be inferred.

## Law Libraries

Previous sections have addressed standards and policies for general library services, some of which addressed legal collections. The ASCLA standards specifically state that they have not addressed standards in law libraries.[109] The ACA standards address access to a law library in section 4–4274, stating "the constitutional right of access to courts requires that inmates who request assistance in preparing and filing legal papers receive the assistance necessary."[110] Katherine Skolnick, in *A Jailhouse Lawyer's Manual*, draws attention to the lack of a clear definition of what an adequate law library entails and the reality that security issues will often trump prisoners' rights to access legal materials.[111] The law library and standards for legal collections or services within a law library have historically been dictated more by litigation than national standards. Specific cases including *Bounds v. Smith* and *Lewis v. Casey*, both of which are pivotal to the role and purpose of the prison law library, will be discussed in more detail in chapters 4 and 5.

In the introductory section in the *Federal Standards for Prisons and Jails*, the U.S. Department of Justice recommends that prisoners should have access to a law library with useful legal materials; if the prisoner cannot make use of the materials himself or herself, a staff person capable of doing so should be made available to the prisoner.[112] Under the ABA Standards for Criminal Justice Standard 23–9.5, access to legal materials is one means of providing meaningful access to the courts. Some examples of acceptable forms mentioned in the standards include access to a law library or electronic access to legal materials. Additionally, within these standards prisoners should be permitted to attain and store their own legal materials as long as these materials are legal in nature and not a threat to the institution's security. As part of these standards, it is recommended that programs be provided for training prisoners on legal matters so that they can assist others.[113] Bosworth details the idea of the "jailhouse lawyer," a prisoner who provides legal assistance to fellow prisoners and often is stretched thin to provide enough consultation to all prisoners.[114]

## *Summary*

Comprehensive policies have been authored regarding prison library services; they could, however, benefit from an update, specifically because of the lack of attention or applicability to modern technology. Within these policies, clear purposes for the prison library have been defined and recommended, as have suggestions for how to administer and manage the library. Additionally, establishing clear policies for collection development and conducting regular needs assessment have been recommended as best practice in nearly all of the applicable standards and policies reviewed. Issues or implications for intellectual freedom, prisoners' rights, privacy and confidentiality, and the appropriateness of law libraries are thornier issues with less documentation. Perhaps these issues are comparable to the fine line a prison librarian has to tread when making selection decisions; what could encourage a security breach versus what is outright censorship? All of these issues will be revisited in chapters 8 and 9 in more depth through surveys and interviews with current prison librarians. It is clear from this chapter's policies and policies in subsequent chapters that national standards are due for an update. The ASCLA's in-depth policy on prison librarianship is nearly 25 years old; certainly technology alone has changed drastically in the last 25 years and is one of many reasons that modern policies on prison librarianship should be authored by practicing library professionals.

# 2

# Current State Policy

*Well, when you're a librarian you're not like anybody else in the institution and they don't readily grasp what you're supposed to be doing and how you're supposed to be doing it. And also that changes with each administration. I'm now on my fourth warden.*

—*Nora, Interviewee from Chapter 9*

*Our current governor has downgraded the status of librarians in the prisons ... and made it more like a paralegal, more like a technical position rather than a professional position. I started out as a professional position and I was downgraded ... to a technical position.*

—*Victor, Interviewee from Chapter 9*

In the last chapter, a number of national policies were reviewed to summarize themes regarding the purposes of the prison library, the necessities for managing a prison library, policies for collection development, and recommendations for gathering prisoners' library needs through annual or regularly scheduled assessments. Additionally, national policies outlining prisoners' rights, privacy and confidentiality, and rights to a law library were analyzed. As mentioned in the previous chapter, many of these policies are out of date: most notably the ASCLA guidelines from 1992. Regardless, many state level prisons abide by the rules and guidelines set out by their respective departments of correction, which may complement or supersede national standards such as the ASCLA standards. This chapter will review and summarize the state policies available from state department of corrections websites. In the interest of providing a summary of all states' generalized approaches, I have included Appendix A, which provides a general overview of each state's approach to providing library service. This information has been summarized from the Directory of State Prison Libraries from Washington State Library. It was last updated in July of 2014, so it is likely that some of these approaches are out of date.[1]

## Method

To ascertain whether outdated national policies are being implemented in state institutions, a review of department of corrections' websites was conducted in September and October 2013. The Directory of State Prison Libraries was consulted to find the Department of Corrections websites for each of the 50 states.[2] Each of the websites was examined for policies concerning library and law library service. Of the 50 websites reviewed, public policies for general library service were found for 50 percent of the websites (25 in total). Forty-eight percent of the websites had public policies for law libraries (24 in total), some of which were included in the general library policies. Policies for either the general library or law library were found for 29 states in total. The remaining states' policies were either not available online or not found via browsing or searching functions on the state's Department of Corrections' website. It is likely that most of these states have policies, but do not make them openly accessible online. Additionally, it should be noted that even if the policies are available openly online, they are not necessarily the current policy being practiced at state institutions. It is also possible, if not likely, that some of these policies may have been updated since the research for this book was completed.

General library policies were reviewed to determine their adherence to the national level policies. Many of these policies referenced national policies from the ACA, as well as the ASCLA policy and previous ACA/ASCLA joint policies. These policies were examined to determine if materials acceptable for inclusion in the library were listed and if a general purpose for the prison library had been established, including whether or not programming and events were to be offered. Since so many of the national policies referenced the paramount nature of security in comparison to providing library service, each of the policies was reviewed to find references to security, especially regarding restrictions on materials, access to technology, etc. Record keeping was discussed in a few policies with very little reference to prisoner privacy or confidentiality.

Management issues such as the educational level or staffing of the librarians were also included in many of the policies, as well as definitions of the space in the library or necessary budget for maintaining a library. Services such as interlibrary loan were mentioned frequently in policies as a supplement to providing access to collections. Services for those in segregation or isolation were also discussed with alternatives provided for those not in the general population. Some institutions recommended that library needs assessments be conducted on a regular basis.

Collection development was frequently discussed in the policies with some mentioning explicit selection criteria. The term censorship was generally not directly addressed with a few notable exceptions. Law libraries or access to legal materials were sometimes listed as services provided by the general library or referenced as a separate service.

Law library policies were reviewed to determine what cases, if any, were cited for reference, with *Lewis v. Casey* and *Bounds v. Smith* appearing most frequently. Additionally, policies were reviewed for references to electronic databases as many prison libraries are offering access to legal databases such as LexisNexis. Lastly, the policies were checked for mentions of alternative legal access whether through inmate clerks, attorneys, law librarians, etc.

## General Library Service

Eighty percent of the policies mentioned some sort of national, state, or association policies for library services in correctional institutions. Of these twenty policies, twelve referred to ACA standards, five referred to the 1992 standards from the ASCLA, two referred to other ALA policies, and five referenced state policies. Only three referenced more than one association or standard writing body: The State of Connecticut Department of Correction mentioned both ACA standards and Connecticut state policies[3]; Hawaii mentioned ACA standards, general ALA standards (the ALA "Library Bill of Rights" specifically), and some state standards for the Board of Education[4]; and New Mexico mentioned ACA standards and ALA standards, but not the 1992 standards published by ASCLA.[5]

Twenty-three or 92 percent of the policies defined an explicit purpose for the prison library. Many of these purposes referenced the need to provide educational and recreational reading materials to prisoners as well as staff. Arkansas' policy, for example, states that the library "provides access for expanding knowledge and self-improvement via collections of reference materials and periodicals involving various media, i.e. hard cover, paper, electronic."[6] Florida's statement mentions the importance of literacy, stating that the library should provide "reference services, readers guidance, self-betterment/educational/cultural programming, resources and services essential to support the activities of the institution's other education and treatment programs, and resources to permit inmates to achieve functional literacy."[7] Hawaii's policy puts forth the idea of preparing prisoners for release so that they are ready "for post-institution life" and that they can "develop reading as a fulfilling leisure activity, a therapeutic release from the strain of institutionalization, and as a positive aid in substituting new interests for undesirable activities."[8] Minnesota's policy also includes a statement that library services can promote "personal growth."[9] Rehabilitation is addressed in Oregon's policy with the statement: "It is the Department of Corrections policy to maintain institution libraries for the educational reinforcement, broadening and strengthening of the rehabilitative program of each inmate."[10] Massachusetts' policy includes a purpose that applies to the greater institution, stating that "the library is an information center for the institution. Library services support, broaden and strengthen the institution's program."[11] Fifteen of the 25 policies (or 60 percent) mention specific programming or events that the library can host including book discussions, movie events, etc.

The public library model is frequently referenced in literature as a guide that should be used when drafting a general library policy for the prison library. Nebraska's policy explicitly states that a mission of the library is "to provide quality library services within the Department of Correctional Services comparable to those of a public library."[12] Of the policies reviewed, only eight, including Nebraska, mention the public library model explicitly, which accounted for 32 percent of the 25 policies.

Of the 25 policies reviewed, 72 percent or 18 policies define the materials to be collected by the library within the policy itself. Seventeen of the 18 policies define books as materials that would be collected in the library. Many state whether hardcover, paperback, or both would be collected. Other types of materials that were listed for collection included periodicals, newspapers, pamphlets, audiovisual materials, among others. Six policies allow for collection of some sort of computer software including CD-ROMs or electronic items. Alaska's policy include a general statement that "materials to aid in release preparation" would be collected.[13] Seventy-six percent or 19 states mention interlibrary loan services in their policies with most encouraging the use of interlibrary loan to acquire titles otherwise unavailable in the general collection. Most policies (80 percent at 20 in total) mention alternative access for those in segregation or isolation.

Of all of the policies, 80 percent, or 20 in total, address security concerns related to library materials in the policy itself. Some of the policies generally mention threats to security with some stating more specific requirements for reading materials. Florida's policy "limits inmate access to publications that contain subject matter detrimental to the security, order or disciplinary or rehabilitative interests of any institution of the department."[14] In Hawaii, the Department of Public Safety's policy states: "Inmates shall have access to publications that do not advocate overt violence or subversive action that is contrary to law, departmental rules and safety, security and health of persons and the good government of the PSD."[15] Illinois mentions two specific restrictions: "in the event that institutional safety or security may be jeopardized" and "where the amount [of library materials in an inmate's possession] poses a fire, sanitation or security hazard."[16] Department of Corrections' policies in Ohio and Indiana both mention general adherence to collect materials that do not threaten security.[17] Massachusetts' policy is less clear with the statement that "each superintendent in cooperation with the librarian should establish procedures to ensure the security of the library and the library collection."[18] Montana's Department of Corrections (DOC) prefers not to accept any materials that do not comply with the "safety and security needs of the facility."[19]

Policies in Connecticut, Michigan, and New Mexico reference general lists of unacceptable materials such as weapon manufacturing instructions, guides for creating drugs or similar substances, materials that might encourage escape or riots, and sexually explicit materials. They also provide general statements of security concerns.[20] Michigan and Minnesota policies refer to other institutional policies on contraband or receipt of mail by prisoners.[21]

Policies frequently ban types of materials that prison administration views as unacceptable. In addition to those mentioned in the above description for policies from Connecticut, Michigan, and Minnesota, taboo items include materials about poisons, bomb making, sexual assault,[22] general lawbreaking,[23] sexist materials, those written in code, promoting gangs, ethnically negative materials, and materials instructing on psychological control.[24] In some cases hardcover materials are banned.[25] In one description, telephone directories are not allowed in the library collection.[26] The description of banned materials from Oklahoma is particularly detailed and specific:

> Library materials will not contain instructions for the manufacture of drugs, weapons, explosives, other unlawful substances, or tattoos; advocate the overthrow of the United States or Oklahoma or other State government; advocate terrorism, criminal behavior, racial, religious or national hatred. Any material that creates an unsafe environment for the offenders or staff, material encouraging unnatural or aggressive sexual behavior, material that is obscene, indecent or is classified as erotica is prohibited.[27]

Policies on technology use in the library remain rather hazy. Very few of the policies include information on technology—only seven of the policies mention any sort of technology (28 percent). Two of these explicitly ban the use of technology. For instance, in New Mexico the following policy exists: "Facility Education Resource Centers shall not provide inmates with access to manual and/or electric typewriters, word processors, computers for personal or legal or non–ERC use, nor supplies for personal inmate typewriters."[28] In Kansas, the policy states that "neither inmate patrons of a library nor inmate library assistants shall be permitted either INTERNET access or access to devices affording INTERNET access."[29] The policy in Arizona allows certain types of devices but also bans

Internet usage, specifically referencing policies for taking courses offered through the education center:

> No course which requires Internet access shall be permitted. The CEPS, CEPM, or CEC may approve courses that require use of CD-ROM or other computer software on a case-by-case basis, depending on security considerations, the availability of computer hardware and adequate staff supervision at the particular facility. Only one such class may be taken at a time.[30]

At Washington State institutions "staff will provide offenders with photocopies of library materials or printed pages from the Internet to fill reference and information requests that meet the educational, informational, and recreational needs of offenders, and to assist offenders with re-entry."[31] This policy does not mention whether or not offenders can use the Internet directly, rather only that staff is permitted to source items for them. The remaining three policies that mention technology are comparatively vague, and are perhaps the most lenient of the policies. In Arkansas and California prisoners can use electronic materials and collections. What "electronic" means in these state policies is elusive; Arkansas only mentions "electronic" as one form that books and media can be accessed in and California provides access to electronic collections without details of what those electronic collections include. It is unclear if those collections are accessed through the Internet or via closed databases.[32] In North Carolina's policy the only mention of technology is that prisoner clerks are permitted to use automated systems to check books in and out.[33]

## Facility Management and Staffing

The 1992 ASCLA guidelines mention adequate space for library facilities, however only four states detail these requirements in state policies (California, Colorado, Michigan, and Nebraska). Sixty percent of the policies (15 in total) mention library budget in some context. Sixty-four percent (16 policies) define recommended education or experience levels for those managing library services. Thirteen of these policies recommend that at least the supervisor of the library have a master's degree in library science; in most of these cases the supervisor either is not on site and/or trains the department and prisoner staff. In Alaska it is permitted to name a prisoner as a librarian.[34]

## Collection Development

Controversial situations often lend themselves to policy development and adherence. Clear policies can support decisions made by management or provide a reasonable method to deny certain requests that might be viewed as infringements. Only 64 percent of the policies reviewed (16 in total) explicitly reference a collection development policy. Twenty in total define selection criteria for a total of 80 percent. Five policies have very similar language regarding selection of library materials including selection to meet the "educational, informational, and recreational needs" of prisoners.[35] Nebraska and Indiana are general in their mentions of selection criteria: Nebraska requires only a "systematic approach" without further description, whereas Indiana allows the local facilities to develop their own processes for selection.[36] Montana's policy mentions criteria of "accuracy; currency; and cultural, inspirational, and/or recreational values."[37]

Many of the policies reference the importance of serving the institution's mission or supporting goals of rehabilitation for eventual reentry. Per Alaska's policy, the library should support "academic, cultural, inspirational, and recreational interests; reading levels; and subject matter, which should not be inconsistent with the objectives of reformation."[38] Washington's DOC mentions that the library should carry "general and specialized reference materials and materials to assist offenders with re-entry."[39] In Oregon, "the library will acquire educational reading materials that supplement and support the facility's education and treatment programs, working in conjunction with designated staff from those areas."[40] Ohio's Department of Rehabilitation and Correction empowers a Library Advisory Committee with decision-making, which "shall ensure that the materials provided in the collection are adequate in quantity, quality, and type to assist in the development of educational skills, treatment programming initiatives, apprenticeship programming efforts, personal growth factors, and that there are materials provided to help facilitate the reentry process."[41]

Selection by committee or review standards are also mentioned in a few other policies besides Ohio's documentation. In Connecticut, a committee is tasked with reviewing what materials are necessary and appropriate.[42] Hawaii's policy mentions either reading reviews of materials for suggestions, or reviewing the materials by hand:

> Books and periodicals are chosen on a selective basis, taking into consideration the accuracy of information, authoritativeness, readability, and social significance of the titles considered for acquisition. Selections are based on favorable reviews from library and correctional journals or based on examination of the material itself, special need for and scarcity of material on a particular subject, demand, etc."[43]

Rhode Island has a similar review policy in place, stating that "materials are selected by first-hand examination, standard library selection publication and guides, reviews, and publishers' information."[44]

Many of the policies acknowledge user needs of the population. Michigan's policy for example states:

> Each librarian shall maintain a comprehensive range of library services. This shall include a collection containing reference, general, and specialized reading materials selected to meet the educational, informational, and recreational needs of the prisoner population. Materials shall be available for various reading levels, languages, ethnicities, and special interests. Educational materials shall supplement those available through the institution's education program.[45]

The public library model is rarely explicitly mentioned in the selection criteria sections. One exception exists in Wyoming's policy where this similarity to public libraries is highlighted, especially with the suggestion that collections be expanded to accommodate diverse languages, literacy levels, cultural heritage, special interests, etc.[46]

Other policies not yet cited in the preceding paragraphs that reference the importance of user needs are California's policy that states that selection will meet the "needs and interests of the entire inmate population"[47] and Colorado's policy in which materials are to be selected for diverse groups with various needs and divergent viewpoints.[48] Only one policy from Minnesota specifically highlights the importance of user feedback: "when acquiring materials, the librarian will actively encourage input from library users. Materials of both permanent and current interest in a variety of subjects will be selected based on the merits of the work in relation to the purpose of the library."[49] Despite the fact that few of the policies mention conducting needs assessment as an explicit way to determine library selection criteria, 11 of the policies (44 percent) include some aspect of getting prisoner feedback on library services.

Only two policies openly discourage censorship: Hawaii and Connecticut. Hawaii's policy is very descriptive regarding fighting censorship in prisons. Specifically:

> Library Services may provide controversial works presenting different points of view, thus enabling inmates to make up their own minds about serious and important questions. The correctional facilities have a population, which is specialized compared to the general public; however, overt censorship cannot serve the aims of redirection. It must be assumed that upon release, persons who have been in correctional facilities will face a wide variety of experiences, and thus must be prepared to deal with these situations."[50]

Hawaii's policy takes the most liberal approach to censorship of all the policies reviewed; this policy was also more documented and expansive than many of the other policies reviewed. Connecticut's policy does not explicitly mention the word censorship, however, it does state: "the Unit Administrator or designee may not reject an item solely because its content is religious, philosophical, political, social or sexual, or because its content is unpopular or repugnant."[51] This stance is particularly interesting in Connecticut, since this was the state of the Hayes trial in 2010 where the press and subsequent Associated Press investigation caused politicians to call for action and change. According to the Connecticut Department of Correction 2010 Annual Report, the policy cited here would have been the policy initiated after the Hayes trial controversy along with another policy on reviewing prisoner mail for subversive or explicit material.[52] This policy, which appeared to be a new directive resulting from political pressure, includes a Library Materials Review Committee. It is surprising that this kind of rejection of censorship was included in the new directive despite the criticisms received from politicians and the media.

Privacy and confidentiality of patron records in prisons, including their borrowing records, is a topic that is infrequently addressed in policies. Only four policies mention any sort of stance on general record keeping related to prisoners' records. Colorado is the most explicit about confidentiality as those employed by the DOC are not to "disclose any record or other information which identifies a person as having requested or obtained specific materials or services or as otherwise having used the library" unless required by subpoena.[53] Policy in Indiana dictates that "library service records maintained at each facility shall include, but not be limited to: inventories, costs, and program participation."[54] Additionally, the same policy states that "the Facility Head or designee and the facility librarian shall recommend to the Director of Education Services operational procedures regarding library services at the facility, including the maintenance of records and inventories relevant to the acquisition, circulation and disposition of library materials."[55] No references to confidentiality or privacy were found in this policy. The Department of Correction's policy in Massachusetts presents the idea of collecting information on patrons related to circulation for "keeping records of the loans."[56] Massachusetts' policy also includes a description of the general information system for the institution, an automated system "that provides processing, storage and retrieval of inmate related information needed by Department personnel and other authorized users within the criminal justice system."[57] The New Mexico Corrections Department authored the fourth policy that mentions recordkeeping in libraries, stating that "circulating materials will be tracked using a record system that identifies borrowers and due dates."[58] Similar to omissions in national policies, the issues of privacy and confidentiality of borrowing records or other patron records are not frequently addressed in state policies. Developing stances on these types of policies may be an action item for current policymakers, including those working on a revision of the 1992 ASCLA standards.

## Law Libraries

I defined a number of simple questions to evaluate each of the law services policies from the 24 states so that overreaching similarities between law library policies could be established. Specifically, the policies were reviewed for cases cited, whether or not access to any sort of technology was permitted, if database access was allowed, and whether or not further legal assistance was mentioned. Policies reviewed included those from the following states: Alabama, Alaska, Arizona, California, Colorado, Florida, Illinois, Indiana, Kansas, Massachusetts, Michigan, Minnesota, Nebraska, Nevada, New Mexico, New York, Ohio, Oklahoma, Oregon, Rhode Island, Vermont, Virginia, Washington, and Wyoming.

The single most referenced case was *Lewis v. Casey*, which was explicitly mentioned in six of the 24 policies (in 25 percent of the policies reviewed). *Bounds v. Smith* was mentioned in three policies, with other cases referenced in four policies. Of the cases in which *Lewis v. Casey* was mentioned, two also mentioned *Bounds v. Smith* among others, and two mentioned other cases along with *Lewis v. Casey*, but not *Bounds v. Smith*. Additional cases mentioned included *Gilmore v. Lynch, Toussaint v. McCarthy, Toussaint v. Rowland, Zatko v. Rowland*,[59] *Johnson v. Avery, Twyman v. Crisp, Ramos v. Lamm, Nordgren v. Mitchell, Petrick v. Maynard, Shaw v. Murphy*,[60] *Booth v. Churner, Porter v. Nussle*,[61] and *Halpin, et al. v. Patrissi*.[62]

Fifty (50 percent) of the policies mentioned technology with 37.5 percent or nine of them allowing or encouraging some form of access to computerized legal services. Those who encouraged this access included Alaska, California, Colorado, Florida, Nevada, Oklahoma, Oregon, Virginia, and Wyoming. Alaska's policy states: "Each institutional law library must contain at least one computer terminal that provides access to legal materials in a digital format."[63] According to California's policy, "each institution shall maintain at least one law library for the use of inmates, in print and/or by means of the Electronic Law Library Delivery System with any necessary print supplements."[64] Colorado allows the usage of certain technology for legal research: "Program tape recorders, DVD/CD players, computers, and laptop computers may be used for the purpose of listening to recordings, viewing video of court and DOC administrative proceedings, or reviewing discovery."[65] Florida's policy encourages the collection of computerized resources[66] while Nevada allows for hardcover copies to be substituted with automated computerized copies.[67] Oregon also allows access to computerized collections but only via CD-ROM.[68] In Oklahoma, prisoners are permitted only to use the law library workstations for purposes of legal research.[69] Wyoming's policy similarly states that computers may only be used for purposes of legal research or legal matters,[70] and Virginia has a more general statement, specifically that the usage of computers should align with facility rules and regulations.[71]

Of the 24 policies reviewed, three ban technology in some form or other in the prison library. These states include Arizona, Kansas, and New Mexico. According to Arizona's policy, prisoners may not use computers for legal research.[72] In Kansas, according to the last date of this policy, prisoners are not permitted to access the Internet in any form.[73] It is likely that this policy is under revision, or that practice in Kansas deviates from this ban, based on the 2015 *Intersect* article on experimentations with Internet access for state prisoners in various states including Kansas.[74] In New Mexico the following policy is in place: "Facility Education Resource Centers shall not provide inmates with access to manual and/or electric typewriters, word processors, computers for personal or legal or non–ERC use, nor supplies for personal inmate typewriters."[75]

Of the nine states allowing some form of technology, seven mention access to databases that can be used for legal research. These states include Alaska, California, Colorado, Florida, Nevada, Virginia, and Wyoming. Alaska's and Colorado's policies mention the database LexisNexis specifically.[76] The other five states' policies mention general electronic resource access. California's policy states: "Inmates shall not access any computer outside of their authorized work, vocational, or educational assignment, or as needed for legal research on the Law Library Electronic Delivery System."[77] Virginia's policy also references an "Electronic Law Library Contract"[78] and Wyoming's policy includes restrictions for printing from electronic resources implying access to database collections.[79] Nevada does not encourage or imply automatic access to databases, rather that hardcover copies may be substituted with electronic versions.[80]

Of the 24 policies reviewed, only two do not mention legal assistance offered through the library or law library. These two states were Illinois and Kansas. Illinois' policy was, however, very limited: It consisted of only a few sentences.[81] The policies cite a variety of methods for alternative legal assistance including knowledgeable librarians, prisoner librarians, prisoner clerks, legal assistants, legal coordinators, attorneys, etc. Many reference the idea of limited assistance only. According to Massachusetts' policy, library personnel may assist with the "instruction in the use of legal materials and reference assistance. However, such assistance shall not include legal advice or direction of legal research on the part of library personnel."[82] Michigan's policy similarly states that staff may be trained to offer legal consultation, "however, neither staff nor prisoner clerks shall provide legal advice beyond instructions on use of the law library collection."[83] It is likely that these provisions are intended to protect staff from providing legal advice; a few interviewees from chapter 9 mention the scope of what they are allowed to provide to prisoners without providing legal advice. One interviewee, Heather, mentions that they are not allowed to provide legal advice and therefore have difficulty addressing certain patron needs.

## Summary

State policies on general library service and law library service reviewed in this chapter adhere to national policies in some regards and either deviate from or omit policy statements in other regards. Law library policies occasionally cite national court cases such as *Lewis v. Casey* and *Bounds v. Smith*. Most states have a clear definition of the purpose of the prison library with many referencing rehabilitation as the primary purpose and others comparing the level of service to that of a public library. Most policies also present clear definitions of the types of materials to be collected by the library with reference to exceptions due to security concerns. Policies on technology in both general library service and law library service are piecemeal with more reference to the usage of computers for legal collections. Management concerns such as space, training level or education of staff, or clear allocation of budget are not consistently addressed across all policies despite these issues having such prevalence in the ASCLA standards from 1992.

Collection development and material selection policies are included in most of the state policies reviewed; these are very similar to national policies and standards. Committees are occasionally used to make selections and user needs are frequently cited as a means of determining what materials to select with some variance on what user needs assessment entails. Few policies discourage overt censorship. Privacy or confidentiality of patron records is rarely mentioned in any of the state policies and is perhaps a subject worthy of further investigation.

This assessment of state policies was not without limitations. Since policies were obtained from respective states' Department of Corrections' websites, it is possible that these documents are not the current policies in place in institutions. Many policies were from 2010 to 2013 and appeared to be relatively current. A few documents dated back to 1984, 1986 and 1999; arguably these documents may not be current. Essentially, I assessed the current state of policies listed publicly on websites. Without confirming with individual institutions in-state, it would be impossible to ascertain whether all of these policies are current or observed. For the instances where policies were limited to only a few sentences or paragraphs such as Florida or Illinois, it is likely that more in-depth policies exist, however, these policies were not found online. The assessment of the 29 states in this chapter should, therefore, not be absolute or complete; rather it should illustrate patterns for library service and adherence to or straying from national policy. Additionally, it should present some of the public-facing policies that correctional institutions tend to observe. Further qualitative information about the practices at individual institutions will be shared in chapters 8 and 9 through a national survey and individual interviews with correctional librarians.

# 3

# Literature on Key Issues
# in Prison Librarianship

*You know, there truly is not enough written about what it's like, really what it's like to be a prison librarian. There's not a heck of a lot of information out there.... It's such an important arm of librarianship. If people only knew.*
—Carrie, Interviewee from Chapter 9

This chapter will present and analyze existing literature on prison librarianship published in the last 40 years. Types of materials include books, scholarly articles, and trade publications. Key points to be touched upon in the literature include the purpose of the prison library, administrative policies and procedures for a prison library, library services generally offered to the incarcerated, collection development policies and procedures, and needs assessment procedures for collection development and services. Additionally, references to intellectual freedom, prisoners' rights and privacy, and access to law libraries will be included. Lastly, the controversial role of technology in the prison library will be discussed.

It appears that more was written on the subject of prison librarianship in the 1970s, perhaps in tandem with the new move towards recognition of prisoners' rights inspired by the previous decade's Civil Rights Movement. Books by Rhea Joyce Rubin, Rudolf Engelbarts, Virgil Gulker, and others centered around the topic of prison librarianship, and were all authored in the 1970s. According to Larry Sullivan and Brenda Vogel, "the 1970s were the golden years of prison library service," especially evident in the more frequent scholarship written during that decade.[1] The trade publications and journals *Wilson Library Bulletin*, *Library Trends*, and *Illinois Libraries* all dedicated issues to the topic of prison librarianship in the 1970s.

Literature became far less frequent in the 1980s through mid–1990s, likely because of the corrections environment during those years. Linkages between rehabilitation and library services were no longer glorified as they were in the 1970s; William Coyle's book was written during this period. Fred Hartz, Michael Krimmel, and Emilie Hartz released a bibliography of works on prison librarianship noting the decline in publications and educational opportunities in the profession. In the mid–90s, an edited book from Rhea Joyce Rubin and Daniel Suvak, as well as Vogel's *Down for the Count*, brought more attention to prison library topics.

In the last ten to 15 years, books focusing on the topic of prison librarianship are less frequent, with a new *Prison Library Primer* from Brenda Vogel, and a joint work from

Sheila Clark and Erica MacCreaigh. Most of the titles published are how-to guides or information about the profession. The scholarly literature is similarly scarce in the last ten to fifteen years when compared to other fields of librarianship. *Library Trends* devoted a 2011 issue to the topic of prison librarianship with notable chapters on U.S. prison librarianship from Vibeke Lehmann. Otherwise, articles on the subject are rare, especially articles of a scholarly nature. Frequently blurbs about programs and cooperation between prisons and public libraries appear to be newsworthy, as are instances where prison libraries are criticized in litigation. Overall, the written coverage of prison librarianship has significantly declined since the 1970s, showing a trend of reduced interest or attention on the topic.

## Purpose of the Prison Library

The prison library began as a place that provided reading materials to prisoners; originally prisoners could only access religious materials including the Bible and related works of Christianity.[2] Public opinion of prisoners having access to books for recreational reading has not always been positive; Rudolf Engelbarts asserts: "the public too often thinks that criminals must be severely punished, and they claim in disgust that many prisons are run like country clubs."[3] Kathleen de la Peña McCook mentions that "long and hard incarceration" is not always necessary and that there are "library connected initiatives that demonstrate a kinder philosophical approach."[4] Robert Stearns states: "To spend tax revenues on library services for thieves, rapists and murderers has the appearance of taking egalitarian principles to the extremes. The entertainment media has fostered the image of the prison library as a place where books are read by sinister characters in order to achieve nefarious goals."[5] Larry Sullivan acknowledges the importance of reading for prisoner populations and the controversy of providing reading materials to the incarcerated: "Reading is good. But the idea of good, indeed the very idea of the book, takes on different meanings for different reading communities."[6] This conflict between offering prisoners respite against idleness and still inflicting retribution for crimes committed is a frequently visited theme in much of the literature on prison librarianship.

Multiple authors cite the varied nature of the prison library as combining elements of a public library, a school library, and a law library.[7] Sheila Clark and Erica MacCreaigh claim that the purpose of a prison library is to provide similar materials to those offered in a public library including materials for recreational reading, lifelong learning materials, literacy support materials, legal resources, job search support services and resources, and a safe haven for free thinking.[8] William Coyle, often criticized for his stance debunking the rehabilitative influence of prison libraries,[9] claims that the purpose of the prison library depends on the stakeholder: some think the purpose is rehabilitation and reentry programs, while others place the most emphasis on bibliotherapy or recreational programs.[10] Sullivan details the history of prison libraries and how materials changed over time to serve diverse purposes of punishment, education, and rehabilitation rather than just provide religious materials.[11] Vibeke Lehmann references the work of Rhea Joyce Rubin in establishing a rubric for roles of the library and presents her own experience in prison libraries fulfilling each of these roles. These roles include provision of popular reading materials, establishment of a learning center, a place for educational support, provision of materials for reentry, a haven for personal retreat, a research center for prison administration, and a mechanism for getting support for school curricula (especially in juvenile facilities).[12] Avi Steinberg, in his memoirs of his time working in a prison library, mentions a number of roles of the prison library including a place where nefarious acts can be plotted, a place to calm prisoners, a place to surveil prisoners, or as a means of passing time. Additionally, he states "the library made the prison safer for everyone, I was told." Steinberg, whose previous and subsequent career is as a writer and journalist, wrote a work that was personal and reflective, not informative or scholarly as many of the other works presented in this chapter. Nor did Steinberg have a long career in prison librarianship, general librarianship, or even preparation in library and information science prior to writing his memoirs.[13]

Steinberg also detailed his time working as an instructor in the prison. This concept of the prison library as an educational epicenter is evident in Virgil Gulker's statements: "This book is also a plea for a greater public awareness of the need for prison libraries. Whatever the need—education, entertainment, emotional release or literary escapism— the paperback library is a multi-faceted vehicle for the personal and social rehabilitation of the inmate."[14] Within his text, Gulker continues to note the importance of the library for supporting educational roles specifically such as providing access to GED or college courses for prisoners.[15] He asserts: "Meaningful educational experiences of this nature enable the library to realize its dynamic potential as a facilitator of learning and growth. This is the role the library can and must play if it is to be a viable and profitable force in the inmates' lives."[16]

Other authors, such as Christine Kirby in an edited essay from Susan McDonald, stress rehabilitation over education and claim "the librarian should provide information to help the inmate cope once he/she is on the outside" including materials that would assist with reentry.[17] Kirby mentions that this is necessary because many prisoners landed in prison due to their inability to survive in the outside world because of lack of basic skills such as getting access to "educational opportunities, job searching, family life, personal finances."[18] Hartz et al. note the importance of rehabilitation as a purpose of the prison library, however, they question the effectiveness of that purpose, since little evidence exists to support the rehabilitative effect of a prison library. Additionally, Hartz et al. claim that prisoners have to make the choice to rehabilitate themselves and that the insistence or encouragement from a prison librarian will never be an absolute road to redemption.[19]

More recent literature also addresses the concept of the prison library as a rehabilitative force that can be used to facilitate reentry to society. Vogel cites a number of goals for the prison library with rehabilitation at the forefront followed by "moral enlightenment," provision of recreational reading materials, and "to provide access to the courts."[20] In Vogel's *Prison Library Primer*, she mentions reentry resources that are important for a library to carry, but states that most literature on reentry does not mention literacy, the role of the library, or the librarian.[21]

As previously mentioned, recreational reading materials were, after the introduction of religious materials in prior centuries, carried in U.S. prison libraries starting in the 20th century. This purpose of providing materials for passing the time has persisted in prison libraries and is often thought of as a constructive use of otherwise idle time. According to a 1973 paper by Rubin, twice as many prisoners read books compared to the average U.S. population.[22] Sullivan also mentions that reading can allow prisoners to escape from the idleness and misery of prison thereby helping with survival.[23] Lehmann references the prison library's role in allowing constructive use of time and access to materials that assist with reentry.[24] Sandra Greenway acknowledges that recreational reading can keep prisoners occupied and at times out of trouble.[25] Diane Campbell claims that prisoners require their information needs to be satiated to be able to survive incarceration and eventually reenter society.[26]

The prison library is not always just a constructive use of time; it can also be a positive socialization experience. Vogel supports this thought: "The prison library as a purveyor of books is more often than not the sole provider of acceptable and essential socialization in the daily regimen of a prisoner."[27] Judith Jordet details the pro-social nature of the prison library in more detail, highlighting the role that collection development can have in promoting a pro-social environment.[28]

Vogel, in two of her publications, mentions the roles and purposes of the prison library of the future, anticipating a need for reform and acknowledging current challenges for the prison library. In an article from 1997, she states that "prison libraries must be transformed from the access-to-the-courts programs and emerge as community information and cultural centers, serving the incarcerated the way libraries traditionally serve their constituencies."[29] More recently, she pleads for change to technology policies claiming that denying access to technology will cause the prison system to revert to emphasis on punishment over rehabilitation:

> Toward the close of the twentieth century, prison libraries, which had become libraries not unlike those in the outside world, were at the mercy of a conservative Supreme Court and a political climate that supported long and hard incarceration. One may conclude that if prison authorities maintain their decision to exclude online access, it would likely mean that the nineteenth-century ethos of the keepers to control reading and information will frame prison libraries in the twenty-first century.[30]

Many of the standards mentioned in chapters 1 and 2 echo these sentiments regarding the purpose of the prison library. Frequent purposes for the prison library include access to recreational reading material, educational programs whether for professional development or to assist with rehabilitation and reentry, and at times access to legal materials. The role and scope of technology is a development worth monitoring, and one that will be discussed in more detail later in this chapter.

## Administration

In chapters 1 and 2, administrative issues were frequently discussed in national and state standards for prison library services. Specific issues that received consistent attention in national and state standards were the space and size of the library, staffing the library with professionals and/or prisoners, and budget issues. Space is infrequently mentioned in the scholarly or trade literature. When referencing space requirements, some authors refer to current ASCLA standards from the time of publication of the author's work.[31] Staffing, however, is often debated; many authors believe that a professional librarian should be utilized more often in prison libraries than they currently are. Additionally, the conflicts with prison administration over decision-making, collection management, etc., are recurrently mentioned throughout the literature.

Many authors stress the importance of hiring professional librarians and the hesitation or inability of prison administration to bring these professionals in. Most authors deem those with master's degrees in library science to be "professional librarians." Lehmann, for instance, mentions that there are not enough professional librarians employed in prisons.[32] Vogel asserts that professionals are needed to ensure proper service.[33] Engelbarts views the prison librarian's position as particularly challenging: "Prison librarians must have special knowledge of sociology, criminology, psychiatry and psychology, must have sympathy and understanding and have strong leadership characteristics and courage."[34] Vogel and others claim that the field of prison librarianship can be incredibly rewarding.[35] Nevertheless, professional librarians in these positions are scarce. In 1990, Linda Lucas published survey results querying state prisons for their requirements for librarians. Lucas noted that specializing in prison librarianship was not possible when getting a degree in library and information science at that time.[36] Thirteen years earlier it was still possible to be trained on prison librarianship during graduate school in library science. In 1977, Harris McClaskey lists a number of educational programs, including master's in library science programs, which offered coursework on correctional librarianship.[37]

Prison librarians also, according to much of the literature, have isolated work conditions and are disconnected from professional development opportunities. Vogel notes a sequestered work experience for many prison librarians: "the awkward paradox of the librarian unleashing pleasure into a cosmos of pain almost mandates isolation from the punishment phalanx."[38] Vogel describes the solitude experienced when dealing with outside libraries and librarians; for example, she claims that public libraries do not often consider serving the prison library part of their duties.[39] In another article, Vogel draws attention to the dichotomy of prison librarians neither being fully integrated members of the librarian profession nor the correctional profession.[40] Glen Singer mentions that it is challenging for a prison librarian to stay abreast of current developments or technologies in the field due to "professional isolation,"[41] while Clark and MacCreaigh discuss the lack of literature and isolation from other librarians both in and out of the profession.[42]

Other scholars discuss the issues with professional literature on prison librarianship. Campbell highlights the nature of much of the literature on prison librarianship, stating "studies should be empirical rather than based on opinion as so much of the literature regarding prisons has been."[43] Hartz et al. question the validity of much of the literature, claiming that many authors are not working in the field of prison librarianship and therefore lack the authority to discuss the topics. They also note the lack of scholarship on prison librarianship in general.[44]

Multiple sources present issues with prison library budgets with Vogel's description providing the most detail. Vogel mentions the effects of the Library Services and Technology Act (LSTA) shifting focus to technology related projects, which ultimately were better suited for the public library than the prison library.[45] This lost funding is only further compounded by budget cuts. Vogel acknowledges that the prison library can potentially suffer major budget losses during tough times: "Prison library programs, the stepchild of all correctional programs, are seldom rewarded with material gain and suffer greater losses than other correctional programs during hard economic and socially frugal times."[46] Gulker also details obstacles in obtaining and maintaining a budget, stating: "Financial and moral support are barely above the subsistence level and are to be obtained only after considerable effort."[47] Certainly managing a prison library's budget seems to be challenging, especially when prison authorities feel compelled to make cuts in education and recreational areas to accommodate prison administration needs.

A recurrent theme in the literature is the constant conflict between the prison administration's goal of incarceration and security coupled with the prison library's mission to provide recreational and/or educational materials. Sullivan acknowledges this challenge, stating: "Library service to prisoners operates on premises that revert to ideas of punishment, confinement, control, discipline, atavistic vengeance, and even exclusion. When we speak of prisons today, we speak in terms of retribution, deterrence, and incapacitation, not freedom to read or surf the Web."[48] This attitude, frequently further disseminated by mass media, leads to a conflict between library service and administrative goals. Libraries attempt to provide the means to reintegrate a prisoner upon release by providing educational services and library materials while the prison administration aims to meet certain goals, including retribution, punishment, and ultimately security. Megan Sweeney acknowledges the complicated and at times contradictory interactions between prison administration and prison libraries, stating "whereas libraries were once deemed a central component of prison rehabilitation programs, libraries and prisons came to be viewed as incompatible institutions."[49] Stearns broaches the fact that the different goals and lack of understanding between librarians and prison authorities can at times even become hostile.[50] Gulker discusses this issue, stating that "the librarian is dependent at all times for all things upon the prison administration," and that "the librarian must work with the administration but he must also work at them. The administration does little more than concede the need for a library."[51] Diana Reese agrees that "it is a fine line correctional librarians must walk between the prisoners' right to information and the administration's goal of a secure facility with active programs."[52] Clark and MacCreaigh discuss the importance of knowing when to push back: "you have to know when to fight for inmates' rights to information and when to back off for the good of the order."[53] Furthermore, Clark and MacCreaigh state that even amongst prison librarians "there are questions about which of librarianship's ethical values to uphold and which to lay aside in the interest of safety."[54] Hartz et al. make an interesting comment regarding the hierarchy in prison administration that may or may not relate to the complicated position many prison librarians may experience: "We need to investigate the reasons why a librarian in a correctional facility has never attained the proper stature in the managerial organization."[55]

Stearns addresses the issue of providing service versus maintaining security as well, but asserts that the library can be used to minimize hostility between correctional staff and library employees if the library also serves the prison administration employees.[56] Additionally, Stearns asserts that if libraries handle correctional issues effectively, they can even help increase safety in the institution.[57] Clark and MacCreaigh echo this sentiment, claiming that "library service inside a correctional institution might have demonstrable *security* benefits," while also fulfilling or boosting accreditation scores.[58]

Multiple authors mention this conflict between the prison library's purpose and the prison administration's agenda as an ethical professional issue. Gerald Bramley's blanket statement that it is the librarian's role and duty to offer service to everyone regardless of their circumstance[59] is an assertion that is challenged and modified based on the needs of the institution and often the prison administration's prerogative. David Wilhelmus states that prison librarians have a constant conflict of interest between adhering to the policies of the institution and complying with the ALA's "Library Bill of Rights."[60] Lehmann also addresses this conflict, stating: "A dichotomy exists, however, between the professional librarian's philosophical and ethical commitment to free access to information and the very real constraints that are or may be imposed on access to reading materials in the prison environment."[61] Coyle acknowledges a role conflict as well, noting that prison librarians have to balance legal and ethical correctional issues with the principles of librarianship.[62] Glennor Shirley, a well-known former prison librarian from Maryland who maintains the blog "prison librarian," states in an article from 2003: "Philosophically, most prison libraries aspire to operate on the same model as public libraries and adopt the "Library Bill of Rights" of the American Library Association. Practically, however, this is difficult because of the restrictions imposed by prison administration whose mission is different from that of the libraries."[63] Furthermore, Shirley lists a number of additional challenges for providing what she considers to be good service, including security issues, unstable budgets, insufficient staffing, isolated work experiences for librarians, lack of opportunity for professional development, and inability to provide technology.[64] This conflict between roles is especially poignant when discussing censorship issues in prison libraries, a topic to be discussed in more detail later in this chapter.

## General Library Services

In chapters 1 and 2, general library services were defined including space recommendations, facility features, hours, services and programs, etc. Engelbarts, for example, cites the important aspects of a prison library, including a schedule with adequate hours of operation, capable staff, financial support, selection of appropriate materials, and marketing or promotion of library services.[65] Rubin, in her chapter on the planning process in *Libraries Inside: A Practical Guide for Prison Libraries*, discusses how to set up a successful prison library program including selecting roles for the library such as an activity center, information center, educational support service, creation of a learning center, a source for recreational reading, or to serve as a reference or research library.[66] Two authors refer to the prison library as a "safe haven" for the incarcerated: Rubin, when discussing prison libraries as legal research centers and effective for treatment groups,[67] as well as Stearns, when he mentions that the library can be used to help transition to the outside world.[68] The literature on prison librarianship frequently references roles that the library can play within the institution. It is still worth noting that most of the literature places less emphasis on standards such as hours or facility requirements, and rather discusses hot topics such as collection development or integrating technology in prison libraries.

## Collection Development and Censorship

Material selection is an oft debated topic in the literature on prison librarianship, since some form of censorship is mandated by most, if not all, prison administrations. As Bramley puts it: "Books were seen as potential threats to prison discipline and security, introducing dangerous and possibly inflammatory ideas. To bring books into a prison could lead to unrest and disorder."[69]

Authors such as Greenway present surveys detailing popular types of materials that are frequently selected for circulation in recreational reading collections, including genres such as fiction, science fiction or fantasy, thrillers and suspense, westerns, ethnic novels, and current events materials such as newspapers or magazines.[70] Greenway acknowledges that collection development and intellectual freedom are complex issues in a prison library.[71] Marjorie LeDonne, in her comprehensive survey from 1974 of correctional institution libraries, presents results that support material selection policies to collect for all reading levels including legal materials and instructional services.[72] Additionally, LeDonne encourages prisoner access to audiovisual collections and services such as photocopying.[73] McDonald lists requests submitted by prisoners including those for crime and prison books, fiction, poetry for composing letters to loved ones, self-help titles, fitness books, books on games, sports magazines and related books, other magazines, legal materials, and reference materials such as dictionaries.[74] Gulker selects materials based on age, ethnicity, and sex to serve a "cross-section of American society."[75] Vogel states that developing a collection should be guided by the same principles librarians use in general librarianship with two exceptions: the prison librarian must assume the materials may be used for alternative purposes that might be negatively viewed by prison administration and must expect that prisoners will have little to no access to the Internet.[76] Sweeney views the situation as more bleak, stating that "penal environments directly influence the availability and circulation of books, as well as the uses that prisoners make of them."[77]

Reese presents a guide on how to do "systematic and continuous" collection development by establishing a process.[78] She discusses the importance of policy for setting goals, scope, assisting with prioritization, making a public statement of the library's mission, assisting with staff training, and providing guidance for budgeting for new collections and weeding existing collections.[79] Vogel has a similar stance, stating that a good collection development policy will withstand criticism and challenges.[80] Furthermore, Vogel recommends referencing the institutional, state, and federal policies for prison libraries to help formulate a better and more accurate collection development policy.[81]

In previous chapters, the issue of maintaining security while aspiring to provide access to potentially dangerous or subversive reading materials was frequently addressed in national and state policies on prison libraries. The ALA acknowledges the tenuous line between censorship and prison security; in the "Prisoners' Right to Read," the ALA establishes a number of exceptions in which censorship is acceptable practice in the prison library.[82] Bramley details types of items that were excluded, or censored, in the 1970s in prison libraries including westerns deemed to be "anti-social," detective books with criminal activity or behavior, newspapers detailing crimes, political works, medical literature, books with explicit sexual content, martial arts materials, works of "introspection," and psychology materials.[83] In general, Bramley appears to oppose arbitrary censorship of materials, but acknowledges that some items may be restricted due to a need to "preserve security and internal discipline."[84] Hartz et al. cite an example of an "Admissible Reading Material Directive" from Florida. Documents such as these may serve as a means for determining which items might cause issues. These items include obscene literature, materials that detail law-breaking activities, anything considered inflammatory that might instigate escape attempts, riots, or similar disturbances, materials that instruct on the creation of weapons or drugs, and any other items that would create legitimate penological concerns, would disrupt rehabilitation, or contradict the goals of the institution.[85] Reese, while defining what an effective collection development policy includes, mentions that the institution's stance on prisoner reading materials should be considered, since the security of the institution is tantamount.[86] Michael Bemis discusses the challenge with selecting materials and supporting an institution's security policies poignantly:

> This is where the prison librarian must walk a fine line. For most of us, it's a natural inclination to be adamantly opposed to censorship, but in this situation, security trumps all. Therefore, certain materials are automatically forbidden: anything dealing with weapons, tattoos, escapes, gangs, martial arts. Ditto on materials that depict or describe sex or nudity. In this environment, knowledge isn't just power—it can be a threat to the safety of those who work here, so a librarian must learn to accept the restrictions.[87]

Other authors present this delicate balancing act that prison librarians must successfully maneuver. Vogel discusses the role that the prison administration and respective department of corrections may play in establishing a censorship policy: "Even now, prison authorities in many states maintain a list of books and magazines that are approved for purchase, and a list of titles that are forbidden. A committee intuitively selects or rejects titles that may provide mass upheaval, or encourage individual evil acts."[88] Furthermore, Vogel mentions that outside institutions and people such as citizens, those working in legislation or justice, or advocating for prisoner rights may have some influence over the collection development policies in place at prison libraries since these groups "mistrust inmate access to information, too."[89] This influence of the state was clearly visible in the Steven Hayes trial, after which Connecticut Senator Kissel requested a revamping of the items censored by Connecticut prison libraries.

Censorship, or limited access to books, is sometimes also related to physical dangers within the institution. Vogel mentions the concern from prison administration regarding the circulation of hardcover books, in which contraband can be smuggled.[90] Steinberg also mentions this issue since concealed items in books or shelves in the library were frequent security problems in his institution.[91] In Gulker's book, only paperback copies were collected for the prison library, perhaps to address security concerns.[92]

In practice, censoring or restricting access to materials in prison libraries appears to conform to many of the policy statements mentioned by authors above and by the standards referenced in chapters 1 and 2 of this book. Materials are frequently censored on the basis of subversive content. Gulker claims that he avoided censoring books that were considered contentious with content such as murders or lynchings. Nevertheless, he acknowledges that conflict can happen as was the case in the banning of the book *Great White Hope* by Howard Sackler at his institution.[93] Greenway, in her survey on prison library services, details responses regarding censored items such as those related to legitimate penological concerns, items that would aid in escape or criminal activities, those related to explosives, weapons, or alcohol, those with explicit sexual scenes, and those that would promote or incite violence between incarcerated groups.[94] During her internship at Oshkosh Correctional Institution Library, Amy Mark observes a number of censorship policies, including the censorship of materials deemed unsafe such as tattoo manuals and racial supremacy materials that might encourage violence such as KKK or Nation of Islam materials. These materials were removed on a case-by-case basis by the librarian in her institution.[95] Mark also mentions that sex offenders had special exclusions, while political books, as long as they were not violent, were deemed acceptable.[96] In Teresa Bowden's article on state prison libraries, she notes that materials on pornography, weapon creation, violence, martial arts, drugs and escapes were banned. Some materials that are occasionally but not consistently banned include materials such as hate literature, literature on gangs, homosexuality, road maps, true crime novels, information on Satanic worship, literature on survival, medical topics, and anything about organized crime.[97] Singer mentions similar topics that are excluded from the prison library: "In addition, certain individual books and types of materials are strictly banned by security on the basis of "penological interest" (e.g. books on martial arts, firearms, organic chemistry, Satanism, etc. as well as those that advocate violence or racial hatred)."[98]

Avi Steinberg's memoir of his time as a prison librarian also includes mentions of censorship. He considers censoring a work by Sylvia Plath because he is concerned of the effects it might have on prisoners: "But just because *Ariel* was art didn't make it less dangerous—in fact, it made it potentially far more so. I had women in my library who were borderline cases, cutters, suicide junkies, who might turn to Plath as an oracle of self-annihilation. Maybe I had a responsibility to shield them from this poem."[99] Steinberg's statement does not reflect the administration's policies on censorship, rather he personally thinks Plath's work is one that might cause potential harm and therefore might need to be excluded from the collection. Steinberg admittedly has no prior experience as a prison librarian and does not have the education required for many of these positions across the United States. It is unclear if Steinberg is aware of ALA stances on intellectual freedom and anti-censorship.

Even religious works have been censored based on prison administration concerns that they might threaten penological interests. Sullivan details instances where religious works such as the teachings of Islam were removed from federal prisons, some of which were subsequently reinstated when protests occurred publicly.[100] Sullivan also mentions a Federal Bureau of Prisons review in which literature is assessed for acceptability in correctional institutions.[101]

Multiple authors refer to the censorship of works from publisher Holloway House, which are viewed as rough street books often incorporating criminal activities in the basic plot lines. Greenway mentions the South Carolina removal of all of these Holloway House books.[102] Mark comments that Iceberg Slim and Donald Goines, both authors under Holloway House, are frequently banned in prison libraries, however, are also the most read items in the collection.[103] McDonald mentions that prisoners request and frequently read books from these two specific authors.[104] Vogel discusses the work of Slim and Goines as well, acknowledging the popularity they both have in prison libraries and the influence their type of "urban fiction" is having on prisoner reading interests.[105]

Frequently, authors criticize institutional policies of censorship, claiming that censoring items does not prevent access to information or to subversive concepts. LeDonne, for example, alludes to the pointlessness of censorship, stating "efforts to control the exchange of ideas have seldom made much sense."[106] Additionally, LeDonne believes that censorship only encourages the violent thoughts and behaviors it was intended to avoid: "Within the institutional milieu, a sure means of lending weight to an idea is to dignify it with attempted suppression. Such efforts immediately bestow an aura of unanswerability."[107] Hartz et al.

share the thought that censorship will not prevent insurrection or bad behavior, believing that reading subversive materials will not "influence an inmate toward disruptive behavior; he knew how to violate the law long before his incarceration—thus his imprisonment."[108] Brenna Doyle, in a recently published article on the freedom to read, similarly asserts that censorship is not supported by any evidence that it dissuades certain actions:

> If those in power believe that reading about violence in books makes prisoners more prone to committing acts of violence in life, then it makes sense that censorship would be employed by the State. This belief, however, does not seem to be backed by any substantial evidence. Instances of censorship reveals that although libraries and book programs within prisons are ostensibly allowing inmates greater access to knowledge, this access is being closely monitored and managed by those in power.[109]

Doyle's suppositions that policies of censorship are not supported by evidence is justified. One must also consider certain exclusions as being protective for the security of the institution, especially in cases where prisoners may educate themselves to commit further crimes, attempted escapes, or to instigate riots. Clearly, policies of censorship are difficult to justify, implement, and maintain. Many decisions made by prison libraries and correctional institutions may be subjective and vary widely from one institution to the next.

Two authors address censorship as a reality of the job. Clark and MacCreaigh claim that all libraries censor in some form or another: "the fact is, every library 'censors' according to the accepted social norms of the communities in which they reside."[110] Daniel Suvak believes that the prison library is not equipped to take on the fight of censorship, stating "even if the sacred cows of intellectual freedom and censorship are the issues, a prison library has neither the money nor the muscle to wage this battle."[111]

## Technology

Many authors of prison library literature encourage the integration and use of more technology in prison libraries, but national and state policies generally do not address technology, perhaps due to security implications or outdated policies. Vogel, who has frequently written about the need to upgrade and implement technology in prison libraries, states: "Right now prison libraries are at a crossroads. They can adapt or they can become extinct. They are caught between the penological politics of the past and the technological potential of the present."[112] Vogel mentions usage of CD-ROMs as an alternative to online databases and asserts that this might be a solution for the future.[113] Sullivan states that "limiting access to this information [the Internet] greatly impedes reentry into the free world"[114] and encourages more Internet access and services for the incarcerated. In Bowden's article, she presents results from a mail survey for prison libraries on the technology they were using in the institution. Most had a mix of print and electronic resources, yet very few offered Internet.[115] All of these articles were published in the late 1990s and early 2000s, but it does not seem that the stance on Internet usage has changed drastically, especially considering the infrequent mention of the Internet or access to online services in the chapter 2 policies from individual states.[116]

More recently, Lehmann provides background on how prison librarians manage challenges for information technology, specifically access to the Internet.[117] In another article, she also mentions the conflict of trying to incorporate technology without threatening the institution by providing LAN or WAN services[118] and presents some institutions that offer LexisNexis access to save money on collection development.[119] Vogel similarly mentions LexisNexis as a means of providing prisoners with meaningful access to the courts and asserts that prisoners must be able to use the computer themselves for the access to truly be considered meaningful.[120] William Payne and Michael Sabath administered a survey to correctional institutions inquiring about information technology implementations in prison libraries. Findings from their survey indicate that there was an increased use of information technology to provide services to prisoners since these alternatives often decreased expenses while also addressing prisoner demands.[121] Shirley mentions computer usage in prison libraries in an earlier paper, completed on the basis of a survey and notes, stating that the use is varied and inconsistent.[122] Computer usage should not be conflated with digital literacy in this section or any other section of this book; access to databases or to basic programs is not a solution for reducing the digital divide for the incarcerated nor is it a means to teach prisoners the critical thinking skills necessary to evaluate digital materials. While basic computer skills may help prisoners once released, technology or computer usage in the prison library may or may not prepare prisoners to have even rudimentary computer skills or higher level digital literacy skills to be able to evaluate online materials.

In later chapters of her book *Prison Library Primer*, Vogel goes into more detail regarding technology in the prison library, claiming that the American Correctional Association has seen the benefit of providing access to computers for prisoners, however, the Internet has generally been difficult to implement in the institution because of concerns regarding prisoners' access to the outside world and potential misuse.[123] She states: "It is unconscionable for the publicly funded prison industry, the ever-expanding behemoth of the U.S. justice system to asphyxiate the prison library program by denying the rewards and reality of the electronic revolution to their wards."[124] Vogel mentions policies in other countries where prisoners have access to the Internet and encourages a technology plan be developed in which telecommunications equipment, copiers, and stand-alone computers will be implemented and regulated. She also encourages library staff to be proficient in the usage of technologies in the prison library in order to be able to assist patrons.[125] Vogel asserts that a "digital literacy gap" exists between the incarcerated, who are often low income minority groups, and the prison librarian can act as a conduit to establishing digital skills that will help prisoners succeed in the outside world.[126] While discussing reentry, Vogel mentions that most of the literature on prison librarianship does not address digital literacy needs and how those needs, if fulfilled, would assist the incarcerated after parole.[127]

Vogel, in another article from 2008, also discusses the digital divide between the incarcerated and the rest of society, claiming that upon release, the previously incarcerated are "digitally dysfunctional people," who have very little chance of succeeding and thereby are limited in their future endeavors, especially since they do not have the "practical skill-sets of information-literate people."[128] She asserts that there is a "vital digital connection that an ex-offender must have in order to at least participate, if not compete, in twenty-first century America" and believes that with the right information technology, Internet access can be supplied that will not threaten security or provide access to commit potential crimes.[129]

According to Lehmann, not even all staff have access to Internet and email.[130] She describes a Colorado intranet that was developed for the prison libraries in network to share resources including manuals, web resources, updates and news, program and events flyers, staff directories, schedules, discussion boards, interlibrary loan web logs, and online training areas.[131] This kind of resource seems to be the exception and not the standard.

Two states have made the news in recent years for their innovative technology programs. Ohio, for instance, allows prisoners to purchase tablets with the goal of helping prisoners connect to the community, thereby increasing chances of reintegration. According to this article, other states including North Dakota, Georgia, Florida, Louisiana, Virginia, Michigan, and Washington also allow tablet usage.[132] In California's San Quentin prison, eighteen prisoners are learning programming skills such as HTML, JavaScript, and CSS. The initiative to teach these prisoners coding skills was established through Code 7370, a course offered in a partnership between the California Prison Authority and the programming boot camp company Hack Reactor. This course is also part of the venture capitalist program "Last Mile," which was established to increase prisoners' chances of employment after release. According to the article, prisoners in the program "are learning essentials like technology, social media, business planning and computer proficiency."[133]

## Needs Assessment

Frequently in the literature, the collection of a prison library is equated to a public library: specifically, a diverse collection to support wide-reaching needs of various groups. Engelbarts states that the prison library exists to stimulate reader interests and should therefore be guided by these interests.[134] Vogel, in a 1976 report on a survey administered with Maryland prisoners, discusses the role that a library can play in stimulating "interest and awareness of information service" to help a prisoner cope and reassess his or her individual situation.[135] Vogel asserts that prisoners have vital needs for information, "which are perhaps more intense and perhaps qualitatively different from persons who are not in prison."[136] These needs are often mistakenly interpreted using librarians' "educated guesses" rather than actual prisoner needs assessment and that "extant research on library services for inmates has focused on evaluating what already exists."[137] Certainly any public library would consider the constituency utilizing their services and accordingly adapt. Many of the authors on prison librarianship encourage the conducting of needs assessments to ascertain interest in different genres or types of materials in the prison library.

In Gulker's project to stock and build a prison library in a Michigan prison, most of the project was administered and run by prisoners. Therefore, the collections accrued were fueled by prisoner reading interests and needs. He states: "the ultimate role of the librarian, then, is to monitor the fluctuating frequencies of inmate interest."[138] According to Gulker, a librarian selecting materials based on personal preferences would be less fruitful than selecting based on prisoner interests.[139] He specifically mentions that not everyone is interested in reading classics.[140] LeDonne also notes the importance of conducting library needs assessments and involving prisoners in the selection process as well as organization of library programs, services, etc.[141] Sullivan details the history of the prison library and the move toward serving prisoners' requests rather than just stocking the shelves with educational materials. He states that "novels and information geared to prisoners' needs" should also be included.[142] Clark and MacCreaigh also mention the value of obtaining feedback from prisoner patrons and consider it especially helpful to inform prisoners when certain requests cannot be fulfilled due to security restrictions.[143]

Collections in prison libraries often span a wide range of reading levels to accommodate prisoners' various educational backgrounds. According to Stearns, "the library is a badly needed resource for inmates struggling with literacy, not a mere indulgence."[144] Lehmann demonstrates that reading interests are often very similar to the public reading interests, but that prisoners frequently have issues with literacy due to their backgrounds: "Incarcerated persons have the same reading interests as individuals in the free world. They do, however, constitute a user group with special needs because of their generally low educational level, their mostly disadvantaged social and economic background, and their high rate of substance abuse and mental illness."[145] Gulker similarly mentions that selection should include books of various reading levels to account for the diverse reading levels of prisoners.[146] Wilhelmus, an academic librarian who describes a potential higher education service partnership with prison libraries, sees a particular challenge with issues of literacy: "A serious problem confronting prison librarians engaged in the delivery of academic materials and services is the low level of literacy among inmates, which is apparent when inmates, as a group, are contrasted to the general population of the United States."[147] Judith Jordet details her investigations as a practicing prison librarian for determining what materials might be most interesting to her prisoners; she conducts her library materials needs assessments based on "common characteristics of the target population" combined with comparisons of her population to the wider public.[148] Jordet, in another article, also discusses the use of surveys to establish gaps between what materials are checked out and what prisoners might be reading that they have not checked out from the library.[149] All of Jordet's aforementioned articles discuss the role of the library in developing pro-social and cultural connections.

Rubin, in her chapter on planning a library from *Libraries Inside*, discusses the importance of needs assessment for building the space, facility, and collections. She specifically encourages data collection of demographics and resources, usage statistics, and similar data analysis measures to gauge interest in services.[150] In Reese's later chapter in the same book, she notes the importance of needs assessment to inform collection decisions.[151] Many prisoners speak languages other than English,[152] which can affect the types of information sought and should inform collection development decisions. Clark and MacCreaigh claim that many prisoners grew up in single-parent situations and frequently have learning disabilities and/or reading comprehension issues.[153]

## Intellectual Freedom, Prisoners' Rights and Privacy

Authors and library service advocates commonly reference intellectual freedom in relation to prisoners' rights. They consider these services necessary to help pass otherwise miserable time while incarcerated. Gulker, for example, refers to the prisoners' "basic mental and emotional literary hunger"[154] and their need to escape emotionally: "society has its synthetic crutches to support escapism but the inmate has only mind and spirit which need the fuel of literature."[155] Doyle claims that "literature 'frees' the mind, conceivably making the fact that the body is oppressively contained somewhat more bearable."[156] Reese encourages collection development policies to include statements on intellectual freedom, nudging librarians in prisons to take a stance on the matter in order to justify challenged material.[157] Greenway mentions the complex processes associated not only with collection development but also intellectual freedom in a prison library.[158] Elizabeth Jahnke and Laura Sherbo discuss the importance of the prison library for guarding intellectual freedom by providing "secure places where people who have lost their freedom are still entitled to intellectual freedom."[159] Oftentimes though, this right is not entirely tangible: Singer claims that concepts and documents such "as the Library Bill of Rights, Intellectual Freedom, and First Amendment freedoms become blurred and subject to pragmatic interpretation" when weighed against the security of the institution.[160]

Intellectual freedom, in this case interpreted as the right to read, is closely associated with prisoners' rights while incarcerated. LeDonne claims that in order to provide quality library services, there must be a "recognition of the constitutionally protected right of all inmates to read all materials available to the general public."[161] Lehmann details prisoners' rights in more detail: "In the United States, inmates in both state and federal prisons are guaranteed certain constitutional and civil rights. They include freedom from cruel and unusual punishment, the right to due process, freedom of speech, freedom of religion, the right to adequate medical care, freedom from racial discrimination, and the right of access to the courts."[162] Clark and MacCreaigh discuss prisoners' rights as they relate to the American Library Association's identified values of librarianship as "access and intellectual freedom, privacy and confidentiality, and social responsibility."[163] Vogel correctly and appropriately assesses the challenges associated with prisoners' rights by acknowledging what she deems to be public opinion on providing certain services to prisoners: "Public opinion has always been rabidly unsympathetic to the idea that an offender retains the right of citizenship and constitutional protections."[164] She addresses in particular the conflict between providing the right of access to the courts to prisoners in light of negative public opinion of such access. She mentions legislation and court decrees, which limit the scope of the prison library, effectively denying certain rights to prisoners[165] and claims that "prisoners are to be estranged from their communities but not from their Constitution."[166] Doyle also acknowledges the challenges associated with providing libraries to prisoners despite essential rights to intellectual freedom claiming that libraries "are there only because the State allows them to be and this beneficence comes at a high price."[167] LeDonne also supports the belief that library services should be provided to support constitutional rights, stating that library services be made available according to the "individual's right granted under the First Amendment of the Constitution to read and have access to all information from all points of view."[168]

Coyle is one of the only authors to contradict this widespread view of essential prisoner rights, stating:

> On the other hand, many of a new generation of service-oriented librarians have taken note of the attention that has been given to the rights of prison inmates and have suggested that library services are one of the things to which inmates have a right, independent of correctional goals. This view has received wide currency in the literature and in professional organizations and probably constitutes the main current of thought.[169]

Coyle's views have been generally ill received by the prison library community due to his opposition of the user-needs based approach modeled after the public library.

Despite Clark and MacCreaigh's claim that privacy is an essential right of prisoners, there is little literature that discusses the prisoner's right to privacy and confidentiality in the context of the prison library. In a previous work, I investigated this issue, finding that the application of privacy policies in prison libraries were at best ambiguous.[170] Clark and MacCreaigh mention privacy in their book, specifically recommending that library identifiers be unique patron identifiers rather than prisoner identifiers used by the entire institution.[171] Furthermore, Clark and MacCreaigh assert that privacy and confidentiality should be maintained as much as possible while understanding that the same standard of confidentiality expected at a public library will not be achieved.[172] They also claim that at times it may be necessary to violate privacy and confidentiality when questioning whether "withholding information about particular patrons' library usage lead[s] to greater harm than the surrender of said information."[173] The only other mention found of privacy and confidentiality of prisoner records including borrowing records is in the 1959 writings from Herman Spector, in which he states that "circulation records are carefully kept and reported quarterly and annually to the prison authority."[174] While Spector does not specifically discuss borrowing records, it does appear that certain records were, at that time, maintained by him and reported to the prison administration that might otherwise be considered confidential in a public library. This case appears to be exceptional and not the standard; Spector was known for his bibliotherapy work at San Quentin prison in California. He was interested in keeping statistics of prisoners' reading habits to ascertain the effectiveness of his bibliotherapy program.[175]

## Law Libraries and Meaningful Access to the Courts

Prison administration has customarily used a law library as one means of fulfilling the constitutional requirement to provide access to the courts; however, in recent years since the ruling of *Lewis v. Casey*, these libraries have subsequently suffered. Some of these libraries have closed or have been drastically cut back to meet the minimum requirements outlined in this landmark court case. According to Sullivan and Vogel in their article "Reachin' Behind Bars," the scope of the prison library, and especially the law library, began to change with the passing of the Prison Litigation Reform Act (PLRA), *Lewis v. Casey*, and the notable omission of correctional institutions in the 1997 Library Service and Technology Act.[176] The PLRA was initiated under the impression that prisoners were clogging up the judicial system with frivolous litigation. However, Vogel, in another article, claims "no research supports the notion that inmates litigate extravagantly, or that their lawsuits are unusually purposeless or frivolous. The media are responsible for this myth."[177] *Lewis v. Casey* was similarly detrimental to the prison library, in Vogel's opinion, as it seemed to reinstate the pre–1960s attitude that the court had little influence or place in enforcing prisoners' rights in correctional institutions, thereby "relieving the court from prison operation oversight, and denying the federal court's obligation to deter violations of prisoners' rights."[178] Vogel claims that fifty percent of prison law libraries were abandoned after *Lewis v. Casey*, an estimate which is higher than those reported by other scholars. Campbell discusses *Lewis v. Casey*'s stance on reversing the burden of proof and claims that those legal developments "changed the focus on legal information for prisoners from ensuring access to making them prove that they have been materially harmed by inadequate access."[179]

Because of reduction or elimination of prison law libraries resulting from the passing of the PLRA and the ruling of *Lewis v. Casey*, Vogel asserts that a prison librarian must have an understanding of legal research to provide the best possible assistance to prisoners making legal inquiries.[180] Clark and MacCreaigh agree that prison librarians must have expertise in providing access and assistance with legal collections, but they acknowledge the challenge of providing service without offering legal advice.[181] Vogel also lauds efforts to include LexisNexis access in prison libraries so that prisoners can access the court via this database or similar electronic resources. She does, nevertheless, qualify this access as only effective and meaningful when the prisoners are allowed to use the computers directly, otherwise "this is not a resource, it is a pitiful and misleading replacement for the print library and no more than a twenty-first century paging system."[182] The right to access the courts will be visited in more detail in chapter 5 with the presentation and discussion of court cases related to this constitutional right.

## Summary

The works investigated in this section reiterated and confirmed many of the policies from chapters 1 and 2 of this book. The purpose of the prison library remains varied with many citing reasons of rehabilitation and facilitation of reentry as major goals of the library. Library administration is oft plagued by budgetary issues and opportunities for staff professional development are limited. Librarians hoping to uphold ethical values espoused by the American Library Association are faced with challenges in dealing with a prison administration that holds conflicting goals. Censorship is often present in materials selection and collection development, sometimes arbitrary and sometimes considered to be justified to maintain the security of the institution. Most authors consider needs assessment to be a valid means of determining what materials to select.

In regards to constitutional rights, intellectual freedom, and rights to privacy and confidentiality, the environment becomes murky and more difficult to define. All authors, perhaps with the exception of Coyle, philosophically concur that prisoners retain constitutional rights including the freedom to read when incarcerated. What happens in practice, on the other hand, is very different: often the goals of the correctional institution supersede assumed prisoner rights. Meaningful access to the courts remains a right that prisoners seem to maintain, albeit in a diminished form in comparison to pre–*Lewis v. Casey* times. In the next two chapters, court cases including this landmark case will be presented and discussed. Chapter 4 will address court cases affecting the prisoners' right to read, followed by chapter 5 in which meaningful access to the courts will be presented.

Recurrent themes that emerge throughout this literature, especially in the literature from practicing prison librarians, are two challenges or issues with the profession that are not addressed in national or state policies. The first is the solitude that many prison librarians are facing on a day-to-day basis that isolates them from professional development opportunities and networking. Also, many of these librarians must accommodate various literacy levels amongst their user bases.

After reviewing this literature, it is also apparent that there is a void of scholarly literature on prison librarianship. Much of the literature presented in this chapter includes "how-to" guides, bibliographies, and other experience essays about the field of prison librarianship. Very few scholars, especially scholars employed in prison librarianship, are writing about research topics related to prison librarianship. User needs assessments, while they may be conducted internally, are not broadly publicized nor are any quantitative statistics regarding usage and experiences from the prisoners' perspectives. Clearly there is a call for more professional literature on the topic of prison librarianship, especially literature of a scholarly nature addressing prisoner needs. The profession needs a new Brenda Vogel, Glennor Shirley, or Vibeke Lehmann to continue discussing the issues of prison librarianship on a national or even international level.

# Part II: Neglect and Disadvantage: The Prison Library as the Forgotten Field of Librarianship

## 4

# Court Cases Affecting the Prisoner's Right to Read

*Education is at your fingertips and the books and materials are available all over and above anything else. And nowadays education is the book you read, because it's the investigation and the writings of others that you've become part of the extension of their life in order to gain your own education. And so I could see the whole world opening up to an inmate ... right now they're behind bars and through the library they could visit all over the world and experience the thoughts of men and women who've recorded their thoughts. My background led me to appreciate diving into a world of knowledge.*

—*Victor, Interviewee from Chapter 9*

Prisoners have frequently instigated litigation regarding their rights while incarcerated and many lawsuits were initiated with the goals of clarifying prisoners' rights to reading materials, library access, and legal materials in prison. This chapter will list a selection of lawsuits in which prisoners or other plaintiffs sued prison authorities regarding their rights to access reading materials. In some instances, the plaintiffs were successful in their attempts to clarify or initiate certain services or rights; in other cases, the prison authorities had justified cause to limit access to certain types of services or materials. Not all cases are directly related to prison library service. Many are cases involving prison mail service and delivery of reading materials. Additionally, a section on legal cases instigated by Prison Legal News will be shared in this chapter since Prison Legal News, also known as PLN, frequently litigates on topics of prisoner access to newsletters and other reading materials. Cases include federal, state, and civil cases in this chapter and the next. Cases from prisoners in jails and detention centers are also referenced.

Cases in which prisoners contested their rights for legal materials in order to obtain meaningful access to the court have not been addressed within this section. These will be presented and discussed in the next chapter in a similar fashion. The number of cases related to access to legal materials far surpass the number in which the dispute involved regular access to library services or general reading materials. Furthermore, many cases considered pivotal for law library services such as *Bounds v. Smith* and *Lewis v. Casey* will be addressed in chapter 5.

The cases presented in this chapter are by no means comprehensive. These are cases that are frequently mentioned in literature, received press, or were located in LexisNexis and cross-checked in Westlaw. These cases were found by keyword searching using various search terms such as "prison libraries," "prison reading materials," etc., with some searches performed using wildcards to include more results. Subject headings from Westlaw were also used to locate additional cases.

Norval Morris and David J. Rothman, as the editors of *The Oxford History of the Prison*, address the concept that prior to the 1960s, courts frequently followed the hands-off doctrine, specifically that "courts were declared not to have jurisdiction or power over the internal management of prisons."[1] Michael Mushlin similarly states:

> While the goal of a humane and rehabilitative penal system remained on the books in some states, in truth, it was more rhetoric than reality. The modern prison was primarily a place of confinement for society's criminals with little regard to how they were kept. The judiciary did little to alter that reality until the beginning of the prisoners' rights movement in the 1960s. The reason was the so-called hands-off doctrine."[2]

In the 1960s, the courts began to take a more active role in policing prison administration with Mushlin's concept that "the hands-off doctrine ends where the abridgement of constitutional rights begins."[3]

There are a number of topics that frequently arise in the cases detailed in this chapter. Mail censorship is perhaps the most frequent topic as prison administration often censors certain publications in the interest of addressing penological concerns and threats. The most notable of these cases is *Turner v. Safley*, in which a precedent was established for dealing with incoming mail in prisons. Within this ruling, the court recommended a test to determine if a prisoner's rights had been violated. This test included four parts to assess whether rights had been compromised including (1) determining the validity of a legitimate penological threat that resulted in a prison administration regulation, (2) if the prisoner was still able to exercise his or her rights to freedom of speech, (3) the potential effect of this free speech on other prisoners or correctional officers, and (4) if there were any alternatives that would be easier to implement than the questioned regulation. This test is frequently referenced in many of the cases both in this chapter and the next chapter and is considered to be very significant "as it applies to all cases where prisoners assert that a penal regulation has violated their constitutional rights, regardless of the type or degree of the deprivation."[4] Censorship of reading materials sent via mail are also disputed in *In re Harrell, Sostre v. Otis, Laaman v. Hancock, Procunier v. Martinez, Carpenter v. State of South Dakota, Hopkins v. Collins, Thornburgh v. Abbott, Guajardo v. Estelle, Clement v. Cal Dept of Corr*, and *In re Andres Martinez*.

Prison administration instigated a "publisher only" rule in some of these cases and the cases from chapter 5 in which mail may only be received directly from publishers, sometimes from those on a specific approved list. These cases include *Johnson v. Moore, Hause v. Vaught, Spruytte v. Walters* and *Ashker v. California Dept. of Corrections*. In cases disputing mail censorship policies, the adherence to a certain due process procedure in evaluating materials was generally viewed as necessary. When such a procedure was in place in the prison and considered to be reasonable, the prison administration was often considered to be justified in limiting access to materials viewed to be dangerous to the safety of the institution.

Censorship restrictions are also litigated in many cases, especially related to the censoring of certain types of media materials. In the case of *Sostre v. Otis, Battle v. Anderson, Jackson v. Ward, Hutchings v. Corum*, and *Beard v. Banks*, questionable materials included newspapers and magazines, whether privately ordered or circulated by the prison library. In *Long v. Parker, Pitts v. Knowles, O'Lone v. Estate of Shabazz, Childs v. Duckworth, Lawson v. Wainwright, Walker v. Maschner, Lyon v. Grossheim, Nichols v. Nix,* and *Sutton v. Rasheed,* plaintiffs claimed infringements of religious rights whether through limitation of access to certain religious materials or restrictions placed on access to the library. *Fortune Society v. McGinnis* and many of the Prison Legal News lawsuits concerned censorship of materials criticizing correctional officials. Censorship of pornographic materials was often deemed an acceptable procedure per *Jones v. Wittenberg, George v. Smith, McCormick v. Werholtz,* and *Amatel v. Reno,* however, per *Aikens v. Jenkins* and *Pepperling v. Crist* categorical censorship without clear procedures was generally not allowed.

The necessity of a library or necessity of providing proper reading space was discussed in a number of cases. Plaintiffs in *Jones v. Wittenberg, Brenneman v. Madigan,* and *Collins v. Schoolfield* filed complaints regarding the inadequacy of their library services. Others were interested in better conditions for reading, for instance plaintiffs *In re Harrell* disputed a prison policy of banning reading materials in cells. The courts in *Jones v. Wittenberg, Collins v. Schoolfield,* and *O'Lone v. Estate of Shabazz* addressed the importance of adequate space for reading in some cases clarifying that adequate light had to be available for prisoners to read.

The following section is a descriptive bibliography including the cases mentioned above. Each legal case will be listed with a citation followed by a summary of the case and quotes from the rulings where relevant. These cases are listed chronologically per section. Only cases have been included that were resolved shortly before the end of or after the Civil Rights Movement; the hands-off doctrine began to dissipate in the late 1960s, so many more prisoners were litigating than might have in the previous decades. Many of these cases were referenced in citations from chapters 1 through 3, or have been noted as interesting cases pertaining to prisoners' rights to library services.

- *Long v. Parker*, 390 F.2d 816 (3rd Cir. 1968).

The plaintiff claimed that his constitutional rights had been violated by religious discrimination and filed two cases that were consolidated into one. One of the claims was that his access to religious literature had been denied. The appeals court ruled that speculation alone was not sufficient justification to deny access to religious materials thought to threaten the security, rather the prison administration must provide evidence that penological interests were indeed threatened by allowing access to this literature. The appeals court remanded the case to the district court.

- In re Harrell, 2 Cal. 3d 675 (1970).

The plaintiffs in this case were prisoners at San Quentin Prison and Folsom Prison in California. They claimed that prison authorities in their institutions limited the material or books that they could hold or possess. Additionally, they were restricted against sharing materials including reading materials. The court ruled that materials that were acceptable for mailing by the US Postal Service could not be excluded or censored by prison authorities. Specifically, the ruling stated that "even persons who have committed anti-social acts warranting their imprisonment may derive greater rehabilitative benefits from the relatively free access to the thoughts of all mankind as reflected in the published word than they would derive from a strictly controlled intellectual diet."

- *Fortune Society v. McGinnis*, 319 F. Supp. 901 (S.D.N.Y. 1970).

New York prisoners filed a civil rights action that a specific prison reform newsletter *Fortune News* had been censored for its critique of prison administrators. The court ruled that there was "no compelling state interest" shown to justify the censorship of publications criticizing administrators.

- *Jones v. Wittenberg*, 330 F. Supp. 707 (D.C. Ohio 1971).

This case detailed a number of civil rights issues with the Lucas County Jail, specifically related to daily operation of the prison and some services that were considered lacking such as library services. Prior to this lawsuit, library services did not exist at Lucas County Jail. The court ruled that a library would be created with materials that had not been censored with the exception that the sheriff could limit pornographic materials as defined by the Supreme Court. Other types of materials that might be censored in other prison libraries were not excluded, i.e., books on bomb-making, escapes, literature that might threaten security, etc. Additionally, there were provisions for improved interior lighting including lighting that would allow prisoners to read in their cells.

- *Sostre v. Otis*, 330 F. Supp. 941 (S.D.N.Y. 1971).

The plaintiff had ordered subscriptions to reading materials, mostly magazines and newspapers. The prison administration withheld a number of the materials. The court asserted that "certain literature may pose such a clear and present danger to the security of a prison, or to the rehabilitation of prisoners, that it should be censored," but that prisoners were entitled to due process when literature is censored. The court therefore ruled that this due process procedure be established at the prison including the initiation of a review board.

- *Pitts v. Knowles*, 339 F. Supp. 1183 (W.D. Wis. 1972).

The plaintiff claimed that his access to the Quran had been limited despite freely available access to the Bible in his prison. The prison library had 700 copies of the Christian Bible and only two copies of the Quran, which resulted in inequitable access to the Quran. The court required the defendants to make the Quran and other requested religious texts as freely available as the Bible.

- *Brenneman v. Madigan*, 343 F. Supp. 128 (D.C. Cal. 1972).

Plaintiffs incarcerated at a pre-trial detention center in Alameda County, California, brought forth this lawsuit with complaints of cruel and unusual punishment during detainment. While library services were not a specific focus of this lawsuit—the scope was general cruel and unusual punishment compared to other detention facilities—library services and access to reading materials were mentioned in this ruling. Specifically, those incarcerated in pre-trial detention facilities should have the same rights to a library and opportunities to read to avoid idleness that are available to individuals posting bail or those in incarceration. Specific services mentioned included daily access to a library and reading room with weekly access to a bookmobile.

- *Collins v. Schoolfield*, 344 F. Supp. 257 (D.C. Md. 1972).

The detainees acting as plaintiffs in this suit made a number of complaints of cruel and unusual punishment at Baltimore City Jail. One complaint included the policies of the institution regarding prisoners' access to literature. In the ruling, the court acknowledged that "in a prison setting, the elimination of some reading matter may be required for security reasons because it is designed to cause severe disruption (as for instance an illustrated pamphlet instructing a prisoner how to destroy jail property or how to interrupt or close down certain jail services and programs)." The court, however, ruled that the prison library collection at Baltimore City Jail was "sparse" and should be reviewed by prison officials to determine where improvements could be made. Furthermore, the court mentioned the necessity of adequate reading light for prisoners.

- *Laaman v. Hancock*, 351 F. Supp. 1265 (D.N.H. 1972).

The prisoner in this case filed a number of complaints including that he was not permitted to receive materials purchased via private subscription. The court ruled that the prison administration may impose restrictions on literature, but that restrictions had to be made based on concrete procedures.

- *Battle v. Anderson*, 376 F. Supp. 402 (E.D. Okla. 1974).

The plaintiff, a prisoner at Oklahoma State Penitentiary, filed a number of complaints including complaints about cruel and unusual punishment. One claim related to cruel and unusual punishment was that the prison authorities restricted access to newspapers and magazines including religious materials in general circulation to the plaintiffs. Additionally, the plaintiffs claimed that inadequate access to the court was provided by the law library and legal assistance program. The court ruled in the favor of the plaintiffs that constitutional rights of the plaintiffs/prisoners had been violated. This decision was affirmed in 564 F. 2d 388 (10th Cir. 1977). Additionally, this case is referenced in a later compliance hearing: 457 F. Supp. 179 (E.D. Okla. 1978).

- *Procunier v. Martinez*, 416 U.S. 396 (1974).

This Supreme Court case addressed class action grievances from prisoners in a California prison regarding mail censorship. The court called for improved procedures for regulating mail and ruled that current processes were unconstitutional. Thurgood Marshall, a Supreme Court Justice on the case, stated that "when the prison gates slam behind an inmate, he does not lose his human quality; his mind does not become closed to ideas; his intellect does not cease to feed on a free and open interchange of opinions; his yearning for self-respect does not end; nor is his quest for self-realization concluded. If anything, the needs for identity and self-respect are more compelling in the dehumanizing prison environment." This quote is also referenced in the "Prisoners' Right to Read" from the American Library Association.

- *Carpenter v. State of South Dakota*, 536 F.2d 759 (8th Cir. 1976).

Prisoners in South Dakota sought damages and relief for the prison administration's withholding of sexually explicit content sent through the mail. The court ruled that the prison administration had implemented proper due process and that sexually explicit material could be withheld on the basis of potential implications on rehabilitation.

- *Aikens v. Jenkins*, 534 F.2d 751 (7th Cir. 1976).

The plaintiff in this case submitted a civil rights action against censorship. The plaintiff claimed that statewide regulations censoring certain types of literature were deemed to be too broad. The types of materials censored included those with content that was sexual in nature and contained nudity, materials degrading race and/or religion, materials that were considered inflammatory or discriminatory, and materials that depicted criminal behavior. The court suggested more specific regulations be implemented rather than broad-based censorship.

- *Hopkins v. Collins*, 548 F.2d 503 (4th Cir. 1977).

The plaintiff in this case claimed that his access to certain publications was restricted, violating his First and Fourteenth Amendment rights. The district court required a full hearing judgment and affirmed that problems existed with censorship in the institution. The appeals court held that certain processes from *Procunier* had to be followed when items were censored via prison mail. Specifically, notice had to be given to the prisoner of the censorship, the prisoner had the right to challenge the decision, and a third party had to evaluate the challenge and initial decision to censor. The appeals court reversed the full hearing judgment from the district court.

- *Jackson v. Ward*, 458 F. Supp. 546 (W.D.N.Y. 1978).

New York plaintiffs alleged that access to materials including books, newspapers, magazines, etc. had been denied without documented procedures or reason. The court reviewed the guidelines for censoring materials and ruled that two guidelines conformed to *Procunier* procedures, specifically those clarifying that the publication should not encourage race or religion based violence nor should it encourage riots or other prison violence. Other guidelines were ruled to be too broad and the court ordered the prison administration to revise these guidelines.

- *Hutchings v. Corum*, 501 F. Supp. 1276 (W.D. Mo. 1980).

Conditions of the jail were contested in this class action suit including lack of access to reading materials both general and legal, and restrictions against newspaper subscriptions. The court ruled that the restriction on newspaper subscriptions was unconstitutional but that the plaintiffs had not shown sufficient evidence that "a state penal institution must constitutionally provide non-legal reading materials in sufficient quantity and quality."

- *Pepperling v. Crist*, 678 F.2d 787, 1982 U.S. App. LEXIS 18789 (9th Cir. June 2, 1982).

Plaintiffs claimed that their First Amendment rights had been violated due to a blanket ban on sexually explicit materials. The district court ruled that the materials were justifiably censored; the appeals court reversed this decision and ruled that further investigations on the blanket restriction on certain publications be conducted.

- *Childs v. Duckworth*, 705 F.2d 915, 1983 U.S. App. LEXIS 28696 (7th Cir. April 20, 1983).

The plaintiff claimed that his constitutional rights to religious freedom had been violated both by the prison administration refusing to acknowledge his religion as a legitimate one and refusing books ordered on interlibrary loan for group study purposes. The prisoner had ordered a number of books on Satanism. The district and appeals court ruled that his constitutional rights had not been violated and that the prison administration had refused certain requests in an attempt to maintain the security of the prison.

- *Guajardo v. Estelle*, 568 F. Supp. 1354, 1983 U.S. Dist. LEXIS 15474 (S.D. Tex. July 14, 1983).

Plaintiffs in this class action suit were in segregation units and claimed violations of their First Amendment rights due to the prison's policy of denying publications received in the mail for all prisoners in these units and only allowing legal books and religious works. The court upheld the "publisher only" rule in place at the institution, but stated that materials may not be censored that inform about grievances, nor may publications simply be censored because they criticize prison authorities—security must be threatened, or the materials must contain information about explosives, weapons, drugs, or riots to justify censorship.

- *Spruytte v. Walters*, 753 F.2d 498 (6th Cir. 1985).

A prisoner claimed that his due process rights had been violated when prison officials refused to deliver a paperback dictionary mailed from his mother. The district court dismissed the complaint and the prisoner appealed. The appeals court reversed and remanded the district court's decision. The appeals court ruled that receiving books from sources other than publishers did not threaten security, a state regulation allowed prisoners to receive materials that did not threaten security, the prisoner's due process rights had indeed been violated, and the prison administration would not receive qualified immunity.

- *Lawson v. Wainright*, 641 F. Supp. 312, 1986 U.S. Dist. LEXIS 22539 (S.D. Fla. July 18, 1986).

Hebrew Israelite plaintiffs in this case claimed that they were denied access to religious materials by the prison administration. The court established that the religious group was a legitimate religion and ordered the defendant, the prison administration, to stock publications related to the faith as well as to implement a number of other allowances related to the observance of this faith.

- *O'Lone v. Estate of Shabazz*, 482 U.S. 342 (1987).

Prison authorities had created new regulations that prevented some Muslim prisoners working off site from returning to the prison to celebrate a Muslim holiday due to security concerns on the part of the institution. When this case went to appeals, the court vacated and reversed the district court's decisions in favor of the plaintiffs, thereby establishing that First Amendment rights can be limited if the prison authorities establish legitimate security concerns as the grounds for the First Amendment right infringements.

- *Turner v. Safley*, 482 U.S. 78 (1987).

This case established precedent in dealing with incoming mail. The plaintiffs filed a complaint regarding the prison administration's practice of reading and banning incoming mail between prisoners at various state prisons, as well as restrictions regarding marriage between prisoners of the correctional system. The court ruled that reading and censoring correspondence between prisoners was appropriate when related to legitimate threats to security, however, not a complete ban on correspondence between prisons. The ruling also stated that the restriction on marriages was unconstitutional. This case is frequently cited in other instances where prisoners' constitutional rights are alleged to have been violated because of its four-part test of establishing an infringement based on limitations due to prison security concerns and freedom of speech violations.

- *Thornburgh v. Abbott*, 490 U.S. 401 (1989).

The court upheld prison authorities' right to review, censor, and ban publications that could legitimately threaten the security of the institution. The court recommended that publications received by prisoners must be analyzed according to the standards outlined in *Turner vs. Safley* (1987). Per this ruling, prison authorities had the right to reject publications if they followed these *Turner vs. Safley* standards and a penological concern was shown.

- *Jackson v. Elrod*, 881 F.2d 441, 1989 U.S. App. LEXIS 11800 (7th Cir. August 7, 1989).

A prisoner claimed that he was denied access to hardcover books and materials that would have helped him treat his alcoholism both by denial of access to the general library and denial of books ordered from publishers. The court ruled that his constitutional rights had been violated since the penal institution could have accommodated his requests by removing book covers or requesting that all items be mailed by a publisher.

- *Johnson v. Moore*, 926 F.2d 921, 1991 U.S. App. LEXIS 3103 (9th Cir. February 28, 1991).

The plaintiff made a number of claims including that his First Amendment rights had been violated partially due to a "publishers only" rule on paperback books. The court applied the Turner test and ruled that nothing was found to support a legitimate penological concern in the blanket ban on paperback books not from publishers. This case was affirmed during appeal in 948 F.2d 517 (9th Cir. October 9, 1991).

- *Lyon v. Grossheim*, 803 F. Supp. 1538, 1992 U.S. Dist. LEXIS 20590 (September 30, 1992).

The plaintiff in this case had ordered religious comic books, which were censored by prison administration pursuant to regulations in place. Prison administration claimed that they represented a threat to the institution. The court applied the Turner test and found no reasonable relationship to a concrete threat to security. The court awarded equitable relief and attorney fees.

- *Hause v. Vaught*, 993 F.2d 1079, 1993 U.S. App. LEXIS 10482 (4th Cir. May 7, 1993).

The plaintiff, a prisoner in South Carolina, disputed a number of procedures of prison administration including restrictions on outside publications. The prisoner suggested a "publishers only" rule to allow books to be received. The court ruled that the blanket ban was legitimately founded on penological interests and affirmed the district court's decision to grant summary judgment to the prison officials.

- *Nichols v. Nix*, 810 F. Supp. 1448 (S.D. Iowa 1993).

The plaintiff claimed that his constitutional rights to exercise his religion had been violated when Church of Jesus Christ publications were censored from the mail due to the prison administration's stance that they could cause unrest in the prison. The court applied the Turner test and concluded that the prisoner's First Amendment rights had not been violated, but that the administration's regulations needed to be revised. The plaintiff received injunctive relief.

- *Gomez v. Kelly*, No. C 94–0041 DLJ, 1994 U.S. Dist. LEXIS 5619 (April 21, 1994).

The plaintiff was housed in a segregated unit and claimed that he was unable to purchase reading materials due to a ban on purchases for prisoners in restricted units. The court ruled that the prison administration had a valid interest in restricting purchases related to penological concerns and that the prisoner did not have a complete restriction of reading materials. Furthermore, the prisoner was able to receive the reading materials by having family order them for him; therefore, no constitutional violation occurred.

• *Amatel v. Reno*, 156 F.3d 192, 1998 U.S. App. LEXIS 22540 (September 15, 1998).

Prisoners sued against the Ensign Amendment, which banned use of federal funding to provide or distribute pornographic or explicit material to prisoners. The court ruled that a connection could be seen between rehabilitative goals and the effects of distributing pornography. The court applied the Turner test and ruled that the regulations in the Ensign Amendment were enforceable.

• *Cuoco v. Hurley*, Civil Action No. 98-D-2438, 2000 U.S. Dist. LEXIS 13970 (D. Colo. September 21, 2000).

The plaintiffs claimed First Amendment rights violations based on the censorship of materials written by other prisoners and also on hardcover books. The administration had apparently censored not just on the basis of a hardcover book, but also taken the content of the book into consideration. The court denied most actions, however, admitted a claim for a violation of constitutional rights by the refusal to provide prisoners with hardcover books and outdated materials on certain topics.

• *Walker v. Maschner*, 270 F.3d 573 (8th Cir. 2001).

The plaintiff made a number of complaints concerning violations to his constitutional rights to religious freedom including the denial of the Torah. The district court concluded that the plaintiff established a constitutional rights violation when prison administration denied access to the Torah. The appeals court reversed and dismissed the case because the prisoner "had not exhausted his administrative remedies."

• *Clement v. Cal Dept of Corr.*, 364 F.3d 1148 (9th Cir. 2004).

The plaintiff made multiple claims regarding infringements of his rights by prison authorities, but was only granted injunctive relief for one of his claims, which was specifically related to the prison authorities' regulations on printed material downloaded from the Internet that a prisoner could receive via mail. In regards to this final claim, the court ordered that the prison authorities had violated the prisoner's First Amendment rights. The court thereby granted the prisoner summary judgment on his First Amendment claim.

• *Ashker vs. California Dept. of Corrections*, 350 F.3d 917 (9th Cir. 2003).

The institution had a policy of requiring vendor labels to be attached to packages of books; if the label was not attached, or the package was not from an approved vendor, the prisoner would not receive the books enclosed in the package. Other objects received in the prison such as shoes and clothing were not required to have a pre-approved label from a specific list of vendors. During the course of the trial, the defendants were unable to justify the requirement of a vendor label for some items and not for others. Per the court's ruling, requiring a book label from a pre-approved vendor was not a rational way to exclude books presenting legitimate penological concerns.

• *Sutton v. Rasheed*, 323 F.3d 236, 2003 U.S. App. LEXIS 4940 (3rd Cir. March 19, 2003).

Prisoners housed in a high-risk facility in a correctional institution in Pennsylvania were denied access to Nation of Islam texts. The court reviewed the Turner test and determined that the officials had not justifiably denied access to these materials per the requirements of the Turner test.

- *Beard v. Banks*, 548 U.S. 521 (2006).

The plaintiff filed a complaint against a Pennsylvania prison policy prohibiting prisoners at a certain level of segregation from having newspapers and magazines. Those at the highest level of segregation were housed there based on violent behavior or egregious actions committed in prison. The court ruled in favor of the prison authorities because the authorities were trying to motivate better behavior amongst prisoners who had already lost nearly all privileges. The court also ruled that the plaintiff had not presented adequate evidence to prove his claims.

- *Daker v. Ferrero*, 506 F. Supp. 2d 1295, 2007 U.S. Dist. LEXIS 62668 (N.D. Ga. August 24, 2007).

The plaintiff claimed he was denied access to fifty-five publications and a number of mailed items by prison administration. Many of the items denied were viewed to be a threat to the security of the institution, however, the administration did not have a proper procedure in place to justify censorship decisions. According to the plaintiff, materials were denied based on the title of the book alone. The court concluded that the institution did not adequately provide reasons for denials.

- *Greybuffalo v. Kingston*, 581 F. Supp. 2d 1034, 2007 U.S. Dist. LEXIS 69476 (W.D. Wis. September 18, 2007).

Documents from a Native American organization were confiscated from a prisoner because the works were considered to be gang literature by prison officials. The prisoner filed a complaint that his First Amendment rights had been violated. The court ruled that in the case of this document (he had brought suit for another document as well), his rights had indeed been violated.

- *George v. Smith*, 507 F.3d 605 (2007).

A prisoner submitted multiple unrelated claims regarding deprivation of his rights. One included the denial of books and magazines, which the court confirmed was in the interest of the institution's security due to pornographic and gang-related content. The court did mention an atlas, which may have been unjustifiably censored, however, the plaintiff did not produce enough facts for analysis. Upon appeal, the district court's decisions were affirmed by the appeals court.

- *McCormick v. Werholtz*, Case No. 07–2605-EFM, 2008 U.S. Dist. LEXIS 110361 (D. Kan. July 22, 2008).

The plaintiff claims that certain books were censored, including one on writing, survival techniques, and *High Risk: An Anthology of Forbidden Writers*, the last of which contained explicit passages about sexual acts. Both the plaintiff and defendant moved for summary judgment. The prison administration was partially awarded summary judgment, with the exception of one book for which censorship was not justified.

- *State of Connecticut v. Steven Hayes*, CR070241859, 2010 Conn. Super. LEXIS 3066 (Conn. Super. Ct. November 26, 2010); CR070241859, 2010 Conn. Super. LEXIS 1667 (Conn. Super. Ct. June 30, 2010).

Prosecutors in the capital case of Steven Hayes attempted to use his reading lists from a previous incarceration as evidence that he had read violent fiction. The attempt to include the reading lists was excluded by the judge, but this case brought national attention to the issue of collection development in prison libraries spurring an Associated Press investigation of prison collection development policies and actions by legislators in Connecticut to more closely control the books allowed in Connecticut state prison libraries.

• *Calhoun v. Corr. Corp. of Am.*, Civil File No. 09–683 (MJD/JSM), 2010 U.S. Dist. LEXIS 102067 (D. Minn. July 16, 2010).

The plaintiff had requested certain books from vendors besides those already shipping to the prison and his requests were denied by prison administration. The court applied the Turner test and determined that the policies implemented in this case had indeed violated the prisoner's constitutional rights.

• *Couch v. Jabe*, 581 F. Supp. 2d 1034, 2010 U.S. Dist. LEXIS 90812 (W.D. Va. August 31, 2010).

A prisoner in Virginia claimed that the general reading library at his institution removed two books from the collection. The prisoner then attempted to purchase the books and was denied access on the basis of the prior banning of the books by the library and prison administration. The court found that the prison had "a bizarre interpretation of a regulation which results in the prohibition of James Joyce's *Ulysees* but the distribution of *Sport's Illustrated* Swimsuit Edition." The court applied the Turner test and ruled that the regulation from the administration was unconstitutional.

• *Jones v. Lockett*, Civil Action No. 08–16, 2010 U.S. Dist. LEXIS 103456 (W.D. Pa. September 7, 2010).

The plaintiff claimed that his civil rights had been violated because African American books had been removed from the prison library's collection. After investigation, it was found that the library collection had not been "dismantled," rather library staff had reorganized the collection. The prison administration defendants moved for summary judgment, which was granted.

• *Lindell v. Wall*, 12-cv-646-wmc, 2013 U.S. Dist. LEXIS 158787 (W.D. Wis. November 6, 2013).

A prisoner, who was incarcerated in Wisconsin, filed a number of complaints concerning what he considered constitutional violations. His claims against the library included that donations of his own materials had been denied, certain library material requests had been denied, hardcover books were prohibited, certain publications were not delivered to him, he was denied interlibrary loan book requests, and certain access to newspapers and magazines had been denied. The court considered the claims to be too broad and ordered the plaintiff to resubmit a narrower complaint within 30 days. The plaintiff submitted the same complaints and was denied reconsideration by the court.

• In re Andres Martinez, 216 Cal. App. 4th 1141, 157 Cal. Rptr. 3d 701 (2013).

A prisoner had ordered the book *The Silver Crown* by Mathilde Madden, which was confiscated by the prison authorities as contraband on the basis that it was considered obscene. The book was werewolf erotica and deemed inappropriate by the prison administration because it contained sex scenes. The court ruled that erotica in this case was not considered pornographic, so therefore could not be regulated or censored on the basis of obscenity.

Many of the cases brought to court by Prison Legal News (PLN) involve mail censorship, similar to those discussed in the first section of this chapter. Most of these cases are civil actions. Mail policies and censorship were the topics of *Prison Legal News v. Cook*, *Prison Legal News v. Lehman* (2003 and 2005), *Jacklovich v. Simmons*, *Prison Legal News v. McDonough*, *Prison Legal News v. Werholtz*, *Prison Legal News v. Schwarzenegger*, *Prison Legal News v. Livingston*, *Prison Legal News v. Babeu*, *Prison Legal News v. Columbia County*, *Prison Legal News v. Livingston*, *Prison Legal News v. Chapman*, and *Prison Legal News v. Umatilla County*. The "publisher only" rule was disputed in *Prison Legal News v. Lehman* (2003) and *Prison Legal News v. Babeu*. A "postcard only" policy was the subject of dispute in *Prison Legal News v. Umatilla County*.[5] A ban on bulk mail was disputed in *Prison Legal News v. Cook* and *Prison Legal News v. Lehman* (2005). In the latter case, restrictions on reading materials in cells were also revoked by the court.

Similar to *Fortune Society v. McGinnis* mentioned earlier in this chapter, Prison Legal News publications also occasionally include the names of correctional officers. In *Prison Legal News v. Washington State Department of Corrections* in 2001 and 2003, newsletters were banned due to mentions of officers' names, which were deemed to be a security risk to the institution and the correctional officers mentioned.

PLN is a frequent litigator; the court cases detailed here are unlikely to be exhaustive. Per the PLN website, "PLN takes the censorship of its publications seriously and litigates to enforce its constitutional rights when necessary." PLN furthermore cites the importance of litigation for maintaining their organization's free speech rights to communicate with prisoners.[6]

The cases mentioned above are described in more detail in the bibliography below. Each case includes a citation and summary of the case with rulings where relevant. Because many of these cases are civil actions, many of the rulings include monetary settlements. These cases are presented in chronological order.

• *Prison Legal News v. Cook*, 238 F.3d 1145, 2001 U.S. App. LEXIS 1729 (9th Cir. February 7, 2001).

PLN and prisoners claimed constitutional rights violations due to a prison policy of banning standard rate mail, which included PLN subscriptions. The district court had granted summary judgment to defendants. The appeals court reversed and remanded the district court's decision due to lack of proof of a legitimate penological concern and an unconstitutional practice of banning standard rate mail.

• *Prison Legal News v. Washington State Department of Corrections*, 11 Fed. Appx. 729, 2001 U.S. App. LEXIS 5165 (9th Cir. March 21, 2001).

Prisoners sued for monetary, declaratory, and injunctive relief because of a ban initiated by the prison administration on one specific issue of a prison newsletter releasing names of correctional officers. The district court ruled that prison administration should receive qualified immunity on claims for monetary relief, however, denied claims for declaratory and injunctive relief. The appeals court affirmed the monetary relief decision and reversed and remanded the denials on the other two claims, suggesting that the *Turner v. Safley* four-part test should be utilized in the institution.

• *Prison Legal News v. Washington State Department of Corrections*, 71 Fed. Appx. 619, 2003 U.S. App. LEXIS 15082 (9th Cir. July 18, 2003).

Prison officials had banned a specific article from a PLN publication in their institution due to the naming of specific guards in the institution and allegations regarding prisoner treatment. The defendants were granted summary judgment by the district court, which was affirmed by the appeals court. The appeals court concluded that the ban was necessary to avert violence in the institution and therefore related to a legitimate penological concern.

• *Jacklovich v. Simmons*, 392 F.3d 420 (10th Cir. 2004).

Prisoners had monetary limitations on the number of materials they could order as publications monthly. PLN had been purchased by family members and friends for prisoners, however, the prison administration refused to deliver them due to penological concerns. The district court ruled in favor of the defendants; the appeals court reversed the decision, ruling that a legitimate penological concern had not been adequately demonstrated. This case also concluded that both prisoner and publisher had to be informed when a work was censored by mailroom staff.

• *Prison Legal News v. Lehman*, 397 F.3d 692, 2005 U.S. App. LEXIS 1556 (9th Cir. February 1, 2005).

PLN claimed First Amendment rights violations through restrictive mail policies at the Washington Department of Corrections. The court granted the plaintiff's motions against the prisons' policies of banning catalogs and bulk mail, granted immunity to administration, and enjoined the defendants not to reject mail solely on the basis of mailing via a standard rate.

• *Prison Legal News v. McDonough*, 200 Fed. Appx. 873, 2006 U.S. App. LEXIS 25377 (11th Cir. October 11, 2006).

PLN sued the Florida defendants due to practices of confiscating or impounding PLN publications intended for prisoners and for restricting prisoner receipt of royalties for items written for PLN. The court ruled that the prison administration had legitimate reasons related to penological concerns for denying compensation to prisoners. Since the proceedings began, the administration, however, began allowing the PLN publications to be distributed to prisoners, therefore the first claim about royalties was ruled moot.

• *Prison Legal News v. Werholtz*, Civil Action No. 02–4054-MLB, 2007 U.S. Dist. LEXIS 73629 (D. Kan. October 1, 2007).

PLN publications had been restricted by Kansas prison authorities on the basis that they represented a penological concern. The court ruled that the defendants had not proven a legitimate penological concern and that prisoners were unreasonably denied access to PLN publications. Within this case, similar to *Jacklovich v. Simmons* and *Prison Legal News v. Washington State Department of Corrections*, prisoners and publishers were to be informed when items were censored by prison administration.

• *Prison Legal News v. Schwarzenegger*, 608 F.3d 446, 2010 U.S. App. LEXIS 11690 (9th Cir. June 9, 2010).

PLN claimed that prisoners' constitutional rights had been violated due to restrictions by prison officials on prisoners' receipts of PLN publications. The appeals court awarded the plaintiff attorney fees, reversed the prior decision and terminated jurisdiction, however remanded and requested that the parties document a record of how the agreement had been fulfilled.

- *Prison Legal News v. Livingston*, 683 F.3d 201, 2012 U.S. App. LEXIS 11108 (5th Cir. June 1, 2012).

The Department of Corrections in Texas banned certain PLN books and publications from prisoners due to content that they believed threatened the safety of the institution. The district court ruled in the favor of the defendants, affirming that the materials were legitimately restricted. The appeals court affirmed the district court's decision. Prison Legal News was, according to the court, not able to demonstrate that the institution excluded books unaffected by legitimate penological concerns. The court determined that the prison authorities did, in fact, have a valid system in place for evaluating whether or not the books or items received demonstrated a threat to the institution's security.

- *Prison Legal News v. Babeu*, 933 F. Supp. 2d 1188, 2013 U.S. Dist. LEXIS 38606 (D. Ariz. March 20, 2013).

A county jail rejected publications, which were not received directly from publishers. Their definition of a recognized publisher was rather vague, only allowing materials from Amazon, Borders, Barnes & Noble, and Waldenbooks. The court agreed that the "publisher only" rule in place in the institution was unconstitutional and required that a new policy be established permitting Prison Legal News mailings. The court did not grant a permanent injunction to Prison Legal News due to lack of evidence to show that their materials would be rejected under the prison's "publisher only" rule. A "postcard only" rule was also upheld in this case in favor of prison administration policies.

- *Prison Legal News v. Columbia County*, 942 F. Supp. 2d 1068, 2013 U.S. Dist. LEXIS 58669 (D. Or. April 24, 2013).

The mail policies of a county jail were challenged in this case as a result of the rejection of PLN publications by the jail administration. The court found that the procedures blocking certain types of publications were unconstitutional. The court required that the defendants stop censoring mail that was longer than postcard length. Prisoners were also entitled to due process when materials were rejected.

- *Prison Legal News v. Livingston*, 683 F.3d 201 (5th Cir. 2012).

PLN claimed that First Amendment rights and due process had been violated by a censorship policy that resulted in the censorship of five books for prisoners. The district court granted the prison administration summary judgment. At appeals, the court ruled that the publisher "had standing" for the First Amendment claims, especially in regards to the books that had not been shared, but that the censorship policy in place did not violate First Amendment or due process rights.

- *Prison Legal News v. Chapman*, 44 F. Supp. 3d 1289 (M.D. Ga. August, 26, 2014).

PLN motioned to enjoin prison administration from the enforcement of mail policies that restricted PLN publications and correspondence from being received by prisoners. The court granted part of PLN's motion by enjoining the defendants from enforcing a ban on PLN's Prison Legal News publication and that the "postcard only" policy in effect at the institution violated due process, but not PLN's right to free speech. All other motions and requests were denied.

- *Prison Legal News v. Umatilla County*, Case No. 2:12-cv-01101-SU, 2013 U.S. Dist. LEXIS 71104 (D. Or. February 27, 2013).

The county jail in this case had a "postcard only" policy, which prevented PLN publications from being delivered. The court awarded PLN some attorney fees and associated costs.

## Summary

The cases presented in this chapter established a number of recurrent themes in prisoner litigation related to reading materials. Mail censorship has frequently been employed by prison administration to further penological goals and, in some cases, is used to prevent perceived risk of unrest in the institution. Some of these restrictions proved to be justified, others were excessive. Prisoners also litigated when facilities were deemed to be insufficient in terms of availability or accessibility of reading materials. Decisions in these cases also vary; sometimes institutions really are not providing enough materials or making them accessible to a certain standard. At other times, the litigation appears to be frivolous.

All of the cases presented in this chapter concerned the right to read, which according to the ALA's "Prisoners' Right to Read" is a fundamental intellectual freedom right. Outcomes in these cases are varied; in some instances, litigation may have been deemed frivolous and, in other cases, prisoners' rights were ruled to have been violated. These cases also further illustrate that practices in individual institutions vary widely; certain procedures may change based on the leadership in that particular institution or on the existence or non-existence of clear policy. These cases are not necessarily representative or generalizable for the climate of prison libraries in the United States. Some prisoners may have more access to the courts to pursue legal action whether those actions are frivolous or not.

The next chapter will discuss and present similar legal cases that are related to the prisoner's right of meaningful access to the court. As discussed in previous chapters, this is a right implicit in the First Amendment of the United States Bill of Rights. Many of these cases involve the prison law library and its collections, which may or may not be offered as part of general library services at the accused's institution.

# 5

# Court Cases Affecting
# the Prisoner's Right of
# Access to the Courts

*They offer us Westlaw training every year—that's our service that we use for our law library ... general libraries (if you think of us like a public library) are a privilege to people that are institutionalized and the law library is a right. It is a legal right. We cannot deny them access to the law library. So anything that supports the law library is kind of pushed forward.*

—Alison, Interviewee from Chapter 9

In the 1960s and 1970s, the Supreme Court began taking a more active hand in enforcing the constitutional rights of prisoners. Previously, the Constitution was rarely taken into consideration in prisons and prisoners had little recourse in court.[1] Per *The Oxford History of the Prison*, the courts' new interest in prisoners' rights contributed to the gradual move toward a rehabilitative focus for the American prison: "the recognition of the needs of inmates for successful integration into society ... paved the way for the recognition of their rights."[2] As rehabilitation became a functional focus of the prison and the courts began to intercede on the behalf of prisoners claiming rights violations, the right of access to the courts became a frequently litigated topic. According to Michael Mushlin, access to the courts is how prisoners establish other constitutional rights.[3] After *Bounds v. Smith* and before *Lewis v. Casey*, a prison law library was an often required means to fulfill this access to the courts requirement. In *Werner's Manual for Prison Law Libraries*, Rebecca Trammell asserts that "the mission of the prison law library is to assist inmates in gaining access to the courts"[4] with the understanding that some prisoners may need more assistance than others.

The right to access the courts, frequently fulfilled by provision of a prison law library, has been the subject of litigation with a number of pivotal cases setting the environment for what should be provided to prisoners in terms of legal collections. Lynn Branham lists a number of cases related to First Amendment rights, beginning with *Procunier v. Martinez*, in which prisoners were permitted to receive legal assistance from law students and paralegals after judgment was delivered.[5] Both Mushlin[6] and Joseph Gerken[7] cite *Johnson v. Avery* as a pivotal case in establishing rights to legal assistance. *Turner v. Safley*, mentioned in the last chapter, established a test to determine First Amendment rights violations, which was often used in litigation as a means of determining potential violations. This test was comprised of an assessment to determine if there was a reasonable relationship between the regulation and the interest for which it was intended, the possibility of the prisoner exercising this right in a different manner, the effect that the claimed right might have on the rest of the prison, and if there were alternatives to fulfill the claim or right that were not as drastic.[8] Branham references *O'Lone v. Shabazz* as a landmark case in determining acceptable limitations for freedom of religion.[9] Perhaps the two most widely referenced cases affecting the prisoner's right to access the court, especially in regards to law libraries, are *Bounds v. Smith* and *Lewis v. Casey*.

The decision on *Bounds v. Smith* was delivered in 1977 and subsequently prison administration was required to either provide law libraries or access to legal assistance. Branham summarized decisions from *Bounds* as requiring "adequate" access to either law libraries or legal assistance, however, without a clear definition of what "adequate" entailed.[10] Wayne Ryan discussed the implementation of *Bounds* including what he deemed to be an acceptable collection for provision of meaningful access to the courts. Ryan states:

> In recent years, it has become a pressing concern to determine how a prisoner may be assured that his right to meaningful access to the courts will not be impaired, even though he is incarcerated and has chosen to prepare and present his own defense. One result has been the establishment of law libraries at prison sites to furnish inmates with access to such materials as law books, treatises, court reporters, and other legal materials."[11]

Others comment on the efficacy of providing law libraries for prisoners. Steven Hinckley claims that providing access to a law library may not necessarily result in "meaningful access" to the courts due to a number of factors, such as illiterate prisoners or those not familiar with the legal system.[12] Most of the subsequent litigation after *Bounds* and prior to *Lewis v. Casey* dealt with legal collections and whether or not these were deemed sufficient to fulfill the meaningful access provisions of *Bounds*. Hinckley claims that the *Bounds* ruling may have contradicted other cases regarding prisoners' rights and suggested a "reevaluation of the constitutional standards on which the right of access is based."[13]

Arturo Flores confirms that furnishing prisoners with law libraries appears to be the most acceptable form of fulfilling requirements of meaningful access to the courts. He also inquires about the effectiveness of law libraries for assisting prisoners in preparing their defenses and questions the correctness of associating access to a library with meaningful access to the courts.[14] Christopher Smith similarly criticizes the effects of *Bounds*, noticing that prisoners rely on the prison library services rather than consulting someone trained in the law: "The substantial reliance upon prison law libraries is doomed to fail in its assigned task of providing access to the courts because the vast majority of prison inmates are incapable of effectively utilizing legal resources."[15] Smith claims that prisoners are reliant on the prison system to provide basic services for survival, they do not have access to the outside world to conduct research or find witnesses, and despite this, prisoners are already heavy litigators, often presenting frivolous cases showing a lack of understanding of the law.[16] The American Association of Law Libraries Standing Committee on Law Library Service to Institution Residents expressed similar misgivings, stating: "Attention should be drawn to the fact that although a law library meets constitutional standards, it is not a panacea for providing access to the courts. Many incarcerated persons are functionally illiterate and unable to frame sufficient legal petitions. Other inmates may not be fluent in English."[17]

Jonathan Abel similarly questions the provision of a law library as offering "meaningful" access to the courts for prisoners who may not have the reading skills to make use of the law library effectively: "Does it make sense to provide indigent, illiterate, often non–English speaking inmates with shelves of library books? Can even the most well-educated prisoners realistically make use of case law and treatises in navigating the court system? Did a prison law library *ever* make sense?"[18] Abel also examines the ambivalence of certain Supreme Court statements, implying that the judges acknowledge the potential inefficacy of prisoners' researching their own legal cases in a law library.[19] He cites various sources who have claimed that legal services with trained professionals are a preferred and appropriate way to satisfy meaningful access to the courts mandates. These sources include Marjorie LeDonne, who conducted an expansive survey on prison law library services, and O. James Werner.[20] Linda Martz references lawsuits in which prisoners claimed that computerized databases were insufficient for providing them access to the courts.[21]

Even writers of library focused publications, such as Werner, assert the stance that prisoners are not necessarily being provided with meaningful access to the courts when they are only provided with a law library. Werner claims that "because of a high degree of illiteracy and the lack of education among inmates, it is unrealistic to expect them to handle their own legal problems above a very simple level."[22] Trammell implies that the effects of *Bounds* created a culture of jailhouse lawyers who assisted less legally savvy prisoners and "prison law libraries were blamed for fostering jailhouse lawyers, and providing the means for excessive prisoner litigation."[23]

*Lewis v. Casey*, resulting out of a dispute in Arizona regarding prisoners' access to the courts, concluded in 1996. The consequence of *Lewis* was a requirement to prove "actual injury" in the case of a denial of meaningful access to the court. David Steinberger claims, similar to Trammel's assertions, that *Lewis* was an attempt to restrict heavy prison litigation despite legitimate issues of access. He states:

> While *Lewis* was an unnecessary attempt at limiting the access precedents, the more disturbing aspect of this case was how the Court constricted this well recognized constitutional right. Specifically, the court found that the prisoners had no standing to bring the suit in the federal courts, having shown insufficient actual injury resulting from the complained of shortcomings of the Arizona Department of Corrections' prison law libraries.[24]

Mushlin discusses the inability to find an abstract violation per the ruling in *Lewis*: "take, for example, the case of an inmate who files a claim, but because of inadequacies in the prison law library lacks the resources to research the case or to determine how to discover important evidence."[25] The prisoner would have no recourse to pursue action in court due to *Lewis*' actual injury requirement. Gerken agrees that the actual injury requirement presents barriers for prisoners challenging deficiencies in the prison law library, stating "the core holdings in *Lewis*, and particularly the actual injury requirement, present a significant impediment to inmates' efforts to obtain court ordered improvements in prison law libraries."[26]

Many scholars of law were perplexed with the decision from *Lewis* since this case, according to some accounts, reversed the decisions from *Bounds*. Joseph Schouten, believing that *Bounds* was the correct interpretation of existing case law, asserts that "because *Lewis* was incorrectly decided, the Court must reconsider the question and bring meaningfulness back to meaningful access."[27] Karen Westwood seems to view *Lewis* as a reversed interpretation of how law library services were measured from *Bounds*: "In reviewing cases that have been decided since *Lewis*, it seems the question has changed from 'Is the law library service *good* enough to meet the *Bounds* standard?' to 'Is any law library service *so* bad as to *not* meet the *Lewis* standard?'"[28]

The effects of *Lewis* were immediate: the state of Arizona, for example, consequently closed all of its prison law libraries.[29] David Wilhelmus mentions the effects of *Lewis* on decisions and strategies employed by prison librarians: "While the decision can be translated into a potential lessening of the need for expensive and space-demanding legal collections, *Casey v. Lewis* means prison librarians will need to develop new strategies to ensure that their inmate-patrons are afforded the opportunity to access appropriate legal documents."[30]

Michael Sabath and William Payne surveyed prisons to determine how they were providing access to the courts in an effort to ascertain the effects of *Lewis v. Casey* 15 years later. Many of the prisons were still providing libraries with updated legal collections. Nevertheless, changes noted by the scholars included a shift from stocking legal materials to providing recreational reading and in some cases completely eliminating the prison law library.[31] Abel claims that many prison law libraries are switching to computer services such as LexisNexis or Westlaw to provide access to prisoners while reducing space and budget requirements for maintaining a physical collection—a move which may or may not provide improved access to prisoners attempting to navigate murky legal waters.[32]

In the same year that *Lewis v. Casey* was decided, the Prison Litigation Reform Act (PLRA) was passed by Congress. According to Mushlin, the major purpose of the PLRA was to "place limits on the ability of the courts to enter injunctive relief in cases brought by prisoners to improve prison conditions."[33] Other authors reference an interest in reduced prisoner litigation from the courts.[34] Major provisions of the PLRA were the exhaustion requirement, the three strikes provision, and the reduction of costs for lawyers. The exhaustion requirement was intended to avoid damage claims that could have been solved with the proper administrative remedies at the prison.[35] The three strikes provision was written to prevent continual access and litigation after repeated unsuccessful attempts that were viewed as "(1) frivolous, (2) malicious, or (3) not a claim for which relief could be granted."[36] Essentially, the PLRA was attempting to prevent these frivolous complaints from clogging up the judicial system.

The PLRA, while it may have alleviated some of the excessive prisoner litigation in the courts, was not without some flaws, according to critics of the Act. Per statements from Margo Schlanger on behalf of the American Bar Association: "The PLRA has successfully ameliorated the burden imposed on prisons and jails by frivolous prisoner litigation, but it has simultaneously created major obstaclees to accountability and the rule of law within our nation's growing incarceration system."[37] Schlanger and the American Bar Association were attempting to lift the ban on physical injury requirements associated with mental and emotional injury. Elizabeth Alexander from the National Prison Project of the American Civil Liberties Union Foundation acknowledges the reduction of frivolous claims in the courts while drawing attention to the PLRA's "disastrous effect on the ability of prisoners, particularly prisoners without access to counsel, to have their meritorious cases adjudicated on the merits."[38] In some ways, it appears as though recent legislation such as the PLRA and litigation such as *Lewis v. Casey* are allowing the courts to return to the hands-off doctrine popular before the 1960s.

The selection of cases presented in the bibliography below include the citation and a brief description of the case. Only cases that occurred after the Civil Rights Movement have been included in this chapter; as mentioned in the previous chapter, this is because courts began more actively hearing prisoner litigation cases due to the fall of the hands-off doctrine. Cases on the right of access to the court could fill an entire book; therefore, these are selections of cases that are either landmark cases referenced frequently in the literature, or cases with specifics that are particularly relevant for the prison law library.[39] Some cases from the previous chapter have been duplicated in this chapter since general library service and law library service sometimes overlap. For cases postdating the *Lewis* ruling and the date the PLRA was effective, cases showing actual injury requirements have been more frequently referenced, as there were a multitude of cases found where these actual injury requirements were not proven. Both *Lewis* and key provisions of the PLRA, such as the exhaustion requirement and the three strikes rule, are frequently mentioned in cases after 1996.

- *Johnson v. Avery*, 393 U.S. 483 (1969).

A prisoner petitioned against a prison rule preventing prisoners from receiving legal assistance from other prisoners. The regulation was initiated by the prison administration to help discipline in prison and encourage prisoners to receive legal assistance only from lawyers. The court rejected this regulation, stating that it disadvantaged prisoners, especially illiterate prisoners. The court held that the prisoners had a right to seek and obtain post-conviction relief on the basis of the importance of habeas corpus relief in the justice system.

- *Gilmore v. Lynch*, 319 F. Supp. 105 (N.D. Cal. 1970).

Often viewed as one of the first cases in which the Supreme Court became involved in constitutional rights of prisoners, this case centered around prisoner complaints that their access to legal materials and assistance had been restricted, which resulted in impaired access to the courts. The court ruled that the available prison law books were deficient and constituted a violation of prisoners' constitutional rights.

- In re Harrell, 2 Cal. 3d 675 (1970).

The plaintiffs in this case were prisoners at San Quentin Prison and Folsom Prison in California. They claimed that prison authorities in their institutions limited the material or books that they could hold or possess. Additionally, they were allegedly restricted against sharing materials, including reading materials. Many of these reading materials were legal materials. Per the ruling, prisoners were permitted to provide legal assistance to or receive legal assistance from other prisoners.

- *White v. Sullivan*, 368 F. Supp. 292 (S.D. Ala. 1973).

The plaintiff prisoner claimed that his Eighth Amendment rights not to be subjected to cruel and unusual punishment were violated due to a number of factors, which included the lack of access to a law library. The few volumes of code in the library were deemed to be insufficient. The court ruled that the prison authorities establish meaningful collections in a law library and provided recommendations for the collection.

- *Procunier v. Martinez*, 416 U.S. 396 (1974).

The plaintiffs claimed the censoring of prison mail and a ban against using law students or paralegals for consultations with prisoners was unconstitutional. According to the court, the ban against mail was a violation of First Amendment rights since the ban was not due to a valid penological concern. The court ruled that the ban on using law students or para-legals provided barriers to the right of access to the courts and should therefore be lifted.

- *Wolff v. McDonnell*, 94 S. Ct 2963 (1974).

A prisoner claimed procedures at a Nebraska prison for inspecting mail and with-holding certain items were unconstitutional. The district court ruled that the restrictions on mail policies including the inspection of correspondence between attorneys and pris-oners was unconstitutional and violated rights to have access to the courts. But the court ruled that prisoner legal assistance in the form that was being provided was not unconsti-tutional. These decisions were affirmed in part and reversed in part by the appeals court, specifically remanding the necessity of reviewing procedures to see if due process standards had been met. This decision was then affirmed in part and reversed in part by the Supreme Court. The Supreme Court detailed some minimum due process requirements. Specifically, mail could be opened by correctional officers in front of prisoners and the prisoners were required to have access to the "capacity of the single legal advisor" who the warden had hired. The court remanded the case back to the district court to determine if the legal assis-tance offered in the prison was adequate.

- *Bounds v. Smith*, 430 U.S. 817 (1977).

The suit was brought forth by incarcerated prisoners in North Carolina, who claimed First and Fourteenth Amendment rights violations. The court ruled that prisoners' Four-teenth Amendment rights had been violated by the lack of access to law libraries. The pris-oners in this case should have, according to the court, been provided with access to the courts through the form of services including office supplies, notarial services, fee waivers, and lawyers. Furthermore, it was ruled to be the correctional institution's responsibility to provide law libraries or assistance from trained legal professionals.

- *Buise v. Hudkins*, 584 F.2d 223 (7th Cir. 1978).

A prisoner had been transferred to a state farm to serve as their prisoner librarian and began assisting other prisoners with legal issues. The prison administration consequently transferred the prisoner to a state prison with worse conditions. The district court ruled in favor of the prison administration. The appeals court reversed the decision and ordered that a law library be established at the farm in the event that the prison administration could not provide "a reasonable alternative means of access to the courts."

- *Fluhr v. Roberts*, 460 F. Supp. 536 (W.D. Ky. 1978).

The plaintiff in this case requested, among other things, a full law library pursuant to *Bounds v. Smith*. The court ordered that establishing a full law library was not necessary, rather that certain core volumes and reference materials were required.

- *Williams v. Leeke*, 584 F.2d 1336 (4th Cir. 1978), *cert. den.* 442 U.S. 911 (1979).

Plaintiffs from prisons in Virginia and South Carolina claimed that their access to legal materials was inadequate in their states and therefore their rights ensured by *Bounds v. Smith* had been violated. In this case, one plaintiff was in segregation in a maximum security prison and another was in a local jail. The court ruled that the prisoner in maxi-mum security was able to receive counsel and was therefore not denied access to the courts. In the case of the jail prisoner, the court ruled that the prisoner should also have reasonable access to the courts and remanded that complaint for further fact finding. This ruling mentions that *Bounds v. Smith* does not necessitate a law library and that there are other alternatives to providing access to the courts.

- *Rhodes v. Robinson*, 612 F.2d 766 (3rd Cir. 1979).

The plaintiff in this case was a prisoner at a Pennsylvania State correctional institution, who made ten claims regarding various services at the prison law library where he was a clerk. The claim that is most relevant to collection development in a prison law library was his claim that certain law books had been destroyed that should not have been destroyed. The court ruled that the prison administration must provide adequate access to the court and since the plaintiff did not prove the inadequacy of the current collection after certain law books had been destroyed, the claim was not founded. The court ruled in the administration's favor.

- *Cruz v. Hauck*, 627 F.2d 710 (5th Cir. 1980).

Prisoner plaintiffs claimed their access to legal materials had been restricted. The court ruled that the prison authorities have responsibilities to enable meaningful access to the courts by providing legal assistance through law libraries or trained legal professionals. The prisoners were, according to the court, not given adequate time in the law library and had little to no assistance from trained professionals. The case was remanded for further fact-finding.

- *Kelsey v. State of Minnesota*, 622 F.2d 956 (8th Cir. 1980).

This Minnesota plaintiff claimed that the law library's collection and hours were insufficient to provide access to the courts. While it was concluded that the collection was inadequate, the court ruled that a law library is only one means of providing access to the courts. Should other programs exist, such as legal assistance, the mandate for access to the courts would be considered adequate.

- *Leeds v. Watson*, 630 F.2d 674 (9th Cir. 1980).

A number of class action claims were made by plaintiffs in this case including issues with the facility itself and claims that constitutional rights guaranteeing access to the courts had been violated. In the case of the right of access to the courts, the court ruled that the prison should investigate either providing legal representation to the prisoners or creating a law library. The court also ruled that prisoners should be made aware of the availability of any services initiated as a result of the inquiry.

- *Jensen v. Satran*, 303 N.W.2d 568, 1981 N.D. LEXIS 220 (N.D. 1981).

The complaint within this case was that the law library was inadequate both in the collection and the number of hours it was open. The plaintiffs claimed that the collection was inadequate because it did not contain certain volumes from a recommended list; the court ruled that the collection, regardless of whether all books from a recommended list were included, was still adequate. The court also ruled that the plaintiffs had not adequately proven that the restrictions with hours and number of prisoners able to use the prison law library impeded their access to the courts.

- *Canterino v. Wilson*, 546 F. Supp. 174 (W.D. Ky. 1982).

Female prisoners in a Kentucky prison sued for, among many claims, a lawyer to assist with legal proceedings as well as an update to the prison law library. The court ruled that legal help was not available, the library was insufficient, and that the women were not being afforded the same services available to male prisoners in other institutions. At appeal, the court affirmed the district court's decision requiring the prison administration to hire part-time legal assistance and update the prison law library due to significant differences between men's and women's services.[40]

- *Corgain v. Miller*, 708 F.2d 1241 (7th Cir. 1983).

Prisoners in an Illinois state prison claimed that their right to access the courts had been impeded due to deficiencies in the collection of state law materials at their prison library. The court acknowledged that the collection in the law library was poor, but found that other means of access existed. Therefore, the claim that library services were inadequate was dismissed as moot with the reasoning that access to the courts can be presented in multiple forms with library services only presenting one possible alternative for providing access to the courts.

- *Cepulonis v. Fair*, 732 F.2d 1 (1st Cir. 1984).

Massachusetts prisoners confined to segregation units claimed inadequate access to the courts due to two issues in the prison law library: infrequent access and the requirement that a prisoner must specify what materials he/she would like to use before utilizing the library. This case was an appeal of a prior case and the appeals court upheld the district court's decision ordering a satellite law library with specific volumes for use by segregated prisoners. The appeals court vacated the prior order that law school students be provided for legal assistance as the provision of library services was deemed adequate to fulfill the directives from *Bounds v. Smith*.

- *Brown v. Smith*, 580 F. Supp. 1576 (M.D. Penn. 1984).

The plaintiff was transferred from a state prison in Massachusetts to a federal prison in Pennsylvania and claimed that he was not given adequate access to the courts due to the lack of Massachusetts state materials in the Pennsylvania prison. The court ruled that a federal prison was not required to carry state legal materials.

- *Brown v. Manning*, 630 F. Supp. 391 (E.D. Wash. 1985).

State of Washington prisoners claimed that they had been denied "meaningful access to the courts" because of an insufficient law library or lack of legal assistance in a county jail. The court ruled that those incarcerated for more than three days should be provided with an "adequate law library or access to persons trained in the law."

- *Morrow v. Harwell*, 768 F.2d 619 (5th Cir. 1985), on remand 640 F. Supp. 225 (W.D. Tex. 1986).

A county jail in Texas was sued for, among other claims, not providing enough access to the courts via legal assistance and a bookmobile. The appellate court ruled that the county was not fulfilling *Bounds v. Smith's* mandates to provide reasonable access to the courts through paralegals certified to practice law and through an existing bookmobile program.

- *Lindquist v. Idaho State Board of Corrections*, 776 F.2d 851 (9th Cir. 1985).

This was a class action suit in which prisoners claimed that their rights to meaningful access to the courts had been infringed upon due to inadequate library services, insufficient legal assistance, and insufficient access to materials or machines, such as copiers and typewriters. The court ruled that the current program was not adequate and approved a six-month plan to bring the program up to standards. At the six-month point, the program and implementations were reviewed by the court and found to be compliant. This case determined a number of minimum requirements for prison law libraries.

- *Berry v. Department of Corrections*, 144 Ariz. 318 (Ariz. App. 1985).

Prisoners incarcerated in an Arizona treatment and detention center for under 90 days had access only to a limited law library without any current code or helpful law books. The court ruled that the Department of Corrections was obligated to provide either an adequate law library or access to other legal assistance for any prisoner held for more than three days.

- *Walker v. Mintzes*, 771 F.2d 920 (6th Cir. 1985).

Prisoners at three Michigan prisons claimed a number of constitutional rights violations, including limitations that had been placed on law library usage after a riot. The court ruled that whether or not prisoners had experienced lack of access to the courts could not be solely based on the hours a library operated after a riot.

- *U.S. ex rel. Para-Professional Law Clinic v. Kane*, 656 F. Supp. 1099, 1987 U.S. Dist. LEXIS 2255 (E.D. Pa. 1987).

Prisoners at a Pennsylvania prison had created a para-professional law clinic run by fellow prisoners to offer legal assistance. The prison administration intended to close the clinic and prisoners filed suit. There was a law library at the institution, however, it did not have current volumes that the court deemed necessary. The court ruled that since no adequate law library was available, the clinic was necessary to provide the prisoners meaningful access to the courts.

- *Flittie v. Solem*, 827 F.2d 276 (8th Cir. 1987).

An inmate legal clerk was dismissed from his position and made a number of claims regarding his dismissal, including restricted access to the courts based on limited hours in the prison law library. The court ruled that the plaintiff's constitutional right to access to the courts had not been infringed upon on the basis of other actions he had been capable of filing.

- *Eldridge v. Block*, 832 F.2d 1132 (9th Cir. 1987).

A prisoner who had been extradited to Maryland made a number of complaints regarding his extradition from California to Maryland, including the lack of access to a law library when in California. Initially, a district court refused the plaintiff's claims, however the appeals court ruled that the prisoner had a constitutional right for access to the courts and reversed the district court's decision.

- *DeMallory v. Cullen*, 855 F.2d 442 (7th Cir. 1988).

A prisoner in segregation in a Wisconsin prison claimed, in addition to other claims, that he did not have sufficient access to an adequate law library. The district court ruled in favor of the defendants, but in the court of appeals, the court reversed the decision. The appeals court ruled that the volumes in the library were insufficient to provide access to the courts; similarly, the legal assistance provided was considered insufficient. The court remanded the case for further proceedings.

- *Coleman v. State*, 762 P.2d 814 (Idaho 1988).

An Idaho prison had a policy of denying prisoner access to a law library for the first ten days of disciplinary detention. The court ruled that this regulation violated constitutional rights of meaningful access to the courts.

- *Giarratano v. Murray*, 492 U.S. 1 (1989).

Death row prisoners in Virginia filed a complaint that their constitutional right of access to the courts had been violated by insufficient access to law libraries or legal aid. The Supreme Court reversed the judgment from the District Court and the Court of Appeals. Both the district and appeals court previously ruled that death row inmates needed special counsel because of their circumstances. The Supreme Court ruled that access did not guarantee continuous access to legal assistance and that no distinction in service offerings were necessary for death row inmates. The Supreme Court also ruled that Virginia's current plan, while not as comprehensive as some in other states, was still sufficient to provide death row prisoners with meaningful access to the courts.

- *Watson v. Norris*, 729 F. Supp. 581 (M.D. Tenn. 1989).

The plaintiff, a prisoner in segregation in a Tennessee prison, claimed, among other things, that his access to the courts was insufficient because of a paging system for requesting books from the prison law library and due to the lack of legal assistance besides access to jailhouse lawyers. The court ruled that the current system was, in fact, insufficient.

- *Griffin v. Coughlin*, 743 F. Supp. 1006 (N.D. N.Y. 1990).

Prisoners in protective custody in New York claimed a number of violations of constitutional rights, including the right to access the courts due to limited library services and legal assistance. The prisoners, who were not afforded physical access to the library, claimed that this affected their ability to properly research legal topics. Additionally, the prisoners could only correspond with law clerks in writing, which impaired their ability to get proper assistance and guidance. The court ruled that the plaintiffs' access to the courts had been impaired.

- *Vaughn v. U.S.*, 579 A.2d 170 (D.C. App. 1990).

The plaintiff claimed that he was subject to cruel and unusual punishment, which included, among other things, lack of access to a law library in the Texas prison where he was serving. The court dismissed his case due to lack of specificity in his claims of unconstitutional practices.

- *Gluth v. Kangas*, 951 F.2d 1504 (9th Cir. 1991).

Plaintiffs in this case were Arizona prisoners, who claimed that their right to access the courts had been impeded due to improperly trained prisoner legal assistants, restrictions preventing prisoners from accessing the law library, and policies on purchasing legal supplies. The district court and the court of appeals both ruled in the plaintiffs' favor and thereby deemed that their access to the courts was inadequate.

- *Geder v. Roth*, 765 F. Supp. 1357 (N.D. Ill. 1991).

A prisoner at an Illinois prison claimed that he was denied "meaningful access to the courts" by limited hours in the law library and lack of access to a law clerk. The court ruled that the prisoner had not properly demonstrated prejudice and that the facility was justified in initiating reasonable restrictions on library facility usage.

- *Nolley v. County of Erie*, 776 F. Supp. 715 (W.D. N.Y. 1991).

A prisoner housed in a New York prison was restricted from using the law library in person due to her HIV+ status. She was able to request cases and books, although she often received the wrong materials. She was only permitted to use the law library to access the typewriter and was banned from touching any law books. She was denied face-to-face contact with legal assistance. The court ruled that the plaintiff's right of access to the courts was violated by the absence of adequate access to the library and lack of access to law clerks or those trained in legal assistance.

- *Chandler v. Baird*, 926 F.2d 1057 (11th Cir. 1991).

The plaintiff was placed in administrative confinement for a period of 16 days and denied access to his lawyer and library services during this time, which he interpreted as a violation of his constitutional right to access the courts. The court ruled that the denials of access were both minor and short-lived and that no injury or prejudice had been shown as required by *Bounds v. Smith*.

- *Johnson v. Moore*, 948 F.2d 517 (9th Cir. 1991).

An incarcerated prisoner claimed a number of constitutional violations, one of which was the limited scope of the legal materials provided in the prison law library. The court concluded that a law library must only be adequate, not unlimited, and that the plaintiff was unable to prove an injury based on the lack of volumes available in the institution's law library.

- *Shoats v. Commissioner, PA Department of Corrections*, 591 A.2d 326 (Pa. Commw. 1991).

The plaintiff had been transferred temporarily to another prison where his access to legal materials from Pennsylvania was limited to a book paging system. This system was restricted to prisoners transferred from a specific prison in Pennsylvania. The plaintiff had been transferred from a different prison and was therefore not eligible to receive materials from this book paging system. The court concluded that the plaintiff had been denied access to the courts because of the book paging system. Both of the parties moved for a summary judgment, which was denied for both parties.

- *Housley v. Killinger*, 972 F.2d 1339 (9th Cir. 1992).

The plaintiff claimed that his right to access the courts had been impaired due to an inadequate collection in the prison law library, limited hours, and lack of legal assistance. The court ruled that the collection was adequate and that federal prisons are not required to carry state reporters and digests, that forty hours a week is sufficient for a library to be open, and legal assistance is not required if the facility has an adequate law library.

- *Shango v. Jurich*, 965 F.2d 289 (1992).

A state prisoner claimed that his access to the courts had been infringed upon due to limited law library hours and also that his due process was violated in a disciplinary hearing. The district court ruled that he had received "constitutionally adequate access to the courts" and awarded only nominal damages for violations of his due process. The appeals court affirmed the ruling on his access to the law library as well as only nominal damages for his due process claims, since the information he required was received before his district court case.

- *Miller v. Evans*, 832 P.2d 786 (Nev. 1992).

The prisoner claimed that meaningful access had been denied by the inadequate nature of the prison law library at a prison in Nevada. The district court found the prison library to be "constitutionally inadequate" and granted the plaintiff's motion for summary judgment The appellate court reversed the district court's decision, stating that the prisoner had not properly demonstrated deficiencies in the current collection in his prison law library. According to the court, the prison law library, supported by legal assistance from librarians and inmate law clerks along with interlibrary loan, was sufficient to provide access to the courts.

- *Petrick v. Maynard*, 11 F.3d 991 (10th Cir. 1993).

A prisoner incarcerated in Oklahoma requested legal materials for his defense of prior convictions in other states that were being used to enhance his Oklahoma sentence. He requested the materials from the other states using interlibrary loan and his request was denied internally due to cost issues. The district court ruled that his constitutional right to meaningful access to the courts had not been violated. The appeals court reversed and remanded this decision, concluding that an injury had been demonstrated and no other means such as legal assistance had been supplied to assist the prisoner with his claim.

- *Martin v. Ezeagu*, 816 F. Supp. 20 (D.D.C. 1993).

The plaintiff, a prisoner in the District of Columbia, claimed that he had been harassed by the prison law librarian verbally including with "racial epithets" when in the law library, he had been banned from the library, and his materials had been confiscated. His complaint claimed that his right to access the courts had been violated among other violations of constitutional rights. The court agreed that the plaintiff's constitutional rights had been violated due to the harassment. The defendants issued a motion to dismiss, which was denied.

- *Oswald v. Graves*, 819 F. Supp. 680 (E.D. Mich. 1993).

A plaintiff from a prison in Michigan filed suit against the prison law librarian with two complaints: that he had not been offered free photocopying and that his time in the prison law library had been limited because his name was on a "library call-out list." The court granted the defendant librarian immunity and ruled that the plaintiff could neither prove injury due to the lack of free photocopying nor the limited library time he received, which amounted to approximately ten hours weekly with a few exceptions.

- *Acevedo v. Forcinito*, 820 F. Supp. 886 (D.N.J. 1993).

The prisoner, whose English was not fluent, claimed that his constitutional right to access the courts had been violated due to the lack of materials available for a non–English speaker and lack of legal assistance in his native language. The court stated that "for prisoners who cannot read or understand English, the constitutional right of access to the courts cannot be determined solely by the number of volumes in, or size of, a law library." The court asserted that assistance should be provided for those who are unable to use a law library, regardless of how comprehensive the library may be.

- *Howard v. Parkman*, 437 S.E.2d 483 (Ga. App. 1993).

The plaintiff claimed that he had been denied access to the courts due to restricted access to the law library and limited or non-delivery of copied legal materials. The appeals court affirmed the decision of the district court that the plaintiff's constitutional rights had not been violated. The plaintiff had received nearly 4,300 copies of legal materials and worked in the law library five hours a week; therefore, he had access to the law library.

- *Allen v. City and County of Honolulu*, 39 F.3d 936 (9th Cir. 1994).

The law library's schedule at the prison conflicted with the outdoor exercise schedule. The prisoner sued for a violation of his Eighth Amendment rights not to be subjected to cruel and unusual punishment. The district court confirmed that forcing a choice of either library usage or outdoor exercise could be considered cruel and unusual punishment. The prison officials appealed for qualified immunity and asked for summary judgment; the appeals court also denied qualified immunity.

- *Lloyd v. Corrections Corp. of America*, 855 F. Supp. 221 (W.D. Tenn. 1994).

The plaintiff was housed in a privately operated detention center in Tennessee before transfer to a federal correctional institution. He claimed that he was denied access to the detention center's law library. Since the plaintiff was represented by counsel during his time at the detention center, the court ruled that his right of access to the courts had not been violated due to lack of law library services.

- *Vandelft v. Moses*, 31 F.3d 794 (9th Cir. 1994).

The plaintiff had been segregated for protective custody and claimed he was denied access to the courts while in segregation because he was not allowed to access certain hard-cover books or reference materials from his segregated unit. He did receive photocopies of cited cases. The court stated that the plaintiff had not adequately shown actual injury to prove that his access to the courts had been impeded. The plaintiff appealed and the appeals court affirmed the decisions of the district court.

- *Walters v. Edgar*, 900 F. Supp. 197 (N.D. Ill. 1995).

Prisoners in segregation across five institutions were not permitted access to a law library and instead were offered a prisoner law clerk system. They claimed that this substitution was a violation of their constitutional right to access the courts and submitted a class action suit. The court ruled that prisoners in three of the five prisons had not been given adequate access to legal materials or assistance comprehending legal materials and that the inmate law clerk system was not sufficient. The court found no issue in the fourth prison. A subsequent case regarding the fifth prison (163 F.3d 430 (7th Cir. 1998)) found no standing in the fifth prison for these claims.

- *Boyd v. Wood*, 52 F.3d 820 (9th Cir. 1995).

A prisoner was housed in an out of state prison in Washington and claimed that he did not have adequate access to the legal materials required for litigation in the state of his alleged crimes (Kansas). The district court dismissed the case and the appeals court affirmed that decision. The appeals court cited other cases in which the state was responsible for furnishing legal materials from out of state when necessary for a prisoner's litigation. The plaintiff, however, brought suit against Washington when Kansas would have been the state that had to supply his legal materials. The court dismissed the plaintiff's action on the basis that he had named the wrong defendant.

- *Brooks v. Buscher*, 62 F.3d 176 (7th Cir. 1995).

A prisoner who was segregated due to violent behavior was denied direct access to the law library and claimed a violation of his constitutional rights. The district court ruled in his favor, but the appeals court reversed the decision determining that the prisoner had been afforded meaningful access to the courts by provision of requested items through a law library along with consultation with the law librarian and inmate clerks.

- *Lewis v. Casey*, 518 U.S. 343 (1996).

This case was a landmark case that influenced the closing of many law libraries in prisons nationwide. Its interpretation of *Bounds v. Smith* denied a right to a law library or legal assistance and rather stated that *Bounds v. Smith* only guaranteed a right of access to the courts. Initially, the district court ruled in favor of the prisoners, calling for reform of Arizona prison law library services. The court found that prisoners in segregation and who were either illiterate or non–English speakers were the most affected. The appeals court affirmed in part, and vacated and remanded in part. The Supreme Court reversed and remanded the decisions. Major points that were established were a (1) "subpar" library or legal assistance program was not enough to constitute actual injury; (2) actual injury caused to two inmates due to either illiteracy or lack of English proficiency was not enough to mandate systematic change; (3) delays in reviewing legal materials were justified if related to actual "penological interests"; and (4) an order from the district court for overarching change to the Arizona library systems was not warranted.

- *Casteel v. Pieschek*, 944 F. Supp. 748 (E.D. Wis. 1996).

Prisoners were given weekly access to a courthouse collection of legal materials. They claimed that this was insufficient and that their rights to access the courts had been violated. The district court awarded summary judgment to the defendants. The case was remanded back to the district court for further proceedings by the appeals court. Upon remand, the district court ruled that the methods the county jail used to provide materials were adequate according to *Lewis v. Casey* and *Bounds v. Smith*.

- *Sabers v. Delano*, 100 F.3d 82 (8th Cir. 1996).

A prisoner in South Dakota alleged that she was systematically denied access to the courts due to an inexperienced contract attorney provided by the prison and an inadequate prison law library. The plaintiff also attempted to amend her complaint as a class action suit. The district court ruled that systematic denial of law library access of legal assistance did not constitute an actual injury and the plaintiff had to demonstrate actual injury. The appeals court affirmed.

- *Ladd v. Hannigan*, 962 F. Supp. 1390 (D. Kan. 1997).

The plaintiff claimed that his constitutional right to access the courts had been infringed upon because of limited access to the prison law library and the lack of attorneys available to assist with legal claims. The court asserted that the prisoner did not have the ability to specify what sort of access constitutes meaningful access to the court, i.e., prison law libraries and legal counsel do not have to be offered simultaneously. The court also noted the plaintiff's frequent usage of the prison law library proved that he had access to the courts.

- *Klinger v. Department of Corrections*, 107 F.3d 609 (8th Cir. 1997).

Female prisoners in a Nebraska prison filed a number of complaints, including a denial of access to the courts due to an insufficient law library and lack of legal assistance. The district court ruled in the favor of the prisoners, asserting that the collection was, in fact, insufficient because it was disorganized and therefore unusable. But between the time the district court ruled and the appeals court ruled, *Lewis v. Casey* was decided, which required actual injury to be demonstrated. Since no actual injury was demonstrated, the appeals court reversed the district court's decision on the meaningful access to the courts claim.

- *Demps v. State*, 696 So.2d 1296 (Fla. 1997).

The plaintiff filed a motion for post-conviction relief based on his inability to meet filing deadlines in Florida since he was incarcerated in Indiana. He claimed that he had been denied access to the courts because he could not use necessary Florida statues or forms in a timely manner to file a motion. The court affirmed his motion and claimed that Florida had the responsibility to supply the prisoner with the necessary statutes and forms.

- *Farver v. Vilches*, 155 F.3d 978 (8th Cir. 1998).

A jail prisoner claimed multiple grievances, including denial of access to the courts through a one-day suspension from law library usage. The district court granted summary judgment in the defendants' favor; the appeals court affirmed and asserted that no prejudice or actual injury had been demonstrated by losing one day of access to the law library.

- *Wilson v. Blankenship*, 163 F.3d 1284 (11th Cir. 1998).

A federal prisoner was housed temporarily at a county jail where no law library was available. He claimed denial of access to the courts based on the non-existence of a law library. The jail administration concurred that there was no law library, but the administration had no funds appropriated to create one. Since the plaintiff had counsel that was assigned to defend him on his criminal convictions and no injury was adequately shown, the appeals court affirmed the decision from the district court to grant the defendants summary judgment.

- *Lambros v. Hawk*, 993 F. Supp. 1372 (D. Kan. 1998).

A federal prisoner, who was apprehended and initially incarcerated in Brazil, claimed mistreatment and violation of his right to access the courts. One of his claims was that he was denied translations of Brazilian laws to contest both his arrest and extradition. The court ruled that actual injury must be shown to demonstrate impedance of his access to the courts per *Lewis v. Casey* and that none had been demonstrated.

- *Jones v. Greninger*, 188 F.3d 322 (5th Cir. 1999).

The plaintiff filed multiple claims including one regarding access to legal materials. The plaintiff was reassigned work duties in an area that had open hours that would prevent him from using the law library as much as he needed. He was limited to only five hours of library time weekly. The court asserted that access to a law library did not have to be unlimited and concluded that five hours weekly would be sufficient.

- *Zimmerman v. Tribble*, 226 F.3d 568 (7th Cir. 2000).

The prisoner acting as plaintiff had been transferred from one institution to another, which had different programs for good time credits as well as less library access. He submitted a complaint against the prison librarian and after doing so, he was no longer allowed to use the library. Per the court's ruling, the good time credits were not inferred to be a prisoner right, however, the plaintiff's claim of retaliation based on the prison librarian's response to his grievance was remanded for further proceedings.

- *Benjamin v. Kerik*, 102 F. Supp. 2d 157 (S.D.N.Y. 2000).

Defendants in this case filed a motion for termination of a number of consent decrees regarding six cases on the basis of the Prison Litigation Reform Act of 1995. The plaintiffs in these cases claimed that the program for law libraries was not adequate for providing access to the courts. The court, citing *Lewis v. Casey*, asserted that an actual injury had to have occurred for a constitutional violation of the right of access to the courts. While the court found a few instances of injury, the court concluded that those individual injuries were not sufficient to warrant systematic change in the institution.

- *Gilmore v. People of the State of California*, 220 F.3d 987 (9th Cir. 2000).

This case reversed a decree from *Gilmore v. Lynch*, in which a certain standard of law library was required. The prison had ceased to follow the decree because of rulings from *Lewis v. Casey,* as well as the Prison Litigation Reform Act. The district court affirmed the decision to terminate the 1972 decree from the original case and denied the plaintiffs' evidentiary hearing request. The appeals court ruled that while the district court read *Lewis v. Casey* correctly in the sense that an actual injury had to be shown, the court did not allow the plaintiffs the chance to demonstrate that injury. Therefore, the court remanded the case for further proceedings.

- *Gomez v. Vernon*, 255 F.3d 1118 (9th Cir. 2001).

A number of inmate law clerks at an Idaho prison claimed that they were retaliated against by prison administration after providing legal assistance to other prisoners. The district court ruled that retaliation was a "policy or custom" against prisoners who were exercising the right of access to the courts and granted injunctive relief to six individual prisoners. The appeals court affirmed this decision.

- *Shaw v. Murphy*, 532 U.S. 223 (2001).

A prisoner had given legal advice via a letter to another prisoner and was subsequently punished by prison authorities for providing this advice. The district court granted the prison administration summary judgment, which was reversed by the appeals court. The prisoner claimed that he had a First Amendment right to give legal assistance as he wished, however, the Supreme Court ruled that the rights acquired from *Turner v. Safley* would not be enhanced to include a First Amendment right to provide legal aid to other prisoners, only a protection of free speech.

- *Colvin v. Schaublin*, 31 Fed. Appx. 170, 2002 U.S. App. LEXIS 4217 (6th Cir. March 7, 2002).

The prisoner plaintiff in this case was in a segregation unit and claimed that because he was segregated, he was denied access to a law library, which in turn affected his ability to file petitions in a timely manner. The appeals court ruled that the prisoner had shown actual injury pursuant to *Lewis v. Casey* and that the prison administration was unable to show a penological concern associated with disallowing segregated prisoners access to the prison law library. Upon remand in 2004, the district court granted the defendants summary judgment. The prisoner appealed again and the appeals court found that he had not provided evidence of injury (113 Fed. Appx. 664 (2004)).

- *Egerton v. Cockrell*, 334 F.3d 433, 2003 U.S. App. LEXIS 11766 (5th Cir. June 13, 2003).

A prisoner attempting to file an appeal on his original criminal convictions claimed that he was not able to do so in a timely manner due to lack of access to necessary law library materials to prepare his case. The district court dismissed his case. The appeals court ruled that in general, prison libraries with less than adequate collections did not guarantee a "state created impediment," however, they ruled that in this case the plaintiff's lack of access to the Antiterrorism and Effective Death Penalty Act of 1996 (AEDPA) had a significant impact on his ability to appeal his conviction. Therefore, his access to the courts had been impeded, the district court's decision was vacated, and his case was remanded for further proceedings.

- *Bolin v. Franck*, 2004 Cal. App. Unpub. LEXIS 11745 (Cal. App. 1st Dist. December 28, 2004).

The plaintiff in this case sued his attorneys who were representing him in a civil rights case against prison administration. One of the attorneys had been suspended from practicing law. The plaintiff had limited access to the law library facilities in his institution and claimed that a number of motions had been unfiled and returned to him. The district court dismissed his case, however, the appeals court reversed and remanded.

- *Kane v. Garcia Espitia*, 546 U.S. 9 (2005).

In this case, the prisoner claimed that he did not have sufficient pre-trial access to the library in order to prepare his case. The plaintiff had four hours of research time in the prison law library before his case went to trial. The district court rejected his arguments and on appeal, the district court decision was reversed. The Supreme Court reversed and remanded the appeals court's decision, ruling that the access to a law library was not part of Sixth Amendment rights to represent oneself.

- *Marshall v. Knight*, 445 F.3d 965, 2006 U.S. App. LEXIS 10395 (7th Cir. April 26, 2006).

The plaintiff claimed that he had been denied access to the courts because of a restrictive policy on accessing the prison law library. The district court dismissed the claims; the appeals court reversed and remanded the decision, concluding that the district court had interpreted *Lewis v. Casey* too narrowly.

- *Koerschner v. Warden*, Nevada State Prison, 508 F. Supp. 2d 849, 2007 U.S. Dist. LEXIS 65237 (D. Nev. August 22, 2007).

The plaintiff, a prisoner in Nevada in segregation, claimed that the "paging system" used to provide legal materials to prisoners was insufficient for providing access to the courts. The prison had initiated a new policy for segregated inmates to replace access to the law library with this system. The court questioned the validity of this system for providing adequate access to the court and ruled appointment of counsel to assist this prisoner with his legal claims.

- *U.S. ex rel. Strong v. Hulick*, 530 F. Supp. 2d 1034, 2008 U.S. Dist. LEXIS 4361 (N.D. Ill. January 18, 2008).

The plaintiff claimed that he was improperly informed regarding his appeal submission deadlines and that he was unable to file due to restrictions on access to the prison law library. The court found that there was in fact a "state-created impediment" that prevented timely filing of the prisoner's petition. The court granted the plaintiff's motion to stay. In subsequent procedures (2009 U.S. Dist. LEXIS 86694 (September 21, 2009)), the court was unable to establish that the plaintiff's access to the courts had actually been impeded.

- *Brown v. Hooper*, Civil Action No. 10–0291 (DMC), 2010 U.S. Dist. LEXIS 82100 (August 11, 2010).

The prisoner plaintiff claimed that requests to use a community law library were denied and he was instead instructed to use LexisNexis for legal research. He was unable to effectively use LexisNexis and sought injunctive relief and damages. Per the court's discussion: "Plaintiff does not have an abstract right to access to a law library and has failed to allege any facts indicating that his lack of access to a law library has caused him actual injury with respect to any of the narrow class of claims protected by the constitutional right of access to courts."

- *Hebbe v. Pliler*, 627 F.3d 338 (9th Cir. 2010).

A prisoner preparing for trial claimed that he was not given sufficient time to use the law library before his state court appeal and that he was forced to choose between law library time and exercise time. He claimed violations of his Eighth Amendment rights to not be subjected to cruel and unusual punishment. The district court denied his claims, but the appeals court reversed and remanded in his favor on both claims.

- *Hicks v. Rowe*, 498 Fed. Appx. 737, 2012 WL 5865897 (9th Cir. November 13, 2012).

The plaintiff was a prisoner in segregation and claimed, as part of his grievances, that he had been provided access to a computer to do legal research, however, was not given a keyboard or a mouse. The courts deemed that the plaintiff was a "vexatious litigant" and had not proven actual injury pursuant to *Lewis v. Casey*.

- *Jacobs v. Woodford*, Case No. CV 07–02618 DOC (RZ), 2011 U.S. Dist. LEXIS 48582 (C.D. Cal. March 10, 2011).

The plaintiff made a number of claims including retaliation for destruction of legal files held in his cell that resulted in an impediment of his right to access the courts. The court ruled that his access to the courts interference claim was not valid, however, ruled that he could continue with the retaliation claim associated with the destruction of his legal materials at trial.

- *Commonwealth v. Rousseau*, 465 Mass. 372, 990 N.E. 2d 543, 2013 Mass. LEXIS 353 (June 5, 2013).

The defendant, on trial for criminal convictions, claimed a number of violations of constitutional rights. Regarding the constitutional right of access to the courts, the defendant was unable to use the digitized law library at the prison due to a ban on his computer usage while incarcerated. Because there were no other means to use the law library, this was viewed by the court as too broad and a violation of his rights. The court recommended that the defendant be permitted to conduct legal research on library computers as it pertained to his case.

## Summary

It is unlikely that the court cases represented in this chapter and the previous chapter are comprehensive; certainly many more cases exist that were not easily discoverable. Additionally, the cases found were not always the final rulings; some were remanded for further proceedings or fact finding. The limitations in finding some of these final rulings was related to difficulties using LexisNexis, which prisoners may also experience as clunky or difficult to understand. Westlaw for instance includes related cases when searching on a certain topic. Additionally, Westlaw includes subject headings so that one can find related cases. Prisoners using LexisNexis might find it very difficult to access or locate relevant cases, especially if they do not have legal expertise. Abel echoes this issue with providing prisoners access to electronic legal collections; he acknowledges that electronic access is easier to use, but states that "computerization comes with a cost, especially for inmates without computer skills." He also cites cases where prisoners have sued because of issues using electronic collections based on computer illiteracy.[41] These prisoners may also struggle with general literacy or English reading comprehension issues.

Practitioners from chapter 9 mentioned LexisNexis usage in their libraries. Beverly discussed challenges she faced when LexisNexis and computerized databases were added in her institution, citing her own issues with technology. Jack thought that the computerized options for legal access in LexisNexis made it a "fabulous product." None of the interviewees explicitly discussed prisoner issues using the databases, nor was this a question that was directly asked.

This collection of case summaries should provide some background about the challenges and issues that frequently cause prisoners to litigate. It is apparent that many more prisoners are litigating about their right to meaningful access to the courts than getting access to general library services. Multiple researchers claim that the right to meaningful access to the courts is one of the only guaranteed rights a prisoner maintains once incarcerated; therefore, it is not surprising that these individuals litigate often on this topic.

The court cases presented in this chapter, especially *Lewis v. Casey*, show a decline in court support of prisoners litigating for their perceived constitutional rights. This is not just a result of *Lewis v. Casey*, but also a consequence of the Prison Litigation Reform Act. While it is sensible to limit frivolous lawsuits from constantly requiring the court's analysis, one must question whether the hands-off doctrine of a pre–1960s America is yet again on the rise. Without access to the courts, prisoners have little recourse to challenge unjust prison conditions or to even maintain basic constitutional rights. Mushlin strikes on this issue as it relates to the PLRA, establishing that access to the courts allows prisoners to "obtain systematic relief from unconstitutional prison conditions."[42] With reduced and limited access to the courts, dire situations could prevail for prisoners that might improve if they were able to dispute their claims in court as they had prior to the passing of the PLRA.

*Lewis v. Casey* is also a directed attempt to reduce what might be frivolous litigation by requiring actual injury. This requirement may thwart efforts to represent those that it is intended to protect: those with actual injuries. The ability to file a claim is in many cases directly related to the meaningful access *Lewis* intends to protect. Mushlin provides an excellent example of the injury prisoners might sustain but be unable to prove: he describes a prisoner who has filed a claim but is unable to properly research or discover evidence due to an insufficient law library.[43] This prisoner has little recourse; he may have an actual injury but does not have the tools to prove what *Lewis v. Casey* requires of him in court. Consequently, prisoners with less means and without this meaningful access may never make it to the courtroom to claim their actual injury. Both *Lewis v. Casey* and the PLRA can cause difficulties for prisoners attempting to improve potentially unjust prison conditions.

# 6

# The Neglected Profession

*I don't think people know enough about correctional librarianship, because it's not part of the curriculum and it really should be ... it's a very important arm of corrections, which is very understated, very underappreciated, and very underpaid.*
*—Carrie, Interviewee from Chapter 9*

*The school does often determine what your opportunities are when you get out. But prison librarianship wasn't offered, it wasn't talked about. They really need to give tours so you can actually see what the physical environment is.*
*—Heather, Interviewee from Chapter 9*

In chapters 1 and 2, federal and state policies on prison librarianship were explored. In chapter 3, literature on prison librarianship from both scholarly and trade publications was reviewed. Certainly policies and literature have been and are being published on the topic of prison librarianship, but how does this body of policy making and scholarship compare to other fields of librarianship?

The idea that prison librarianship has been frequently ignored by the general library and information science community is not new. Fred Hartz, Michael Krimmel, and Emilie Hartz, who compiled their bibliography in 1987, begin their foreword by commenting on this issue:

> Historically, prison libraries and training for correctional librarianship have, with few notable exceptions, been largely ignored by librarians, library schools, and professional library organizations. There has been a lack of professional leadership in the area of correctional libraries throughout this century, at least until the passage of the Library Services and Construction Act of 1966.[1]

The methods I intend to employ during this chapter are efforts to reinvestigate whether this standard of neglect is still the case.

As mentioned in chapter 1, many of the national policies such as the *Library Standards for Adult Correctional Institutions* were written more than two decades ago. In order to understand if this frequency of updates is less than other disciplines of librarianship, I compared the frequency of publication of public policies for other national and international groups of librarianship including academic and public organizations. National groups such as the American Library Association (ALA) and its subdivisions were reviewed as well as international groups including the International Federation of Library Associations and Institutions (IFLA).

In comparison to other fields of librarianship—such as public, academic, corporate, or special librarianship—prison librarianship is not a prolific topic for many scholars. Perhaps librarians with experience in prison librarianship are not expected to share their professional experiences to the degree that, for instance, academic librarians are encouraged. These professionals may be actively discouraged or simply do not have the time. There may be little reward for them to publish or pursue professional development opportunities.

It may also be the case that many of the librarians or library staff running prison libraries are not trained as professional librarians in the same way as public or academic librarians. Two of the librarians I spoke to in chapter 9 did not have master's degrees in library or information science. Many of those I spoke to stated that it was not a requirement for them and it might have been something they minimized during their job interviews for correctional librarianship. It is important to remember that these librarians, whether they had library science degrees or not, are the active librarians in the profession. Many librarians in other states did not volunteer to participate in interviews or participate in my survey so their voices are not represented.

While the research in this chapter cannot necessarily determine the reason less works are published on prison librarianship, it certainly shows a disparity between the field and other fields of librarianship. Within this chapter, I also reviewed the citations of top library and information science journals to, where possible, compare the frequency of publications on prison librarianship compared to other areas of librarianship. For the citations found on prison librarianship, I reviewed whether the topic of prison librarianship was ancillary or central, i.e., was the article or monograph written solely about the prison library or was it about censorship and included sections about the prison library? I also attempted to determine what the role of the author was at the time of publication; for instance, was the author actively employed as a prison librarian or employed in another type of institution?

Lastly, I reviewed the existence or non-existence of prison librarianship paths and courses at American Library Association accredited schools for receiving a master's in library and information science (MLIS). This approach is similar to that presented by Harris McClaskey in his 1977 article on correctional librarianship. At the time of publication, McClaskey reported that nine library schools, both ALA accredited and non-accredited, offered some form of correctional librarianship educational program.[2] The lack of MLIS programs geared toward correctional librarianship has also been discussed on the ALA prison listserv in the last few years. I reviewed websites and course catalogs from accredited programs to determine if any tracks or coursework were offered on the specific topic of prison librarianship.

## Policymaking

As discussed in chapter 1, many policies on prison librarianship are decades old, in particular the *Library Standards for Adult Correctional Institutions* from the Association of Specialized and Cooperative Library Agencies, which was authored in 1992. There have been subsequent international and national policies published by the American Library Association, such as the "Prisoners' Right to Read," which was first published as the "Resolution on Prisoners' Right to Read" in 1982, adopted in a version of its current form in 2010, and recently updated in 2014. Within the context of this chapter, I was interested in understanding what other kinds of national policies were in place for other types of institutions and also if they were more frequently updated than national policies on prison librarianship.

First, I reviewed the American Library Association's website to find policies, dates amended, and number of updates. The American Library Association has a category on their website for advocacy and issues on which many national policies have been published. In particular, there are a number of interpretations of the "Library Bill of Rights" on ALA's website, including the aforementioned "Prisoners' Right to Read" policy. Additionally, many policies are available in the *Intellectual Freedom Manual* online. I reviewed both of these sources for published policies, noted the focus of the policy, i.e., what type of institution it targeted, as well as the dates of amendment so that I could calculate frequency of amendment. The policies found in these two areas that relate to prison librarianship are listed in Appendix B.

Of these 31 policies reviewed under the ALA advocacy sections and in the *Intellectual Freedom Manual*, two explicitly stated that they applied to all types of libraries ("Advocating for Intellectual Freedom" and "Services to Persons with Disabilities"). Another five applied to various types of libraries, and likely could be applied unilaterally to different types of libraries ("The Freedom to Read," "Libraries: An American Value," "Code of Ethics of the American Library Association," "Resolution on Workplace Speech," and "Policy Concerning Confidentiality of Personally Identifiable Information about Library Users").

Only one policy, the "Intellectual Freedom Principles for Academic Libraries" was clearly focused on academic librarianship. Six referred to "publicly funded libraries" of some sort and one of these in particular titled "Privacy" likely was applicable at other types of institutions as well. One policy, "Access to Resources in the School Library Media Program," targeted school libraries specifically. One policy, the above-mentioned "Prisoners' Right to Read," specifically addressed needs of prison libraries. The remaining 15 policies did not specify what type of institution the policy was designed for, however, three of the 15, because of the inclusion of youth or minors in the policy title ("Access for Children and Young Adults to Nonprint Materials," "Access to Library Resources and Services for Minors," and "Minors and Internet Activity"), were likely targeting school libraries and public libraries with youth services programs.

On average, policies had been updated or published three times since inception with as many as seven updates and as few as none. The policies that had been amended most frequently were overreaching policies such as the "Library Bill of Rights," or policies that included some sort of technology dependent statements such as "Labelling and Rating Systems." A list of policies that relate to prison librarianship and years of updates is in Appendix B.

I also reviewed each of ALA's divisions, since many divisions often publish their own policies. I reviewed the websites of the American Association of School Librarians (AASL), Association for Library Collections and Technical Services (ALCTS), Association for Library Service to Children (ALSC), Association of College and Research Libraries (ACRL), Association of Specialized and Cooperative Library Agencies (ASCLA), Library and Information Technology Association (LITA), Library Leadership and Management Association (LLAMA), Public Library Association (PLA), Reference and User Services Association (RUSA), Young Adult Library Services Association (YALSA) and United for Libraries. I reviewed any website sections on advocacy issues, publications, guidelines and standards, and any other sections that might include stances on issues or explicit policies. I did not include guidelines or standards published in books for sale from any of these associations. No policies, per these review procedures, were found on the AASL, ASCLA, ALSC, LLAMA, PLA, or United for Libraries websites. Standards and policies were, however, found on ACRL, ALCTS, LITA, RUSA, and YALSA pages. Seventy-four policies were reviewed within these divisions; I noted the focus of the policy, the dates amended and calculated the number of instances of a publication of the policy based on the amendment dates. There are a few "position papers" from YALSA, which have been included. These were included because they have been approved by the YALSA Board of Directors and are listed on YALSA's guidelines website. While they are not named as policies per se, they contain a board approved message designating them as guidelines or standards.

The Association of College and Research Libraries (ACRL) had many policies listed on their website, so almost half of these policies (34) were geared toward academic library services. Four policies from the Young Adult Library Services Association were specific to public libraries ("The Importance of a Whole Library Approach to Public Library Young Adult Services: A YALSA Issue Paper by Linda W. Braun with contributions from Sarah Flowers and Mary Hastler," "The Benefits of Including Dedicated Young Adult Librarians on Staff in the Public Library by YALSA with Audra Caplan," "The Need for Teen Spaces in Public Libraries, by Kimberly Bolan," and "YALSA's Public Library Evaluation Tool"). The remaining publications (36 in total) could be applied in various contexts and were from the divisions Association for Library Collections and Technical Services (ALCTS), Library and Information Technology Association (LITA), Reference and User Services Association (RUSA), and YALSA. Prisons were not mentioned in any context, which is not surprising. Policies on prisons might have been more likely to be found in the Association of Specialized and Cooperative Library Agencies (ASCLA)'s division website, however, ASCLA did not have an easily located policies section compared to these other divisions.

The policies were published an average of about 1.75 times, so on average, a policy was amended one time. Those published more than 3 or 4 times were from ACRL and RUSA with one exception where YALSA had multiple versions of one standard.

I also reviewed the International Federation of Library Associations and Institutions' (IFLA) website to find specific policies on different areas of librarianship. IFLA published seven policies on issues related to and addressing public library service. IFLA also published four policies specifically tailored to librarians and museums handling special collections. Three policies addressed public sector or government library policies ("Guidelines for Legal Deposit Legislation," "Guidelines for Legislative Libraries," and "Guidelines for Libraries of Government Departments"). Two policies were authored with academic libraries as the target group: one which proposed guidelines for library and information science education and one which addressed e-resource issues faced by academic libraries. School libraries were given guidelines in "IFLA/UNESCO School Library Guidelines." Prison libraries were targeted in one policy, "Guidelines for Library Services to Prisoners," a policy which was mentioned and discussed in chapter 1. Seven general policies were written to address multiple types of institutions. Seventeen policies did not specify a target library type and could apply to various types of institutions.

Determining the number of amendments that had occurred was more difficult in IFLA documents. Often these documents were PDF versions without clear listings of previous dates of publication. Most would list an edition version, which allowed me to count the number of published instances. I did find a "List of IFLA Standards" from 2014, which was created to present to the IFLA Committee on Standards in January 2012. This document, for the most part, included the dates for various editions.[3] I used this document to fill in gaps on dates for policies I had found on the IFLA website; the document itself includes many historic policies that are no longer featured on the IFLA website.

The IFLA document "International Resource Sharing and Document Delivery: Principles and Guidelines for Procedure" had the most amendments and publications with five editions. The policy on prison libraries was in its third edition with prior publications in 1992, 1995, and 2005. Three other IFLA standards were revised three times: an academic publication "Guidelines for Professional Library/Information Educational Programs," and two other policies "IFLA Principles for the Care and Handling of Library Material" and "Multicultural Communities: Guidelines for Library Services," were in their third edition. On average, all policies on the IFLA site that had editions noted had been published an average of 1.5 times.[4]

The IFLA policy was published more recently than the ASCLA policy, with the last revision occurring in 2005. The IFLA standards in general are more expansive than the ASCLA policy; the ASCLA policy is limited in scope to federal and state prisons, whereas the IFLA policy does not limit to type of institution. Perhaps this is because it would be very difficult to establish international regulations with various national groups determining their countries' policies. Additionally, the IFLA policy does include a section on information technology and the importance of access to technology in prisons; the ASCLA policy is far too outdated to include this kind of information.[5]

Overall, it does seem that some sort of prison library policy is maintained at least on a national or international level by associations. There is a lack of public display of prison library policy in divisions such as the ASCLA, where such a policy would likely be well placed and used. As mentioned in chapter 1, the ASCLA's current work to revise the 1992 publication on library standards in prisons is a timely and warranted update.

## Citation Analysis

In addition to analyzing the frequency of policy updates on prison librarianship compared to other areas of librarianship, analyzing the number of citations in scholarly journals over a period of years also shows the limited coverage of prison librarianship topics. Hartz et al.'s citation analysis includes citations from January 1, 1945, through December 31, 1985. These authors found 511 entries on the topics of correctional libraries with approximately 12 citations yearly.[6] Hartz et al. reference previous citation analyses such as David Gillespie's analysis from 1900–1966 and Rudolf Engelbarts' review from 1900 to 1969. Gillespie's research shows lower citation counts per year than that from Hartz et al. with approximately three entries published per year.[7] Hartz et al., echoing Gillespie's statements, also state that the infrequent publications on prison librarianship may be due to a lack of leadership in these institutions.[8]

Concluding that lack of scholarship or publication on prison librarianship may not be as simple as stating that this is related to lack of leadership. It may be worth noting that in reality many prison librarians may be discouraged from publishing on their experiences, whether due to security restrictions, culture within their institutions, or other issues. In many situations, these librarians may also operate as "one-man-shows" in their institutions, leaving very little time for making contributions to the profession. There may also be no reward for participation in these kinds of activities. As Hartz et al. and other authors note, much of the scholarship written about prison librarianship may be written by those who have never worked in a prison library, which is certainly the case in this book. Again, this leads one to believe that there may be other forces at work besides lack of leadership.

Within this section, I present results of analysis from searching for citations on prison librarianship published between 1993 and 2013. These citations were worldwide and not limited to publications in the U.S. These publications were included for a few reasons: some featured issues of journals included research or case studies from foreign countries, but may have been published by a U.S. journal. Additionally, some of the monographs may be authored about foreign institutions or worldwide trends. Without carefully reviewing the contents of each of these items, it would impossible to ascertain if they focused exclusively on the U.S. The analysis should illustrate worldwide trends for publishing, rather than U.S. trends.

Most of this research was completed in 2014, so I endeavored to research the last two decades with the prior year as the end date for citation searching. Searching for books was simpler than searching for journal citations; WorldCat can be used to find books that are catalogued at any library using Online Computer Library Center (OCLC) cooperative services.[9] OCLC includes over 332 million bibliographic records from libraries using their services.[10] While these numbers will not be comprehensive of all holdings in the world, especially if member libraries are carrying materials not cataloged with OCLC, using WorldCat as a starting point is still more comprehensive and accurate than simple Google searching.

Tracking journal articles was more complicated. Because there are hundreds of journals from which I could base this search, I have used Laura Manzari's 2013 article "Library and Information Science Journal Prestige as Assessed by Library and Information Science Faculty" as a means of uncovering what journals were deemed to be the most reputable in the field of library and information science according to recent research.[11] I reviewed citations in the journal titles ranked with a mean average of 1.31 or above. Where possible, I exported records to a RefWorks program[12] for closer analysis. In the case that records were not easily exported, I searched the journal's websites and subject indices for articles on prison libraries. Both of these methods may not be entirely comprehensive for uncovering all literature written on prison librarianship; if a book is not cataloged by a member library in OCLC, it will not be discoverable on WorldCat. Similarly, consulting a selection of highly rated journals rather than all library and information science topic journals could and did lead to excluded citations. For instance, the journal *Behavioral and Social Sciences Librarian* was not included in the journals with an average rating of over 1.31. This journal contains a number of articles on prison librarianship including those from Robert Stearns and Amy Mark.[13] Due to the sheer volume of journals, however, selecting a group of highly rated journals should be an appropriate mechanism to display an exploratory example of the lack of scholarship in library science oriented publications that focus on prison librarianship.

I should note that there is an obvious gap in this analysis; many prison librarians and prison staff may be publishing articles on prison librarianship in other disciplines such as corrections, social work, and education journals. Including all of these disciplines for this type of analysis is simply too large of a task. This problem with citation analysis is not exclusive to prison librarianship; many academic librarians, for instance, may publish in education journals that are not considered to fall under the library science discipline. Citations from journals of other disciplines have been included throughout the literature review in chapter 3 and throughout other chapters of this book.

Many books or articles that include topics on prison librarianship are not centered on the topic exclusively. For instance, an article or book may be written on topics of prison administration including the management and implementation of a prison library. For this reason, it was also interesting to look at whether the topic of prison librarianship was central or ancillary to the individual work's topic. I reviewed the titles and abstracts of those works containing some reference to prison librarianship and classified them according to their primary topic of discussion. Additionally, after finding both monograph and journal article citations, I attempted to ascertain what the author's role was at the time of publication. To do this I checked any biographies included with the citation and searched for information about that author online from other publications' websites or from LinkedIn profiles.

Ninety-two non-fiction WorldCat records were found that related to prison librarianship with these terms displayed either within the title or the description. A complete list of these citations is available in Appendix C. Seventy-two of these were monographs, not articles or theses. Theses were excluded because OCLC cataloging policies related to theses and dissertations vary from institution to institution; therefore, it would not be possible to get a clear idea of how many theses or dissertations were published on the topic of prison librarianship using OCLC records. Only 72 citations were found from the journals based on Manzari's list. These citations included some aspect of prison or jail librarianship in the title or mentioned these institutions in the abstract. This amounted to a total of 144 citations found between the period of 1993 and 2013 for an average of nearly seven citations yearly.

The general trend in the last few years shows an up-tick in citations on prison librarianship within the channels analyzed. However, this may or may not be meaningful, especially if compared to previous analyses such as those from Hartz et al. in which 12 citations were published yearly on average.[14] In this case, if one were to look at more decades, a downward trend might be visible.

Some years seemed to have more peaks in citations. In 2011 for instance, 11 citations were found on prison librarianship. All of these citations were journal articles, with seven of 11 appearing as part of a special issue of *Library Trends* on prison librarianship. A similar peak in 2009 is explained by the publication of nine policy documents on individual facilities in Washington State, which were cataloged in OCLC. 2009 was also the year that Brenda Vogel published *The Prison Library Primer*, one of the most referenced books on prison librarianship. Peaks in 1993, 1995, and 1999 of ten citations each were not related to any particular group publications.

It was also worth noting what citations centered on the topic of prison librarianship compared to those that simply mentioned prison librarianship as part of a broader topic such as prison administration or education in prison. Of both monographs and articles, 89 citations (61.81 percent) centered on the topic of prison libraries or prison law libraries. Seventeen citations (11.81 percent) broached broad topics on prisons such as prison administration. Sixteen citations (11.11 percent) discussed multiple types of institutions with a section or mention of prison libraries. These citations included books such as *True Stories of Censorship Battles in American Libraries*; *International Resource Book for Libraries Serving Disadvantaged Persons: 2001–2008: An Update to the International Resource Book for Libraries Serving Disadvantaged Persons: 1931–2001*; *Providing for Special Populations*; among others, and articles such as "Briefs" or "Late Bulletins" in magazines such as *Public Libraries, American Libraries,* and *Library Journal.* Ten citations (6.94 percent) focused on the topic of reading in prison including books such as *Reading Is My Window: Books and the Art of Reading in Women's Prisons*; *Rethinking Corrections: Rehabilitation, Reentry, and Reintegration*; and *Prison Reading Groups: What Books Can Do Behind Bars: Report on the Work of PRG 1999–2013.* Articles addressing the topic of reading in prison discussed themes such as children reading with incarcerated parents ("From a Distance"), reading programs for juveniles in detention centers ("From Classroom to Courtroom"), and the article "People were literally starving for any kind of reading: The Theresienstadt Ghetto Central Library, 1942–1945." These articles appeared in magazines such as *School Library Journal, Public Libraries*, and in the journal *Library Trends.* Five citations (3.47 percent) centered on topics related to education in prison with ancillary mentions of prison libraries. Three (2.08 percent) were focused on public library services and included mentions of outreach services to prisons. Two citations (1.39 percent) discussed legal assistance in prisons such as through jailhouse lawyers. The remaining two citations were publications about library services in a secure hospital and a general monograph on career options in libraries (*A Day in the Life: Career Options in Library and Information Science*). Generally, there were more articles written about prison librarianship specifically than there were monographs. Forty-nine of the 72 article citations (68.06 percent) were focused on prison librarianship whereas 40 of the 72 monographs (55.55 percent) focused exclusively on this topic. Clearly, monographs can include much more content than an article so it is not surprising that less monographs take this narrower focus.

Hartz et al. and Coyle[15] both mention that very few of those publishing on prison librarianship have ever worked in a prison library. In order to ascertain if this was in fact the case, I reviewed biographies and attempted to find online resumes or information about the authors of the monographs and articles. Many of the articles, for instance, included biography statements with information about the individual authors. Where no biographical information was found, I searched online for LinkedIn profiles that included dates of employment, looked on academic websites where some may have been employed, and found personal websites with work history details. Hartz et al. and William Coyle's statements appear to still be true: only 16.67 percent of those publishing on prison librarianship were either currently or previously employed in a prison library. Many more were either associated with an academic institution (20.14 percent), working as an editor for a magazine or journal (20.83 percent), or working for a state, organization, or association library (20.14 percent). Eight (5.56 percent) were employed as public librarians, many of whom had positions where they facilitated outreach programs with prison libraries. Six (4.17 percent) were not affiliated with any institution at the time of publication (and had also never worked in a prison or prison library). These authors were considered to be independent researchers. Four (2.78 percent) were graduate students at the time of publication. Two (1.39 percent) were attorneys and another two (1.39 percent) worked as law librarians outside of a prison. One was authored by a prisoner, another by a school librarian, and a third by a librarian working in a special library. Each of these respectively accounted for 0.69 percent of citations. For three of the citations, affiliation or information about the author could not be found. In four cases, the author was employed in some other context. For instance, one was a PR assistant for a specific project that provided information services to prisoners. In two other cases the authors were consultants of some type; one was a "Communications and Media Consultant," and another was contracted by an external authority to write the material. One citation was classified as "other" because the piece was written by an editor, but contained an interview with a public librarian who conducted outreach activities with prison libraries.

This analysis supports the thesis that many prison librarians choose not to or cannot publish about their field of librarianship. Only 24 of those publishing had worked in a prison library at some point during their career out of 57 named authors[16]; and even then, many of these authors were retired and might not have faced the same challenges with publishing as they did when employed by a correctional institution—whether related to restrictions by administration or simply lack of time with so many duties. Additionally, this lack of research on the topic may be due to the lack of professional librarians working in many of these institutions; those who do not have any degrees or certifications in library science may be less likely to pursue these kinds of opportunities. Some of those publishing on behalf of state, organization, or association libraries may have had more experience or interaction with prison populations, but all of these publications were monograph publications. They were not case studies, research, or even personal experiences encountered by an author while employed as a prison librarian. Certainly academics, including faculty, academic librarians and independent researchers, have less institutional hindrances to publishing about prison librarianship among other topics.

Upon initially embarking on my research, I had hoped to classify article citations according to the type of institution about which they were written. This proved to be more complicated than anticipated, so while there are some interesting findings from this part of my research, they cannot be assumed to be generalizable due to challenges in collecting and analyzing citations. I was able to collect comprehensive citations details for the last two decades in RefWorks for 23 of the 41 journal titles with a mean average over 1.31. Most of the remaining journals did not have online systems in which I could efficiently export years of citations to RefWorks. Within these collected citations, I removed book reviews, editors' introductions to the scholarly articles, corrections, responses, conference proceedings summaries, author biographies, website reviews, acknowledgments, advertisements, appendices, calls for papers, etc. Then I reviewed the remaining 18,625 citations by reading titles and abstracts to determine the institutional focus of the work. This also proved to be difficult; many topics, especially technology topics, span multiple types of institutions. An article written on information retrieval, for example, could be written from the perspective of any number of institutions. Where it was not clear in the title or abstract, I marked the type as "unknown." Nearly 9,000 of the citations (8,786 or 47.17 percent) did not have clear details as to where the research took place or which type of institution the article was written about. Academic, research, or scholarship topics accounted for the largest percentage of the remaining citations at 30.09 percent, most of which were written by members of an academic institution or were targeted for this audience. Corporations and similar organizations were next with 8.64 percent of the citations. Many of these topics included competitive intelligence and management. Government, public sector, nonprofit, and public policy papers followed with 6.65 percent of citations. Articles written about public libraries accounted for 2.28 percent of all of the citations. Medical libraries or health sciences libraries were the topic of 1.90 percent of the remaining citations and school libraries were just under 1 percent at 0.84 percent. Special libraries and museums accounted for 0.88 percent of citations. A total 1.47 percent of the citations described some combination of institutions, for instance, an academic library partnering with a public library wrote about an initiative at the two institutions.

Comparably, only 14 citations were found that focused on prison librarianship at 0.08 percent. This is, of course, far less than the 72 articles found in the above mentioned sections on citation analysis. It is, however, significant to note that of the remaining 58 articles not represented in these 14 citations, only five of these articles were from peer-reviewed journals as defined by Ulrich's Periodicals Directory at Ulrichsweb.com. The resulting 53 articles were from trade journals such as *Public Libraries, Library Journal, American Libraries*, or *School Library Journal*. So if one were to look at my limited analysis of 23 peer-reviewed journal titles, one could conclude that there is, in fact, significantly less peer-reviewed scholarship being written on the topic of prison libraries than for instance in academia or the public sector.

Overall this section, through a mixed methods approach to uncover citations on prison librarianship, showed that professional writing about prison librarianship is scarce. Often topics that include some mention of the prison library will not focus on this topic exclusively. Furthermore, writing that does occur is more frequently written by non-practitioners rather than practicing prison librarians. The methods used in this section were also not comprehensive and therefore not generalizable; more in-depth research is needed to determine actual quota of citations compared to other fields of librarianship. It would also be valuable to cross reference publications not only in the field of library and information science, but also to consider contributions from corrections, social work, and education disciplines.

## Prevalence of Prison Librarianship Curricula at U.S. ALA-Accredited Library and Information Science Schools

Researching the prevalence of prison librarianship at library and information science graduate schools is easier in the twenty-first century than it would have been when McClaskey analyzed the number of schools offering programs in 1977 since most library and information science schools prominently display their curricula and programs on the Internet. I was interested in understanding two questions: are these schools offering the opportunity to specialize in prison librarianship and do any of these schools offer courses designed to teach the skills necessary for the specific field of prison librarianship? I researched whether these schools also had specializations related to other specific types of institutions such as academic, public, school, or special libraries and if these schools had courses solely focused on any of those types of institutions.

I limited my research to ALA accredited schools located in the United States since all other research from previous chapters and subsequent chapters was also limited to the

United States. I was looking at programs that offered a master's degree in library science, a master's degree in library and information science, or the equivalent. Of the 63 schools listed on the ALA's website as holding accreditation at the time of my research, I reviewed the websites of 50 U.S. library and information science schools in December 2014 to determine if they offered prison librarianship tracks or any courses in prison librarianship. I did not review programs in Canada or Puerto Rico. Program pages were reviewed for degree requirements, descriptions, specializations, and tracks. I accessed course catalogs to review course titles for library and information science tracks.

Of the 50 schools reviewed, none had any sort of specialization, career path, or track for prison librarianship. Forty-three of the 50 mentioned programs for school librarianship or school media specialist certification. Eighteen mentioned academic and public tracks; if a program had a specialization in one of these areas, they offered a specialization in the other area. Twenty-four offered specializations in something related to special libraries, such as special collections, archives management, etc. These special library focuses might include some topical coverage of prison libraries, but this was not explicit in any of the program definitions. Five programs did not offer specializations that were institution specific or no specializations were found. Two offered broader specializations: University of Michigan's information school has specializations titled as "librarian" and University of North Texas had general programs of study such as "Youth Librarianship" or "General Program of Study."

Similarly, of the schools with course catalogs online, no schools were found that offered courses targeting future prison librarians. I was unable to find course catalogs on two of the schools' websites. Of all schools with catalogs online, 37 had some course specifically targeting academic librarianship with titles such as "The Academic Library" or "Academic Libraries." Thirty-six had a public librarianship course with a similar focused title. Thirty-seven had specific school librarianship courses and 33 offered courses with some form of special collections librarianship or archives management programs. Many courses were also offered that targeted other types of special librarianship such as music, health sciences, corporate, etc. In many cases these courses were offered in immediate succession in the course catalog: In the case of University of Rhode Island the course catalog lists "School Library Media Services," "Public Library Service," "College and University Library Service," and "Special Library Service" in successive order. Again, special library courses might include some coverage of prison librarianship, however, it is not the main focus of any courses.

Only one university mentioned outreach with prisons as any sort of career opportunity for library and information science graduates: St. Catherine University in Minnesota listed a number of career paths for MLIS graduates and included "Law Librarian for the Prisoner's Program at MN Law Library." No other references to prison librarianship as a career were found on the other MLIS granting library school websites in the United States. Some librarians may be able to prepare for prison librarianship by taking law librarianship courses, however, no explicit courses were offered at any institution that solely addressed working in a prison library.

It seems that the field of prison librarianship has only suffered further neglect by accredited library and information science schools in the nearly three decades since the publication of McClaskey's article. At that time nine schools were offering some sort of correctional librarianship education, whereas none were found that currently offer curricula for this area. It should be noted that there are considerably less library schools offering the MLIS or equivalent than there were in 1987, however, the complete absence of prison librarianship from library school curricula is noticeable.

## Summary

The outlook from this chapter is rather bleak. Policies on prison librarianship tend to be scarcer than other fields of librarianship, scholarship and publications on prison librarianship are infrequent and published by non-practitioners, and library schools neglect to focus on this particular career opportunity. What can the community do to encourage more discussion on this field of librarianship?

Perhaps a first start would be more open publication of policies on prison librarianship. The ALA does have a well-placed policy in the "Prisoners' Right to Read." As mentioned in previous chapters, a revisiting of the ASCLA's *Library Standards for Adult Correctional Institutions* will be a valuable contribution from the association and would mirror efforts that IFLA has made to continue to update their policies for underserved populations. It is possible that ASCLA has other policies in place that are not well publicized on their websites; if these do exist, perhaps the community would benefit from more strategically distributed policies on the ASCLA division website.

It does appear from my limited research that less is being written about prison libraries than was written over 25 years ago when Hartz et al. published their annotated bibliography. At this time even Hartz et al. lamented the lack of literature on prison libraries. While some may attribute this to lack of leadership in the field, it may also be difficult for many of these practitioners to publicly share their work and experiences due to a number of potential challenges. Interviews in chapter 9 may provide some reasons that professional development opportunities like these might not be supported or sustainable in a prison library setting.

Lastly, few new librarians are aware of or encouraged to go into this field of librarianship. No ALA accredited library schools in the United States are currently offering any specializations or even courses on prison librarianship, which was not the case when Hartz et al. investigated these programs in the 1980s. Vacancies for these positions still exist; in 2014 and 2015, I received a number of solicitations and announcements about positions in the California Department of Corrections and Rehabilitations, which were publicized via the ALA prison libraries listserv as well as via the California Library Association's calix listserv. These calls for applications mentioned a number of openings and the need for more applicants. It may be that many potential applicants are apprehensive at the thought of working in a prison, nevertheless, the possibility of educating potential applicants during their tenure at library school is an untapped possibility. With waning and limited jobs in traditional library science fields, this particular field of librarianship seems to be unjustly excluded from library science curricula.

7

# The Prisoner as the
# Public Library Patron

*I think if you were to try to explain it to someone who was in public libraries, let's
say, and they wanted to know how would my day-to-day change if I went to work
for a prison library—there wouldn't be that many changes, you're still helping people
find stuff. You have much more limited resources, but you still check out books to
people, you still help them with their legal work. You don't do research exactly, but
you do give them books and talk to them and you give them little tutorials on the
computer. So you're still doing the same kinds of services to a slightly different population and the subject areas are much more narrow. You're still doing programming,
if your facility allows it, you can do several different kinds of programs just like you
would do in a public library. So I guess a big difference is really the environment.
You're working with custody officers, people who have been convicted of crimes—
some of them violent crimes—but overall they're a very calm group.*
—Heather, Interviewee from Chapter 9

According to the policies and literature from early chapters of this book, various
authors and organizations recommend that the services of the prison library be modeled
after public library services. On a national level, in an older edition of the American Correctional Association's *Standards for Adult Correctional Institutions*, the public library model
is cited as a potential source for policy development. This policy encourages prisons to
partner with public libraries to acquire materials not owned by the institution through
interlibrary loan.[1] State policies also mention the public library model for policy development; as presented in chapter 2, Nebraska's Department of Corrections recommends that
the library should "provide quality library services within the Department of Correctional
Services comparable to those of a public library."[2] Seven other policies from state-level
Department of Corrections authorities similarly mention the public library model.

Sheila Clark and Erica MacCreaigh, in their book *Library Services to the Incarcerated:
Applying the Public Library Model in Correctional Facility Libraries*, define implementation
of the public library model as a willingness to apply at least three of ALA's 11 core values
of librarianship. The specific three values they deem crucial for correctional libraries applying the public library model within their institutions are "access and intellectual freedom,
privacy and confidentiality, and social responsibility (in which customer service can be
defined as a commitment to equitable treatment of all library users)."[3] Clark and Mac-
Creaigh additionally state that "belief in equal access and equal treatment of all library
patrons ... must be unwavering" and that correctional librarians, if they do in fact embrace
these values by following the public library model, will be required at some point "to defend

these values."[4] Other authors such as Glen Singer mention the public library model as the one most frequently used within prison libraries, which can create a "normalizing environment."[5]

In Marjorie LeDonne's comprehensive survey of library services in correctional institutions, she cites the importance of interactions with local public or state libraries, claiming that services should be either provided by these institutions, or existing services should be complemented with these outside services.[6] Additionally, LeDonne cites the importance of providing reentry materials both during and after incarceration. She specifically mentions partnerships with outside institutions, which can provide resources after incarceration, stating that "public, school, and academic libraries should recognize their responsibility to develop new methods of gathering and sharing reentry information."[7]

William Coyle, whose book *Libraries in Prison: A Blending of Institutions* brought criticism for its rebuttal of the public library model as a realistic option for prison libraries, provides his opinion on the reasons for the public library model's usage in prison library policies:

> On the other hand, many of a new generation of service-oriented librarians have taken note of the attention that has been given to the rights of prison inmates and have suggested that library services are one of the things to which inmates have a right, independent of correctional goals. This view has received wide currency in the literature and in professional organizations and probably constitutes the main current of thought. Adherents of this view have generally promoted the development of library services based on the multi-service, user-oriented model of the public library.[8]

Coyle rejects the theory that prison libraries should emulate their public peers, claiming that the model is flawed because of two assumptions: (1) prisoners have a right to library services, and (2) prisoners benefit from materials provided based on their own needs.[9] Furthermore, Coyle asserts that aligning library services to the "interests of inmate users might well be more detrimental than beneficial to constructive change."[10] Other statements from Coyle contradict literature written by prison librarians, such as the opinion that recreational reading in prisons is not beneficial to prisoners; the prison librarian's role should, according to him, support only rehabilitation and punishment.[11] Essentially, Coyle considers the public library model to be ineffective since decisions are often made at the Department of Corrections or state level.[12] Coyle's ideas and call to abandon the public library model have not appeared to have gained much traction in the prison library community; since the publication of his book in 1987, policies continue to be written by state authorities referencing the public library model as a guideline. Additionally, much literature, including books from Clark, MacCreaigh, and Vogel, mention the public library model as a functional means of providing prison library service. A prison librarian who wants to employ the public library model has to believe in this model, acknowledge the benefits of such a model for the library's constituency, and garner support internally from administration.

Prison libraries, while they may embrace the theoretical principles of the public library model, often seek support from public libraries to supplement and enhance services and materials. Most prison librarians who publish cite the importance of such partnerships, sometimes giving examples or tips for establishing collaborations. Brenda Vogel suggests that many public libraries may consider the prison outside their realm, however, these public libraries are in fact receiving tax funding from prisoners who had either lived or will live in their communities before and after incarceration.[13] She makes suggestions on how community partnerships with public libraries can be fostered, mentioning that most of the burden will be on the prison librarian to establish these collaborations as the library's collections will not be as flexible or expansive as those in a public library.[14]

Glennor Shirley similarly encourages these collaborations between public and prison libraries. Shirley sent a questionnaire to 110 librarians listed in the Directory of State Prison Librarians to determine who might be involved in these types of partnerships. She states: "Prison librarians should try to convince public librarians that eventually most prisoners return to their communities and may need service from their community libraries."[15] In an interview with Stephen Lilienthal, prison librarians Glennor Shirley and Loretta Cimini both mention the importance of these increased partnerships between prison and public libraries, encouraging public libraries to also initiate more collaboration.[16]

Clark and MacCreaigh, who author their book from the perspective of a jail librarian and a public librarian with a history of collaborating, see a great opportunity, especially "with the public library profession emphasizing greater outreach."[17] As the ultimate under-served community, prison patrons can benefit from a prison librarian acting as a "gatekeeper to information in an information-hostile environment."[18] The authors show awareness of some of the issues with applying the public library model within a correctional institution. They state: "If you truly want to apply the public library model behind bars, it is absolutely critical that you reconcile constant mindfulness of criminal intent with a commitment to provide equitable—and excellent—library service to criminally minded people."[19] While they acknowledge that traditional public library service cannot be mirrored exactly due to the security needs of the institution, they mention that programming such as events or workshops might be even more useful in a prison library than a public library. This especially applies to reentry related programming.[20]

## Policies at Public and Prison Libraries

As discussed in depth in previous chapters, prison libraries may have a number of purposes depending on the policy initiated at the institution. The ASCLA 1992 guidelines, for instance, mention purposes such as rehabilitation, staying connected with the world outside, having opportunities to learn new vocational skills, accessing legal materials, discovering information about reentry into the community after parole, recreational reading, and to support lifelong learning.[21] While many of these purposes are not necessarily commonly prioritized services in public libraries, especially those that relate to rehabilitation and reentry, prison libraries aspire to serve their specific constituencies much like public libraries do.

In 2014, the Public Library Association's (PLA) Board of Directors approved a new strategic plan, one which acknowledged the need for public libraries to adapt to suit the needs of their patrons. This strategic plan highlighted the importance of the library as a tool for personal development and enrichment with the ultimate goal of providing crucial literacy services:

> The library provides a pathway to a better future for all community members by serving as the principal destination for individual learning, enrichment, and economic opportunity. Community members are attracted by the library as a learning space where they will find expert assistance, relevant resources and tools for

research, content sharing and creation, and opportunity for cultural enrichment. By also providing critical literacy services, enriching formal education, and supporting lifelong learning, public libraries are learning spaces that make America a literate nation.[22]

Topics are consistent between the ASCLA guidelines and the PLA's strategic plan. Prison libraries that provide resources or programming on rehabilitation, reentry, or legal issues are supplying "relevant resources" that help prisoners to learn and be enriched. The PLA mentions employment assistance in a subsequent section of the strategic plan, which correlates to one of the ASCLA guidelines in which the prison library should provide an outlet for developing vocational skills. Similarly, the Public Library Association mentions the role the library plays in supporting lifelong learning, a purpose frequently mentioned in the ASCLA policy. The PLA may not explicitly mention recreational reading, but public libraries nationwide continue to maintain collections and organize programming around reading, including recreational reading. According to the PLA strategic plan, the library is positioned to continue its role as a public learning space.

A prisoner's right to read persists regardless of incarceration. The ASCLA acknowledges this in the 1992 standards, specifically referencing ALA policies such as the "Library Bill of Rights," "Resolution on Prisoners' Right to Read," "Policy on Confidentiality of Library Records," "Freedom to Read Statement," and the "Freedom to View."[23] With the exception of the "Prisoners' Right to Read," these policies also apply to other institutions, including public libraries. According to the ALA, all types of libraries should be abiding by a core set of principles that support basic human rights and endeavor to support free expression of ideas.

It is no question that prisoners lose certain rights during incarceration and there cannot be unfettered access to information due to security needs of the institution. Basic human rights though, such as those defined by the UN's *Universal Declaration of Human Rights,* are maintained. The ALA, with their publication and subsequent updates to the "Prisoners' Right to Read," similarly assert these basic human rights even for prisoners. Both prison and public library populations maintain the right to read, regardless of their circumstances.

Kathleen de la Peña McCook, a library scholar and activist, researched programs and connections between public libraries and prisoners by searching public library websites to find examples of libraries doing outreach with prisons or jails. She mentioned that "there have been few recent articles that provide insights into single library programs" and prepared the column with the intent of sharing the importance of establishing such partnerships.[24] Because of the lack of articles assessing library outreach programs to prisoners, she states that "we must rely upon Web site coverage or brief mentions in articles."[25] In her web searching she finds examples of various libraries with such partnerships in the U.S. including Alameda County Library in California, Arapahoe Library District in Colorado, Monroe County Public library in Indiana, Montgomery County Public Libraries in Maryland, Hennepin County Library in Minnesota, and Chesterfield County Public Library in Virginia.

Little has changed in the last ten years since the publication of McCook's article. As shown in the previous chapter, citations on prison librarianship, especially of a scholarly nature, are infrequent at best. Such programs and partnerships are mentioned in some of the articles reviewed in previous chapters. Additionally, others are featured on websites and in news releases. In order to understand what kinds of partnerships currently exist between public and correctional libraries, I undertook a similar approach to that of McCook. I also searched databases for mentions of such partnerships in scholarly and trade journals, and completed web searches to try to locate library websites and news announcements publicizing these partnerships. I did find more partnerships than McCook found in 2004, likely due to the ever growing nature of the Internet. Many of the collaborations McCook found are still in place. Some partnerships are state mandated, for instance, the state of New York requires public libraries to participate in correctional library service.[26] Throughout the next sections I will detail the public and prison library partnerships that were found in the literature and from web searching. It should be noted that many of these partnerships are with local jails or detention centers. In previous chapters and subsequent chapters, I have concentrated on state and federal prisons, who more often than not have an established prison library program that is likely funded, at least in part, by the institution. Many of the prisoners in jails and detention centers may only be incarcerated for a short time, therefore, library service is often limited. In this case, public library service can substantially complement existent or non-existent library services.

Additionally, the programs presented below may or may not still be administered. All of the discussed programs were based on web research and it is possible that some of the programs have been discontinued. It is even more likely that many partnerships have not been publicized and that this list of programs is incomplete.

## Current Collaborations between Public and Prison Libraries

I found 14 articles from scholarly or trade journals and 23 websites, which included library websites and news announcements that discussed one or multiple collaborations between public and prison libraries. These articles, websites, and news items discussed general outreach principles, programs for materials donation, family and early literacy initiatives, educational programs such as workshops conducted in and out of prison, book discussion groups and book talks, and provision of reentry materials for current or previously incarcerated prisoners by public libraries. Two documents were found from state authorities in Indiana and Wisconsin that defined some overall guidelines for provision of jail or prison library service by public libraries.

One document, a chapter of an unnamed book or set of guidelines for Indiana public librarians, defines jail services and what kinds of outreach initiatives should be considered. This document was found as a PDF through a Google search. These services include materials donation and distribution, conducting readers' advisory, storytelling, "Changing Lives through Literature Programs," interlibrary loan services, GED resources as well as reentry materials, and promotional visits to encourage current prisoners to utilize the public library upon release.[27] The chapter also lists some Indiana libraries that have conducted successful outreach programs with prisons. This resource appears to be chapter 26 of a larger resource from the state library, which was last revised in 2008. Reference to this document was not found upon searching and browsing the state library's website. It is possible that this document is no longer used and is just an artifact on the web.

A similar document was found on the Wisconsin Department of Public Instruction's website, which was titled "Early Initiative for Wisconsin Public Libraries." This document focused on how to target different types of patrons in the community with early learning initiatives. One of the specific target groups was "Parents in Jails and Prisons." The document gives tips for setting up collaborations with prisons, such as setting up an audio recording program for prisoners to read children's books to their children, as well as facilitating the use of children's books during visiting hours. The resource also provides guidelines for whom one might contact in a prison to instigate such a partnership.[28]

## Materials Donation Programs

The New York Public Library has a very in-depth Correctional Services outreach program with a staff of four as well as volunteers. This program serves 12,400+ patrons yearly. The goal that the New York Public Library presents on their website is "to offer regular, sustainable, and quality library services to justice-involved people and their families in and around New York."[29] In the case of materials donation, they take donations and have an exhaustive list of the kinds of materials they can accept. Donations for which a need exists include popular fiction, urban lit, fantasy fiction, Spanish language literature including fiction and non-fiction, and educational titles. For popular and fantasy series fiction, a list of recommended authors is provided as well as a request that items have publication dates after 2011. Specific titles for educational books, such as the TASC[30] workbooks, computer books, Microsoft Office 2010 books, and almanacs are mentioned, most with publication dates not older than one to two years. Controversial urban lit author Donald Goines is included on the list of titles sought. Only paperback books are accepted by the New York Public Library Correctional Services.[31]

Brooklyn Public Library, who also partner with New York Public Library to reach additional jails in New York, offer mobile libraries that are located within the campuses of four correctional institutions. Brooklyn Public Library's mission is to connect "incarcerated New Yorkers to their communities and families through robust access to information and innovative family programming."[32] Similar to many other public libraries, their correctional services fall under outreach services. In Buffalo and Erie Counties of New York, the public libraries have a division to provide services to two institutions in Erie County. On their website they define the space and number of books offered to prisoners in these institutions.[33]

McCook mentions Arapahoe Library District in her article, stating that a partnership exists between the public library there and the local jail. This partnership is also the subject of Clark and MacCreaigh's book mentioned in previous sections. Arapahoe Library District, according to their website, offers materials at county jails and also classes on literacy.[34]

Hennepin County's initiatives with jail libraries, led by Daniel Marcou, are also often cited in literature for various outstanding programs, such as the "Freedom Ticket," which will be described in more detail in a later section of this chapter. Hennepin County serves shut-in, senior housing, and rehabilitation center patrons in addition to prisoners in county correctional institutions. The purpose of the Outreach Services program at Hennepin County is "to bring the library to the nontraditional or under-served patron through programs and services." Adult Correctional Services offered by this library include, but are not limited to, a book donation program and providing requested materials to patrons in men's and women's prisons. In the local Public Safety Facility, the library also distributes paperback books and offers additional services for homeschooled students and juveniles in detention centers. The program appears to be at least partially funded by the Hennepin County Friends of the Library.[35]

In Indiana, Monroe County Correctional Center (MCCC) partners with the Monroe County Public Library (MCPL). According to the Monroe County Public Library's website, the following arrangement is in place between the two institutions: "MCCC provides the space for the library within the jail, as well as funds for books and other library materials. MCPL provides staff members to operate the library three afternoons and to maintain the collection."[36] Statistics from the program are also listed on the website, albeit from 2011. In the reported year, the library in Monroe County Correctional Center was visited 3,500 times with 70 patrons visiting weekly and with 15,674 checkouts. Prisoners in this facility are permitted to access the library once every two weeks. The budget for the library is provided by Monroe County Correctional Center. On Monroe County Public Library's website, they also detail the types of materials that the prisoners are interested in accessing:

> Inmates typically want the same blockbuster titles and high demand authors that are popular among other library customers. Even though many of the requests parallel the main library's clientele, there are some subjects, trends, and materials that hold particular interest for the jail population. The jail library collection has been developed to meet the recreational, educational, and informational needs of the inmates. Highly requested non-fiction subjects include recovery and substance abuse, reentry, bibles and other religious materials, test preparation, career resources, reference, parenting materials, health and fitness, and legal materials. Highly requested fiction genres include westerns, science fiction, urban fiction, horror, and mysteries.

Donations for the program are received by Monroe County Public Library's Friends of the Library organization.[37]

In Massachusetts a faith-based mission Concord Prison Outreach facilitates a program between the Northeast Correctional Center and the Concord Free Library to loan books from the library to prisoners. The program brings books to the prisoners bimonthly, which prisoners request and volunteers collect from the library for delivery. According to the program's website, "inmates' book choices range from the very practical books on house painting or plumbing, to ancient history, and modern novels."[38]

Multnomah County Library in Oregon, also frequently lauded in news articles and announcements, provides library service for county jails. According to the library's "Jail Services" page on their website, book selection occurs as follows: "We select books for each of the living units in the county jails. Recreational reading is geared to inmate literacy, language and reading interests. Informational reading includes recovery, jobs, life skills, domestic violence and other practical subjects." The library also organizes a book club within county jails.[39] The Coastline system in Coos County Oregon similarly provides reading materials to correctional institutions, including provision of items to a jail and a juvenile detention center.[40]

Alameda County Library in California is cited in multiple articles as a system offering prison library service as an outreach service. According to the website, the program serves more than 4,000 incarcerated patrons in county jails with 75 percent of the materials received coming from local donations. Genres that are particularly popular according to the library's website are "bestsellers, westerns, poetry, African-American fiction and non-fiction as well as books focused on self-help and recovery." This library provides tutoring in county jails and maintains a blog on prisoner literacy.[41]

Also in California, the Lompoc Public Library has been bringing books to a local federal prison for the last 20 years according to their 2012 annual report. They state that they
have provided 5,000 books to prisoners. According to the library's annual report, the GED
study courses in prison are taught using library materials and a recently downsized reference
collection was also donated to the prison.[42]

In North Carolina, a prison book donation program began as a research project
between a criminal justice professor and an academic librarian, who were investigating
"how book collections fit into the overall management of the jails and the potential threats
they presented." The researchers conducted a study with jail administrators, the results of
which were summarized in this article as follows:

> Jail administrators who participated in the study shared that library services are important in giving inmates
> something productive to do, and they noted that happier inmates contribute to a safer environment. Some
> also described access to reading materials as a right rather than a privilege, and noted that the role of jails,
> unlike prisons, is custody and care, rather than punishment. However, jail administrators also described the
> enormous challenges jails face in providing even rudimentary library services. The facilities lack not only
> funding to purchase materials but also space for books. Several jail libraries consisted of a single movable
> book cart and in one case the collection was in a locker. In addition, the facilities have limited staff available
> to maintain the collections and coordinate library services.

The researchers in this article determined that expanding topics of books in the jails to
include educational materials and reentry resources could enhance the current collections.
Based on these results, the librarian involved in the research project initiated a program with
the local public library system, the Fontana Regional Library System, to update the collections
in local detention centers. The program accepts donations for paperback materials, especially
popular fiction, educational resources, westerns, legal forms, and self-help non-fiction. They
are in the process of attempting to acquire a newspaper subscription for one of the detention
centers. This article also provides tips for those looking to emulate the program elsewhere.[43]

In Maryland, a study published by Margarita Rhoden and Molly Crumbley evaluates
the outreach services at the Calvery Library and includes details of institutional services.
According to the authors, "institutions are provided a rotating temporary collection of
library materials, each of which is tailored with the customers in mind."[44] The library cir-
culates a special outreach collection with the expectation that many materials will never
be returned. According to the statistics in the article, the library made 618 institution visits
over a period of three years as part of their outreach program.[45]

There are also materials donation programs in effect between academic libraries and
prison libraries. In an article from *American Libraries*, Jennifer Burek Pierce details a program from the University of Wisconsin, Madison in which library and information science
students collect donated books to give to a local Wisconsin jail.[46] In a feature on prison
libraries in *Library Journal* entitled "Arts on the Inside," one case study is shared about an
Indiana University Professor, who provided a small library of Shakespeare classics to prisoners in solitary confinement. The results of the small library she donated along with classes
she held with prisoners in Wabash Valley Correctional Facility were shared in her book
*Shakespeare Saved My Life: Ten Years in Solitary with the Bard*.[47] In Vogel's *Prison Library
Primer*, she mentions an interlibrary loan program between California State University
Bakerfield and Taft Correctional Institution that began in 1999.[48] LIS graduate student
Kathrina Litchfield at The University of Iowa facilitates a prison reading group and received
a grant to buy books for the prison.[49]

One of Cornell University's libraries implemented a "Prisoner Express Program" that allows prisoners to make requests for books that, when available, are mailed to the prisoners. This library also manages a newsletter for prisoners to share their own writing and creative endeavors. The program is managed by volunteers and student assistants.[50]

Additionally, some non-profit institutions have programs for sending books to prisons. For example, the Prison Book Program serves many states in the United States. States not serviced by the program are listed on the Prison Book Program website with details on local programs in those states that process book donations.[51]

In some states, partnerships are being developed between prison libraries, academic institutions, and community organizations. The website "Incarcerated in Iowa" claims a goal to "to highlight, create, and foster connections between Iowa prisons and surrounding communities, especially the University of Iowa community." This group organized a symposium with a number of speakers ranging from prison administration to academic and community partners.[52]

## Family and Early Literacy Initiatives

Family and early literacy initiatives, especially "Read to Me" programs are frequently mentioned throughout the articles and websites reviewed for this chapter. Renea Arnold and Nell Colburn, who were public librarians writing about a program from Multnomah County Library in Oregon, describe an initiative where prisoners are taught the importance of early literacy for their children and are shown potential books that they could share with their children on dealing with the challenges of having an incarcerated parent. The class culminates with a videotaped session of the prisoner reading a children's book to his child, the recording of which is mailed to the child.[53] A similar service is offered by Dane County Library Services in Wisconsin called the "Kids' Connection" program.[54] Hennepin County Library, a library with many outreach programs in collaboration with the county jail, offers a "Read to Me" family literacy program where recorded stories are shared with prisoners' children.[55]

These programs are common in other states as well. In New York, the New York Public Library has a similar family literacy program called "Daddy & Me" where recordings are made of prisoners reading stories to their children.[56] Additionally, the New York Public Library partners with Sesame Street on "Little Children, Big Challenges: Incarceration." This program from Sesame Street has a kit with strategies for comforting children of incarcerated parents. It includes videos, resources, and activities.[57]

In Maryland, Glennor Shirley established a program called "Family Literacy @ Your Library" to encourage prisoners to read with their children and experience a "positive interaction." This program also aspires to improve the participating children's academic performance. She enlisted help from the Howard County and Enoch Pratt Libraries, who provide training to prisoners on storytelling techniques and book selection.[58]

In another article, Shirley details an outreach program by the Maryland Department of Corrections to get prisoners' children into public libraries with the intended purpose of also encouraging prisoners to visit the public library once released. In a partnership with a local public library, children and their prisoner parents participate in the "Summer

Reading Games." Children are encouraged to sign up for library cards at the sessions. The program had clear learning outcomes related to improving the institutional behavior of prisoner participants, decreasing recidivism, fostering positive interactions between the prisoners and their children, providing proof of participation for parole hearings, and the prison benefitted from the positive news coverage.[59]

An initiative at Brooklyn Public Library also encourages joint reading and literacy through telestories: children read aloud to their incarcerated parents via teleconferencing. The New York Society for Ethical Culture Social Service Board partners with Brooklyn Public Library and Cisco provides equipment.[60] Librarians from the Carnegie Library sing and read to children following family visits at Allegheny County Jail.[61]

## Other Educational Programs

Prisons and public libraries also collaborate recurrently to deliver educational programs. Daniel Marcou, the correctional librarian from Hennepin County Jail, collaborates with the Hennepin County Library on the "Freedom Ticket," which is mentioned in trade journals and also on Hennepin County Library's website. This resource is a compilation of services that can help prisoners once they are no longer incarcerated.[62] This program has received accolades nationwide, with Marcou participating in interviews with *American Libraries* and *Library Journal* on the program as well as presenting on successful outreach opportunities between public and prison libraries at national conferences. The "Freedom Ticket" includes workshops and programs delivered by library staff at the correctional institution with the public library offered as a point of reference upon reentry.[63]

The "Freedom Ticket" inspired other programs, including a program at the Los Angeles Public Library. Jacquie Welsh, who was subsequently nominated as an American Library Association Mover and Shaker for 2015, created an eight-month pilot "Pathways from Prison" to introduce former prisoners to library services. Some highlights include setting up library accounts for computer access to search for jobs or complete educational pursuits, as well as instructional workshops for finding jobs, managing finance, on literacy, and on health topics.[64]

Other public libraries are partnering with prisons to provide additional literacy skills to prisoners. For instance, the Carnegie Library of Pittsburgh partners with the Allegheny County Jail in a program called "Literacy Unlocked," which offers workshops on getting a job or managing finances. This particular program concentrates on providing skills, not just bringing donated materials to the prison. According to a news article written about the partnership, the Carnegie Library is considering expanding this program "by working with halfway houses to offer computer classes to ex-inmates." Dan Hensley, the librarian running the program, mentions that this program should make prisoners aware that they can visit the public library upon release.[65]

A number of public and prison partnerships are mentioned in Lilienthal's article "Prison and Public." These include Colorado initiatives headed by Diane Walden, coordinator of institutional library development, in which financial literacy is taught to prisoners including how to recognize online scams. A Denver Public Library program teaches prisoners computer skills.[66]

Educational partnerships are not just limited to public libraries. Joseph Bouchard and Linda Kunze describe a partnership between a correctional library and a school library in which prisoners are taught research skills.[67] Felicia Smith details a program created by an outreach librarian at Notre Dame to interact in a classroom setting with juveniles in a local detention center. Within this class, the librarian uses "Freedom Readers" as a means of empowering juveniles who were participating so that they can "use information to get the appropriate knowledge necessary to keep them free, physically and mentally."[68]

Three articles or websites mention outside groups organizing book discussion groups or book talks. Sheila Clark and Bobbie Patrick describe a program where public librarians give book talks at Colorado prisons.[69] Hennepin County Jail and Hennepin County Library partner on a book club for women called "One Read."[70] Multnomah County Library in Oregon organizes a book club for prisoners.[71]

## Provision of Reentry Materials or Workshops

Public libraries often offer reentry materials to current and released prisoners with the intent of attracting recently released prisoners to the public library as patrons. New York Public Library, for example, published a 290-page guide in 2015 with services for previously incarcerated individuals. This guide is published annually and includes resources on job hunting, services offered by the public library, organizations that they can join for support, educational opportunities, housing, financial assistance, counseling and family services, etc.[72]

The Long Branch Free Public Library in New Jersey initiated an award-winning program called "Fresh Start" for those who have been newly released from prison. The program began in 2011 with workshops offering training in computer and technology as well as assistance with job research and resume writing.[73] In Colorado, Denver Public Library created lists of resources for those reentering the community including advice on job searching, handling one's criminal record, access to computer labs, and other resources in the community.[74] An additional program at Denver Public Library called "Free to Learn" was funded by an LSTA grant and is an open computer lab session for women who have been incarcerated. Volunteers and a librarian are available for assisting the women with questions and the women can use the computers for whatever other purposes they would like.[75]

In San Diego County Library in California, librarian Hildie Kraus offers training sessions to those recently released from prison and modifies lesson plans to suit the specific attendees' needs.[76] Newark Public Library hosts an online guide of resources for reentry, most of which are local services.[77] In Buffalo and Erie County, the public library compiles a guidebook for the newly released and links to a list of suggested websites for those reentering the community.[78]

## Summary

Large portions of public library budgets are funded through taxes from constituents, some of whom may be incarcerated. It is important that outreach services to local prisons, jails, and detention centers continue so that these former and future members of the community are served with public library offerings. Certainly no public library has unlimited funding; nevertheless, partnerships with prison libraries can have a significant impact for otherwise unserved members of the population. Opportunities for public relations for both the public library and the prison are abundant.

Many of these programs can positively affect both the incarcerated and the greater community. Materials donation programs assist correctional institutions with supplying or supplementing their library collection that otherwise often are limited by budgets. Family and early literacy initiatives such as the "Read to Me" programs at various institutions create positive experiences between prisoners and their children, encourage reading for all parties involved, and in some cases may affect the mental wellbeing or even academic performance of the children taking part in the programs. Programs like Marcou's "Freedom Ticket" and other initiatives to educate prisoners may address goals of rehabilitation and decreasing recidivism. Public libraries who offer reentry materials or support for prisoners serve a new constituency that stands to benefit heavily from such support, especially with programs such as the "Fresh Start" program in New Jersey or the "Free to Learn" program in Colorado.

Many public libraries are doing exemplary jobs of reaching out to or serving incarcerated and previously incarcerated patrons. Some of these libraries are sharing these successes broadly by posting announcements on websites, inviting press coverage, or publishing articles about programs and services. I assume that many more public libraries are involved in prison outreach services that have not disseminated this involvement widely. If this is the case, they should—these kinds of programs provide valuable services to a disadvantaged population while reaching a whole new group of library patrons. For those public libraries who are not currently collaborating with a local correctional institution or vice versa, I hope that the examples in this chapter provide inspiration for establishing more partnerships between public and prison libraries.

8

# Current Policies in Prison Librarianship: An Expanded Survey

In November 2010, I conducted a simple exploratory eight-question survey of prison librarians in the United States. I was interested in understanding two key concepts: collection development policies and practices, as well as circulation records retention practices in U.S. prison libraries. I only publicized this survey via the ALA prison listserv and received 17 usable responses. The survey responses were so interesting and in many cases so ambiguous compared to the national policies in effect that I published this exploratory research in 2012 in *Library Quarterly*. This initial survey provided the basis for expanding my research, both in the form of an expanded survey in this chapter and interviews in the following chapter.

Seventeen responses for a survey is certainly not statistically significant, so it was necessary to expand the survey and collect more responses, preferably from more states. I wanted to discuss more issues in addition to the original questions from this survey, which addressed material selection, purposes for the libraries, collection development, censorship issues, and privacy of records issues. I wanted to get additional demographic information about the individual prisons to see if there was a correlation between some of the policies and the demographics of the institution. I wanted to understand if librarians working in prisons normally had a master's degree in library and information science, and if these degrees seemed to be preferred by administrators filling prison librarian positions. I also wanted to understand the location of the prison library within the hierarchy of the institution, i.e., did the prison library report directly to wardens and upper level administration, or was it located under, for instance, the education department. I also wanted to understand how important library needs assessments were for the prison library and how much influence prisoners as the patrons had in collection development decisions. Many prison libraries serve a purpose in providing legal services to prisoners: for this reason, it was important to ask a few questions about how those libraries were offering legal services and whether or not these legal services comply with court cases such as *Lewis v. Casey* or *Bounds v. Smith*. In my previous survey, I had asked about computer software as a potential item in the collection that prisoners could use or access. It was important to expand this question to understand not only whether prisoners have access to computers, but also to ascertain what kind of access prisoners have to Internet resources.

The final survey instrument included 43 questions with sections for demographic information, administration and facility details, purposes of the library, collection development policies, restricted materials policies, services and programs offered in the institution, needs assessment, availability of legal materials and services, technology in the prison library, and policies on privacy of records. Questions for both this expanded survey and my initial exploratory survey were developed after reviewing national and state standards, in particular the 1992 ASCLA publication *Library Standards for Adult Correctional Institutions*. Participants were encouraged to provide contact information if they were interested in conducting more detailed phone interviews. This survey was approved by my institutional review board and prepared in both an online and paper form. Both the online and paper form required that participants consent to the research terms, specifically agreeing that their responses could be used in an aggregated and confidential version for my research.

In order to obtain more responses from more states than my previous survey, the survey was distributed in these two forms. An online survey was prepared using Google Forms, which was publicized in mid–May 2014 on the American Library Association's prison libraries listserv. This listserv reached 435 subscribers as of May 2014. Reminders about the survey were sent three weeks later. Additionally, a BCC email was sent to 181 librarians who had emails listed in the Directory of State Prison Libraries[1] soliciting participation at the end of May 2014. Approximately 20 of these emails resulted in return to sender messages. 41 responses were received from all of these inquiries by June 9, 2014. One prison administrator emailed me to inform me that their librarians were not able to participate pursuant to orders from their Department of Corrections. This state was removed from any further communications. With a total reach of 596 individuals either listed in the Directory of State Prison Libraries or subscribing to the ALA prison libraries listserv, the online survey had a response rate of nearly 7 percent. It is possible that this response rate is higher than 7 percent as some of those targeted with mailings may have also been subscribers of the prison libraries listserv. Also not every subscriber to the prison libraries listserv is a prison librarian, which may also increase the response rate.

So that more responses were elicited, I also mailed this survey to states where I had not received online survey responses. The paper format of this survey was prepared using InDesign and formatted to fit on 11 × 17 double-sided paper, so that the survey had four pages that were attached to one another. The questions on this paper survey and the online survey were identical, including order. I also included a cover letter, which provided details about my survey and a request that responses be returned by August 30, 2014. This cover letter, the four-page folded survey, and a business reply envelope were included in each mailing.

Based on the online survey responses, I excluded states from the mailings where I had received more than two responses. Eight states were eliminated based on these response rates. The state that had disallowed their librarians from participating was also removed from this mailing. At the end of June 2014, 500 mailers were sent to federal and state prisons in 41 states. These prisons were selected by cross-referencing prison contacts listed in the Directory of State Prisons with the *2013 Directory of Adult and Juvenile Correctional Departments, Institutions, Agencies, and Probation and Parole Authorities*, which is a yearly publication of the American Correctional Association. Wherever possible, mailers were addressed to named librarians, library technicians, or other library program managers. Institutions with individual contacts were prioritized over those with no contacts. In states where no library staff names were listed as a contact in either the online directory or the ACA directory, inquiries were sent addressed to the "Library Services Program Manager." Nineteen of all 500 mailers were returned to sender.

Fifty-one responses were received from this mailer, the last of which was received in October 2014. Additionally, one online survey response was added to the pool of 41 for a total of 42 online survey responses. Based on the timing of this survey submission, I assume that this survey was submitted by a participant who had received a mailed copy of the survey. With the inclusion of this survey response, the total response rate for mailed surveys was approximately 10.4 percent. In total, 93 responses were received for my survey with both online and mailed responses for a total response rate of 8.5 percent.

I was contacted by two states who asked me to submit research directives to allow their librarians or library staff to participate in my research. One of these states had clear instructions on their websites banning any staff participation in research activities, therefore a research directive was not submitted. In the second state I submitted a research directive, which was subsequently denied. I did, however, receive five mailed responses from these two states despite their central offices requesting that their staff not participate. After discussions with my institutional review board, I chose to exclude these two states from further analysis. I also excluded one response from a foreign country, one response from a jail—as this survey only addressed state or federal prisons—and combined two respondents' duplicated participation into two individual responses instead of four. This left a total of 84 usable responses. Responses were received from 35 states and countries; one of these was a foreign response, two of those states were excluded as mentioned above, and one did not report the state, leaving responses from 31 U.S. states for analysis.

The results presented in this chapter may not be statistically significant due to a number of factors. With 1,369 federal, state, and privatized prisons in the United States as of the end of 2012,[2] roughly 90 responses would have been needed for statistical significance if these were calculated at a confidence level of 95 percent and a confidence interval of 10. The original amount of 93, which were received before any exclusions were applied, was close to this statistically significant recommended sample size (at a high margin of error). There are, however, challenges with working with this population that make it difficult to obtain an absolutely statistically significant representation through a survey. The most significant of these challenges is the barrier that many prison administrators or central department of corrections may be initiating to prevent their staff from participating as research subjects. As mentioned before, I was contacted by three states and asked either to submit a research directive with little chance of approval, or informed to discontinue any research with that state. These exclusions limited my ability to produce more statistically significant results. Furthermore, this may have been the case in other states where the emails or mailers were received: administration may have requested that the surveys not be completed without informing me, as the researcher, of this decision. Without sponsorship from a major funding agency such as the U.S. Department of Education, similar to what Marjorie LeDonne obtained while working in cooperation with the ACA in the 1970s,[3] it is unlikely that any researcher embarking on this type of research would be able to produce statistically significant results at high confidence intervals. The learning from this survey is therefore not generalizable, rather it provides more qualitative details about what is happening at 84 adult correctional institutions in the United States.

Furthermore, it was challenging to compare responses from online and mailed formats. Online responses tended to be longer and more detailed, likely due to the printed form requiring handwritten responses. Some of the written responses were hard to decipher and, in a few cases, some answers to questions were not entirely legible in the respondent's hand-writing. Also, in order to reduce time required to complete the survey online, the questions were removed when a respondent had answered in a manner that did not require further clarifications on that item, for instance if the respondents claimed that their institutions were not restricting access to materials, no further questions on this topic were asked in the online survey. In the mailed survey, respondents were encouraged to skip to subsequent questions when a further response was not necessary on a topic, however, a few respondents wrote in answers to questions on topics they should have skipped. This was not possible in the online form so therefore there are some discrepancies between the two mediums.

In order to understand any possible significance of the survey, especially in regards to demographic coverage, I compared demographic questions to the national standards and statistics published by various administrative bodies. In some cases, these statistics can be confusing. The ACA's 2013 directory provides some conflicting and in some cases estimated data that makes it difficult to make direct comparisons. For instance, a report on the number of adult state-run facilities and privatized prisons, and projected change in facility capacity for the 2013 fiscal year showed deficiencies between the numbers of facilities in each state and the totals calculated by the report.[4] The reports on gender in institutions also showed large discrepancies: a report on "Adult Inmate Population by Gender and Race" counted more individual prisoners than reports on "Adult Inmate Population by Gender and Age" as well as "Adult Inmate Population by Gender and Security Level."[5] Descriptions or footnotes on these various reports do not address the discrepancies between reports. It seems to be very difficult to centralize and summarize data about state and federal institutions; a learning that extended into my experience surveying this population.

Some demographic questions asked about the institution included whether or not the institution was adult or juvenile; if the prison was federal, state, private or another type of institution; in which state the respondent was employed; the gender of prisoners in the prison whether male, female, or co-ed; the number of prisoners incarcerated in the institution, and the security level of the institution. All responses were from adult institutions at various types of prisons in 31 states.

Survey respondents reported their individual states in their responses, but pursuant to my institutional review board documentation, I decided to group the responses from states into divisions to protect the identities of individual survey participants. Divisions were defined using the United States Census Bureau regions and include New England and the Middle Atlantic in the Northeast; the South Atlantic, East South Central; and West South Central in the South; East North Central and West North Central in the Midwest; and Mountain and Pacific in the West.[6] New England includes the states of Connecticut, Maine, Massachusetts, New Hampshire, Rhode Island, and Vermont. The Middle Atlantic includes New Jersey, New York, and Pennsylvania. East North Central includes Illinois, Indiana, Michigan, Ohio, and Wisconsin. West North Central includes Iowa, Kansas, Minnesota, Missouri, Nebraska, North Dakota, and South Dakota. The South Atlantic includes Delaware, Florida, Georgia, Maryland, North Carolina, South Carolina, Virginia, and West Virginia. East South Central includes Alabama, Kentucky, Mississippi, and Tennessee. West South Central includes Arkansas, Louisiana, Oklahoma, and Texas. Mountain includes Arizona, Colorado, Idaho, Montana, Nevada, New Mexico, Utah, and Wyoming. Lastly, Pacific includes Alaska, California, Hawaii, Oregon, and Washington.[7]

The division with the most responses was the East North Central (Midwest) at 26.19 percent of survey results. An equal number of responses were received from the South Atlantic and Pacific states, which both amounted to 15.48 percent respectively. Remaining divisions were as follows: Mountain, 10.71 percent; New England, 8.33 percent; Middle Atlantic, 7.14 percent; West North Central, 7.14 percent; West South Central, 4.76 percent; East South Central, 3.57 percent; and one response, 1.19 percent, did not record the state of employment. These response rates were compared to the percentage of institutions in each division as defined by the ACA *2013 Directory*. Survey results were in some cases very representative of the percentage of facilities in those individual divisions compared to other divisions, in particular those in the Middle Atlantic (with a difference of 1.11 percent between percentage of responses and percentage of institutions in those divisions) and in the West North Central (with a difference of 1.12 percent). For the divisions East North Central and Pacific, the survey response rates were significantly higher (15.06 percent and 8.7 percent, respectively) than the percentage of facilities in those divisions. Other divisions had less than a 4 percent difference in either one direction or the other; East South Central, Mountain, and New England were well represented in the survey responses to a certain extent when compared to the percentage of total facilities in those divisions. Two divisions had major deficiencies in terms of the number of responses: South Atlantic and West South Central had differences of 16.67 percent and 11.89 percent, respectively, however, it should be noted that these two divisions include states such as Florida and Texas, where the percentage of institutions is considerably higher than in most surrounding states or in states in other divisions. Florida and Texas have 151 and 133 state and federal prisons respectively according to the ACA *2013 Directory of Adult and Juvenile Correctional Departments, Institutions, Agencies, and Probation and Parole Authorities*, and the Federal Bureau of Prisons listings,[8] which account for 33 percent to 55 percent of the institutions within that region. If even one of these state department of corrections requested that the survey be ignored, the results would be understandably skewed.

Most of the survey respondents were employed at male correctional institutions (88.10 percent) with 8.33 percent employed at female correctional institutions and 3.57 percent working in co-ed institutions. When compared to the ACA's *2013 Directory of Adult and Juvenile Correctional Departments, Institutions, Agencies, and Probation and Parole Authorities* data from 2012 on adult prisoner population by gender and race, the percentages are similar. The population by gender in state and federal prisons was reported to be approximately 6.76 percent for institutions housing females compared to 93.23 percent for institutions housing only males.[9]

On another demographic question, survey participants entered actual numbers for the prisoners incarcerated rather than ranges. As part of my normalization of the data, I entered these responses into ranges. Over 70 percent of the survey participants worked at large institutions that incarcerated over 1,001 prisoners. In the Bureau of Justice Statistics data on "Prisoners in 2013," state and federal institutions were filled at 110 percent capacity on average.[10] No granular data on prison sizes or capacity was found from a centralized body such as the Bureau of Justice Statistics or the Sentencing Project.

I also asked two demographic questions regarding the individual survey participant: specifically, what the participant's working title or position name was as well as the highest level of education that participant had received. In comparison to my previous exploratory survey, many more respondents were working in positions that were not necessarily librarian or library specialist positions. This could be attributed to the fact that the previous survey was only administered to subscribers of the ALA prison libraries listserv, which consists of many prison librarians who are members of ALA. The mailed portion of this expanded survey included more responses from those working in or with the prison library with a title that was not necessarily a traditional library worker title. Over 70 percent (72.62 percent) of all responses held titles that included librarian, library director or manager, or library technician or specialist. A small percentage had titles that included some aspect of the law library including law library coordinator or law library supervisor (2.38 percent). Responses were received from a number of educators working with the prison library (16.67 percent) and these job titles included director of education, education program manager, education technician, teacher, instructor, and other education related titles. All of the respondents who reported job titles with some form of education or instruction in them were received via mail, therefore it was assumed that many of these educators are not following the ALA prison libraries listserv and may not be active members of ALA.

A majority of respondents (52.38 percent) reported that the highest level of education they had completed was a master's in library and information science (MLIS) or a master's in library science (MLS). A smaller percentage reported having both this master's and another master's degree or a law degree (5.95 percent). 20.24 percent reported holding a master's degree in another subject. A small percentage reported either having a doctorate or a pending doctorate (2.38 percent). 11.90 percent had completed bachelor's degrees, 1.19 percent associate's degrees, and 3.57 percent had completed high school or the equivalent. A small percentage reported completing a library technician certificate program (2.38 percent). It should be noted that this question was problematic, especially in the online form as there was no option to check multiple master's degrees. In this case respondents both online and in mailed surveys either entered their double degrees in the "Other" box online or wrote both in on the mailed form.

According to the ASCLA 1992 standards, a central library coordinator is required to hold an MLS or the equivalent. A local library director is also required to hold an MLS or the equivalent. Even the Assistant Librarian must hold either an MLS or a bachelor's degree with at least 15 credits in library and information science.[11] Most of those (80 percent) with librarian titles reported having either an MLIS/MLS or an MLIS/MLS as well as an additional degree such as a second master's degree or a law degree. Four librarians indicated they had master's degrees in a topic other than library and information science (8 percent). Four librarians (8 percent) had bachelor's degrees only. Two had library technician certifications (4 percent). All of the library managers had an MLIS or an MLS, or in one case, a doctorate in library science. The institutions in which the individuals were employed appear to be mostly conforming to the ASCLA standards when hiring librarians, especially if a different master's is viewed as "equivalent." All of the librarians with a bachelor's degree reported their titles as full librarian, not assistant librarian. Had their titles been "assistant librarian," they would have potentially fulfilled the requirements set in the ASCLA standards if they had coursework in library and information science.

Three library technicians or specialists had MLIS/MLS degrees and another three had other master's degrees (33.33 percent, respectively). One had a pending doctorate and one had a high school diploma. The respondents who were technicians were overqualified when compared to the ASCLA standards, which require an associate's degree or two years of college. Seven of eight respondents had master's degrees or were completing even higher levels of education. Perhaps these over-qualifications directly correlate to a broader issue in library science where few positions are available to MLIS graduates[12] and many are accepting or staying in positions for which they are overqualified. This trend may also support the possibility that these positions in prisons are being de-professionalized in states across the nation.

## Administration

The next section of the survey included administrative questions such as the number of hours the library was open on average, the parties involved in strategic planning and policy writing, whether or not the prison library budget had its own line item, and to which department or authority the prison library reported. I was particularly interested in seeing how closely these institutions adhered to the ASCLA 1992 library standards.

Survey respondents were asked how many hours the library was open to the prisoner population on a weekly basis. Most respondents wrote in the digits in hours. A few respondents (six in total) wrote in a range of hours. Hours were averaged for those who provided a range. Overall, respondents reported that prison libraries were open for an average of 36.5 hours weekly. The minimum open hours reported were 10 per week and the maximum 100 per week. All institutions appeared to be adhering to the ASCLA standards to be accessible for "at least five (5) hours per week."[13]

Respondents were asked in an open-ended question who authored strategic plans, procedural documents, or policy documents at their institution. Seventy-eight of the 84 respondents answered this question. Many mentioned various stakeholders including local administrators, local departments such as the library or the education department, and central offices authoring wider policies. The highest percentage (29.48 percent) reported that some variation of local administrators, departments, library staff, or committees were authoring these types of documents. For instance, one respondent mentioned a policy committee that works with a school superintendent, principal, and the librarian to author plans and policies. Another respondent mentioned that s/he creates forms, slips, and signs, but policies are authored by a "prison policy team," which, according to the respondent, may or takes librarian feedback at its discretion when creating those policies.

Nineteen respondents (24.36 percent) mentioned stakeholders were involved in policy authoring who were not local to their institutions, including those at central offices or state officials. One respondent detailed the multiple parties that provide feedback while developing procedures depending on what kind of policy or plan is being authored: "Anything concerning security follows a chain of command beginning with the commissioner. Policies & procedures are recorded by committees and are found in administrative directives. Strategic plans are issued by our school ... and goals are developed by me and approved by an administrator." Another respondent mentioned that central institutions participate in an advisory manner and they "guide library staff training, collection decisions, etc., and make sure that the DOC libraries statewide remain consistent in policies and practice."

An unexpected 20.51 percent reported that their library or specific library staff were solely responsible for authoring these types of documents. One of these respondents, however, despite noting that his or her local library had the autonomy to author documents, stated that "it would probably be myself and the Senior Librarian, but we don't really have time for it."

Six respondents (7.69 percent) reported that a central library office created policy and strategic documents. The same number and percentage of respondents mentioned only central institutions, not restricted to central library offices, as those authoring strategic or policy documents. Seven respondents (8.97 percent) stated that local administrators such as wardens or department heads were responsible for this type of documentation.

As mentioned in chapter 1, both the ASCLA and Vibeke Lehmann and Joanne Locke recommend that the library hold its own line item in the budget.[14] Nearly half of the survey respondents (45.24 percent) indicated that their budget, if they had one, was included with budgets from other programs or services. Only 34.52 percent reported that they maintained their own line item as recommended by standards. Fifteen respondents (17.86 percent) were not sure if their library had a separate line item in the budget or not. Two respondents (2.38 percent) did not respond to the question. The discrepancies between the ASCLA standards and the actual practice are troubling, especially to the future ability of prison libraries to continue to sustain a certain level of service.

I also found it interesting to understand where the prison library tended to be positioned in the prison administration hierarchy. The majority responded that they reported solely to the education department (54.76 percent). A total of 13.10 percent stated that they reported to programs or program services and 8.33 percent reported to rehabilitation services. Three respondents (3.57 percent) stated that they reported to multiple or combined departments with two reporting to both Education and Programs and one reporting to Education and Rehab Services. Some (9.64 percent) reported to upper prison administration such as the warden or the assistant warden. A total of 8.33 percent reported to central department of corrections units, with four stating only the DOC and three mentioning the state DOC library. Two respondents (2.38 percent) did not respond to the question. One interesting correlation between this question and the previous question about budgets was that 23 of the respondents who did not have a separate line item for the budget responded that the prison library reported to the education department; eight of the 14 who did not know whether or not there was a separate line item in the budget also reported to the education department. Since reporting to the education department seems to be a trend in the majority of these prison libraries, it is not surprising that the budgets might be compressed into one budget for education. This, of course, also has implications for the library collection and service offering, since there are many programs and services competing for the same funding. In responses to other questions, respondents indicated the problematic nature of not having enough funding.

## Purpose of the Prison Library and Collection Development Policies

In my 2010 survey for my 2012 article on prison libraries, I asked a number of questions about the purpose of the prison library and collection development policies. In the expanded survey presented in this chapter, I included seven questions on the purpose of the prison library, the types of materials offered to patrons, materials selection processes including decision makers, and information on existence of collection development policies, frequency of updates to these policies, and stakeholders involved in authoring policies.

In both surveys, I used reasons defined in the ASCLA 1992 standards for the purpose of the prison library.[15] Respondents had the option of checking a number of purposes for the prison library from a list including rehabilitation, maintaining contact with the outside world, enhancing vocational skills, providing legal materials, information about reentry into the community after parole, recreational reading, lifelong learning, and an "Other" field with the option to enter additional purposes. Respondents could check as many boxes as applicable. Eighty-three respondents (98.8 percent) indicated that recreational reading was a purpose of the prison library. Sixty-nine provided information about reentry into the community after parole and 66 claimed that their library played a role in rehabilitation. Sixty-six mentioned that the library served a purpose in providing legal materials to prisoners, amounting to 78.57 percent of respondents. This percentage was higher than anticipated, especially when considering legislation such as *Lewis v. Casey*, which had, according to some interpretations, reneged the *Bounds v. Smith* requirement of law materials housed in a prison library. Sixty-two respondents mentioned the purposes of both enhancing vocational skills and lifelong learning for the prison library.

Only 46 of respondents agreed that the prison library served a purpose in maintaining contact with the outside world. In retrospect, this option may have been confusing to participants: this could be interpreted loosely and could, according to my interpretation of the ASCLA standards, include providing access to newspapers and periodicals that keep prisoners in touch with the outside world. Many participants may have interpreted this purpose as a means of maintaining contact with actual individuals in the outside community. The ASCLA standards were also authored over two decades ago: certainly access to the Internet for purposes of maintaining contact with actual people in the outside world would not have been addressed within this purpose when it was authored.

Nine respondents wrote in additional purposes for the prison library including: researching college assignments, accessing materials on addiction, "exploring creativity," and supporting curricula. Two of these nine respondents mentioned legal purposes explicitly; one mentions a "Legal Writer program" to help prisoners conduct legal research. Two others mentioned purposes that might have been covered under existing survey options including for basic reading and literacy, as well as to access "recreational and educational media." Survey option responses are detailed in the graph below.

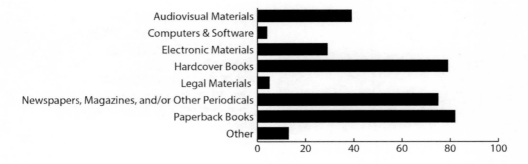

**Fig. 1. Purposes of the Prison Library.**

In my previous survey, I asked participants about what materials were offered to prisoners in libraries, specifically to see if they had access to paperback and hardcover books, newspapers and periodicals, audiovisual materials, and computer software. In this expanded survey I eliminated the computer software option as I intended on asking more specific questions relating to technology and computers. I did, however, include an option for electronic materials. I also gave the participants the option to write in additional materials under "Other."

Most respondents (82) allowed their prisoners to access paperback books. Comparably, 79 respondents allowed access to hardcover books. The restriction on hardcover books has been frequently mentioned in the literature, since hardcover books can be used to conceal contraband including weapons. Based on the frequent banning of hardcover books in the literature and in state policies, it was surprising that so many of the institutions (94.05 percent) allowed hardcover books. Seventy-five respondents allowed prisoners to use newspapers, magazines, or other periodicals. Thirty-nine respondents allowed usage of audiovisual materials; one explicitly wrote in cassettes only. Twenty-nine of the respondents mentioned access to electronic materials was allowed. Four respondents wrote in additional materials such as computers or computer programs, and five mentioned legal books, publications, or legal computer resources. Thirteen wrote in additional "other" materials including eReaders, calculators, CD-ROM, eBooks, computer-based encyclopedias, jigsaw puzzles, local job ads, puzzles, typewriters, playaways (audiobooks), workplace/employer databases, etc.

Eighty of the 84 participants provided long answer responses detailing their process of selecting materials. One respondent in the Pacific region detailed a very descriptive process of steps including reviewing statistics on what kinds of materials adult males in that state were reading, reviewing state book sales statistics for literature targeted at adult males, considering demographics of the prisoners in that state's prisons and in the individual institution, conducting prisoner surveys to ascertain author recognition and ranking top genres, and conducting activity surveys across the prison to compare usage of library books as compared to other prison activities. Another respondent from the South Atlantic region detailed a seven-step process in which s/he consults circulation statistics, takes requests from both prisoners and prison staff, reads publication announcements and reviews, compiles a "wish list," determines if the wish list books are available and affordable, replaces missing or damaged items in the current collection, and chooses some materials based on

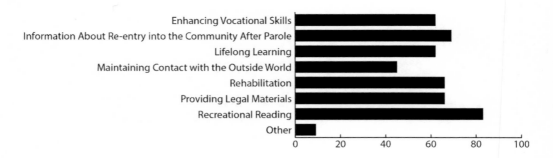

**Fig. 2. Materials Held in the Prison Library.**

day-to-day interactions with prisoners. One respondent, also from the South Atlantic region, broke down the process into three simple questions. "Is it cheap? Will it circ[ulate]? Will someone pay for it??"

Another respondent detailed a back and forth interaction with the state central library in which certain percentages and splits must be addressed when purchasing materials; the respondent gave two examples of reentry materials and materials written in Spanish as items that are prioritized. Another respondent from the East North Central region detailed his or her process as the following: "When funds become available and/or subscriptions end, the presumed continued use or use of a new item is prioritized. Keeping in mind restrictions for content choices are made based on funds, expected use, and restrictions dictated by the governing entity."

A few respondents mentioned the collection development policy as a guiding document in making selections in the prison library. One in particular from the East North Central region referenced the policy as the first step, followed by reviewing *Library Journal* and *Booklist* for items that would appeal to the local population and be appropriate for their reading levels.

A number of respondents mentioned reviews and rankings as a method for narrowing selection. One respondent from the West North Central region stated, "I use various sources (*Publisher's Weekly, Baker and Taylors Forecast*, Amazon, offender suggestions, etc.) to choose books that meet offenders' interests, as well as educational goals, and transitions. Another respondent from the South Atlantic region mentioned the importance of reviews, stating, "All books ordered must have a favorable review from a reliable source." Others cited additional sources that they consult including bestsellers lists, purchasing guides, Kirkus, etc. Two respondents discussed security concerns that must be taken into consideration when selecting materials.

Needs assessment is frequently mentioned as a means of developing the library collection through informed analysis of the prison population's interests. This kind of needs assessment is specifically related to the library; it is not to be confused with prisoner needs assessments' conducted by the entire prison. One respondent from the East North Central region initiated yearly needs assessments "where about 10% of our inmate population is asked to participate in the survey. Each inmate is asked to list 5 newspapers, 5 magazines, 5 book titles, 5 authors, etc. and other services that he would like to see at the library." Another respondent in the West North Central region had more interactive means of collecting requests from prisoners:

> I really try to listen to what offenders want—I keep a 6 ft. tall piece of butcher block paper on the end cap of a bookshelf where they can write suggestions. I started in this job 9 months ago, so I've been busy trying to fill in the gaps of series fiction. Lots of bestsellers and books on popular topics—drawing, spirituality (as opposed to religion), dictionaries, and URBAN FICTION (they can't get enough of it).

A respondent in the Mountain region acknowledged the challenge in using only circulation statistics to gauge usage since the prisoners in his or her institution have restricted and limited access to the library. This respondent mentioned the importance of soliciting prisoner requests to inform purchasing decisions.

Four respondents specifically mentioned modeling their collection development decisions after public libraries. One in the Pacific region reviewed public library collections to determine what might be applicable in his or her institution. Another respondent in the

Middle Atlantic stated that that they use the "same process as a public library, although with some restrictions placed on content."

Donations are frequently mentioned as a source for new material amongst respondents. One respondent from the East North Central region described his or her process for selection in the case that funds are available for purchasing additional items:

> Most are donated, but if we do have funds we use bestseller lists, patron requests and other collection development tools (including librarian experience and judgement as to the gaps in the collection) to select materials to add to the collection. Security is always a consideration as well, as materials are covered in administrative code.

A respondent from the Pacific region also mentioned budget issues, or lack of a budget whatsoever:

> We really have no budget. If we did, I would attempt to fill in the gaps of existing book series, solicit recommendations from institutional teachers and other staff, improve re-entry materials, use medical library core lists to update medical collection, increase easy reader selections using teacher catalogs, and mostly, use suggestions and requests from prisoners.

Budgetary issues and constraints are frequently cited in the responses to this question; at least five respondents mentioned budgetary issues, including lack of allocations for new purchases.

Seventy-nine respondents answered a question regarding what parties, people, or groups were involved in collection development and materials selection. These answers were coded according to their responses into similar stakeholder categories as administrative questions on the survey, including local administrators, local departments such as the library or the education department, and central offices. More than 85 percent of the parties involved in collection development were local parties without input from state or other officials. Fifty percent of decisions were made amongst library staff, 32.05 percent were some sort of local combination including library staff, education staff, administrative staff, or other departments, and 3.85 percent of those making decisions were prison administrators only. This was particularly interesting when compared to the percentages from the question on who authored strategic plans and policies: only 21.05 percent of the respondents on that question authored those plans in the local library. Local administration was also far more involved in that process than the collection development and selection process with 9.21 percent compared to 3.85 percent.

Central institutions and central libraries were also less involved in the collection development and selection process than they were in strategic plans and policy document authoring: only 3.85 percent of respondents included the central library offices in selection decisions (compared to 7.89 percent with plan and policy authoring). Similarly, only 8.97 percent had to involve central institutions such as the DOC or other governing bodies in the selection process, compared to 25 percent for strategic plan and policy authoring. All in all, local institutions, and in particular local libraries, seemed to have more autonomy when it came to selecting materials for their specific prisoner populations. This result might not have been surprising in another type of institution where strategic planning is frequently done at a higher or more centralized level, but since selection decisions have often been the focus of bad press, it was surprising that many institutions were still allowing their prison libraries to have so much autonomy in collection development decisions.

According to survey participants, collection development policies were often in place in prison libraries; 67.86 percent responded that their institution maintained a collection development policy statement. Twenty respondents did not (23.81 percent) and seven (8.33 percent) were not sure if their institution had a policy or not. Of those who did maintain a policy, most updated it every two to five years (38.60 percent). A total of 28.07 percent updated it yearly or more frequently, and 15.79 percent waited more than five years before updating the policy. 15.79 percent, or nine respondents, were not sure how often the policy was updated though they were aware that one existed. One respondent (1.75 percent), who had indicated a collection development policy existed, did not answer the question regarding frequency of update.

Library administration and staff also retained much of the decision making power when it came to authoring collection development policies: 61.40 percent of respondents indicated that the library staff was responsible for this document. Nine respondents (15.79 percent) mentioned central institutions and local institutions working together to author the policy. The education department was also occasionally involved in the process at two reporting institutions (3.51 percent). The Department of Corrections and/or the central library services department authored policy 7.02 percent of the time according to respondents. Prison administration was also solely responsible in four cases (7.02 percent). In one instance prison administration and the library staff collaborated without involving other outside institutions. One respondent did not respond to the question despite indicating that s/he had a collection development policy in his or her institution. One respondent did not know who was responsible for such policies.

## Restricted Materials and Policies

As mentioned in previous chapters, and throughout the literature on prison librarianship, items are frequently restricted, or censored, from the prison library collection in the interest of protecting the security of the institution. The ALA's "Prisoners' Right to Read" acknowledges that prison administration may have to censor items that are deemed to threaten the security of a correctional institution, therefore it is not surprising that so many institutions have policies about what kinds of materials are restricted, nor is it surprising that there is so much literature on the topic of censorship in prison libraries. In my survey from 2010, many of the respondents discussed censorship within their responses on collection development. As part of the discussion for this survey, the natural questions to ask are whether or not items are restricted in the institution, what kinds of materials are restricted, and who made decisions about what was restricted or banned.

As part of my survey, I asked a clarifying question about whether or not the institution had a policy for restricting certain materials. Participants were given the option of "yes," "no," or "I don't know." Most (94.05 percent) of institutions reported that they restricted access to some type of material in their library. Three respondents claimed that nothing was restricted (3.57 percent) and one respondent was unsure if items were restricted (1.19 percent). One respondent did not answer the question. Respondents who selected that their institution did restrict materials were forwarded to two subsequent questions. One respondent, who participated via a mailed survey, checked that his or her institution did not restrict items, however, wrote in a number of restricted materials under a follow-up question.

Respondents also provided more details about what types of materials were restricted within their institutions in long answer form. Many of the answers mirrored answers received during my survey from 2010. Some respondents appeared to have cut and pasted their policies directly from their central documents, as some texts are identical between respondents from the same state. Commonly censored topics in many of the respondents' institutions included anything describing the making or manufacture of weapons or firearms; discriminatory materials that might incite violence between two groups due to racial, religious, ethnic, or other differences; any types of materials that might be gang-related or related to congregating as a potentially violent group; sexually explicit items or materials; any materials that might threaten the security of the institution or the employees of the institution; and any materials that support law-breaking or criminal activity in general. One respondent from the South Atlantic region summarized these general guidelines well:

> Anything deemed "detrimental to the safety and order of the institution," including, but not limited to the following: bomb or weapon-making instructions, inflammatory propaganda, overly graphic (pictures or words) depictions of torture, rape, etc., writing that promotes riot or revolt, materials of sexual nature that graphically depict penetration (primarily pictures), detailed maps of the area, nude photographs of children.

Another respondent from the Pacific region answered similarly but with other examples:

> Books that described the making of any weapons, explosive, poison, or destructive device. Books [sic] that depicts, portrays, or describes a sexual assault upon a correctional employee. Maps depicting any area within a 10-mile radius of a facility. Obscene material: material when taken as a whole, to the average person, applying contemporary statewide standard ... depicts or describes sexual conduct, which, when taken as a whole lacks serious literary, artistic, political, or scientific value.

Many respondents named specific titles or authors that are banned within their institutions. One mentioned the Sleeping Beauty series by A.N. Roquelaure (pen name for Ann Rice) and Boris Vallejo art books. Another gave specific examples, such as *The Black Hand: The Story of Rene "Boxer" Enriquez and His Life in the Mexican Mafia* by Chris Blatchford, as well as magazines with titles such as *Cleavage, Close Shave, College Girls, Eager Beavers, Erotic Stars, Faery Stone*, and *For the Connoisseur of Submissive Females*. Popular urban literature author Donald Goines is mentioned but as an author who is allowed to be included in that institution: Goines and another urban literature author, Iceberg Slim, were mentioned in responses to my 2010 survey, since these two authors are particularly popular in correctional libraries. Another respondent from the South Atlantic region talked about issues with urban literature and attempted to include more of these titles in the collection:

> And sometimes they ban books that would be carried by mainstream books stores. Urban lit takes quite a hit in some prisons although, so far, not so much in the prison I serve. I have a prepared statement I use when this issue comes up that is really quite well thought out, I think. It seems to diffuse staff concerns about these books and helps staff understand First Amendment protections from the legal perspective.

Urban literature, frequently a discussion in the literature from previous chapters, continues to be of interest to prisoners, which is complicated by restrictions within individual institutions.

Oftentimes, respondents referred to Department of Corrections committees or to lists produced by these committees. One respondent mentioned a "Disapproved Publications Committee," which produces a list of disapproved titles. Another respondent mentioned a quarterly list compiled by legal personnel in a central office. Other respondents referred to local lists compiled by their individual institutions. One respondent detailed a proactive solution by a network of prison librarians in his or her system, stating:

> We do not maintain a list of "banned books." And it's interesting, because very recently, the DOC Contraband policy changed, but none of the librarians were told that it had changed! The new Contraband policy actually seems MORE lenient than the old one—the new one only refers to censoring or books that include PICTORAL displays of nudity, sodomy, etc. But the policy basically doesn't discuss books with stories that contain those types of things, just without pictures. At our Spring librarians meeting, we decided that as a group, we would come up with language about what libraries are, what we do, and what we want to do, so that when a book IS challenged, we have a united front. We are also going to start maintaining a database of books that are challenged/removed at our institutions…. Currently, a book may be totally allowed at one institution and banned at another. There seems to be very little rhyme or reason, so we've decided to be proactive.

This kind of joint effort appears to be helpful, at least to this institution's librarian, in establishing more statewide best practice for censorship decisions.

A few respondents also mentioned their own decision-making power when determining which books are restricted. One respondent restricted "any items that I feel are not suitable for the inmate population." Another respondent referred to lists and standards that are in place, but asserted that "the judgement of the librarian is trusted when purchasing." Another respondent from the Pacific region added comments in an open-ended response field at the end of the survey regarding further details about his or her selection process:

> Since there is no browsing unit in my institution, books are delivered to the units. The only books limited to check-out are reference books, non-fiction books, books in series, and classics. That way the book shelves on the units have mostly fiction. The only non-fiction is a set of encyclopedias and maybe ten titles with rehabilitation from addiction themes. Inmates can order true crime novels and own them, however that genre will not be placed upon library shelves or available for check-out. This is not a statewide decision, only the decision of myself in order to provide more room for fiction. In each unit of 130 men, there is room for only 650 books. My check out non-browsing book room only holds 2,000 books. There is a chapel library separate from mine with 5,000 books and an education library separate from mine of about 1,000 books for ABE/GED level reading.

This respondent provided very detailed responses about selection processes and restricted items regulations, perhaps due to the space constrictions s/he was faced with in his or her institution.

Participants were asked who decided what materials were restricted or banned. They had options to select library administration and library staff, prison administration and staff, department of corrections staff, or to fill in an "Other" field. Multiple selections were allowed. Twenty-one respondents (26.58 percent) reported that the decision-makers consisted of library administration and library staff, prison administration and staff, as well as Department of Corrections staff. A total of 24.05 percent of respondents observed rules determined solely by central offices either from the Department of Corrections or other central entities. Prison administration and staff were reported to be sole decision-makers at 11.39 percent of the institutions at which the respondents worked. The library was solely responsible for the decisions in only 5.06 percent of responses. The remaining 32.91 percent of responses were split in various ways: 8.86 percent of responses listed decision makers that included some sort of review committee, whether local or at the state level. These responses mentioned various stakeholders including involvement from some local administrators (library and prison administration or staff) as well as some configurations including state or central authorities. A total of 15.19 percent of respondents checked two or three of the options in the survey. Mail room staff were included as decision-makers in implementation of restrictions in three responses (3.81 percent). Two responses mentioned the education department (2.54 percent). One respondent checked "Other," but did not elaborate. One respondent, who confirmed that his or her library did have policies for restricting materials, did not respond to this question.

## Additional Library Services

I was also interested in understanding if prison libraries were offering many of the services available at public libraries. Respondents were queried as to whether their institutions offered services such as readers' advisory services, assistance with obtaining GEDs or high school diplomas, assistance with college-level entrance exams, correspondence courses, seminars or classes on reentry, referrals for legal service requests, and assistance with legal questions or research. These options were based on services defined in the ASCLA 1992 standards.[16] Additionally, respondents had an option to write in other programs or services they offered in their respective institutions.

Fifty-two respondents (61.90 percent) indicated that they were providing assistance with legal questions or research, while only 33 respondents (39.29 percent) provided referrals for legal services requests. Thirty-eight (45.23 percent) responded that they were providing assistance with completing either GEDs or high school diplomas. Others organized other types of courses; 20 (23.8 percent) were offering assistance with college-level entrance exams, 25 were offering correspondence courses (29.76 percent), and 17 (20.24 percent) were providing seminars or classes on reentry. Thirty-two (38.1 percent) had some sort of readers' advisory service. Twenty (23.8 percent) wrote in responses to the "Other" field. Six mentioned that a book club program was offered. Other responses included "consequential thinking seminars"; "creative programs like art, writing, poetry, etc.," training of law clerks; writers groups or clubs, "stress reduction through humor," and study groups.

Prison libraries also frequently offer interlibrary loan programs. In the institutions queried, 66.6 percent offered interlibrary loan programs and 32.14 percent did not. The remaining one response wrote in "No, 'Intra' only." All respondents seemed to be aware of existence or nonexistence of an interlibrary loan program, as no one checked the box "I don't know."

## Needs Assessment

Needs assessment can be a pivotal means of collecting information about what kinds of resources patrons really need. In the context of this book, I am discussing library needs assessment for making decisions about library collections and services. This does not include needs assessments for the general prison population about overall prison services. In the ASCLA 1992 standards, assessment measures are mentioned as an effective means of developing a collection to suit the local needs.[17] Of the 84 respondents queried, 55 (65.48 percent) were conducting some sort of needs assessment. Twenty-five (29.76 percent) were not conducting needs assessments, two (2.38 percent) were unsure if they were, and two did not respond to the question. One respondent that mailed a response indicated that his or her institution was not conducting needs assessments, however, subsequently checked the option for "interviews with inmate patrons." This comment was excluded from the following analysis.

Of the 55 that were conducting some sort of needs assessment, 42 were collecting information from interviews with prisoner patrons (76.36 percent). Just over half (50.9 percent) were administering user satisfaction surveys, and 14 respondents (25.45 percent) were using information from intake forms. Sixteen respondents noted other methods that they were using to conduct needs assessment. These included annual surveys, a "book request form," circulation records and statistics, informal discussions with prisoners, suggestions from staff, "reader's suggestions on the suggestion wall," other suggestion forms, and notes from reference transactions, among others.

## Legal Materials in Prison Libraries

Access to legal materials is a frequently discussed topic in the literature on prison libraries, especially the contradictions between court cases such as *Bounds v. Smith* followed by the more recent *Lewis v. Casey* ruling. I was interested in understanding if institutions were still following recommendations from *Bounds v. Smith* to provide legal materials in their libraries, or if many had used *Lewis v. Casey* as a justification to abandon these practices in favor of other less cost-intensive legal services. Questions throughout this section were problematic for a number of reasons. Most of those responding to this survey were employed in or involved with the general library collection at their institution, and often a law library was a separate facility. This meant that the survey participant may not have been fully aware of the services of the other facility. Answers throughout this section should, therefore, be viewed with a critical eye as many of the questions may not have been appropriate for those specific library employees to answer. Nevertheless, it is interesting to see their perspectives, whether erroneous or not, about how legal materials and services are offered in prison libraries.

Survey participants were first asked how legal materials were offered to patrons within their institution. Those who responded "via a select collection of legal materials included with the general library collection" and "via a separate law library in the institution," were forwarded to additional questions about legal materials and services. Also, any respondent who entered "Other" and a corresponding text was also forwarded to additional questions on legal materials. Those who responded that they either did not offer access to legal materials or responded that they only received legal materials through interlibrary loan only were asked to skip the next section of questions on legal materials.

Exactly half of the respondents reported that they had a separate law library in their institution (42 respondents; 50 percent). Twenty-two respondents reported that they had a select collection of these materials in their general collections (26.19 percent). Only 4 (4.76 percent) did not offer any access to legal materials. Another 16 claimed they had other situations than the listed answers (19.05 percent). Of these 16 responses, many mentioned LexisNexis or electronic law library access. Another mentioned librarian supported searching of databases, i.e., reference questions would be researched and responded to by librarians using online databases. Another respondent claimed that they use a combination of two of the responses and stated:

> We do both #1 and #2—a librarian ... comes to each prison once/month and we mail them legal kites almost every day (ones that we can't handle in house) AND we have a law library (a separate room within the library that houses our Core Collection of law materials (the core collection is the same across all the ... DOC libraries.) We also offer Lexis on 4 law computers (via an external hard drive that is updated every 3 months).

On the basis of some of the answers, this question could have been open-ended as it was not simple to group these types of libraries or services into straightforward categories.

Next, I was interested in understanding what kinds of standards were being referenced to develop legal collections. Again, this may not have been the best audience to answer this question as many of the respondents were, as they themselves mentioned, disconnected from the collection development process for selecting legal materials. Respondents could choose from a number of options and multiple selections were possible. Thirty-eight respondents indicated that their institutions referenced local, state, or federal policies to make purchasing decisions on legal materials. Twenty respondents referred to court cases or litigation on the topic. Eight consulted the American Association of Law Libraries (AALL) publications. Eight wrote in some form of "not applicable." Another 16 wrote in "Other" responses. Other responses included prisoner suggestions, other local or state authorities' documents, national publications and policies, mandated materials to be purchased through state directives, LexisNexis access, etc.

Respondents were asked if they or their staff were trained in providing legal assistance. Of the 78 responses received to this question, 49 (62.82 percent) had not received legal training while 29 (37.17 percent) had received some sort of legal training. Respondents were asked if they felt their training was sufficient to be able to answer the kinds of legal questions they received. This too was a problematic question: if these staff were not asked any legal questions at all, they may have reported that they felt comfortable answering questions, since they were not confronted with legal questions. Regardless of this issue, perhaps it can be interesting to note that of the 69 responses to this question, 31 (44.92 percent) felt equipped to answer these questions while 29 (42.03 percent) did not feel equipped. Nine responded that they did not know if they were equipped to answer these questions (13.04 percent).

In my previous article on prison librarianship, three court cases were referenced due to their relevance to prison libraries' policies and principles of intellectual freedom. These cases included *Lewis v. Casey, Turner v. Safley,* and *Procunier v. Martinez.* Much of the literature, and many of the policies in individual states that are available online, reference the precedent before *Lewis v. Casey: Bounds v. Smith.* Participants were asked if they referenced any of these court cases in internal policy documents. Additionally, an option was given to fill in any cases not mentioned under "Other" and there was an option for those who did not reference any court cases in any of their policy documents. Respondents had the option to select as many boxes as were applicable.

Twenty-six respondents indicated that they referenced *Lewis v. Casey* in policy documents. This was considerably more than I had noticed in my chapter 2 analysis of state policies in which reference to *Lewis v. Casey* was only explicit in six state policies. Twenty-five claimed that their policy documents included mention of *Bounds v. Smith.* Thirteen respondents indicated that *Procunier v. Martinez* was referenced somewhere, and 12 indicated they referenced *Turner v. Safley*. Twenty-six respondents indicated that they did not reference any court cases in their policy documents for law libraries, with one indicating in a note that it was possible they did reference these cases, but s/he was unaware of it. This may be the case with other respondents; they might not have known if the cases were referenced or not in their policy documents. Nineteen respondents wrote in other court cases. These included *Cepulonis v. Fair, Stone v. Boone, Gilmore v. Lynch, Toussaint v. McCarthy, Zatko v. Rowland, Toussaint v. Rowland,* and *Spates v. Manson*. Three of the respondents did not appear to understand the question as they indicated that these cases were available on LexisNexis in their institutions. It is possible that many of the respondents did not understand the question but recognized certain court cases also from LexisNexis or similar resources they offered in their institutions.

In another question, respondents were asked what legal assistance programs were offered in their institutions and given the option to check as many as were applicable. Options included law librarian assistance, access to paralegals, legal assistance through local law schools, and jailhouse lawyers or inmate clerks with legal experience. Respondents had the option to write in an "Other" field for additional types of assistance offered. Fifty-nine responded that they had jailhouse lawyers or inmate clerks with legal experience offering legal assistance to their prisoners. Twenty-seven had law librarian assistance and 15 provided access to paralegals. Ten had programs with local law schools to offer assistance. Twenty-one wrote in additional responses detailing the services they offered, which included more detailed inmate legal clerk programs. One respondent indicated that "each institution has a law clerk who works with the librarian (the law clerk is an offender)—he is specifically NOT to offer legal advice—he only fills legal requests (cases, DOC policies, etc.)." A few mentioned certification programs for inmate law clerks. One said that the public defender had a local office. Multiple respondents referred to legal writing programs with support from prisoners, legal resource centers, clinics offered by law schools, law order service, monthly law librarian visits, electronic law library, and LexisNexis. One respondent stated, "we (staff & inmate clerks) are not allowed to give any legal advice but can direct and show inmates how to find and research on their own."

One respondent, in a final section allowing comments from survey participants, opted to provide more information about legal services at his or her institution. S/he stated:

> Library staff and inmate clerks provide legal research assistance, but we do NOT provide any sort of legal advice, counsel, interpretation of law assistance. We are NOT licensed attorneys, and as such may not practice law. Also, jailhouse lawyers exist, but they do not function as part of any program. Our legal research is Internet-based with a secure direct connection to the LexisNexis database site at login with NO Internet functionality at all for inmates once logged in.

This participant, who opted to add additional details, provided perspective and clarifications to some of the less than optimal results received in this section. The idea that the library staff can support but not advise has also been mentioned in literature from the first few chapters of this book.

I was also curious to understand whether or not a clear policy was in place for providing legal materials in the institutions, as some of these policies were difficult to find online when I was researching for chapter 2. Seventy of the 78 participants who responded to this question (89.74 percent) indicated that a policy did exist. Three said that one did not exist (3.84 percent) and five were not sure if a policy existed.

In retrospect, it may have been too difficult to try to survey general library services and legal library services as part of the same survey; some of LeDonne's work in the 1970s included a focused legal services survey, which was clearly directed to the legal library services stakeholders in prison libraries at the time.[18] More research is needed that focuses on legal services and collections in prison law libraries, since these services can be integral, supplemental, or completely separate from general library service. In the next chapter this becomes even more apparent; many interviewees separated general library service from law library service in their responses as well.

## Technology in the Prison Library

Technology, and more specifically access to computers, is a service that has been contentious in some prison libraries. Brenda Vogel laments the issues with denying prisoners access to computers, detailing the disadvantages they face in a digital world upon reentry.[19] During my 2010 survey, about half of the 17 respondents mentioned that they had access to some sort of computer software and none provided Internet access,[20] therefore I was interested in seeing if anything had changed and asked more pointed questions about technology in the library. I was asking about any technology whatsoever; I acknowledge that simple computer access or access to electronic legal access is not equivalent to providing the opportunity for digital literacy. Prisoners are often not supplied with anything more than rudimentary access to technology and current approaches are, for the most part, not sufficient for addressing the digital divide. Also, this question addressed technology in the library; many education departments may have more robust technology programs and educational offerings.

Participants were asked a clarifying question about whether or not prisoners were permitted to use computers in the library. They had the option of selecting "yes," "no," or "not currently, but in planning." The last option was important to include because it shares potential future intentions and commitments to addressing issues with prisoners' lack of computer skills or at least providing some electronic access. Those who answered "yes" were forwarded to two additional questions including one about what services prisoners were permitted to use on computers and a further clarifying question on whether or not prisoners were allowed to use any services requiring usage of the Internet. The same three options were presented to the last question, and again those who answered "yes" were asked two additional questions about Internet usage. These questions included long answer questions about what services prisoners were and were not permitted to use on the Internet.

I was surprised by the number of institutions that were allowing their prisoners to use computers for accessing certain software or services: 66 respondents (78.57 percent) were permitting some sort of computer access. Sixteen respondents (19.05 percent) did not allow prisoners to use computers. Two respondents (2.38 percent) claimed that they were planning on allowing prisoners to use computers.

Of the 66 "yes" responses received on the prior question, 53 (80.30 percent) indicated that the computers were used for legal purposes, to prepare legal documents in word processors, to access legal databases, etc. Thirty of those respondents (45.45 percent of all of the respondents on this question) exclusively offered access to legal services with no other services available on computers. One respondent in the Pacific region explained this well: "They are only allowed to use the law computers (Electronic Law Library Delivery System). This system has case law and secondary legal research materials on them. They do not have MS Word, Excel, Internet connection, PDFs or any other application or program. They cannot print from them or fill out forms on them." Others indicated that the software versions of LexisNexis or other electronic law libraries provided superior access in comparison to the paper copies that the libraries may or may not be purchasing.

Fifteen of the respondents (22.73 percent) used computers for educational purposes. Some programs or services offered included access to the Khan Academy, typing practice or training, web development tutorials, Google Sketch-Up, AutoCAD, QuickBooks, Rosetta Stone with training in English and Spanish, GED tutoring, driver's education and training, and financial literacy training or tutorials. Eight of the respondents (12.12 percent) indicated that they allowed prisoners to access job listings or services on the computers as well as provided them with applicable programs to create resumes. One respondent in the West North Central region for instance stated, "computers are used to learn keyboarding, word processing, spreadsheets, databases, and to type legal or college work." Another respondent in an unreported region provided more granular information including approval processes for software or computer services: "Legal, Jobs and Family services information, Monster. com, typing tutor, these are all in the library. Administrative office technology program, CDL driving practice …, computer labs with educational programs. All computer access has to be approved through the Education Superintendent." Three respondents mentioned computers being used by prisoners working for the library. One respondent in the Pacific region stated: "only approved clerks can use computers for basic tasks (library catalog, excel spreadsheets) to complete their job duties." This respondent also mentioned access to legal services on computers and computers in classrooms. Four respondents claimed their institution's prisoners had access to email of some sort. Many mentioned usage of the library catalog on computers.

Of the 66 respondents who indicated that prisoners were allowed to use computers, only eight of them allowed usage of services that required Internet access (12.12 percent). Two were planning to allow certain Internet services (3.03 percent). Fifty-six respondents (84.84 percent) indicated that they did not offer access to any services that required use of the Internet. Of the eight who allowed usage of services that required Internet access, most did not provide access to anything other than a select suite of sites. These included state job and housing search engines, Monster.com, "family services," a "work opportunities tax credit program" in which prisoners provide a service to an employer for a tax credit, LexisNexis, and email programs. One respondent noted that prisoners were not allowed to use Facebook or do any web searching.

One respondent added information on technology at the end of the survey in the comments section, stating: "I would like to offer e-books to the inmate population as soon as a secure reading device can be allowed. There are 1000s of public domain books that could be offered, and this would give the inmates a taste of real-world technology." Allowing access to technology seems to be a challenging endeavor at a prison library due to security concerns and various restrictions. Certainly the prison library is not offering the same level of access to technology currently available at a public library. None of the survey respondents mention any of the initiatives from chapter 3 for distributing tablets or other similar devices. There is, however, a desperate need for more technology in prisons, especially to equip future released prisoners with the digital literacy skills necessary to survive in modern times. Current access offered is often too simplistic and gated to allow a prisoner to learn how to use a computer or a device, especially since so few allow prisoners to connect to the Internet. Furthermore, without technology prisoners cannot be educated on how to evaluate online information. While some institutions appear to be attempting to bridge digital literacy gaps, security needs and constrictions seem to make it very difficult for meaningful progress to be made.

## Privacy of Records

Privacy is a luxury that most prisoners are not afforded. Confidentiality of records, however, is a fundamental principle of librarianship, set forth in the ALA's "Policy on Confidentiality of Library Records,"[21] and generally treated as something that should be protected. My 2012 article was initially fueled by the contradiction that I saw between public libraries and prison libraries with the management of their borrowing records. Public libraries frequently attempt to protect privacy by implementing borrowing record deletion procedures. This did not seem to be the case at prison libraries. The results of my initial exploratory assessment led me to believe that policies were ambiguous; often privacy was not a top priority concern when so many other overreaching issues such as security and censorship take precedence.

In my expanded survey, I asked four questions about privacy of records, specifically related to checkout records. The first was how prisoners were uniquely identified, since associating a prisoner with his or her institutional code could allow associations to be made and records of individuals to be tracked more easily. Secondly, I asked what happened with checkout records once an item had been returned. I provided multiple choice options due to my previous experience collecting responses in free text form. I also asked whether or not a policy existed regarding privacy practices for prisoner library records. Lastly, I was interested in knowing who had access to checkout records as a technical administrator.

Sixty-four of the respondents (76.19 percent) indicated that they tracked their prisoners' library usage with institutional inmate codes. Only nine respondents (10.71 percent) generated a library code for their prisoners. Seven respondents wrote in responses of other methods that they using to track their prisoners' circulation records. One stated that they used both institutional and library generated codes; one used inmate badge ID numbers; another used the name, the number, and the cell of the prisoner; and another mentioned a written card system to check items out. Four respondents did not answer the question or wrote in that they did not understand the question.

There was less ambiguity in the responses regarding the length of time that checkout records were maintained in this iteration of my survey compared to my 2010 survey. Forty-four of the respondents (52.38 percent) maintained the records indefinitely. Eighteen kept records until the item was checked out by another patron (21.43 percent). Three respondents wrote in that the records were kept until the patron left the institution permanently (3.57 percent). Only six respondents (7.14 percent) selected that the records were immediately deleted when an item was returned, despite this being the recommended practice by many public libraries. Thirteen respondents wrote in "Other" responses. Some of these responses included retention periods of three years, two years, one year, or as short as 45 days; until the book was removed from the collection; or on the card system until the cards were replaced. One respondent stated that policies were different depending on what type of record it was: "any trust withdrawals from damaged or missing books are kept for 7 years, regular check out history approximately a year or less." One respondent did not answer the question.

The existence or non-existence of policies about privacy of records was more ambiguous. Only 34 respondents (40.48 percent) knew of a policy addressing privacy practices for prisoner library records within their institution. Forty-one (48.8 percent) stated that one did not exist and six (7.14 percent) were unsure if one existed. Three respondents did not answer the question.

Lastly, survey participants were asked which parties could access checkout records as an administrator. Participants were encouraged to check all that applied with the options of library non-prisoner staff only, library staff including prisoner staff, or prison administration. The respondents also had an opportunity to enter "other" parties who had these rights. Thirty-two (38.09 percent) of the respondents claimed that library non-prisoner staff were the only ones who had access to these records. Thirty-three respondents (39.76 percent) checked that library staff including prisoner staff had access. Forty-one respondents selected prison administration. Ten wrote in other responses. Some of these responses included the IT department in the prison, legal staff, the principal or warden, the research department, etc. One respondent from the South Atlantic region stated, "It has never come up but I would not deny access to administration staff if they wanted it. I would consider the request unusual but not unreasonable." Overall the results for this question were more ambiguous. It is possible that this question was confusing to understand due to the usage of the word administrator, which was meant to imply a technical administrator with access to administrator level privileges in a circulation program.

I also asked participants if they would be interested in participating in a more detailed phone interview, the results of which will be discussed in the next chapter. Those who were interested provided their email addresses or phone numbers. I also provided a comment box for those who had additional feedback about the survey or any additional comments or clarifications. Relevant additional comments that were submitted have been interspersed with the narrative above.

## Summary

The 84 responses included in the analysis were very helpful for providing an initial look at how closely (or not closely) many of these institutions are adhering to the most recent, and at the same time outdated, standards for library services in correctional institutions. A few questions, because of limitations in my survey instrument, were problematic once administered, in particular the security levels of the institutions and degrees received by survey participants. Legal questions in general were problematic and inconclusive. For any future research, it is important to break these out separately. Many of the surveyed institutions have separate law libraries or separate stakeholders who are responsible for these services. Surveying the librarians managing the general collection was generally less effective as many of them were only remotely involved with legal materials collection and reference.

While the results presented in this chapter may not be statistically significant across all states and all types of institutions, there appear to be some consistencies in terms of certain policies. These consistencies, especially in the case of restricted materials, seem to conform to recommendations from ALA and state authorities. Most institutions appear to offer similar materials, services, and abide by a set of principles for the purpose of the prison library. It is very difficult to administer a statistically significant survey due to some of the challenges encountered when working with specific states' research directives. In this regard, a statistically significant survey would have to be administered or even mandated by someone employed by a central authority such as the American Correctional Association. Otherwise, it seems very difficult to produce generalizable results, especially as an outside researcher.

Overarching principles and services may be consistent in prison libraries, but many more detailed services and functions become more ambiguous when institutions' survey respondents' results are compared. Libraries report to various departments depending on the state and the institution with no real conclusive precedent. Budgets also appear to be set on an institution by institution basis. Many institutions are conducting some sort of library needs assessment, however, many may not have the staff to administer these initiatives or the budget to make actionable choices on the basis of the data. Privacy of checkout records also continues to be a contentious topic in which prisoners are not necessarily treated like public library patrons; a few of the respondents' institutions emulate public library policies to delete records, but most appear to be maintaining the records at least for some time. Technology as a whole is generally troublesome, as many of the prisoners are likely in need of training in basic computer skills, but have only limited, if any, access to computers, programs, and Internet services.

Interviewees from the subsequent chapter mentioned that many practitioners, who are active in the Association of Specialized and Cooperative Library Agencies, have been pushing for a revision to the 1992 standards. It is good news that a national policy update for prison library services is under consideration by ASCLA, since the current version is over two decades old. Certain elements of these standards require further clarification twenty years later, especially access to technology and Internet services. Institutions that offer no computer or technology access may be limiting the success rates of their prisoners when they re-enter the community as many of them may have limited computer skills and will therefore have difficulty transitioning. Per data from the Sentencing Project, prison sentences during the War on Drugs era caused an ever growing increase in the number of incarcerated individuals.[22] A Pew Center on the States Report from June 2012 confirms that prison sentences have increased by 36 percent in the last two decades.[23] The digital divide only continues to grow, especially as prisoners serve longer terms, which remove them from even more technological advances necessary to succeed in modern society. Changes to policy, especially to update the policy to reflect twenty-first century technology services, are needed.

In at least one instance a survey respondent indicated struggles with being informed of policy changes. In that particular case, that respondent banded together with other prison librarians in his or her state to establish best practices across their institutions. An updated national policy could supplement and support these kinds of initiatives by providing guidelines for not only the states but for the individual institutions.

# 9

# Prison Librarianship in Practice: Interviews with Prison Librarians

This chapter includes summarized results from eleven interviews with prison librarians in various states. The survey from the last chapter provided some insight into day-to-day operations in a prison library and how the librarians in these positions adhere to or deviate from policy; in-depth interviews take this research a step further. Actual practitioners were interviewed about their decisions to work in prison libraries, opportunities for professional development, partnerships with outside institutions and organizations, and general experiences administering a prison library. Because of their conversational nature, interviews allow a researcher to experience something from the subject's perspective.[1] As a non-practitioner, it was important to have these conversations to learn from insider perspectives.

Interviewees were selected based on feedback from the survey presented in chapter 8, which was conducted in the summer of 2014. A final question in the survey asked if the survey respondent would be interested in participating in an in-depth telephone interview. Initially I had hoped to speak to at least five prison librarians and was both surprised and pleased to have 33 respondents from 19 states volunteer for in-depth interviews.

Since I had multiple volunteers from some states, with as many as six in one state, I initially selected a handful of prison librarians to contact based on the U.S. region in which they were employed. Within each state, I selected the respondent with the most senior working title as this person would likely have the most years of experience in a prison library. I did not exclude those who did not have librarian titles; I was aware that the profession had, in many states, been reduced to technician or specialist status. Many of the professionals working in these positions had been trained as librarians. I also did not exclude those who did not have MLS or MLIS degrees. In some cases, other graduate degrees had been accepted as sufficient to hold the position in the library. After conducting a few interviews, I proceeded to contact and schedule interviews with prison librarians and staff in additional states. I did not contact multiple people in any one state in order to avoid skewing responses—in one region, I had six librarians willing to speak to me from one state, only one from another state in that region, and none from the remaining states. Rather than have multiple responses from one state where a central policy was likely in existence, I chose to select one librarian, preferably one with the most senior status, to represent that state. Additionally, I did not speak to a librarian in every state where I had volunteers. For instance, I had many volunteers from states in New England, but New England did not have as many prisons as the South Atlantic region, so I chose not to talk to librarians in all of the New England states where I had volunteers. In total, I contacted 21 potential interviewees.

In four cases, the librarians who had responded to my survey had left their posts by the time I contacted them for interviews. Another librarian was not reachable after multiple attempts due to a full mailbox. I had initially hoped to schedule interviews for the fall of 2014, however the survey had extended longer than expected due to mailings that continued to arrive after my planned cutoff date. Therefore, I pushed back interviews for early 2015. It was not surprising that some of the librarians in these positions had moved on or were unreachable since six or more months had passed. One interviewee asked for permission from superiors before agreeing to talk to me. I assume that permission was not granted, as I did not hear back from this librarian. In the interest of reducing risk to study participants, I did not contact her further. Four librarians did not respond to an initial email or a follow-up email.

Phone interviews with 11 prison librarians or library staff were conducted from February 2015 through April 2015. Interviews were scheduled at the best times for the interviewee; most seemed comfortable conducting these interviews at work. Only two happened after working hours, one of which was with a prison librarian who had recently retired. Based on some of the challenges I had with individual states from the previous survey research, I had expected less librarians to be so willing to talk and also expected that most would want to talk to me in confidence outside of working hours. This was not the case. Most were comfortable talking about their work while on the job.

Few studies conclusively identify the number of interviews necessary for saturation in these kinds of projects. Mario Luis Small discusses the challenges and approaches for selecting cases when conducting field research and determines that some tools such as "sampling for range, snowballing, and identifying unique cases" may help to "build better vessels" or provide effective qualitative research, however, he does not identify what number is appropriate.[2] Sarah Elsie Baker and Rosalind Edwards collect a number of expert opinions about sampling and cases to answer the question of how many qualitative interviews is enough. Ultimately, they are unable to provide a definitive answer—rather the answer that results from their study is "it depends."[3] Greg Guest, Arwen Bunce, and Laura Johnson determine that data saturation occurred at 12 interviews in their study of West African women in which 60 women were interviewed.[4] Certainly there were overreaching themes that emerged in my research after only five or six interviews. It was, nevertheless, interesting to talk to practitioners from as many states as possible, since procedures did appear to vary between the states and at times even between institutions in a state.

An important point to note is that many of these librarians were recruited through the ALA's prison libraries listserv and nine of them had a graduate degree in library and/or information science. They were interested in participating in my survey, as well as willing to spend additional time for an interview. This may be atypical for many of the librarians and library staff working in prison libraries. The few that I spoke to were pro-active and interested in their professions; they are likely invested and eager to share learning, perhaps more so than prison librarians and library staff in states that are not represented. It was more difficult to get interviews with library technicians, specialists, or other Department of Corrections staff. Very few non-librarians volunteered to participate in additional interviews; only one from the group of 11 was a library technician. During the survey, it was much more likely for a librarian to agree to be contacted for an interview than it was for other types of library or education department staff. As mentioned in chapter 8, I was also contacted by three administrations to ask that I not contact their staff further for inquiry.

All of the interviewees in this chapter will be referred to by pseudonyms and their state will only be identified as part of its greater region. This precaution was taken to protect the individuals who were so gracious to allow me to interview them; most were not hesitant to tell me about the positive and negative experiences they had within their institutions and with their individual administrations. Additionally, in some states, only a handful of librarians are working in these capacities in prison libraries; sharing responses from participants in specific states could make these individuals identifiable.

Interviewees were asked a series of 14 to 17 questions, depending on their survey responses and depending on responses to questions within the interview itself. The interviews lasted on average between 30 and 45 minutes, with a few eager interviewees who were willing to talk to me for nearly 90 minutes. Prompts to the questions were also on hand in case the interviewee answered with short responses. Some general questions included motivations for working in a prison library, whether or not the respondent had worked in another type of library, what kind of education the respondent had, and if that education had been helpful in the prison library. There were also a series of questions about professional development and opportunities to network within their current positions. Additionally, there were a number of questions about administration, such as staffing (both prisoner and non-prisoner), processes for selecting materials, interactions with administration, services for prisoners in segregation, and situations in which a prisoner's access might be restricted. I was interested in ascertaining what kinds of cooperation might be in place between prison libraries and other institutions including interlibrary loan services and programming partnerships. Lastly, I had two questions about technology in the prison library. Access to technology does not appear to be a service as frequently offered as it is in public libraries, but would be a beneficial addition to reducing the digital divide for the newly released.

Before conducting the interviews, I wondered how the interviewees would perceive me, the researcher. I had no experience working in a prison library and all my current perceptions of the field are research based and external only. My experience in prison libraries is limited to a tour of a state prison facility, including brief discussions with the librarians on staff. Authors such as Coyle and Hartz et al. mention the issue that most literature on prison libraries is written by non-practitioners. This is certainly true in my case. However, this chapter should be the voice of the practitioners and their experiences rather than an overview of existing literature, which may or may not be written by practitioners. Regardless, my concern that these librarians might be hesitant or even hostile to me as an outside researcher was unfounded; overall the librarians I interviewed were pleased that someone was researching this field and publishing results. Many claimed to be eager to see the results, especially to see what respondents in other states were saying or doing in their institutions. A few asked a number of questions about where I was publishing and stated that they were interested in being notified regarding publishing timelines. Some even expressed interest in purchasing it. I had not expected this kind of interest or support, but in retrospect found that the supportive conversations I had are representative of many of the interactions within the community of librarianship. Even though many of these librarians may have to adhere to policies that in some ways violate stances on intellectual freedom from the American Library Association or are disconnected from the profession in terms of professional development involvement, they still had a fundamental interest in seeing something about their work as a librarian disseminated.

Interviewees were professionals working in library positions in prison. Most were librarians; ten of the interviewees were classified as librarian or library managers within their institutions. One had been reclassified or demoted to a technician position and while this interviewee did not have an MLIS, most others holding his position in his state did have an MLIS or MLS. These practitioners had various levels of experience; some had as many as 15 to 20 years in prison libraries and some had under two years of experience.

## Motivations for Working in a Prison Library

Very few of the interviewees had actively pursued a career in prison librarianship. Some mentioned location and proximity as the driving force in their choices to become prison librarians; others came into the prison library after careers in other libraries for reasons such as higher pay, superior benefits, MLS requirements, etc. Only two of those interviewed had actively sought prison library positions. Kelly, a librarian in New England, became a prison librarian because she felt a need to work for the greater good. She stated:

> If you're not really working to help people, you're not really doing much with your time. So I was deciding, well, which of these career paths makes the most sense in terms of helping people? And as much as I love historic preservation and looking at really pretty buildings, I didn't really think that was changing anyone's life, so I said, well, of all these being a librarian makes the most sense. And then I said to myself, well what kind of libraries are there? Where is there a library that there's probably a lot of need and probably people who don't necessarily want to work there? And I said, hot damn, there are prisons in this world that have libraries. I've seen *Shawshank Redemption*.

Kelly had actively pursued opportunities for internships in graduate school in prison libraries, unlike any of the other interviewees. Kelly, while in graduate school, spoke to advisors about pursuing prison librarianship. Her advisors were not able to place her anywhere and, according to Kelly, admittedly did not know much about prison librarianship as a career path. To find an internship, she found contact information on local correctional institutions and managed to get a response encouraging her to intern. She said that the experience "pretty much clinched it," leading her to pursue a career in prison librarianship.

Jennifer, a librarian in the Midwest East North Central region, also pursued librarianship with the intention of becoming a prison librarian. She stated the following about her job application process and choice to become a prison librarian:

> At that time, I didn't realize how few people wanted to become prison librarians. You know, my experience is quite a bit different than most people because I was very interested. I did a lot of research on the subject before I became a librarian. As I was becoming a librarian, I wrote several papers, did several different types of independent studies, and that kind of thing. But I've been really happy with my career choice. I've worked in a prison for over 20 years now and it's mostly been rewarding.

Jennifer was the only interviewee who mentioned having family members who had also been employed in corrections.

Others mentioned the contribution to rehabilitation as the reason for seeking out work in a prison library. Olivia, a librarian in the South Atlantic, states that "everyone is supposed to be united for their rehabilitation and the caring staff who work here are all sort of ... counselors. And I like that part of the job." Olivia worked with female offenders and was particularly interested in helping that segment of the population. Victor, also a librarian in the South Atlantic region, talked about working with offenders and helping them as the main reason for becoming a prison librarian. Linda, a librarian in the Pacific region, cited her passion for rehabilitation, mentioning literacy as a way to support her institution's mission. Another interviewee, Nora, who was a librarian in the East South Central region, had worked with students in secondary school alternative programs and "had that connection to juvenile justice."

Heather, a librarian in the Pacific region, talked about her previous career in a public library and how benefits through the state department of corrections far surpassed what she was able to earn through a local public library. She described her reluctance to work in a prison library, stating: "At first I was a little hesitant, but someone I knew had applied to a prison library and he didn't think it would be that horrible. So I went through the whole process and got hired, and it actually turned out that I really liked working here. So what motivated me was strictly money, but it turned out to be a good thing." Heather was not the only librarian who applied to the job because of benefits or pay. Jack, a librarian in the South Atlantic region, described a certain curiosity about the career and an impetus to apply based on superior pay and benefits.

Sarah, a librarian in the Mountain region, mentioned her initial uncertainty in applying for a prison library job, which reduced after she talked to a friend who had worked in the environment. She said, "you worry about behavior, things you see in the media," and followed by recounting her conversation with the friend who said that offenders did not behave in the way that might be expected. She stated, "it's a privilege for the prisoners to come to the library and they appreciate it and they're well-behaved." Sarah was encouraged to apply for the position after getting an opinion from someone who had experience in a prison setting.

A few interviewees mentioned proximity to their homes as the main factor in their decisions to work in a prison library. Alison, a librarian in the Midwest East North Central region, applied to a prison library because it was one of the few local institutions that required that she have a master's degree in library science to work in the position. Carrie, a recently retired librarian from New England, also chose her position based on location due to family reasons. She described her interview process, giving details about how difficult it might be for a candidate to agree to work in a prison library:

> Well, it's just very difficult because you cannot bring a candidate into the prison unless maybe it's minimum security. I mean, I don't know how other states handle that, but in [*interviewee's state*], you sit before a panel of people and that's how you're interviewed and then you go through a rigorous background check.... I walked into a dungeon, a dungeon for my library.

While Carrie had not singled out prison librarianship as a path during graduate school, she did speak of her previous employment as a prison librarian with a great deal of nostalgia.

## Prior Library Experience

Most, but not all, of the librarians interviewed had prior experience working in another sort of library. Four had worked predominantly in public libraries before transitioning to prison librarianship. One had worked in academic librarianship and another in a school library. Two had worked at a mix of institutions including both academic and public libraries. Three had never worked in a library outside of the prison library. Two of these three had degrees other than the master's in library science; they had graduate degrees in education.

When asked how the environments differed from the other environments these librarians had worked in, the answers varied, but a few key themes emerged. The pressures of regulations and security were mentioned by a few participants. Additionally, the solitary nature of prison librarianship was described by more than a few, not just in response to this question, but as overreaching commentary and in answers to other questions.

In regards to security, Sarah stated that "the most important thing is that everything is secure, it's safe rather than access to library resources." Nora similarly said that "there's a lot more policy and regulations in this job" though she equated the services offered to those offered in a public library. Three librarians talked about being a "solo librarian" in response to this question including Jack, Jennifer, and Sarah. Jack stated: "Here in corrections, we're kind of a one-person show, a one-man show, so to speak. You literally are responsible for everything that surrounds the library and we hire inmate staff/inmate crew to do the work."

Jennifer talked about having peers and mentors at her previous workplace who helped her figure out how to succeed within her environment. She stated:

> I was really mothered by the staff, they helped me figure out what to wear, what not to wear, what to do, you know, how to be a good librarian and so that librarianship in a large library, knowing reference collections really helped once I became a prison librarian because now I have to be everything. I'm the library director, and the library changer, and I have to do all the collection development, I do all of the cataloging and I do all of the jobs. So from that aspect it's a lot like running a very small library, you know, you're the person who's in charge, you have to worry about the carpet getting cleaned and the copier not working as opposed to a big library, you just call somebody and they do those kinds of things and you just do your job.

Sarah mentioned similar aspects of performing her duties as a "solo librarian," admitting there were some challenges transitioning to that type of position. Ultimately though, Sarah claimed that this challenge was also positive: she was often able to make her own decisions without consulting with other librarians.

Jack, who had at least a decade of experience in other types of institutions, expanded upon previous comments about being not only a solo librarian, but also the only paid person in the library:

> I guess the major differences are that in all those other libraries I was working with other paid professionals and in some cases I was a supervisor and in some cases I wasn't. Here I'm the only, effectively the only, paid person. Certainly the only paid professional and the only person who gives a hoot of any sort about the library. My inmate workers are paid 95 cents a day and they almost never come with any type of library experience—they might have some prison experience from another facility but not here. Rarely do they have college education or a degree.

Very few of the respondents had additional paid staff in their library. Most of the librarians were working alone without any support from additional non-inmate staff. Specific details on this will follow in the subsequent section on staffing.

Heather asserted that the main difference between working in public and prison libraries was the environment. She stated:

> You're working with custody officers, people who have been convicted of crimes—some of them violent crimes—but overall they're a very calm group. I personally have not had any unpleasant experiences working

with inmates—anything that was threatening—and I've worked at three different prisons, ... and I haven't had as much trouble with prison public as I have with the public library public. I actually feel safer in prison then I did out in the streets.

Heather was not the only librarian to describe the environment as a safe one; others also confirmed that they felt perfectly safe working within their prison libraries.

Both Alison and Heather mentioned that they still perform reference interviews in a prison setting; this was not something that everyone confirmed as part of their job duties. Alison addressed the differences in intellectual freedom due to the restrictions of the prison setting. She stated:

> As far as the information you can give people—so as I mentioned I have a library science degree. I know one of the major pillars of librarianship is that we give free information to anyone and everyone and we give them the information freely. Here that's not the case so I had to retrain myself in what information they could actually have. And another pillar is separating yourself from the issue and so that is a big thing for me that I still work through on a daily basis. Like if someone comes and asks me a question and I can't give them the answer because of security concerns and I have a basic fundamental understanding of why they can't have it, but at the same time I feel like people should have access to any information that they want to have because that's the way I was trained and that's really what I believe.

Nora also mentioned intellectual freedom stating that the mailroom does not give "a lot of latitude regarding intellectual freedom" when sorting and allowing materials. Jennifer also discussed issues with access to information and misconceptions librarians have who are new to the prison library setting:

> I think many librarians are surprised and bothered when they first start the job on some of the censorship that we have to do. 'Cause, you know, as a librarian it's like free information, let's get you information, as much as you need, especially when I was first in library school, you know, the Internet was just starting to come along and databases and being able to expand and find out all kinds of things. In the prison setting, we do a lot of restrictive kinds of things. I have to be aware of what we buy and what we borrow through interlibrary loan and what we do for prisoners because prisoners use this information in a lot of ways that is really surprising to the public and the amount of danger and contraband and those types of issues are things that the average person doesn't think about in how a library would work in a prison setting.

It was surprising that only a handful of librarians mentioned issues with censorship and intellectual freedom, especially considering how this was interwoven into many of the policies presented in chapters 1 and 2. Certainly many of them talked about selection restrictions and restricted environments, but they did not necessarily focus on censorship or limitations to First Amendment rights.

In Linda's case, as well as others, she had been responsible for setting up the entire prison library. She talked about the challenges of establishing a physical library in her institution, "this was like the Garden of Eden—you just walk in and nothing is named and there's nothing there." Carrie, who did not have previous experience in another type of library, also described building a library from the ground up: "I took pictures of the old library and all of its changes as long as I was there, and believe me, many changes took place."

Many scholars and authors on prison librarianship debate about the prison library being modeled after the public library. Most of these scholars and authors supported the implementation of the public library model. Two of the librarians I spoke to did not view their library as following the public library model, rather they insisted that prison libraries are more of a special library than a public library. Nora, however, did make a point to mention this model when describing the similarities between the prison library and other libraries she had worked in. She stated: "the American Correctional Association, which recertifies us every three years, requires that the prison library be as much like a public library as possible." Her statement implied that the institution itself needed to be recertified every three years, not the individual libraries or librarians. Some interviewees, such as Sarah, established similarities between the work in public and prison libraries, stating that similar issues might be encountered, such as "dealing with, you know, the homeless population, or people with behavioral issues, mental health issues."

## Education

All of the librarians and library staff interviewed had a master's degree of some sort, though not all were required to have a master's degree in library science or any other subject to hold their position. Nine had a master's degree in library science and two had master's degree in education. Nora, Linda, and Sarah all mention that the MLS was not a requirement for their positions. Nora, who thought she might be the only librarian in her state with an MLS, stated "they would like for you to have it, but over the years, before I came, they stuck anybody in the library who wanted the job." Linda also concurred that there was no requirement for an MLS or a master's degree and said that "during the interview I made sure not to mention that." Linda continued to describe her interview process and how she did not highlight her master's degree: "And so during the interview I never talked about library school, I never talked about having a master's degree even though it was on my resume. I talked instead about evidence-based practice, and when I studied the org in the Department of Corrections, I saw again and again how important that was to the direction they want to go."

In other states, the master's degree may have been necessary at one time, but in some states the job titles and descriptions for prison librarians were being modified to allow for less education, and in most cases, less pay. In particular, Jack and Victor talked about the environment in their states, where requirements had been reduced along with the status of the librarian. Other interviewees also expressed hesitation at the state of affairs with the perception of the master's degree, or in some cases the classification of the prison library professional as a whole. This discrepancy is perhaps one of the most poignant examples in the gaps between policy and practice in prison libraries. Many national and even state policies call for a prison librarian to have a master's degree, nevertheless in practice this qualification appears to be on a downtrend. Many states are de-professionalizing the role of the prison librarian by not requiring the education recommended by national policies.

Participants were also queried as to whether an MLS had been a requirement for their positions. Many of the state prisons did require an MLS, but not all of them, and certainly there was no consistency within regions. As mentioned above, Jack and Victor both discussed how the MLS had been required at one time, but how requirements or salary had diminished over the years since they had been hired. Kelly also mentioned that within her state a bachelor's degree was necessary with some library classes, but that an MLS was not required. She said, "we're hoping to change that, but no, it does not require it." Heather also detailed a history of hiring individuals without MLS degrees stating that many of them are "excellent librarians." She also mentioned that the requirements have changed and that "you do have to have some library school under your belt before you're hired, and then you do have to be able to complete your degree."

I also asked interviewees if they felt that their studies, whether in library science or education, prepared them to complete their day-to-day duties as a prison librarian. Alison stated that she learned reference and related skills in library school, but not about the security side of working in a prison library. She mentioned that this should be provided as on-the-job training and not necessarily something handled in the curriculum for an MLS. Jack felt that his MLS degree did help him to feel prepared even though he had not studied prison librarianship during his degree. He talked about coursework in prison librarianship, stating, "I don't recall there being any offered either, but certainly I could have read in the literature about it." Linda discussed the concept of applying the theory from library science curricula to the prison environment from her experiences in graduate school as a student:

> So you see my library science, the students were all complaining about "it's all theory, it's all theory" but they explained to us that you have to be able to understand the theory so that when you go out into the world and the technology changes on you, and all of your tools are changing all the time you have to be able to adapt and that adaptation has to be based on sound theory. So that's what prepared me to work in a prison library. I feel a little bit like, what was that guy's name? Livingston, Dr. Livingston I do presume ... he was a medical doctor and then he went to the Congo? Well I don't know enough about him but ... he just disappeared off the map. And he was a trained medical doctor and somehow he brought medicine and healing and science to the Congo. And he didn't have the tools. So that's sometimes what it's like to be a prison librarian. You have to know the theory to adapt and then you can find the tools and the way to network and collaborate.

Both Jennifer and Carrie talked about the prison environment not being taught in library schools. Carrie stated: "You learned the practical side of librarianship, the book learning so to speak, but to go into a prison library and you basically work alone. There is nobody there to help you." Jennifer also mentioned struggles that new librarians might have in a prison library, stating:

> There's a big gap between what is offered in library schools and what is reality inside a prison. And I talked to many librarians who get started at the job for whatever reason and then just quit because they are either stressed out by their clientele, or stressed out by operating in the kind of restrictions that working in a prison, you know, reporting to a structure and a supervisor that doesn't really know what you do and all they really want is for you to not cause them any problems. So.... That's difficult for a lot of people.

Olivia had an LMS certification rather than an MLS, but also possessed a graduate degree in education. She mentioned the issues that a new prison librarian might have as related to the lack of technology in the prison:

> I mean most library courses today are geared toward making librarians pretty much system managers. Because of the technology. And so I had a lot of that. It was a certification for school librarians and of course schools have moved toward technology, and Internet and computers and helping students navigate that and setting up appropriate firewalls and helping teachers do technological displays. None of that applies here because they're not allowed by [*her state*] law, offenders aren't allowed access to the Internet. It kind of concerns me that anyone coming out of librarian school, any sort, whether it's a certification or a master's, has all this technology under their belt that is pretty much at this point a moot point in prisons. So you have to come into it being really motivated to work with the special population.

Olivia's concern that technology skills would wane once starting in a prison library was something mentioned by other interviewees, which will be discussed more in subsequent sections on technology.

Overall most of the librarians I spoke to had master's degrees in library science; all had master's degrees in either library science or education. This was irrespective of whether or not a master's degree was required for the position within their individual states. Additionally, answers from those with an MLS or MLIS were varied about the preparedness they might have after leaving library school. Some felt very prepared to approach the theoretical and practical tasks at a prison library. Others felt very underprepared, especially for the environmental and cultural change of working in a prison library.

## Professional Development and Networking

Interviewees were asked if they were members of any professional associations. Seven out of 11 were not current members of any national or state professional associations, though one mentioned that she would like to join the Special Libraries Association (SLA). Victor, who was not a member of any associations, expressed disappointment that he had not really been able to participate in associations due to lack of institutional support. He stated: "A prison librarian is somewhat not supported into their endeavors to participate in groups outside of the prison structure." Other librarians who do not have current memberships stated that they had been in ALA at one point in time. Two stated that they are not sure how joining those professional associations might bring them value; Kelly, for instance, said, "I don't feel that they do a lot to serve me or represent me" and had let her memberships lapse. Jack was a member of his state association only. Sarah was a member of both ALA and her state association; she also considered joining the Correctional Education Association. Carrie and Nora both maintained memberships in organizations as well. Carrie was a member of ALA and SLA while Nora was a member of ALA, the National Education Association, and the National Association of Social Workers. So out of 11 interviewees, only four had memberships to associations and three of these had multiple memberships.

In regards to staying abreast of professional development via publications, few had the time to keep up with the literature and most did not have budgets to purchase any sort of materials to support their work in the prison library. A few mentioned the ALA prison listserv as a resource they frequently read. Carrie lamented that not enough is written about "what it's like to be a prison librarian" and wished more people were publishing. Alison acknowledged the challenges with working alone, having a lot of responsibility, and finding the time to invest in professional development: "I have to do everything, so there's honestly not a lot of time for professional development. In my institution or my organization they— I don't want to say that they don't support professional development—but it has to come out of your own pocket. And so you get to be really choosy about what you want to do and what you have time to do."

A few of the interviewees mentioned correctional publications, many of which were purchased by their institutions. Others cited state resources or newsletters that were distributed within their institutions. Linda talked about *Corrections Today* as a publication that she had frequently read in the past, however found that the discourse in the magazine had become less rehabilitative in nature: "Now it's been taken over by the knuckle draggers and they're all talking about great equipment like Tasers and stuff like that. And then tirades about how soft the prisons have become on prisoners and, oh man, it's become so discouraging I stopped reading it."

Respondents generally did not have the time or the resources to do much reading beyond listservs and when they did, often the publications were on corrections topics, rather than librarianship. A few who had ALA memberships also mentioned receiving and reading *Library Journal* with many acknowledging how little information was applicable to them from such publications.

As part of my research, I also did a cursory web search of those I interviewed to determine whether or not they were involved in publishing or presenting at conferences. I found that participation in publishing was limited. Two had published articles in either library science journals or corrections trade publications. One had written public opinion pieces on prison librarianship and another authored a book review on an unrelated topic. Two of the librarians were mentioned by name in articles on librarianship. Another had clearly given presentations at regional and national levels. Overall though, most were not publishing or presenting frequently.

Opportunities to network with other library professionals were scarce on a day-to-day basis, though many of the interviewees did have chances to network at association meetings, conferences, and training sessions. Jennifer, who was a senior librarian within her state, invited new prison librarians to visit her facility to get an idea of what her day-to-day work entailed. Carrie talked about meetings and networking between librarians in her state through informal, sometimes social gatherings. Most had some sort of in-state network whether through local colleagues, state meetings, email correspondence with other prison librarians in local prisons, local listservs, etc. Olivia and Jack both discussed the demise of some networking opportunities due to budget cuts. Jack mentioned that due to organizational changes, the previous meetings were not happening anymore. He stated: "So it's kind of just like unintentional mission drift. You go for months and months and months without talking to people. Or, in this case, we go years without meeting. Everybody kind of goes off on your own direction in many ways, out of necessity. Out of what is being asked of you by your institution. By your population." Olivia also mentioned the cutting of in-state meetings as an unfortunate consequence of budget circumstances. She talked about a yearly meeting that had allowed for networking between presentations and at lunch that no longer existed.

Those who were able to network with other professionals either in-state or out-of-state did feel that these kinds of interactions were helpful. Heather, who had come into the prison library from a public library, described how her interactions with other local prison librarians had helped her assimilate to her job:

> When you're new they're very helpful because there's nothing to orient you. I mean they throw you into the job and it's like here's the lights, here's the key. And they kind of do that with public libraries, but you're working in a building with more people so you always have a little support staff. And here you're kind of working alone, so they really don't help you with that too much.

Jennifer also discussed how interacting with other peers had helped her find new solutions or approach tasks differently, especially if she met those peers outside of her institution. She stated that this distance helps her think about her job more critically.

When asked about professional development in the form of conferences, training, webinars, or other events, most talked about local training organized by the prison. Few were going to national conferences—only three mentioned attending a national conference and only one of those three was funded by the institution to attend. Others attended state conferences when possible both financially and in terms of covering shifts. Jack described this well:

> They don't exclude the prison libraries, it's just that there's so few of us and we're so sequestered, that it's really … it takes a great deal of initiative of the part of the prison librarian. In addition to that, if we close—

if I close, if I'm gone because I'm going to training, we probably don't have a substitute—so if I close the library closes. And that has, you know, internal impacts, of providing access to inmates—so you always have to balance that against the service.

One librarian talked about attending an ASCLA online course on correctional librarianship. There was an asynchronous course offered by ASCLA in March and April 2015 on correctional librarianship, as well as another course on portrayals of prison in juvenile literature.[5] Another interviewee emailed a link to me after the interview, which led to a webinar on what kinds of programs public libraries and prisons were offering, both collaborative or individual.[6] Many of the interviewees mentioned general training, security training, and CPR training as programs that they attended within their institution or which were sponsored by their institution. Two talked about motivational interviewing seminars that were helpful for dealing with incarcerated patrons. A few also described educational seminars organized by education departments for their staff; many of these librarians fell under the supervision of an education program. LexisNexis and law library training was also mentioned since many facilities have stringent requirements for providing access to legal materials. Some states had minimum requirements for professional development activities to warrant re-certification of the librarian.

I was also interested in knowing whether the institutions were providing support for professional development activities such as reimbursements or time off. Of the 11 interviewees, three were reimbursed and received time off for professional development activities. One was reimbursed sometimes and received time off depending on the budget that year. Three received paid time off, but had to pay their own expenses. Four did not receive reimbursements or time off, so were taking vacation days to attend conferences or meetings.

Nora felt that lack of support for these kinds of activities was because "there's really nobody to take my place if I'm gone." Nora participated in local activities instead. Victor stated that prior to bad budgetary years, he could attend an event yearly, but time off and paid trips had been eliminated when the budgets had become scarcer. Linda claimed that she is not supported because the institution does not care about the library. Jack acknowledged that while he may not receive a lot of support, this type of support varied from institution to institution. He said that some institutions provide exceptional support, whereas in others "we don't get a dime. They almost view us as being, you know, an unwanted appendage." Jennifer stated that her situation varies depending on budget restrictions or the event she wanted to attend. She mentioned that sometimes she has had everything paid for, sometimes certain things were paid for, and sometimes she only received time off. She also stated that "it depends on what it is that you're going to do and how you can sell it to your supervisor as being important for what you're going to learn." Alison received paid time off, but stated that she did not often ask for the time off since she carefully vetted different professional development opportunities and was selective about what she tried to get pre-approved by her administration.

## Staffing

Staffing recommendations are presented in the ASCLA standards and in many of the standards discussed in chapter 1. Based on responses to the survey from the last chapter and interviews in this chapter, it seems unlikely that many institutions are following suggested staffing recommendations. Nine out of 11 librarians were a one-man show at least in terms of paid, non-prisoner staff. Only two institutions had multiple librarians and in both of these cases, the librarians were serving multiple campuses. One interviewee mentioned that he had a "backup librarian" who could fill in for him when he was absent. This backup librarian was a part-time employee who was on call as needed. One library had a volunteer who ran a listening lab with media such as CDs, DVDs, etc. Most of the librarians had inmate clerks who worked for the library and some had more support or prisoner staffing than others. A few interviewees insinuated that they have to push administration to get continued prisoner staffing at the levels that are useful for them.

## Collection Development

Interview participants provided a lot of detail about their collection development and selection procedures. I was not specifically asking about censorship policies or items that might be restricted, as I had already addressed that in the prior survey, which all the interviewees completed. Instead, I asked them to describe how they would go about selecting materials. In a few cases, these descriptions were hypothetical: seven of the librarians had no budgets to work with and either had to work with donations or try to find community partnerships to get materials.

A few librarians discussed their regular procedures for selecting materials. Most talked about stocking the library with popular materials. Kelly followed reviews on the *New York Times*, *NPR*, in official library publications, or other websites but also considered what the prisoners liked to read. She stated:

> It's a combination of, you know, keeping up with the stuff everybody wants to read, so every frigging book that James Patterson publishes gets purchased, much to my chagrin. And obviously there are other authors that are incredibly popular. And putting in things that I think people would like even though it might be a lesser known author, but I'll say, "Oh, this person's kind of like that person, I think people here will like it." Trying to fill in some gaps in the collection.

Alison also mentioned that popular series were well read. She talked about James Patterson as well as other authors including John Grisham and Dan Brown. Because of the popularity of some of these books, she maintained extras to swap out when damages occur. Alison also detailed a partnership with a state community organization where she received free books:

> So they have it open for me and it's almost like free shopping. I just go in there and I go through the books and I get what I want. They usually ask me for a list of what I want and they try to collect in the areas of what I want before I come in and they also ask for things that I don't want so they don't waste their time getting those books out. So if I'm like, oh, you know, last time I really needed a lot of westerns that just is kind of fizzled out, I don't need any westerns right now. They help me with that.

Olivia also mentioned a non-profit organization that she worked with to get donated materials. This organization also allowed her to suggest certain materials she would like them to purchase.

Many of the librarians I spoke to and some of the survey respondents indicated that they did not have a budget from which to buy materials and had to rely on donations. These donations came from outside sources such as organizations and non-profits, from prisoners, and sometimes from commercial stores. Jack talked about a hypothetical situation if he were to have a budget. He took prisoner requests for books and kept those requests in a folder, so he would review those requests if he were to have a small budget. He stated:

> If I did get money, these days it would just be a few hundred dollars—maybe $500. What are you going to do with $500? I would look around for some really cheap law materials that would be useful. Like, take for instance, if I could find a decent $10- or $20-law dictionary, I would be inclined to buy a few of those. I would—if I could find a cheap set of a popular trilogy that was out. For instance, *Hunger Games* when it was popular. If I had some money I would've bought a set of those. So to some degree I try to go with the popular stuff, because the truth is you don't have any money and when stuff is popular it tends to cost more.

Carrie talked about getting donations from local stores, specifically Barnes & Noble, where she is a frequent customer. She said, "I'm like a bull in a china shop" and "you have to beg, borrow, and steal." Carrie detailed the connections she had made with local businesses and how these connections helped her to get donated materials, particularly books. She acknowledged that occasionally she was given a budget for purchasing books, but normally she would have to build her collection with donations.

Librarians in these institutions were most often selecting based on their local population. Olivia, who worked in an institution with female offenders, described the types of materials she included most often in the collection:

> I gear myself to female—at least in non-fiction—to psychology, a lot of recovery materials, a lot of materials relating to domestic abuse, trauma, suicide, sexual abuse, health, yoga, a lot of the Dummies books. I get tons of the Idiots' Guides, Dummies, because they're just perfect for this population—the way they're laid out. Dealing with personal finances, things they need to know when they're going to be released, everything that can prepare them for successful release, books that because they're not exposed to technology keep them abreast of, you know, what an iPhone is, how to use the Internet, what Facebook is, what Twitter is. They're really interested in that sort of thing. As far as fiction goes, they just—what's popular is what's new. They're all into the vampire novels, the shape shifters, all that paranormal stuff. They love that. They like urban books. I get a select number of those, not a lot but I get some. They like some of the Christian urban. They like the Amish books, the Christian books, they like detective, thriller … and then just whatever is popular fiction, what appears in magazines as the newest thing, they like that.

At Heather's institution she acquired recreational reading materials based on prisoner requests and previous usage. She listed popular genres as fantasy, sci-fi, thrillers, military fiction, and westerns. She mentioned that her state Department of Corrections maintains a list of restricted titles and subjects, but stated: "that's not a big issue, it's pretty much what's prohibited in public libraries although it's a bit stricter."

Jennifer provided details about how she administered an annual library survey with the prisoners in her institution. She also maintained a suggestion box in multiple library locations. She mentioned that there is a "policy that prohibits certain materials for prisoners that depict crimes against minors and depict escape." Sarah also talked about administrative concerns with certain types of materials, especially non-fiction materials such as true crime books. She stated that her predecessor had not collected true crime books, however, under new administration, she had been able to collect and circulate these types of books when donated. Linda also listed true crime books as controversial, stating that her institution would not add those types of books to the collection, but that prisoners could purchase true crime as well as urban fiction, if the books were received in accordance with mailroom policies.

A few of the interviewees mentioned issues with damaged books when the materials included pictures of the female form. Specifically, prisoners had cut out graphics and images in books that they collected. Sarah explained:

Another issue that I hadn't thought of before I started working in prison libraries is that if they like the pictures, a lot of times they'll just cut out the picture from the book, so just being aware that that can happen. So I do have books in my office that they can check out, but they check them out through special permission and check and make sure all the pictures are there when the book comes back and if anything's missing then that person can't check them out again.

Nora also addressed the topic of restricting materials, but detailed her interactions with her internal affairs group who manage the mailroom staff. She stated that she had correspondence with her internal affairs group every other month or so discussing denials of certain materials. She said, "some things I know they're not going to allow. Other times I'll call them and get a definite answer on it so that we're going to be on the same page."

## Library Services to Segregated Units and Restricting Access to Library Materials

The ASCLA standards, other national standards, and many of the individual states' policies on library services define the necessary level of service to prisoners in segregation or other restricted units. I asked the interviewees how they were providing services to prisoners in such situations. Most of the collections offered to segregation unit prisoners were collections specifically for those units. Many interviewees mentioned that the books they distributed in these units were paperback, even though they might have hardcover books in the regular library collection. Carrie detailed a process in which the correctional officers took around a book cart weekly to those in segregation and allowed prisoners to take out two to three books. She said that she never expected to receive the books back. Nora also mentioned that the segregation unit in her institution had its own collection, which was wheeled around on a cart and consisted only of paperback books. She visited the unit weekly to confirm that the collection was sufficient, to take back any items for repair, and to see if the prisoners in those units required books on particular subjects. Jack also described a system that included a book cart of recreational reading materials combined with a paging system where materials were delivered via the institutional mail. He also visited the prisoners within the segregation unit to get requests in person, since "you're kind of relying on someone to express themselves in writing, which you can never count on here." Kelly also described a cart system with paperbacks, however, stated "now I have heard tale that in some buildings they ... stick their hand out the little trap door and they grab a book and that's the book they get." She stated that she did not have any immediate contact with prisoners in the segregation units, but did try to give them some variety. She stated that she boxed up books, which were sent over to segregation units.

Linda talked more about the content of the books that she provided to prisoners in segregation:

And the other thing is in segregation, I've read up about it.... The first three days are pretty okay but after the third day it's hard to concentrate. You think you'd be able to, but apparently it's really hard to concentrate and so guys need to have high powered, plot-driven books and graphic novels. And so I was trying to keep it supplied with graphic novels. Because also if it's on the units they'll all be destroyed and stolen. So any graphic novel that I've gotten a hold of, which is hard to get from a public library and also the guys seldom donate those, but anytime I was able to get some, I would put them on segregation...

In most of the interviews, interviewees viewed the collections that were offered to their prisoners in segregation as less popular, enticing, or complete as those they have in their general libraries. Many of these restrictions seemed to be security based—most were only able to circulate paperback books. In other cases, it appeared that there simply was not enough funding to go around to provide quality materials to prisoners in general population as well as segregated units.

I was also interested in understanding when access to library materials might be restricted and if these restrictions were generally library or administration initiated. The answer to this was ambiguous and depended on the institution. Some institutions restricted library access only when the prisoner had violated library policy while others restricted the privilege to general library access when a prisoner had disciplinary problems.

In Nora's institution, access to the general library could be restricted for six months if the prisoner violated library policy, but she said that that rarely happened. Olivia also had library initiated restrictions if prisoners frequently checked out books and lost them. She mentioned that prisoners often passed around the books and if there was a pattern she would restrict access only to the most popular, newer books, which tended to be urban fiction. Jennifer talked about restricting access to books to give prisoners incentives to be respectful and responsible:

> I use that as my incentive to be a good library user and to encourage them to take responsibility for themselves. I mean, you know you borrowed the book, don't borrow more books than you can read in the time frame you have them. You're responsible for the book you borrowed, you need to return it. Books belong to everybody, you can't take the pages out of them or write gang signs in them.

Sarah also restricted access to books if needed. She mentions two contexts in which a prisoner might have restricted access. The first instance was for segregated prisoners, who were not permitted to come to the library in her institution. In the case of these prisoners, she generally still provided a collection of uncatalogued books for leisure reading. For prisoners who were permitted to come to the library, she restricted access for those who had stolen books and been caught or those who had many overdue books.

Jack said that access can be restricted by the library, but that often there is no pay-off to punishing a prisoner this way:

> One obvious way is if they are "in violation of library policy," but that becomes kind of a balancing act, severity vs. output of effort. Let me give you an example. Somebody has overdue materials. They refuse to turn them back in. It's a long road to actually get money back and it requires a lot of paperwork. And in the process, you agitate the inmate and the money if it's gained in compensation for the material doesn't actually come back to me. I always hesitate to go all the way down that road unless I have to because, to me, it's a lose-lose situation. The inmate loses money, assuming he even has any, I've pissed him off, and I don't get the book or the money. So it's the last thing I try to do is to go down that particular road. You know, you're always weighing the benefits of enforcing the policy against any particular inmate. I mean, what good does it do to restrict this guy from reading material when he's got a thousand days on confinement? Is he the type of person who would steal the book? Does he have a record that suggests that type of behavior? What are his other infractions over the course of time? You know, there's just so many factors. I'm always trying to, especially on confinement, trying to get them reading material. One thing that might surprise you is that if you could imagine a tier of cells, the books that these guys might get from me are shared around, they're passed around. And yes, I can hold them responsible for these things and I do, but you also have to remember your main mission down there. And just then by virtue of having something additional to do for their 23 out of 24 hours of confinement, I believe, strongly, pays benefits not necessarily to just me in the long run because this guy's going to get off seg and end up back in my library, but it's all part of doing things to help keep the peace and keep the chatter down and keep things as calm as possible.

Other interviewees also discussed whether or not there was a benefit to restricting library access for prisoners if they have violated library policy. A few of the interviewees asserted that access is seldom, if ever, restricted to legal collections, due to mandated access to the courts. Some of these librarians were managing both the general library collection and the law library collection. There was—similarly to the previous chapter's survey responses— not a lot of consistency in regards to who managed these services among the interviewees.

Other interviewees mentioned that the institution had the power to restrict library access as part of disciplinary procedures. Victor talked about prisoners in segregation or "disciplinary confinement" who can only have access to either legal or religious materials. Carrie stated that those on suicide watch might be restricted from using the library or library materials, but that otherwise the only restrictions were on those in segregation. This limitation was interesting; in many cases library materials are touted to have therapeutic purposes, both by practitioners and in the literature. The fact that access would be restricted for someone on suicide watch seems counterintuitive in this context. In Alison's institution, the general library was considered a privilege. She stated: "If they've had discipline problems, they can lose privileges and they can lose privileges across the board. And that includes recreation time, library time, that kind of thing. So they can lose library time just for discipline outside the library."

There was no clear consistency regarding policies for restricting library access, rather it seemed to be determined on an institution-by-institution basis with some restricting for library infractions, some for disciplinary actions, and some for both reasons. One respondent talked about limiting access to the library based on actions within the library; in her institution she dealt with "inappropriate touching" in the library and was concerned that the library might develop a reputation as the place where prisoners can "hook-up."

## Collaborating with Outside Institutions

I was interested in understanding whether these prison librarians were collaborating with outside institutions, either to access interlibrary loan services or for partnerships such as event programming in the prison, regular donation services, educational programs, etc. Five of the librarians did not participate in interlibrary loan; one mentioned that his institution had previously been in a state network, but no longer had access. The remaining six had access to interlibrary loan services with various levels of usage. Victor asked his prisoners requesting books through interlibrary loan to give him 10 to 15 choices of materials they would like to receive so that he could at least deliver one of them. He said that normally he was able to receive one in eight requests and had about six to ten books that were received monthly. The reason he gave for only being able to fulfill one in eight requests was the outdatedness of the collections he was able to get from the local library. These collections, because of limited budgets at the local libraries, often did not include the newest fiction that prisoners were requesting. Nora provided more detail about those who used her interlibrary loan services:

> It just complements what we don't have. The majority of our inmates don't have that much reading skill, so I have some that can't read at all. Occasionally we'll have one or two with a master's degree. So, and they're like the general public, their interests span everything. I have one right now who's really into farming books.

And I have a few, but I've gotten several more for him. And then those that are taking college classes at night, they'll come and I'll help them find things that will be suitable for their research.

Jennifer also fulfilled requests for interlibrary loan materials and received these materials from two local libraries and other local prison facilities. Two librarians mentioned that interlibrary loan was not heavily used. Heather stated, "it's not really something they rely on. If it was something they needed, we definitely would get it for them." Olivia also provided interlibrary loan services to her patrons, but said that it was very ad hoc and often just something they borrow from a local library or local prison to support specific educational needs of individual prisoners.

Within these discussions about interlibrary loan, a few mentioned funding for interlibrary loan. Heather had access to an interlibrary loan program, but was not using it heavily. She mentioned that prisoners had to pay for interlibrary loan of legal materials. Nora claimed that she tried to find free opportunities for interlibrary loan. Otherwise, none of the participants addressed the issues with determining who would pay for interlibrary loan services, especially when prisoners with low hourly salaries were asked to pay for these services.

In regards to collaborating with outside organizations on other services, the results were very similar. Six had partnerships with outside organizations or individuals to provide either event programming or to get donations. Five did not have any such partnerships. Alison talked about a book club that is offered within her institution. This was in addition to a state non-profit that she worked with to get donated books. Kelly recruited volunteers for book discussion groups on an ad hoc basis. She also talked about educational programs offered such as basic education, GED programs, and classes offered through a local community college that would allow a prisoner to earn an associate's degree. Linda described a program much like the "Read to Me" programs in chapter 7, in which prisoners can record stories for their children. Linda also accepted books from a local community college and facilitated a reading competition within her institution in partnership with a public library. Olivia worked with a state non-profit that provided books to prisoners. She was able to make requests for popular materials. Sarah, who had been in her position for under two years, was interested in implementing more programs and was starting to investigate opportunities. She received donations from bookstores and was investigating a national program that might donate books to her institution. Jack also received donations from local community colleges and libraries but did not have partnerships beyond book donations.

Two of the participants who did not have partnerships with outside organizations to provide services or materials talked about the difficulties of such partnerships. Victor stated:

That's pretty difficult to do in a prison setting. I wish we had access ... we do have the right to bring in speakers, interested parties of that nature, but there's not that many people out there in the real world that want to come in and do that. In my nine years, I don't think that I've had anybody that has taken advantage of that. The religious area, yes, but not the library.

Heather discussed issues with trying to get volunteers security clearance to her institution since the prison ran background checks on those who were visiting the facility. She mentioned that a workshop for a legal issue or family law questions would be valuable for her prisoners, yet the challenge was trying to provide those kinds of service without actually having the volunteers offer legal advice. She stated, "it's hard to work with outside organizations. They can't really come into the facility to work with us." Jennifer mentioned that they had previous partnerships to borrow legal materials from her state law library, but that that service was no longer in operation.

## Technology

Computer skills are a concern for prisoners who have been incarcerated as technology advances, especially because many prisoners are likely to be released and may have poor computer skills that prevent them from finding employment. Because of the dichotomy between the importance of reducing the digital divide and the restrictions on technology mentioned by the survey respondents, it was important to explore how many institutions were offering some sort of computer access within their institutions. Nine of the 11 interviewed allowed prisoners to have direct access to computers, however, all of them were restricted to certain applications or services. Nora and Sarah only offered access to the library catalog and holdings on their computers. Five of the librarians offered computer access in connection with legal law library requirements. Victor, Heather, and Jennifer all offered some access to computerized databases such as Westlaw or LexisNexis. Carrie allowed prisoners to listen to legal transcripts on laptops in the library and her prisoner clerks were permitted to use the computers for circulation transactions. Linda also offered access to legal materials via library computers and prisoners were allowed to have USB drives. Jack and Olivia were the only two who offered access to additional educational services. In Olivia's institution, the law library was separate from the general library, but they still offered educational software and programs on the computers in the general library. She stated:

> We have about, I think, it's five or six in the library and what they have on them is educational software. I have Microsoft Encarta, which gives them a little bit of feel for the Internet because it contains links. It has a typing program on it. It has all the applications that they can fool with. But the only thing I'm allowed to print is school related work. They can't write personal letters and have me print them. They can't write legal letters in this library, they have to go to the legal library which is separate from me ... but they do have computers they can use and the college students do use them to print their papers—to produce their papers and I print those.

Jack mentioned a number of services offered in his library. Legal materials were included in his library, so the prisoners had access to a law database as well as standalone legal content that he transferred to the computers using a USB drive. He also stated that they had word processing software, typing tutors, programs with information about commercial drivers' licenses, Microsoft Encarta and WorldBook. He also saw value in training his inmate clerks to be computer literate: "I've made it my point to involve all of my library workers, my library aides, to use computers in some way shape or form. So they perform tasks at least some of which require all of them to use computers."

Even though none of these institutions mentioned above offer Internet access in their institutions, some of the librarians mentioned initiatives to bring more technology to the prisoners. Linda stated that prisoners are permitted to have MP3s and that her Department of Corrections preferred offering access to MP3s over CDs because of security concerns.

In Olivia's institution and state, she noticed a trend toward providing more online services to prisoners. She mentioned the implementation of kiosks in units, which allowed prisoners to download music. She discussed the potential additional services that her Department of Corrections may offer to their prisoners and the caveats of offering those services:

And, I think, just recently they are going to move towards—and this is all controlled on the units—email, some email access to accounts that are setup with specific people just like how they have a visitors list. Nobody except those people on the list can visit them. They will have an email list and they can only email those people. I think that DOCs across the country are seeing the value of that technology because it can reduce cost—it can reduce the need for mail room personnel. And no contraband can ride in on an email, so you know, I think they're seeing certain advantages to that technology. And I think that's a good thing. On the other hand, I would like to say, I think some of these are privatized concerns. These inmates don't get that downloaded music for free. And what they have to pay for it is just crazy as compared to you and I using iTunes. I can't give you exact figures, but there is an increasing privatization of some of these things that I think is what you and I would consider a rip-off and that concerns me. It's just like the food they buy on canteen. You know the most they ever make is 65 cents an hour—that's like a great job within the prison. Most of them earn more like 35 or 40 cents an hour doing their prison jobs or money that's put on their account, yet all the items on their canteen cost as much as you and I would buy it at a grocery store. A can of tuna or a candy bar or what have you ... that bugs me. You got what I'm saying? People are making money off people who have nothing.

Olivia was the only respondent to acknowledge or discuss the growing privatization of many prison services and the disadvantages that privatization had for prisoners in her institution.

In two institutions, prisoners had no direct access to computers. In Alison's institution, she answered reference questions using a computer, but the individual prisoner was not permitted to access a computer in her library. She was the only person in the library with Internet access, which was locked in her office. She stated, "they can't touch the computer. They can't even really be in here when I'm on the Internet." Kelly also mentioned an initiative within her organization to purchase computers, which were unfortunately deemed a security risk and never implemented. In interviews with librarians, it was evident that many of them acknowledged the problems that lack of access to technology is creating for their prisoners, especially upon release into a digitally literate world.

Alison talked about additional initiatives to incorporate more technology in the prison. She mentioned kiosks that her institution was interested in investigating and possibly purchasing. She described the kiosks as having access to a suite of services including Westlaw and access to other legal materials, commissary shopping, and capability of handling Skype-like video visitation. When asked what she thought about that initiative, she stated:

I think it's great, I want them to have it. I want them to have access to technology because, you know, as I talk to some of the guys here—they don't know how to use the Internet. They don't know how to use the computer. And so, you know, our job is to prepare them go out in the world and be a law-abiding citizen and not to come back and that's really hard when you don't know how to use the Internet and you don't know how to use a computer 'cause if you go to, I don't know, Walmart for example to apply for a job, they set you at a computer—you don't fill out an application. And so there's a gap there. But filling in that gap is a challenge because there's a whole security side to it too.

Alison did not discuss what implications this technology might have for actual in-person visitations, rather she was excited by the opportunities that prisoners might have to learn computer skills. Alison's comments reassert the desperate need for improving digital literacy skills of prisoners; legal database access or access to gated services is not sufficient to address the skills that many prisoners are lacking upon release if they cannot use a computer or assess online information critically.

Many interviewees also discussed the lack of technology having a negative impact not only on the incarcerated, but also on the non-prisoner individuals working in prison library positions. Carrie said that "in prison you don't have computers, so it's almost like if you don't use it, you lose it." Heather also acknowledged a disadvantage for new prison librarians, who may forget many of their technology skills once working in a prison library. She stated: "That, I think, is the biggest obstacle for the new librarians coming in. That they won't be able to use half of what they learned in school in terms of technology." Olivia also echoed these sentiments, stating that "I do fear people will ... not be attracted to it because of the dearth of technology."

## Interacting with Administration

A theme that continued to emerge throughout the interviews, especially in the interviews with prison librarians who had been in the institution for many years, was the importance of the administration's support to ensure enough funding, support, and attention to the prison library. Carrie, who had been through six or seven superintendents over the course of 15 years, stated: "If you do not have your administration's full support that gives you the autonomy that one needs to be a great prison librarian, who is dedicated to deliver the absolute best library services you possibly can in that environment and under the law and giving them what they're entitled to, then ... you really are a loner." Carrie also discussed the challenges of being a woman in corrections along with the attitude of some administrators that libraries are not important. She stated, "certain administrators that believe that women don't belong in corrections, number one, or that, what the heck, what they hell do they [the prisoners] have to read for?"

Many of the librarians I spoke to had limited interactions with administration within their prison, seeing them only on occasion or when an issue needed to be resolved. Linda detailed the isolation between everyone in the institution as an experience shared by many prison librarians. She mentioned that she might see a correctional officer walk through her prison library twice daily. She also talked about the difficulties of being isolated from your coworkers:

> Because of the hierarchical structure as well as the isolation of everyone from each other, there's a tendency for rumor and gossip to have a very common place in all corrections and it's very distressing because it can destroy your reputation. I think it has to do with the culture of black and white thinking and how severe the culture is between this is ok and this is not ok. So, there's not very much forgiveness if you make a mistake and there are stereotypical boxes that people can find themselves in.

Linda also discussed how she has learned that effectiveness within her job and in her institution depends largely on being able to communicate with her manager.

Most others reported positive and cordial relationships with their administration. Victor attributed this to the individual librarian's personality and ability to get along with other people. He stated:

> The relationship between a program staff, such as library and security staff, will be based upon the personality of the program staff person and in my case I'm very bubbly and outgoing and they have a tendency to like that, to enjoy that, so my relationship with them has been very good over the years. Somebody who comes in and has a negative personality in that job, or has a more firm personality, more abrupt personality, they're going to go crossways with security real quick. Somebody who doesn't like to follow rules is going to go crossways with them very quickly. Me, I take it as an act of God when they tell me something and they like that, so I follow their directions as if I have no alternative. If I have a beef I handle it privately. It seems to meet their needs, their egos, very successfully. It would depend upon the person who's running the library; everyone will be different.

Kelly mentioned the personalities of the administration as also indicative of what kind of interactions she will have with them. She described two extremes of personalities: those who "don't care about anything" and those who are "controlling of the minutia of the library." She summarized this as "it's either completely lackadaisical, don't care, or completely 'I run this space and I don't care who you are or what you do, I will control how it's run.'" Jennifer talked about keeping her administration informed about issues that might be problematic. She stated that "some bosses want to know before you do something. Some bosses don't want to know, but they also don't want to ... be surprised." She claimed to have adapted her behavior based on the types of administration she has dealt with.

Generally speaking, few librarians I spoke to talked about major issues with their administration. Many adjusted their behavior based on the personalities and management styles of those in positions of power. All appeared to respect the decisions of the administration with a few willing to speak up when they felt the need to fight for the library. Most described cordial interactions that happen infrequently due to the isolating circumstances of the institutions.

## General Comments about Prison Librarianship and Prisons

At the conclusion of each interview, I asked participants if they had any additional comments to add about their experiences working in a prison library. Most of the interviewees talked about general overreaching themes and misconceptions about their profession, some told stories about specific prisoners, and a few talked about the solitude of their job.

A few mentioned skewed perceptions about prison libraries, especially by librarians who might otherwise have considered a career opportunity in a prison library. Carrie talked about the problem of not including correctional librarianship as part of the curriculum in library schools. She described the reading levels of prisoners and their challenges with literacy. She also talked about how rewarding it had been for her to help prisoners get access to reading materials and improve their literacy. She characterized the hiring process as disadvantageous for attracting candidates because those candidates often were not able to see where they would be working until their first day of work and must go through a vigorous panel interview and background check.

Jennifer also discussed the difficulties of working in a prison and encouraged those interested in the profession to visit someone in a prison library and shadow them. Despite the solitary nature of the job, she stated that librarians interested in these careers had to have social skills:

> Many people who go into librarianship somehow think they're going to go sit in a corner and read a book. We have to be able to go out there and talk to people. And the thing is, prisoners can be really difficult clients because they're angry, because they're used to intimidation and you know this scaring people and so somebody can really play into their own fears. And without feeling real confident that you are aware of what you can and can't do. And being willing to talk to prisoners. You can't hide in your office and not tell the prisoners, "No, you can't get this." And "No, that's not what policy says." And "Yes, you can have this." You have to be fair.

Some institutions seemed to allow visitors periodically in their prison libraries, whereas others closed access. For instance, it is unlikely that Carrie would have been able to have someone shadow her in her institution to get an idea of whether or not the career would be an appealing one. Heather mentioned the importance of understanding the physical environment and not being scared of working in a prison. She described her library as being filled with at least ten people regularly as well as having correctional officers within earshot. She stated that many librarians may be hesitant to pursue careers in corrections because of safety, but that these fears are unfounded.

Heather spoke the most highly of the job as compared to a public library job she had previously. She talked about job security and reaching the underserved people of the community in a way that wasn't possible in a public library. She also talked about the positive challenges that she had in her career, citing that as a potential attractor to those wishing to make a difference. She also felt safer in a prison library than she did working in a public library. She asserted that most prisoners are respectful and that it was possible to work through a difficult interaction with a patron in a prison library much more easily than with one in a public library.

Sarah called herself the "book shepherd" who forwarded books to other state institutions. She mentioned one of the biggest challenges was getting books back from prisoners. She shared some strategies she learned from other local prison librarians to encourage prisoners to return materials including the threat of a cell search. She viewed her job very positively, mostly because she felt that she had a supportive supervisor and coworkers, which, according to her, made a job more tolerable regardless of whether or not she was working in a prison. She talked about being disconnected from the outside world, "because I can't bring in my cell phone. I can't get on Facebook and tell people what I'm doing." Despite the solitude she still felt that she has "the best job in the prison. I don't have to talk to them about their problems or what brought them to prison. I just talk about books."

All participants alluded to or mentioned solitude as something they dealt with regularly working in a prison. As mentioned under the staffing section, most of these librarians were working as one-man shows within their libraries. Alison described her sense of isolation in the most detail:

> We're very isolated. In my department there's other teachers—and there's multiple teachers—but there's no other librarians, no other library staff, so and in one respect that's good because you can only get mad at yourself if something doesn't go right but on the other hand, you're by yourself and there's just not enough time. Like I mean if there's something super pressing or I'm not really sure about this, I will email a colleague or email our central offices and ask our person that's over there for libraries.... But the day-to-day like, oh, did this get done or collaborating in this, or did you see this article on this librarian blog or anything like that, it just doesn't happen because we're just so isolated. It is what it is. I guess when this facility opened ... there were multiple librarians or multiple library staff. I believe there's always just been one librarian and I'm going to call the librarian the person with the master's in library science. But there was support staff and as they left or retired they were just never replaced. And so now here we are and there's just one of us. So I would say isolation is something that I just never even considered would be an issue but it's just a very different experience than the other library experiences that I've had as far as the isolation.

While almost all interviewees mentioned isolation in some form, some saw the isolation as positive as well. Many had more authority to make their own decisions than they would have had in another library setting. Most seemed to view the isolating conditions as the most challenging part of working in a prison library.

Multiple interviewees also talked about working with prisoners, even telling stories about some of their experiences. Carrie discussed the growing population in prisons and the need for communities to be ready to support them upon their release. She said, "pretty soon they're gonna outnumber the people that are walking the streets." She touted the library as the "information center" that can help them have continued access to information in the outside world. She acknowledged that prisoners have committed serious crimes, nevertheless, that her role was not to pass judgment, but to correct behavior so that prisoners could be successfully released to their communities after parole.

Jennifer talked about the frustrations of dealing with prisoners who often have not been good at following rules. She said that "most people don't know anything about the law until you come in conflict with it." Jennifer found the job to be difficult at times because of frustrated prisoners, but that being "firm but fair" was the successful way to deal with this kind of population. Carrie similarly talked about the need to maintain a sense of order in the prison library in order to garner respect from prisoners:

> We are not behind a glass shield ... they come to the library in the flesh, they're there. You have 60 odd people: inmates, serial killers, rapists, child molesters, murderers, armed robbers—they're all sitting in your library. I mean, I was never behind a cage. I was there ... a lot of them don't like being told no. And believe me I was not afraid—you develop a respect for the fear of being in that working environment and that respect means that you have to know at all times. And you obey the law. You don't give out to inmates anything other than what they're entitled to by law and if you hold true to that in your policy and procedures, you really can't go wrong.

Both Jennifer and Carrie found that the strict approach to dealing with prisoners was the best way to maintain order within their libraries.

Linda told stories about some prisoners whom she had encouraged to be successful upon release. She talked about one prisoner in particular who had misused library services. Her institution had started a program encouraging prisoners to write essays in response to disciplinary problems. After an issue in her library, she asked this prisoner to write an essay and described what happened:

> And so when he comes back I tell him, this is the essay that I have in mind. At such and such a date you are going to be released to this county. And you have housing and you have a minimum wage job and you have a bicycle with a helmet. Now the parole officer you have is really a perfectionist and he is going to want you to meet with him every other day. He's going to give you drug tests unexpectedly any of the times and he's going to come over to your place and he's going to search your place up and down at least once a week. And so you have this minimum wage job and you have this bicycle. And if ever you don't wear your helmet you're going to be pulled over by the police and written up. And if you're late to work you're going to be told upon and it's going to be really possibly frustrating. But you happen to have found ... three friends and those three friends have never broken the law and they have access to transportation and they enjoy doing interesting things but none of them involve alcohol, or drugs, or breaking the law. So I want you to describe to me your first year and what you do with your free time and what your plans are ... and you're going to have this minimum wage job for a year and at that end of the year, you can decide to either buy a car or get a better apartment. And he wrote the best story ... and so I said can you see yourself out there in [the county where the prison is located] even if you have the worst parole officer, even if the police know you and stop you all the time, can you see yourself succeeding and not coming back to prison?

Linda continued her story to talk about an interaction she had with another employee:

> As another employee said to me ... "We only see the second act. The first act is what they did to come into the second act. And we have them for the second act and we will not get to see the third act of how it turns out. And we just cannot be attached to the outcome." And when some guy is just happy go lucky, he could be manipulating you. He could be telling the change agent what the change agent wants to hear. We won't know, but we still have to keep the message going of providing some kind of direction and hope, respect and encouragement to hope that these guys don't come back.

I had the impression from many of my interviews that those librarians I spoke to had very rewarding careers with the potential of making an impact on underserved populations. Carrie said, "it's a wonderful career and it takes a certain kind of person. And it takes a person to have passion." Certainly some of the interviewees had experienced defeat or solitude within their institutions, but many if not all of them still had interactions with prisoners and colleagues that gave them some sense of achievement.

## Summary

Speaking to 11 prison librarians about their day-to-day experiences in prison libraries added clarity and actual practical experience to an otherwise removed research experience. It was surprising that these librarians were keen to speak to an outside researcher and that they were also intrigued to see something published, regardless of the fact that it was being written by someone not in a position similar to theirs.

Most of these librarians had master's degrees in library science and if not, they had advanced degrees in education. Nearly all of the librarians stumbled upon the job; only two had actively sought positions as prison librarians. All but three of the librarians I spoke to had previous library experience, which was varied and abundant. They were able to relate their experiences in a prison library to experiences they had at public, academic, and school libraries. The biggest differences between their positions in prison libraries and those from the outside were related to the secure environment or the special population they were serving. Most of these librarians, with the exception of two, were solo librarians in their institutions with little to no additional staff support other than prisoner staff.

Despite having advanced degrees, not all of the librarians interviewed felt that their studies had prepared them to do the work required in a prison library, especially any special requirements of the job. Some talked about the theory being relevant and helpful; others felt that it would be very difficult for a graduate program to prepare them for such an environment. Professional development was also a difficult topic: many did not have the support or the time to actively keep up on published trends, attend professional development events, or attend conferences. Few were publishing on the topic of prison librarianship; those who had published or presented did so far less frequently than might be expected from an academic librarian. They had sufficient training opportunities though, which mostly seemed to be supported in some way by the institution. Networking was also difficult because they were so sequestered: most who were actively engaged in networking in the field either had networks set up in-state by their administrations or initiated their own opportunities.

Technology was out-of-date and mostly inaccessible to both prisoners and staff in prison libraries. Most of the institutions did have computers, but services on these computers were often limited to gated networks for legal services, software programs for learning basic computer skills, or typing programs. This trend does appear to be changing. Many of the interviewees mentioned programs that are being initiated in their states, much like the coding program at San Quentin, or the usage of tablets in Ohio prisons.[7] These types of programs could potentially bridge an ever increasing divide between digital literacy in the prison and in the outside world by providing access to digital technologies close to those a non-incarcerated individual might experience.

Few interacted on a daily basis with their administration and interactions were mostly cordial when they occurred. Interviewees cited a number of misconceptions about the field of prison librarianship and that it was disappointing that so many librarians were hesitant to work in those environments. Most seemed to view their work as rewarding in some sense and mentioned how interesting it was to work with underserved prison populations. All interviewees alluded to the isolating nature of the work.

Again, it was very beneficial to speak to individuals working in prisons to get stories and to personalize their experiences. These experiences, combined with the survey results from the previous chapter, have provided a rich pool of practice to compare policy to practice in prison libraries. In the conclusion, I will delve more into the similarities or discrepancies between policy and practice by comparing the discussion from chapters 1 through 7 with the results from chapters 8 and 9.

# Conclusion: Revisiting the Role of the Prison Librarian

Conducting the survey and interviews from the previous two chapters of this book illustrated many of the challenges and rewards that prison librarians face on a day-to-day basis. It also added context to compare what is happening within these institutions to national and state policies on prison library services. The interviews in particular were an informative means of representing insider perspectives from 11 librarians in 11 states. These stories and experiences made much of my previous reading and research come to life, especially the more personal stories about rewarding interactions working with prisoners or serving special populations.

Throughout this book, there have been certain topics addressed within each chapter, which were also addressed in my qualitative research. Within chapters 1 and 2, I discussed national and state policies on prison library services. Topics within these chapters introduced the prescribed purposes of the prison library, administration, general library services such as programming and interlibrary loan, collection development procedures and policies, and needs assessment for library collection development and services. I also discussed the conflicting role of intellectual freedom in a prison library, as well as murky definitions of prisoners' rights including any limitations to their privacy. I have mentioned law library issues and court cases throughout this book, albeit my investigations more thoroughly review general library services. Law libraries are not consistently offered in all states, even though many states have some form of recreational reading and many appear to have library facilities for these purposes. More research on law libraries, perhaps with the institutional buy-in at which Marjorie LeDonne completed her research in the 1970s, would be appropriate for assessing or reviewing law library service in U.S. prison libraries.

What has become clear after reviewing policies and speaking to practitioners is that, much like Larry Sullivan and Brenda Vogel mention in their "Reachin' Behind Bars" article,[1] there appears to be a paradigm shift underway in U.S. prisons. While many policies acknowledge the role of rehabilitation in the prison structure, some of the survey results and interviews seem to indicate that punishment is taking precedence to rehabilitation. This may be influenced by the broader public's views of incarceration. The prison library has, according to historians' accounts of its development, flourished under paradigms of rehabilitation. It remains unclear what this potential paradigm shift might mean for future general libraries in prisons.

In this conclusion, I will mostly compare the national and state policies mentioned in chapters 1 and 2 to the survey results and interviews from chapters 8 and 9. In the interviews I also asked a number of questions about professional development, which are generally not addressed in policies from institutions or national bodies. I will compare some of the research from chapter 7 regarding lack of scholarship and educational opportunities to the statements from interviewees in chapter 9. By comparing these sections to one another, I hope to draw conclusions about the influence or importance of policies, whether state or national, in the individual institutions of survey and interview participants.

## Purpose of the Prison Library

Survey participants answered a core question about the purpose of the prison library with options mirroring those suggested in the ASCLA 1992 standards and mentioned frequently in other national and state policies. Nearly all participants acknowledged the role that recreational reading has in a prison library. Between 73 percent and 82 percent agreed that the prison library also fulfilled purposes of providing information about reentry, assisting in rehabilitation, enhancing vocational skills, and contributing to lifelong learning. Almost 80 percent acknowledged the role that the library had in providing legal materials to prisoners. Only a little over half of the respondents acknowledged that maintaining contact with the outside world is a role of the library. This could be attributed to potential confusion over the wording of the question; maintaining contact in modern times is often done via technology and digital connections. Other survey respondents mentioned additional purposes for the prison library of varying natures. These results support the need to revisit and revise the ASCLA 1992 standards. As a few of the interview participants shared and participants on the ALA prison listserv have mentioned, these conversations have started amongst prison librarians at conferences and on the listserv itself.

Regardless of the purpose that the prison library has within an institution, the overreaching goals of security within the institution tend to trump any and all aspects of the services offered. Many of the survey participants mentioned issues with collection development or with offering certain services to prisoners. Interviewees told stories or gave examples of administrative issues concerning contraband that could be transported in library hardcover books. They also shared procedures for maintaining security in isolated units whose prisoners have less access to all prison services. Many acknowledged the challenges they faced in providing library service due to the constrictive nature of the prison. Some stated that those pursuing careers in prison librarianship will have to be comfortable with these kinds of restrictions and control. Trained librarians, who are encouraged to fight censorship and support intellectual freedom, may experience discomfort in a prison setting when their core values and ethics are challenged by security needs of the institution. Some rise above this discomfort using the skillsets they have learned as librarians by attempting to protect and maintain prisoners' rights. In some interviews, librarians had fostered communication with their administration to find compromises.

## Administration

Many standards including those from the ACA and the ASCLA define space requirements for general libraries. Some of these policies include facility requirements such as lighting and hours of operation. Policies also include collection requirements based on the size of the facility, preferred educational background of non-prisoner staff employed in the library, and recommendations for budget independence of the library.

In my research, I did not generally ask about facility requirements meeting the standards of the ACA or ASCLA other than recommended open hours. Interviewees confirmed that their libraries were separate facilities or rooms within an institution or campus. We did not discuss square footage or ratio of books to prisoners, etc. These details, while they would have allowed me to compare facility requirements to actual practice, are often details that are, among others, reviewed during ACA accreditation visits. All institutions conformed to ACA and ASCLA requirements for open hours.

Educational background was a much more ambiguous and complicated comparison between policy and practice. Most standards recommend that librarians in these institutions hold master's degrees in library science. Only 52 percent of survey participants held master's degrees in library science, and 20 percent had other master's degrees. After speaking to interviewees about their credentials and hiring processes, it seemed that there were inherent challenges with the MLIS or MLS in the prison library culture. Four participants indicated that their states did not require an MLIS or MLS to hold their positions at the time of their hiring. One of these participants indicated that some library training or certification was required. In another state, a participant indicated that his state was no longer requiring an MLIS or MLS, but had required it in previous years. In one state, an interviewee talked about difficulties filling positions with MLIS or MLS graduates due to the lack of applicants. While at least four states had essentially devalued the MLIS or MLS degree for prison librarians and, in some cases, devalued the whole position by reducing it to a technician, other states had difficulty filling positions. Therefore, it was unclear if this inconsistency in educational requirements was due to issues filling positions or to an actual devaluing of the profession by prison administrators. Perhaps it is due to a combination of both or perhaps it depends on the state.

A minority of institutions had budget independence in line with the ASCLA 1992 standards. A little under 35 percent of survey participants indicated that they had their own line item in the budget. Many of the survey participants and some of the interviewees indicated that they had no budget whatsoever. Often those with a budget were sharing budgets with other departments, such as education. Sharing a budget with education was logical, since the library frequently reported to this department. Many of the interviewees discussed budgetary troubles associated with the recession, mentioning that many services had been cut back and that the library was often a victim of staffing and fiscal reductions.

ASCLA standards also recommend that the library director have equal footing in the hierarchy to other departments managed by a director. This did not appear to be the case in most institutions, similar to the discrepancies between standards and budget actualities. Under 20 percent of the respondents in the survey reported directly to prison administration or to a central agency in the state. All others reported to various programs with most (nearly 55 percent) falling under the education department. In regards to strategic planning and policy development, 55 percent collaborated either with prison administration or a central agency and 20 percent were able to author their own documents in this regard. While the library was not often hierarchically placed where the ASCLA standards would recommend, it appears that many of these institutions were still allowing their library staff to remain invested and involved in the planning of their areas.

Staffing was bleak at most of the interviewees' institutions. Only two were not "solo librarians" and both of these interviewees were serving multiple campuses alongside various levels of local staff, including non-prisoner staff and prisoner-only staff. Levels of prisoner staffing also varied across the interviewees' institutions. Some seemed to have support for hiring multiple prisoners, while others experienced reductions in their prisoner staff.

## Library Services

The IFLA standards specifically mention a number of services that should be offered in prison libraries, including readers' advisory services, instruction, interlibrary loan, and reference service. The ASCLA standards detail similar services that are mostly educational or rehabilitative in nature, with some inclusion of law library services. Assistance with legal inquiries was offered in nearly 62 percent of survey respondents' institutions, which was the most frequently offered service that fell under ASCLA recommendations. A little under 40 percent of the institutions were offering readers' advisory services. Over 45 percent were providing services for those completing GEDs and high school diplomas. Between 20 and 30 percent were offering other educational or rehabilitative programs such as correspondence courses, college entrance exam assistance, and seminars on reentry. It seems that in practice institutions are not able to adhere to the policy recommendations regarding library services and programming, since none of these services—with the exception of legal services—were consistently offered in a majority of institutions. This may well relate to the constantly reoccurring issues that prison librarians seem to face: lack of additional permanent staffing and no ability to distribute work within the prison library to non-prisoner employees.

Both the Department of Justice and the ACA mention the importance of addressing gaps in the collection through interlibrary loan. In practice, a majority of the institutions were providing interlibrary loan services to their patrons with nearly 67 percent reporting this service in the survey responses. During interviews, it became clear that interlibrary loan was more prevalent in years past in prison libraries than it is now. One interviewee indicated that his library had been involved in interlibrary loan before systems had changed and that the prison libraries had been unfortunately excluded with no immediate plans to be added back to the network. He was hopeful that the services would return. Another interviewee addressed the challenges in receiving materials and asked that his prisoners request multiple titles to ensure that they would receive something from a public library that was also underfunded.

The public library model, as mentioned in the IFLA standards and by Bayley et al., has frequently popped up in the literature as an approach and standard that should be utilized in prison libraries. Of the state policies reviewed in chapter 2, 32 percent mention the public library as a model for prison library services. In survey responses, four participants explicitly mentioned the public library model when responding to questions about collection development. Additionally, multiple interviewees cited similarities between previous jobs in public libraries and the prison library. One explicitly referenced the usage of the public library model in her organization. Two of the librarians interviewed denounced the public library model for their institution, both claiming that the prison library should be treated as a special library. There are apparent gaps between national recommendations, state policies, and statements from interviewees regarding the implementation of the public library model in the prison, which is perhaps part of the reason for authors, such as Coyle, to develop what is viewed as controversial opinions on prison librarianship.

Most of the national standards do not explicitly recommend or mention what types of partnerships prison libraries should have with outside organizations. The Department of Justice standards, for instance, mention the possibility of partnering with public or community libraries, but the recommendations are more focused on filling in holes in the collection or using outside organizations to acquire materials. No standards were found that explicitly detail additional types of collaborations. In practice, about half of the interviewees had some sort of partnership with outside organizations, with most of them receiving book donations from these types of institutions. Only three of the 11 interviewed were partnering with organizations for other programs such as book discussion groups or "Read to Me" programs.

The situation regarding technology was less dire than in 2010 when I first began investigating this topic. Nevertheless, few standards address modern technology concerns. The ASCLA standards discuss technology inclusion in prison libraries, but the technology mentioned is outdated and not representative of the kinds of hardware or software that a prisoner might encounter upon release today. State standards remain hazy on the topic of computers in libraries; 20 percent mention technology in policies and may allow computers for legal or educational purposes. None appear to offer access to any sort of Internet services according to state policies. In practice, survey respondents indicated that computers were frequently allowed and utilized in institutions with 78 percent permitting some sort of computer access, albeit often gated to legal services only and not necessarily helpful for reducing digital literacy gaps. Many of these computers were offered to fulfill mandates regarding access to the courts; 80 percent of respondents who allowed computer usage indicated that legal services are available on workstations. Of this same group, 45 percent exclusively offered legal services on computers. LexisNexis was frequently referenced in survey responses and was also referenced in state policies. This database, often offered in an offline form in prison libraries, appeared to better suit many institutions' needs for providing access to the courts. Nearly 23 percent offered access to computers for educational purposes. Surprisingly, some institutions even allowed their prisoners to access the Internet. Of the librarians surveyed, more than 12 percent offered access to Internet services such as job listings, family services information, etc. An additional two respondents claimed that their institutions planned to offer access to the Internet in some form in the future.

In the interviews, technology was discussed in much more detail. Nine of the 11 interviewees offered some sort of computer access in their institutions. Many of these instances included gated computer access to legal databases, so also were not huge steps to reducing issues with digital literacy. Furthermore, this legal access cannot be equated to what one might encounter outside of a prison, since none of the interviewees offered services to prisoners that required Internet access. There were some hints of development in offering Internet access: a few detailed plans within the institution or at other institutions to start offering these types of services, including MP3 downloads, devices that prisoners could purchase and use for emailing, and kiosk services. While the technology offered in prisons in no way mirrors that available in the public, it does appear that there are, at times and in more progressive states, efforts underway to reduce the digital divide.

Conversely, the digital divide appears to be worsening for librarians working in these positions. Three librarians talked about issues for those new to the profession who had been trained in technology and would not be able to use those skills in a prison library. One concluded that not using technology regularly would worsen any skills acquired in library school. Two feared that many were not and would not be attracted to the profession because of the lack of technology.

## Needs Assessment

The ASCLA 1992 standards encourage prison libraries to conduct annual library needs assessment of prisoners to determine if services and collections are useful for the constituency. In practice, this was not consistently applied across institutions. Of the institutions surveyed, 65 percent were conducting some sort of needs assessment. Of those collecting this type of data, 75 percent were getting information from interviews with prisoner patrons, 50 percent were administering user satisfaction surveys, and 25 percent were utilizing information from intake forms. Information on the frequency of these methods was not collected, so it is not clear if these kinds of activities were occurring on an annual basis as suggested by the ASCLA standards. Nevertheless, it is concerning that nearly 30 percent reported that they were not assessing their prisoners' needs. Based on some of the feedback from the interviews, one might assume that there simply is not enough time to manage these kinds of processes, especially in institutions where one librarian may be solely responsible for library services.

One reoccurring theme from the interviews was prisoners' literacy challenges. A few of the librarians mentioned reading levels as a hurdle in determining what services or collections a prisoner might benefit from. One stated that a ninth-grade reading level is rare and very high. Another talked about the difficulty some of the prisoners might have in expressing themselves in writing to make requests. Certainly literacy challenges are appearing to affect collection development decisions and even programming decisions, yet there do not appear to be many library specific policies, either national or statewide, to instruct librarians on how to approach these types of populations with various reading levels.

## Collection Development

The ASCLA, the ACA, IFLA and Bayley et al. reference the importance of a collection development policy to define processes for acquiring materials in a prison library. Reviews of state policies from chapter 2 also support the need for a collection development policy with 80 percent of the state policies defining some sort of selection criteria. These types of policies and procedures are particularly important in institutions where collection decisions may be questioned and criticized in efforts to support actual or supposed security issues. The majority of survey participants echoed this collection development policy requirement; nearly 68 percent knew of the existence of a policy within their institution. Many of the respondents had authored the policies. A little over eight percent were not sure if their institution had a policy, so it is possible that policies were in place at a few more institutions than 68 percent. Additionally, the library retained much of the authority in defining these policies. Over 60 percent of participants who had a policy in place indicated that the staff in the library was responsible for writing and updating the policy.

Most national policies and many state policies recommend that materials be selected based on the needs of those incarcerated in that institution. Some of the state policies define overreaching broad collection goals whereas others recommend specific materials that are suggested for or banned from the collection. Survey responses were similarly varied. Some mentioned following specific, defined procedures from their local Department of Corrections; others had developed their own processes based on what was most effective within their institutions. Some reviewed local or publisher statistics to determine what might be useful, others took requests, some read reviews, and some incorporated materials on the basis of library needs assessments. In the interviews, some of these responses were duplicated; interviewees mentioned similar procedures, especially related to getting prisoner feedback on determining what materials might be most popular. Regardless of needs assessment or collection development policies, a few participants from both the survey and the interviews were only able to represent a hypothetical collection development process. Many of these participants did not have allocated budgets and had to rely solely on donations from outside organizations.

Inherent security risks also make collection development decisions more complicated than what might be encountered at another type of library, whether public, academic, or special. Restricting or censoring materials based on risks to the institution's security are standard practices in most prison libraries and that frequently ruffles librarians' feathers, especially those who are proponents of free and open access to information. Almost all survey participants claimed that censorship occurred within their institution; nearly 95 percent confirmed that a policy was in place at their institution restricting access to certain types of materials. Survey respondents provided examples of restricted materials that were very similar to those that might be considered problematic in the context of the ALA's "Prisoners' Right to Read," or Bayley et al.'s recommendations. Survey responses also mirrored many of the state policy recommendations for materials that should be restricted or censored to maintain order in the institution. Some mentioned "disapproved publications" lists maintained by the institution or a central organization. True crime appeared to still be a hot topic issue; these types of books were mentioned in survey responses and interviews. They were not categorically banned from institutions, rather it seemed to vary on a case-by-case basis. Urban fiction, another popular type of material in a prison library, was also intermittently available in institutions. Some libraries were able to offer these materials and others were not. Again, these types of restrictions seemed to be implemented on an institution-by-institution basis.

Most libraries were not solely responsible for censorship decisions, instead internal or external organizations were at least participating in the decision-making process about what to censor. At least 70 percent of the survey participants indicated that decisions on censorship were being made above them by prison administration or the central offices, or that some combination of central or local administration was working with the library to determine what materials should be censored. Only 5 percent of respondents indicated that the library had the sole responsibility for making these decisions. Censorship is an unfortunate reality in most prison libraries, whether to protect the institution from real or falsely perceived threats. Clearer policy, or updated policy, could facilitate easier communication and best practice on these topics.

## Services to Segregated Units and Restricting Access

The ASCLA standards and other national standards require that library access in some form be available to all prisoners in an institution, regardless of where they are housed. Prisoners in segregation in particular are, according to these standards, supposed to be offered some sort of alternate service if they are not able to visit the physical library. Interviewees confirmed that these types of services were available to prisoners in segregation, nevertheless these prisoners were sometimes offered a lesser quality of materials. Interviewees fulfilled book requests, distributed books on book carts, and maintained separate collections for prisoners in segregation. They expressed various levels of satisfaction with the services they were offering; some mentioned that the materials available to prisoners in segregation were not as popular or well circulated as those in the regular collection. Others were afraid that those in segregation did not have a lot of choices about what materials they could select. Regardless of the quality of services, all were meeting the standards to provide services to segregated prisoners.

The *Federal Standards for Prisons and Jails* and the ASCLA both require that prisoners have access to a library or library materials over a period of a few days or for a minimum number of hours. All survey participants indicated that they were meeting these requirements in terms of open hours since all were open more than ASCLA's recommended five hours. Prisoners undergoing some sort of disciplinary action may have been limited in terms of what they have access to. Interview participants, when asked if and how a prisoner's access to the library might be restricted, responded with ambiguous answers that implied that decisions were made on a case-by-case basis by the institution. Some claimed that library access could not be taken away by administration and that the library was the only organization that had the right to restrict access as a form of punishment for bad library behavior. Others stated that their institutions could ban library access if the administrators had a disciplinary reason to do so. The likelihood of the institution fulfilling this policy in practice seemed to be related to internal disciplinary issues and security needs.

In both the survey responses and the interviews, the theme of security superseding most services in the prison was recurrent. A few survey respondents and interviewees discussed the challenges of offering hardcover books in their regular collections or collections for segregated prisoners. It was easier for prisoners to conceal contraband in hardcover books and therefore in some cases, only paperback books were offered. One interviewee specifically talked about prisoners smuggling sandpaper in hardcover books so that they could sand off the logos on their jeans. She intimated that they were not necessarily trying to conceal the logos to escape, rather they were just interested in having regular jeans and not constantly feeling like a prisoner.

## Privacy

When incarcerated, prisoners forfeit many rights, including rights to privacy that they would have otherwise maintained in the outside world. Few policies are available at either the state or national level that address what degree of privacy prisoners retain once incarcerated. Procedures in the prison libraries also seem to imply that very few rights to privacy are retained, especially not those they might enjoy at a public library. The majority of institutions were tracking their prisoners' library usage with institutional inmate codes instead of anonymous library codes that might be generated by an integrated library system. More than 75 percent were retaining records beyond the recommended immediate deletion standards at public libraries; there, records of circulation are purged once the item is returned. Library staff were aware of privacy policies in place at only 40 percent of the institutions from which survey responses were received. It was not clear from this analysis whether retention had justified benefits for the institution or if records were maintained simply because it was less work to retain them than to purge them. This may be another area where ethics of librarianship conflict with the needs of the institution.

## Law Libraries

Meaningful access to the courts continues to be an inherent right of prisoners, notwithstanding recent cases discouraging frivolous prisoner litigation. State policies maintain standards on meaningful access to the courts and national policies indicate the importance of providing this fundamental right. But overall approaches to prison law library services—and perhaps to legal services in the prison in general—are led by litigation, not national standards. Court cases such as *Lewis v. Casey* have established recommended levels of commitments required by institutions rather than institutions being encouraged to abide by standards devised by the ACA or other national bodies.

According to participants, institutions were, nevertheless, establishing the benefits of computerized access to legal services by offering LexisNexis, WestLaw, or similar programs to their prisoners, either within their general or law libraries. These programs were frequently implemented in such a manner that prisoners could not access the Internet, but most institutions offering these databases appeared to let the prisoners conduct their own research on computers in the facility. As a few interviewees mentioned, technology access also seemed to be shifting in prisons as more and more were offering, or planning to offer, legal services and other services via computers, tablets, kiosks, or similar devices.

Legal services in prisons, even if only focused on legal library services, are a topic worthy of much more research than this book has afforded them. The administration of law libraries is not always consistently offered as a service of the general library, so contacting individuals within general libraries was not always conducive to receiving informed details about how the libraries in their institutions were tackling the need to provide access to the courts. Survey questions were also not sufficient to address the complexity of these services. A targeted study focusing only on prison law libraries would be much more appropriate to be able to analyze how these institutions are adhering to national policies or court decisions.

## Topics Worthy of Further Research

Even with the participation from prison librarians in chapters 8 and 9, this research is still exploratory. My online and mailed survey had a combined response rate of 8.5

percent from a pool of 1,096 contacts. The National Prison Library Survey from 1990 mailed surveys to 521 institutions and received 323 responses for a total response rate of 62 percent. This survey was conducted by the Standards for Adult Correctional Institution Libraries Committee of the Association of Specialized and Cooperative Library Agencies.[2] If the ASCLA or the ACA were to sponsor a new prison library survey, I would hope that the response rates would be considerably higher than my 8.5 percent, rather it may be closer to the 62 percent reported in 1990. Marjorie LeDonne's work from the 1970s, which was a collaboration with the ACA and sponsored by the U.S. Department of Education, might be something worth revisiting in a modern context. The possibilities for authoring reliable and up-to-date policies based on the prospect of a new national survey is exciting; I can only hope that some of these associations are considering the benefits of analyzing their current prison library offerings nationwide. Since most of my survey and many of my interview questions were based on the ASCLA 1992 standards, perhaps these standards are an appropriate starting point for such a survey. Topics worthy of investigation certainly include topics discussed throughout this book; the purpose of the prison library, administration, library services, library needs assessment, collection development, intellectual freedom and prisoner rights, and privacy.

Even exploratory research on prison librarianship should be encouraged. As demonstrated in chapter 6, prison librarianship is underrepresented in scholarship when compared to other library science topics. The lack of scholarship is even more dire when one considers that most of those writing the scholarship are not prison librarians. The profession needs to hear from more practitioners; new advocates for the profession should step up to further the knowledge on the topic and use examples such as Brenda Vogel, Glennor Shirley, Vibeke Lehmann and Daniel Suvak to learn how to get involved and contribute.

## Other Topics

National standards do not address the solitude that one might experience working as a prison librarian. The literature from prison librarians such as Vogel, Clark and Mac-Creaigh, and Singer all discuss the isolating nature of the work as the only librarian or library staff. Survey respondents did not explicitly mention solitude as a challenge within their organizations, but interviewees frequently touched upon this topic. Most of the interviewees were the only non-prisoner professionals in their libraries. They were confronted with administration that did not always understand what the role of a librarian was and what kind of qualifications or experience were necessary for the job. Additionally, these interviewees had infrequent contact with other professionals working in similar positions, unless they exerted some self-guided initiative in pursuing networking opportunities. Few had adequate support to pursue professional development activities where they might network with other professionals. Some seemed to enjoy the solitary nature of their job at times, since there was a lot of autonomy in being a one-man show. Most saw the solitude as one of the major differences between employment in a public, academic, or special library versus a prison library. It is not surprising that few of these prison librarians were trying to publish or present on their work since they were, at times, so disconnected from communities of scholarship or dissemination.

## Summary

As a librarian working outside of a prison, the approach used in this book was helpful to have a better understanding of conflicts between policy and practice in prison libraries. Reviewing national and state policies set some context for the literature published by both practitioners and researchers. Researching court cases provided background for overreaching policy decisions. Assessing the state of prison librarianship in the curricula for library school, determining the existence of policies on prison librarianship for national library organizations, and reviewing the frequency of citations on the topic led to the clear conclusion that prison librarianship does not receive anywhere near the coverage or attention from which other types of libraries benefit. While some public libraries and other organizations are successfully partnering and collaborating with prison libraries, there could be many more partnerships that would benefit both collaborators. Additionally, in a time where traditional librarian positions are waning, there is a missed opportunity for collaboration between prison libraries and library schools. As noted in chapter 6, no ALA accredited master's programs in library and/or information science are offering any sort of coursework on prison librarianship. Only one library school mentions a prison position as a potential career path; overall, the path is overlooked. New alternatives such as taxonomy and search work are shared with MLIS graduates as a reason for attending library school. Meanwhile, in states such as California, Department of Corrections' librarian positions take months to fill. In a profession where jobs are not currently abundant, it seems logical to forge partnerships between the prison libraries and the library schools.

The research conducted as part of the final two chapters of this book has highlighted some of the realities of prison librarianship that are not conclusively defined in policy. Even though the results are not generalizable, the 84 individuals who provided survey feedback and the 11 of those who allowed me to interview them clarified many open questions I had about what it was "really like" working in a prison library. I was impressed and heartened by the commitment many of these librarians have to the profession, especially by those who acknowledged how meaningful their work might be to an incarcerated patron who had otherwise lost nearly all rights and certainly his or her freedom. As has been presented and discussed in this chapter, policies are still ambiguous. Local administrators and local libraries often determine how library services will be offered, regardless of what the ACA, ASCLA, or ALA may recommend.

I may have represented and presented the stories of some individuals working in prison libraries, but many more institutions remain unrepresented in my research. Librarians may not necessarily be employed by the nearly 1,400 prisons in the United States; some may be operating libraries combined with other services or potentially not offering library services at all. The unfortunate consequence of focusing on prison librarians within this study is that these other institutions remain nebulous, especially considering the ambiguities found between policy and practice in institutions where librarians are present. I can only hope that the unrepresented institutions have someone who believes in access to information and the rehabilitative potential of reading and who can offer their patrons some respite from hard time.

# Appendix A

# Summary of State Approaches to Prison Library Services

All of the state approaches listed below, with the exception of Nebraska and Iowa, have been summarized on the Directory of State Prison Libraries from Washington State Library (http://wiki.sos.wa.gov/ils/). It should be noted that this list is no longer kept current. The last listed update was on July 10, 2014.

| State | State Approach to Prison Library Services |
|---|---|
| Alabama | State has one professional librarian managing the statewide program. |
| Alaska | State provides library services through the education department. |
| Arizona | State has a well-developed library program and employs multiple professional staff members distributed across facilities. |
| Arkansas | State has a well-developed library program and employs multiple professional staff members distributed across facilities. |
| California | State has a well-developed library program and employs multiple professional staff members distributed across facilities. |
| Colorado | State has a well-developed library program and employs multiple professional staff members distributed across facilities. |
| Connecticut | State provides library services, library contacts are in each facility, but they may or may not hire professional librarians. |
| Delaware | State provides library services, but they may or may not hire professional librarians. |
| Florida | State provides library services, library contacts are in each facility, but they may or may not hire professional librarians. |
| Georgia | State provides library services, library contacts are in each facility, but they may or may not hire professional librarians. |
| Hawaii | State provides library services, library contacts are in each facility, but they may or may not hire professional librarians. |
| Idaho | State has one professional librarian managing the statewide program. |
| Illinois | State has a well-developed library program and employs multiple professional staff members distributed across facilities. |
| Indiana | State provides library services, library contacts are in each facility, but they may or may not hire professional librarians. |
| Iowa | State provides library services, but does not require professional librarians per information from prison librarian. In Iowa; no contacts are listed on the Washington State Library directory. |
| Kansas | State provides library services, library contacts are in each facility, but they may or may not hire professional librarians. |
| Kentucky | State provides library services, library contacts are in each facility, but they may or may not hire professional librarians. |

| *State* | *State Approach to Prison Library Services* |
|---|---|
| Louisiana | State provides library services, library contacts are in each facility, but they may or may not hire professional librarians. |
| Maine | State does not hire professional librarians or provide library contacts. |
| Maryland | State provides library services, library contacts are in each facility, but they may or may not hire professional librarians. |
| Massachusetts | State provides library services, library contacts are in each facility, but they may or may not hire professional librarians. |
| Michigan | State has a well-developed library program and employs multiple professional staff members distributed across facilities. |
| Minnesota | State has one professional librarian managing the statewide program. |
| Mississippi | State provides library services, but they may or may not hire professional librarians. |
| Missouri | State has one professional librarian managing the statewide program. |
| Montana | State provides library services, but they may or may not hire professional librarians. |
| Nebraska | Nebraska is not included in the Washington State Library Directory; per the library policy quoted earlier in this chapter, Nebraska requires that the library be supervised by a professional librarian. This policy was last reviewed in 2015. It is not clear if a professional librarian needs to be in each institution, or if each institution has to have access to a central professional librarian. |
| Nevada | State does not hire professional librarians or provide library contacts. |
| New Hampshire | State provides library services, library contacts are in each facility, but they may or may not hire professional librarians. |
| New Jersey | State provides library services, but they may or may not hire professional librarians. |
| New Mexico | State provides library services through the education department. |
| New York | State has a well-developed library program and employs multiple professional staff members distributed across facilities. |
| North Carolina | State has one professional librarian managing the statewide program. |
| North Dakota | State provides library services, but they may or may not hire professional librarians. |
| Ohio | State has a well-developed library program and employs multiple professional staff members distributed across facilities. |
| Oklahoma | State provides library services, but they may or may not hire professional librarians. |
| Oregon | State provides library services, library contacts are in each facility, but they may or may not hire professional librarians. |
| Pennsylvania | State has a well-developed library program and employs multiple professional staff members distributed across facilities. |
| Rhode Island | State provides library services, law library contacts are in each facility, but they may or may not hire professional librarians. |
| South Carolina | State provides library services, library contacts are in each facility, but they may or may not hire professional librarians. |
| South Dakota | State provides library services through the education department. |
| Tennessee | State provides library services, but they may or may not hire professional librarians. |
| Texas | State has a well-developed library program and employs multiple professional staff members distributed across facilities. |
| Utah | State provides library services, but they may or may not hire professional librarians. |
| Vermont | State does not hire professional librarians or provide library contacts. |

| State | State Approach to Prison Library Services |
|---|---|
| Virginia | State has one professional librarian managing the statewide program. |
| Washington | State has a well-developed library program and employs multiple professional staff members distributed across facilities. |
| West Virginia | State provides library services, but they may or may not hire professional librarians. |
| Wisconsin | State provides library services, library contacts are in each facility, but they may or may not hire professional librarians. |
| Wyoming | State has a well-developed library program and employs multiple professional staff members distributed across facilities. |

# Appendix B

# ALA Advocacy Policies

The advocacy policies listed below are those that are applicable to prison librarianship that were reviewed as part of the policymaking discussion in Chapter 6. Many more policies from ALA were reviewed to ascertain the number of dates, dates of amendment and focus of the policy.

| Policy | Focus | Dates Amended | Number of Updates |
|---|---|---|---|
| Library Bill of Rights | Not specified | 1939, 1944, 1948, 1961, 1967, 1980, 1996 | 7 |
| The Freedom to Read | Various | 1953, 1972, 1991, 2000, 2004 | 5 |
| Code of Ethics of the American Library Association | Various | 1939, 1981, 1995, 2008 | 4 |
| Privacy | Publicly funded libraries mentioned, though this likely applies to more | 2002, 2014 | 2 |
| Prisoners' Right to Read | Prisons | 2010, 2014 | 2 |
| Universal Right to Free Expression | Not specified | 1991, 2014 | 2 |
| Policy Concerning Confidentiality of Personally Identifiable Information about Library Users | Various | 1991, 2004 | 2 |
| Development and Implementation of Policies, Regulations, and Procedures Affecting Access to Library Materials, Services, and Facilities | Publicly funded libraries | 1994, 2005 | 2 |

# Appendix C

# List of Citations on Prison Librarianship

This list includes books and articles on prison librarianship, published from 1993 to 2013. OCLC's WorldCat engine was used to uncover cataloged books worldwide. To discover articles, I selected a subset of highly rated library and information science journals based on Laura Manzari's 2013 *Library Quarterly* article "Library and Information Science Journal Prestige as Assessed by Library and Information Science Faculty." Using this smaller list, I uncovered citations by either exporting records from the journals' homepages or searching their indices using various keywords. This list was compiled to find out how frequently the topic of prison librarianship is discussed in library and information science literature. This list and the text from Chapter 6 illustrate the dearth of literature on the topic.

## Books

*Airway Heights Corrections Center Branch Library: Airway Heights, Washington.* Washington State Library. (Book, 2009).

*Arizona Department of Corrections Listing of Arizona Corrections Facilities.* Jennie L. O'Leary, Arizona Department of Corrections. (Book, 1993).

*A Bibliography and Guide to Legal Research for Jailhouse Lawyers.* John E. Siska, J. Robert Keena, National. Lawyers Guild, Prison Law Project. (Book, 1995).

*The Bill of Rights: The Eighth Amendment.* Richard Minsky, Larry E. Sullivan. (Book, 2002).

*BookMarks: Reading in Black and White: A Memoir.* Karla F. C. Holloway. (Book, 2006).

*California Department of Corrections Libraries.* California Department of Corrections. (Book, 1994).

*Clallam Bay Corrections Center Branch Library: Clallam Bay, Washington.* Washington State Library. (Book, 2009).

*Coyote Ridge Corrections Center Branch Library: Connell, Washington.* Washington State Library. (Book, 2009).

*Criminal Justice: A Brief Introduction.* Frank Schmalleger. (Book, 2012).

*The Development of Performance Indicators for Prison Libraries.* Susan D. Lithgow. (Book, 1995).

*Directory of Librarians in Penal Establishments in the United Kingdom.* Anne Milton. (Book, 1994).

*Directory of Librarians in Penal Establishments: 2000–2001.* Library Association, Prison Libraries Subject Group. (Book, 2000).

*Down for the Count: A Prison Library Handbook.* Brenda Vogel. (Book, 1995).

*Electronic Resources in Ohio Prison Libraries.* Virginia A. LaPoint. (Book, 1997).

*Guidelines for Library Services to Prisoners, 2nd Edition.* Frances E. Kaiser, International Federation of Library Associations and Institutions. (Book, 1995).

*Guidelines for Library Services to Prisoners, 3rd Edition.* Vibeke Lehmann, Joanne Locke, International Federation of Library Associations and Institutions. (Book, 2005).

*Guidelines for Prison Libraries.* Liz Boden, Roy Collis, Library Association, Prison Libraries Group. (Book, 1997).

*Higher Education in Prison: A Contradiction in Terms? American Council on Education Series on Higher Education.* Miriam Ed Williford, Washington, D.C. National University, Continuing Education Association, Washington, D.C. American Council on Education. (Book, 1994).

*How Do the Washington State Library's Institutional Branches Benefit Washington's Taxpayers, State Government, Communities and Families?* Washington State Library. (Book, 2013).

*Implementation of the New Prison Library Specification.* Richard White, Great Britain Department for Education and Skills, National Foundation for Educational Research in England and Wales, et al. (Book, 2006).

*Institution Libraries Eligible for LSCA Funding.* Connecticut State Library, Division of Library Development and Administrative Services. (Book, 1994).

*International Resource Book for Libraries Serving Disadvantaged Persons: 2001–2008: An Update to the International Resource Book for Libraries Serving Disadvantaged Persons: 1931–2001.* Joanne Locke, Nancy M. Panella, International Federation of Library Associations and Institutions (Netherlands). (Book, 2010).

*Interrupted Life Experiences of Incarcerated Women in the United States.* Rickie Solinger, Paula C. Johnson, Martha L. Raimon, Tina Reynolds, Ruby C. Tapia. (Book, 2009).

*Law Library Service to Prisoners: In and Out of Prison for Ten Years.* Karen E. Westwood, Law Library Service to Prisoners, Minnesota State Law Library Outreach Services Department. (Book, 1996).

*Libraries in South Australian Prisons: Report Prepared for the Department of Correctional Services (SA).* Claire Ohannessian, University of Adelaide. (Book, 1998).

*Libraries Inside: A Practical Guide for Prison Librarians.* Rhea Joyce Rubin, Daniel Suvak. (Book, 1995).

*Library and Information Services to Incarcerated Persons: Global Perspectives.* Vibeke Lehmann. (Book, 2011).

*Library Services to the Incarcerated: Applying the Public Library Model in Correctional Facility Libraries.* Sheila Clark, Erica MacCreaigh. (Book, 2006).

*A Library That Changes Lives.* Gerry Maclean. (Book, 2004).

*Literacy: A Way Out for At-Risk Youth.* Jennifer Sweeney. (Book, 2012).

*Literacy Efforts in Prison Libraries: A Sampling of Programs.* Christine Long. (Book, 1995).

*Long Range Plan for Library Service, 1993–1996.* Allen J. Overstreet, Florida Department of Corrections. (Book, 1993).

*McNeil Island Corrections Center Branch Library:* *Steilacoom, Washington.* Washington State Library. (Book, 2009).

*Minnesota State Law Library: 1994 Annual Report.* St. Paul Minnesota State Law Library. (Book, 1994).

*Offender Literature: A Report to Correctional Services Canada.* Peter Strong, Correctional Service Canada. (Book, 1996).

*Orality, Literacy, and Malcolm X.* Anthony J. Palmeri. (Book, 1993).

*Planning and Design Guide for Secure Adult and Juvenile Facilities.* American Correctional Association. (Book, 1999).

*The Planning Process for Wisconsin Institution Libraries.* Rhea Joyce Rubin. (Book, 1997).

*The Prison and the American Imagination.* Caleb Smith. (Book, 2009).

*Prison Law Library Guidelines.* American Association of Law Libraries, Standing Committee on Service to Institutionalized Persons. (Book, 1994).

*Prison Librarians Needed: A Challenging Career for Those with the Right Professional and Human Skills.* Vibeke Lehmann. (Book, 1999).

*Prison Libraries Committee: Report of the Departmental Committee on the Supply of Books to the Prisoners in H.M. Prisons and to the Inmates of H.M. Borstal Institutions.* Great Britain, Parliament, House of Commons. (Book, 2007).

*Prison Libraries: Roles and Responsibilities.* Standing Committee on Prison Libraries. (Book, 1993).

*The Prison Library Primer: A Program for The Twenty-First Century.* Brenda Vogel. (Book, 2009).

*Providing for Special Populations.* Information Today, Inc. (Book, 2001).

*Reading Is My Window: Books and the Art of Reading in Women's Prisons.* Megan Sweeney. (Book, 2010).

*Rethinking Corrections: Rehabilitation, Reentry, and Reintegration.* Lior Gideon, Hung-En Sung. (Book, 2011).

*Return to the Common Reader.* Beth Palmer. (Book, 2011).

*Rights and Wrongs ...* Chicago, IL, Special Committee on Youth Education for Citizenship American Bar Association. (Book, 1996).

*Roster and Statistics of Oklahoma Public and Institutional Libraries, July 1, 1993–June 30, 1994.* Oklahoma Department of Libraries. (Book, 1995).

*Running the Books: The Adventures of an Accidental Prison Librarian.* Avi Steinberg. (Book, 2010).

*Shut Up and Read.* Colin Will. (Book, 2003).

*Stafford Creek Corrections Center Branch Library: Aberdeen, Washington.* Washington State Library. (Book, 2009).

*State of Corrections: Proceedings ACA (American Correctional Association) Annual Conferences, 1992.* American Correctional Association. (Book, 1993).

*True Stories of Censorship Battles in America's Libraries.* Valerie Nye, Kathy Barco. (Book, 2012).

*Twin Rivers Corrections Center Branch Library: Monroe, Washington.* Washington State Library. (Book, 2009).

*Washington Corrections Center Branch Library: Shelton, Washington.* Washington State Library. (Book, 2009).

*Washington Corrections Center for Women Branch Library: Gig Harbor, Washington.* Washington State Library. (Book, 2009).

*Washington State Library and Department of Corrections Library Needs Assessment: Inmate and Staff.* Washington State Library; Washington (State) Department of Corrections; Washington (State) Department of Community, Trade, and Economic Development, Research & Evaluation Unit. (Book, 1994).

*Washington State Penitentiary East Complex Branch Library: Walla Walla, Washington.* Washington State Library. (Book, 2009).

*Werner's Manual for Prison Law Libraries.* Rebecca Trammell, Arturo A. Flores, O. James Werner, American Association of Law Libraries. (Book, 2004).

*Why Does a Large Prison Population Yield So Few Participants in a College Program Offered at Prison Sites?* S. M. Steve Walsh. (Book, 2000).

*Within These Walls: Prison Library Services in Victoria: Recommendations and Future Directions.* Australian Council of Libraries and Information Services, Victorian State Committee, Working Party on Prison Libraries. (Book, 1993).

*Women in Prison.* JoAnne O'Bryant, Library of Congress, Congressional Research Service. (Book, 2004).

## Articles

*Affordable Justice.* Donna Seaman. *American Libraries.* (Article, 1993).

*Arizona Shuts Down Its Prison Libraries.* Edith McKormick. *American Libraries.* (Article, 1997).

*Arts on the Inside.* Unknown. *Library Journal.* (Article, 2013).

*Bailing Out Prison Libraries.* Brenda Vogel. *Library Journal.* (Article, 1997).

*Behind Adobe Walls and Iron Bars: The Utah Territorial Penitentiary Library.* Melvin Bashore *Libraries & Culture.* (Article, 2003).

*Beyond Books: Restorative Librarianship in Juvenile Detention Centers.* Isaac Gilman. *Public Libraries.* (Article, 2008).

*Birthplace of my Redemption.* Larry Bratt. *American Libraries.* (Article, 1996).

*Books Open Worlds for People Behind Bars: Library Services in Prison as Exemplified by the Muenster Prison Library, Germany's "Library of the Year 2007."* Gerhard Peschers. *Library Trends.* (Article, 2011).

*Breaking Out of the Box: Reinventing a Juvenile-Center Library.* Veronica A. Davis. *American Libraries.* (Article, 2000).

*Briefs.* Unknown. *American Libraries.* (Article, 2000).

*Briefs.* Unknown. *American Libraries.* (Article, 2001).

*Broward County Inmates Sue to Stop Libraries Closing.* Unknown. *American Libraries.* (Article, 2004).

*Castro Defenders.* Nat Hentoff. *Library Journal.* (Article, 2004).

*Choose Freedom Read: Book Talks behind Bars.* Sheila Clark and Bobbie Patrick. *American Libraries.* (Article, 1999).

*Collection Development and Circulation Policies in Prison Libraries: An Exploratory Survey of Librarians in U.S. Correctional Institutions.* Suzanna Conrad. *The Library Quarterly.* (Article, 2012).

*College Stocks Prison Libraries.* Michael Kelley, Meredith Schwartz, Lauren Barack and John N. Berry III. *Library Journal.* (Article, 2012).

*Court Ruling Could Hurt Prison Libs.* Norman Oder. *Library Journal.* (Article, 1996).

*Defendant Denied Access to Prison Library.* Unknown. *American Libraries.* (Article, 2005).

*The eGranary Digital Library.* Nick Patten. *Educause Review.* (Article, 2012).

*Escape Reading.* Unknown. *American Libraries.* (Article, 1997).

*Federal Prisons to Return Religious Books.* G.M.E. *American Libraries.* (Article, 2007).

*For the Underdog.* Editor (article is about Diane Walden). *Library Journal* (Article, 2011).

*From a Distance.* Renea Arnold, Nell Colburn. *School Library Journal.* (Article, 2006).

*From Classroom to Courtroom.* Kathy McClellan. *Public Libraries.* (Article, 2009).

*Global Reach.* Unknown. *American Libraries.* (Article, 2000).

*The Greatest Morale Factor Next to the Red Army: Books and Libraries in American and British Prisoners of War Camps in Germany during World War II.* David Shavit. *Libraries & Culture.* (Article, 1999).

*How the World Sees Us.* Unknown. *American Libraries.* (Article, 2011).

*Inmate Challenges Ban.* Associated Press. *American Libraries.* (Article, 2006).

*Iowa May Close Prison Law Libraries.* Unknown. *American Libraries.* (Article, 1999).

*Iowa Prison Law Libs. On Death Row.* Norman Oder; Michael Rogers. *Library Journal.* (Article, 1999).

*Jailhouse Informants.* Russell Eisenman. *Journal of Information Ethics.* (Article, 2007).

*Kudos for Books in Prison* Merilyn Grosshans. *American Libraries.* (Article, 2011).

*Late Bulletins.* Unknown. *Library Journal.* (Article, 1997).

*The Least of Our Brethren.* Larry Sullivan. *American Libraries.* (Article, 2000).

*Libraries in Hell: Cultural Activities in Soviet Prisons and Labor Camps from the 1930s to the 1950s.* Ilkka Mäkinen. *Libraries & Culture.* (Article, 1993).

*Libraries in Lock-Up.* Jenn Hooker. *Public Libraries.* (Article, 2013).

*Library Services in Spanish Prisons: Current State of Affairs.* Margarita Pérez Pulido, Christina De Angelo. *Library Trends.* (Article, 2011).

*The Long Development of Prison Libraries in France.* Odile Cramard. *Library Trends.* (Article, 2011).

*The Mistreatment of Iraqis at Abu Ghraib Prison.* Russell Eisenman. *Journal of Information Ethics.* (Article, 2006).

*A New Emphasis for Correctional Facilities' Libraries.* David W. Wilhelmus. *The Journal of Academic Librarianship.* (Article, 1999).

*Out-Sorcerer.* Editor (article is about Daniel Marcou). *Library Journal* (Article, 2009).

*A Part of What I Do: An Interview with Mark Salzman.* Brendan Dowling. *Public Libraries.* (Article, 2004).

*People Were Literally Starving for Any Kind of Reading: The Theresienstadt Ghetto Central Library, 1942–1945.* Miriam Intrator. *Library Trends.* (Article, 2007).

*Picturing Classification: The Evolution and Use of Alternative Classification in Dutch Public Libraries.* Rachel Ivy Clarke. *Public Libraries.* (Article, 2013).

*Prison Law Librarianship: A Lesson in Service for All Librarians.* Karen Westwood. American Libraries. (Article, 1994).

*Prison Librarian Fired in Reprisal for Giving Access to Law Library.* E. McC. *American Libraries.* (Article, 1995).

*Prison Libraries Change Lives.* Julia Schneider. *American Libraries.* (Article, 1996).

*Prison Libraries in Italy.* Emanuela Costanzo, Giorgio Montecchi. *Library Trends.* (Article, 2011).

*Prison Libraries in Japan: The Current Situation of Access to Books and Reading in Correctional Institutions.* Kenichi Nakane. *Library Trends.* (Article, 2011).

*Prison Libraries in Poland: Partners in Rehabilitation, Culture, and Education.* Elzbieta Barbara Zybert. *Library Trends.* (Article, 2011).

*Prison Library Suit Reinstated.* Unknown. *American Libraries.* (Article, 2000).

*Prison Scam Used Books.* Unknown. *American Libraries.* (Article, 2006).

*Prisons Limit Religion Titles.* Lynn Blumenstein. *Library Journal.* (Article, 2007).

*Prisons Remove Religious Books.* Unknown. *American Libraries.* (Article, 2007).

*Prisons Say Rulings Won't Affect Inmates' Access to Libraries.* Leonard Kniffel. *American Libraries.* (Article, 1994).

*Public Libraries and the Ex-Offender.* Brendan Dowling. *Public Libraries.* (Article, 2007).

*Raunchy "Prison Classics" Pulled from Prison Libraries.* Thomas Gaughan. *American Libraries.* (Article, 1995).

*READ/Orange County: Changing Lives through Literacy.* Shari Selnick. *Public Libraries.* (Article, 2004).

*Reading in American Prisons: Structures and Strictures.* Larry Sullivan. *Libraries & Culture.* (Article, 1998).

*Recent Trends in UK Prison Libraries.* Carole Bowe. *Library Trends,* (Article, 2011).

*S.C. Scraps Innovative Prison Library System.* Ron Chepesiuk. *American Libraries.* (Article, 1995).

*A Theory of Life in the Round.* Elfreda A. Chatman. *Journal of the American Society for Information Science.* (Article, 1999).

*Two Cons Escape While Using PL.* Michael Rogers. *Library Journal.* (Article, 1999).

*Welcoming Children and Families Affected by Incarceration into Public Libraries.* Megan Sullivan. *Public Libraries.* (Article, 2013).

*When Is a Prison Not a Prison, an Inmate Not an Inmate, and a Guard Not a Guard?* Russel Eisenman. *Journal of Information Ethics* (Article, 2005).

*"You Work Where?"* Michael Bemis. *Library Journal.* (Article, 2011).

# Chapter Notes

## Introduction

1. American Correctional Association, *2013 Directory Adult and Juvenile Correctional Departments, Institutions, Agencies, and Probation and Parole Authorities*, 74th ed. (Alexandria, VA: American Correctional Association, 2013), 29.

2. "Incarceration," *Sentencing Project*, accessed December 28, 2015, http://www.sentencingproject.org/template/page.cfm?id=107.

3. Steven Raphael and Michael Stoll, *Why Are So Many Americans in Prison?* (New York: Russell Sage Foundation, 2013), 4, 27–31; Steven Raphael and Michael Stoll, *Do Prisons Make us Safer?* (New York: Russell Sage Foundation, 2009), 28.

4. Brenda Vogel, *Prison Library Primer* (Lanham, MD: Scarecrow Press, 2009), xvii.

5. Association of Specialized and Cooperative Library Agencies, *Library Standards for Adult Correctional Institutions* (Chicago: American Library Association, 1992), 1.

6. Vibeke Lehmann and Joanne Locke, "Guidelines for Library Services to Prisoners," 3rd ed., in *IFLA Professional Reports*, no. 92 (The Hague: International Federation of Library Associations and Institutions, 2005), 6.

7. American Correctional Association, *2013 Directory*, 65.

8. Rhea Joyce Rubin, "U.S. Prison Library Services and their Theoretical Base" (occasional paper no. 110, Graduate School of Library and Information Science, University of Illinois, 1973), 3.

9. Norval Morris and David Rothman eds., *The Oxford History of the Prison: the Practice of Punishment in Western Society* (New York: Oxford University Press, 1995), 156.

10. Adam Jay Hirsch, *The Rise of the Penitentiary: Prisons and Punishment in Early America* (New Haven: Yale University Press, 1992), 19.

11. Megan Sweeney, *Reading is My Window: Books and the Art of Reading in Women's Prisons* (Chapel Hill: University of North Carolina Press, 2010), 27–29.

12. Larry E. Sullivan and Brenda Vogel, "Reachin' Behind Bars: Library Outreach to Prisoners 1798–2000," in *Libraries to the People: Histories of Outreach*, ed. Robert S. Freeman and David M. Hovde (Jefferson, NC: McFarland, 2003), 114.

13. Hirsch, *The Rise of the Penitentiary*, 16.

14. *Ibid.*, 18–20.

15. "History of Eastern State Penitentiary, Philadel-phia," *Eastern State Penitentiary*, accessed January 10, 2016, http://www.easternstate.org/sites/default/files/pdf/ESP-history6.pdf.

16. Hirsch, *The Rise of the Penitentiary*, 65.

17. Larry E. Sullivan and Brenda Vogel, "Reachin' Behind Bars," 114.

18. Gerald Bramley, *Outreach: Library Services for the Institutionalized, the Elderly, and the Physically Handicapped* (Hamden, CT: Linnet, 1978), 71.

19. Janet Floyd, "Dislocations of the Self: Eliza Farnham at Sing Sing Prison," *Journal of American Studies* 40, no. 2 (August 2006): 313.

20. Rudolf Engelbarts, *Books in Stir: A Bibliographic Essay about Prison Libraries and About Books Written by Prisoners and Prison Employees* (Metuchen, NJ: Scarecrow Press, 1972), 27.

21. Kathrina Litchfield, "A Critical Impasse: Literacy Practice in American Prisons and the Future of Transformative Reading" (master's thesis, University of Iowa, 2014), http://ir.uiowa.edu/cgi/viewcontent.cgi?article=5194&context=etd. Litchfield summarizes extensive information about the history of reading in prisons.

22. Jonathan Abel, "Ineffective Assistance of Library: The Failings and the Future of Prison Law Libraries," *Georgetown Law Journal* 101, no. 5 (June 2013): 1180.

23. New York Prison Association, *Catalogue and Rules for Prison Libraries to aid in the Suitable Selection and Economical Maintenance of Reading Matter in the Prisons and Jails* (Albany: The Argus Company, 1877).

24. Bramley, *Outreach: Library Services*, 71.

25. Litchfield, "A Critical Impasse," 33.

26. Vibeke Lehmann, "Challenges and Accomplishments in U.S. Prison Libraries," *Library Trends* 59, no. 3 (2011): 494.

27. *Ibid.*, 170.

28. Eric Cummins, *The Rise and Fall of California's Radical Prison Movement* (Stanford: Stanford University Press, 1994), 21–22.

29. William J. Coyle, *Libraries in Prisons: A Blending of Institutions*, New Directions in Information Management 15 (New York: Greenwood Press, 1987), 57.

30. Lehmann, "Challenges and Accomplishments in U.S. Prison Libraries," 492.

31. Cummins, *Rise and Fall of California's Radical Prison*, 38.

32. Litchfield, "A Critical Impasse," 52.

33. Gervase Brinkman, "Correctional Libraries and LSCA Title IV-A," *American Libraries* 7, no. 4, April 1970, 383.

34. Michael B. Mushlin, *Rights of Prisoners*, 4th ed. ([United States?]: Thomson/West, 2009), 1:10.

35. Morris and Rothman, *The Oxford History of the Prison*, 171.

36. Abel, "Ineffective Assistance of Library," 1178.

37. Mushlin, *Rights of Prisoners*, 3:136.

38. *Ibid.*, 186–190.

39. *Private Prison Information Act of 2007, and review of the Prison Litigation Reform Act: a decade of reform or an increase in prison and abuses?: Hearings on H.R. 1889, Before the Subcommittee on Crime, Terrorism, and Homeland Security of the Committee on the Judiciary, House of Representatives*, 107th Cong. 149 (2007).

40. Caroline Wolf Harlow, "Education and Correctional Populations," special report prepared at the request of the Bureau of Justice Statistics, January 2003, 1.

41. *Ibid.*, 2.

42. American Correctional Association, *2013 Directory*, 61.

43. Laura Winterfield, Mark Coggeshall, Michelle Burke-Storer, Vanessa Correa and Simon Tidd, "The Effects of Postsecondary Correctional Education: Final Report" (Washington, D.C.: Urban Institution, Justice Policy Center, 2009), v..

44. *Ibid.*, 12.

45. Gerald G. Gaes, "The Impact of Prison Education Programs on Post-Release Outcomes," (presented at the Reentry Roundtable on Education, Jay College of Criminal Justice, New York City, March 31 and April 2008).

46. *Ibid.*, 11.

47. Vogel, *Prison Library Primer*.

48. Brenda Vogel, "Bailing Out Prison Libraries," *Library Journal* 122, no. 19, November 15, 1997, 35.

49. *Ibid.*, 36.

50. *Ibid.*, 37.

51. Vibeke Lehmann, "The Prison Library: A Vital Link to Education, Rehabilitation, and Recreation," *Education Libraries* 24, no. 1 (2000): 6.

52. Sheena McFarland, "Inmates See Prison Libraries as Tools to Making a Better Life," *Salt Lake Tribute*, May 11, 2010.

53. Julia Schneider and Ron Chepesiuk, "Prison Libraries Change Lives," *American Libraries*, 27, no. 10, November 1996, 46.

54. Jenna Scafuri, "Best in Business: Prison Libraries Make a Difference in Colorado," *Corrections Today*, June/July 2012, 30.

55. William Glaberson, "Prison Books Bring Plot Twist to Cheshire Killings," *New York Times*, July 10, 2010, http://www.nytimes.com/2010/07/22/nyregion/22cheshire.html.

56. *Ibid.*

57. Leanne Gendreau, "Lawmaker Wants Answers on Prison Library Policy," *NBC Connecticut*, July 22, 2010, http://www.nbcconnecticut.com/news/local/Lawmaker-Wants-Prison-Book-Policy-in-Light-of-Cheshire-Case-99007644.html.

58. Pat Eaton-Robb, "Conn. Prison Inmates Have Choice of Violent Books," *Associated Press*, October 3, 2010, http://www.washingtonpost.com/wp-dyn/content/article/2010/10/03/AR2010100301715.html.

59. *Ibid.*

60. *Ibid.*

61. *Ibid.*

62. *Ibid.*

63. Beverly Goldberg, "Ban Violent Books from Prison Libraries, Urges Connecticut State Senator," *American Libraries*, October 12, 2010, http://www.americanlibraries magazine.org/article/ban-violent-books-prison-libraries-urges-connecticut-state-senator.

64. "Connecticut Department of Correction Annual Report 2010," *Connecticut Department of Correction*, last modified July 1, 2010, http://www.ct.gov/doc/lib/doc/PDF/PDFReport/annualreport2010.pdf.

65. "Inmate Communications," *State of Connecticut Department of Correction*, last modified June 19, 2012, http://www.ct.gov/doc/LIB/doc/PDF/AD/ad1007.pdf.

66. "Title 18—Correctional Institutions and Department of Correction," *Department of Correction*, last modified March 7, 2015, https://eregulations.ct.gov/eRegs Portal/Browse/RCSA/%7B4EED71A5–398E-4A4F-A487-ABECF98318C4%7D.

67. "Connecticut Department of Correction Annual Report 2007," *Connecticut Department of Correction*, last modified July 1, 2007, http://www.ct.gov/doc/lib/doc/PDF/PDFReport/annualreport2007.pdf; "Connecticut Department of Correction Annual Report 2008," *Connecticut Department of Correction*, last modified July 1, 2008, http://www.ct.gov/doc/lib/doc/PDF/PDFReport/annualreport2008.pdf;

"Connecticut Department of Correction Annual Report 2009," *Connecticut Department of Correction*, last modified July 1, 2009, http://www.ct.gov/doc/lib/doc/PDF/PDFReport/annualreport2009.pdf;

"Connecticut Department of Correction Annual Report 2010," *Connecticut Department of Correction*, last modified July 1, 2010, http://www.ct.gov/doc/lib/doc/PDF/PDFReport/annualreport2010.pdf;

"Connecticut Department of Correction Annual Report 2011," *Connecticut Department of Correction*, last modified July 1, 2011, http://www.ct.gov/doc/lib/doc/PDF/PDFReport/annualreport2011.pdf; "Connecticut Department of Correction Annual Report 2012," *Connecticut Department of Correction*, last modified July 1, 2012, http://www.ct.gov/doc/lib/doc/PDF/PDFReport/annualreport2012.pdf;

"Connecticut Department of Correction Annual Report 2013," *Connecticut Department of Correction*, last modified July 1, 2013, http://www.ct.gov/doc/lib/doc/PDF/PDFReport/annualreport2013.pdf;

"Connecticut Department of Correction Annual Report 2014," *Connecticut Department of Correction*, last modified July 1, 2014, http://www.ct.gov/doc/lib/doc/PDF/PDFReport/annualreport2014.pdf. The 2014 numbers were not included in the calculation above because they do not appear to be accurate. The numbers reported in the 2014 report were identical to those reported in 2013.

68. Daniela Altimari, "Prison Book Policies Under Review," *Hartford Courant*, August 28, 2013, http://articles.courant.com/2013–08–28/news/hc-prison-reading-0829–20130828_1_books-library-shelves-new-yorker.

69. Matt Berman, "What You Can and Can't Read in Connecticut State Prisons," *National Journal*, August 30, 2013, http://www.nationaljournal.com/s/71586/what-you-can-cant-read-connecticut-state-prisons.

70. "Inmate Library Services," *State of Connecticut Department of Correction*, last modified September 1, 2011, http://www.ct.gov/doc/LIB/doc/PDF/AD/ad1016.pdf.

71. "Raunchy 'Prison Classics' Pulled from Prison Libraries," *American Libraries* 26, no. 2 February 1995, 126. Megan Sweeney also discusses the plethora of true crime novels in a women's prison in North Carolina. She claims that employees from the institution estimate that 75 percent of requests in the library are for true crime books. Megan Sweeney, "Living to Read True Crime: Theorizations from Prison," pts. 1 and 2, *Discourse* 25, no. 1 (Winter 2003); 25, no. 2 (Spring 2003): 55–80.

72. Ron Chepesiuk, "S.C. Scraps Innovative Prison Library System," *American Libraries* 26, no. 6 June 1995, 501.

73. *Ibid.*, 501.

74. Colin Dayan, "Words Behind Bars: Do Prisoners Have a Right to Read What They Want?," *Boston Review,* November 1, 2007, http://www.bostonreview.net/colin-dayan-words-behind-bars.

75. *Ibid.*

## Chapter 1

1. Megan Sweeney, *Reading Is My Window: Books and the Art of Reading in Women's Prisons* (Chapel Hill: University of North Carolina Press, 2010), 41.

2. Suzanna Conrad, "Collection Development and Circulation Policies in Prison Libraries: An Exploratory Survey of Librarians in U.S. Correctional Institutions," *The Library Quarterly* 82, no. 4 (2012): 407–427.

3. The ALA prison listserv is an electronic email discussion list maintained by the American Library Association. The listserv is open for anyone to subscribe to.

4. American Correctional Association, *Standards for Adult Correctional Institutions,* 2nd ed. (College Park, MD: American Correctional Association, 1981), 5.

5. Vibeke Lehmann and Joanne Locke, "Guidelines for Library Services to Prisoners," 3rd ed., in *IFLA Professional Reports,* no. 92 (The Hague: International Federation of Library Associations and Institutions, 2005), 4.

6. William J. Coyle, *Libraries in Prisons: A Blending of Institutions,* New Directions in Information Management 15 (New York: Greenwood Press, 1987), 2.

7. Linda Bayley, Leni Greenfield, and Flynn Nogueira, *Jail Library Service: A Guide for Librarians and Jail Administrators* (Chicago: American Library Association, 1981), 3.

8. ABA Standards for Criminal Justice, *Treatment of Prisoners,* 3rd ed. (United States of America: American Bar Association, 2011), 246–7.

9. Mary Bosworth, *The U.S. Federal Prison System* (Thousand Oaks, CA: Sage Publications, 2002), 69.

10. Bayley et al., *Jail Library Service,* viii.

11. John W. Palmer, *Constitutional Rights of Prisoners,* 8th ed. (Newark, NJ: LexisNexis, 2006), 71.

12. Bayley, *Jail Library Service,* 44.

13. Association of Specialized and Cooperative Library Agencies, *Library Standards for Adult Correctional Institutions* (Chicago: American Library Association, 1992), 18–20.

14. Lehmann and Locke, *IFLA Professional Reports,* 8.

15. Bayley et al., *Jail Library Service,* 33–35.

16. Association of Specialized and Cooperative Library Agencies, *Library Standards,* 14–16.

17. U.S. Department of Justice, *Federal Standards for Prisons and Jails* (U.S. Department of Justice: 1980), 18.04, 18.06.

18. American Correctional Association, *Standards for Adult Correctional Institutions,* 4th ed. (College Park, MD: American Correctional Association, 2003), 158–159.

19. Lehmann and Locke, *IFLA Professional Reports,* 9–10.

20. Bayley et al., *Jail Library Service,* 11.

21. Linda Schexnaydre and Kaylyn Robbins, *Jail Library Service: A Guide for Librarians and Jail Administrators* (Chicago: American Library Association, 1981), ix.

22. Association of Specialized and Cooperative Library Agencies, *Library Standards,* 13.

23. Coyle, *Libraries in Prisons,* 3.

24. Association of Specialized and Cooperative Library Agencies, *Library Standards,* 17; Lehmann and Locke, *IFLA Professional Reports,* 11.

25. Association of Specialized and Cooperative Library Agencies, *Library Standards,* 17.

26. Bosworth, *The U.S. Federal Prison System,* 69.

27. American Correctional Association, *2013 Directory Adult and Juvenile Correctional Departments, Institutions, Agencies, and Probation and Parole Authorities,* 74th ed. (Alexandria, VA: American Correctional Association, 2013), 38–39.

28. U.S. Department of Justice, *Federal Standards for Prisons and Jails,* 18.07.

29. Association of Specialized and Cooperative Library Agencies, *Library Standards,* 21.

30. *Ibid.,* 11.

31. *Ibid.,* 21; Lehmann and Locke, *IFLA Professional Reports,* 14.

32. American Correctional Association, *Standards for Adult Correctional Institutions,* 4th ed., 158.

33. Bayley et al., *Jail Library Service,* 4.

34. *Ibid.,* 60–69.

35. U.S. Department of Justice, *Federal Standards for Prisons and Jails,* 18.08–18.09.

36. American Correctional Association, *Standards for Adult Correctional Institutions,* 4th ed., 158–159.

37. Lehmann and Locke, *IFLA Professional Reports,* 4.

38. Sheila Clark and Erica MacCreaigh, *Library Services to the Incarcerated: Applying the Public Library Model in Correctional Facility Libraries* (Westport, CT: Libraries Unlimited, 2006), 13.

39. Bayley et al., *Jail Library Service,* 44.

40. Coyle, *Libraries in Prisons.*

41. Association of Specialized and Cooperative Library Agencies, *Library Standards,* 23–24.

42. Lehmann and Locke, *IFLA Professional Reports,* 9.

43. "Prisoners' Right to Read," *American Library Association,* last modified July 1, 2014, http://www.ala.org/advocacy/prisoners-right-read.

44. Brenda Vogel, "Two Million on the Wrong Side of the Digital Divide," *Interface* 30, no. 1 (2008).

45. U.S. Department of Justice, *Federal Standards for Prisons and Jails,* 18.03.

46. Bayley et al., *Jail Library Service,* 24–26.

47. Lehmann and Locke, *IFLA Professional Reports,* 15.

48. Bayley et al., *Jail Library Service*, 32.

49. Lehmann and Locke, *IFLA Professional Reports*, 15.

50. Association of Specialized and Cooperative Library Agencies, *Library Standards*, 23.

51. American Correctional Association, *Standards for Adult Correctional Institutions*, 4th ed., 158.

52. Lehmann and Locke, *IFLA Professional Reports*, 12.

53. Bayley et al., *Jail Library Service*, 55.

54. Lehmann and Locke, *IFLA Professional Reports*, 12.

55. Association of Specialized and Cooperative Library Agencies, *Library Standards*, 23. The standards define the number of materials that should be purchased based on the size of the institution. For books, at least 5,000 books should be made available in the collection, or 15 per inmate up to 2,500 prisoners. For magazines, at least 50 should be carried or one for every ten prisoners. Newspaper requirements vary depending on location and the institution. There should be at least 100 audio recordings or materials, or one for every five inmates. At least 20 videos should be in the collection or at least one for every thirty inmates. Additionally, it is recommended that interlibrary loan services be used to supplement the collection. The materials should be similar to those found in a public library or school. The collection should be weeded periodically. (23–24). Lehmann and Locke also list minimum amounts for the book, magazine, newspaper, audiovisual, and software collections based on inmate population and basic standards (2005, 14).

56. American Correctional Association, *Standards for Adult Correctional Institutions*, 4th ed., 158.

57. Lehmann and Locke, *IFLA Professional Reports*, 11.

58. Bayley et al., *Jail Library Service*, 24–26. Bayley et al. mention that any materials selected should support library programming, should be current in nature, and should reflect any diverse populations' needs. Lists should be maintained of items that were considered for inclusion and gifts may be accepted, but each item must be evaluated individually (99–100). Recommendations are also provided for getting materials through interlibrary loan from public library collections, purchasing materials directly, accepting gifts, using community programs and institutions, or getting donations from other individuals or groups (50–51).

59. "Bill of Rights," *American Library Association*, last modified January 23, 1996, http://www.ala.org/advocacy/intfreedom/librarybill.

60. Association of Specialized and Cooperative Library Agencies, *Library Standards*, 11. Microform is also listed as a type of material within this standard. In a 2012 article, I determined, based on survey results, that libraries were unlikely to be using microform.

61. Lehmann and Locke, *IFLA Professional Reports*, 13.

62. Bayley et al., *Jail Library Service*, 45–48.

63. "Prisoners' Right to Read," *American Library Association*.

64. ABA Standards for Criminal Justice, *Treatment of Prisoners*, 246–247. The right to media of some sort is also mentioned in the U.S. Department of Justice's *Federal Standards for Prisons and Jails* (1980).

65. Association of Specialized and Cooperative Library Agencies, *Library Standards*, 12.

66. Lehmann and Locke, *IFLA Professional Reports*, 7; Bayley et al., *Jail Library Service*, 50; U.S. Department of Justice, *Federal Standards for Prisons and Jails*, 18.09.

67. "Prisoners' Right to Read," *American Library Association*.

68. "Bill of Rights," *American Library Association*.

69. Bayley et al., *Jail Library Service*, 98–99.

70. Palmer, *Constitutional Rights of Prisoners*, 72. Palmer also mentions that the courts should make prison administration more accountable instead of leaving "little to no analysis of the process and standards used to reach that decision" when decisions are made regarding restriction of reading materials or mailed items (72). Furthermore, Palmer addresses the issues of receiving obscene material in the mail, which is not protected under the First Amendment, and concludes that "If the decision to exclude literature as obscene is left to a prison center, without meaningful administrative or judicial review, the inmates' rights will often depend on highly subjective decisions" (73).

71. United Nations, Resolution 217 A, "The Universal Declaration of Human Rights," December 10, 1948, http://www.un.org/en/documents/udhr/index.shtml.

72. "Prisoners' Right to Read," *American Library Association*.

73. *Ibid.*

74. *Ibid.*

75. "Bill of Rights," *American Library Association*.

76. Lehmann and Locke, *IFLA Professional Reports*, 4.

77. Rabun C. Sanders Jr., Hazel B. Kerper, George G. Killinger, and John C. Watkins, "Prisoners' First Amendment Rights Within the Institution," in *Criminal Justice Monograph* 3, no. 3 (Huntsville, TX: Institute of Contemporary Corrections and the Behavioral Sciences, Sam Houston State University, 1971), 65.

78. Association of Specialized and Cooperative Library Agencies, *Library Standards*, 10.

79. U.S. Department of Justice, *Federal Standards for Prisons and Jails*, 1.10; American Correctional Association, *Standards for Adult Correctional Institutions*, 2nd ed., 87.

80. Daniel Suvak's scathing review of Coyle's book is best summarized through his statement: "He calls for a complete rethinking of the model on which prison library service is based, namely, the public library model. He then asserts that this is the wrong choice of models, because public libraries are, and prison libraries should not be, responsive to the needs of their users. The arguments he invokes do such violence to accepted canons of library service that examining them may shed light on the broadest goals of librarianship." Daniel Suvak, "'Throw the Book at 'Em': The Change-Based Model for Prison Libraries," *Wilson Library Bulletin* 64, October 1989, 31.

81. Coyle, *Libraries in Prison*, 2.

82. "Prisoners' Right to Read," *American Library Association*.

83. *Ibid.* The "Prisoners' Right to Read" also highlights the principles from the "Bill of Rights" that, according to the ALA, still apply to prisoners. These include a written collection development policy, policies for challenging materials, needs assessment for material selection, ability to select materials without administration veto, accom-

modations for non-English speaking patrons, accessible materials for people with disabilities, the tenet that non-traditional materials should not be banned without legitimate cause, that sexual content is acceptable as long as it does not violate laws, and that prisoners should have access to computers and the Internet (2014).

84. American Library Association, "Resolution on Guantanamo and the Rights of Prisoners to Read," *SRRT Newsletter* 11, 2009, 11.

85. Bayley et al., *Jail Library Service*, 1.

86. *Ibid.*, viii.

87. U.S. Department of Justice, *Federal Standards for Prisons and Jails*, 18.01.

88. Association of Specialized and Cooperative Library Agencies, *Library Standards*, 21.

89. Lehmann and Locke, *IFLA Professional Reports*, 7.

90. U.S. Department of Justice, *Federal Standards for Prisons and Jails*, 18.05.

91. Association of Specialized and Cooperative Library Agencies, *Library Standards*, 12.

92. American Correctional Association, *Standards for Adult Correctional Institutions*, 4th ed., 73; Association of Specialized and Cooperative Library Agencies, *Library Standards*, 21–22.

93. Association of Specialized and Cooperative Library Agencies, *Library Standards*, 11.

94. "The Prison Litigation Reform Act: Know Your Rights," *American Civil Liberties Union*, last modified August 1, 2011, https://www.aclu.org/prisoners-rights/know-your-rights-prison-litigation-reform-act. The Prison Litigation Reform Act also required that filing fees be paid in full and that three strikes would apply to those submitting frivolous or malicious lawsuits.

95. "Fair Information Practice Principles," *Federal Trade Commission*, last modified 2012, http://www.ftc.gov/reports/privacy3/fairinfo.shtm (page discontinued).

96. *An Act to Deter and Punish Terrorist Acts in the United States and Around the World, to Enhance Law Enforcement Investigatory Tools, and for Other Purposes*, H.R.3162, 107th Cong. (2001).

97. "Resolution on the USA Patriot Act and Libraries," *American Library Association*, last modified June 29, 2005, http://www.ala.org/offices/sites/ala.org.offices/files/content/wo/reference/colresolutions/PDFs/062905-CD20.6.pdf.

98. "American Library Association 'Inimically Against' Bill to Extend Section 215 of PATRIOT Act Without 'Urgently Needed Change,'" *American Library Association*, last modified April 22, 2015, http://www.ala.org/news/press-releases/2015/04/american-library-association-inimically-against-bill-extend-section-215.

99. ABA Standards for Criminal Justice, *Treatment of Prisoners*, 217–218.

100. "Policy on Confidentiality of Library Records," *American Library Association*, last modified July 2, 1986, http://www.ala.org/advocacy/intfreedom/statementspols/otherpolicies/policyconfidentiality.

101. "Resolution on the Retention of Library Usage Records," *American Library Association*, in *Intellectual Freedom Manual*, 8th ed. (Chicago: American Library Association for Intellectual Freedom, 2010).

102. "Policy Concerning Confidentiality of Personally Identifiable Information about Library Users," *American Library Association*, last modified June 30, 2004, http://www.ifmanual.org/piipolicy.

103. Bayley et al., *Jail Library Service*, 37.

104. The author does not address how long after check-in the circulation records should be kept.

105. Bayley et al., *Jail Library Service*, 38.

106. "Code of Ethics of the American Library Association," *American Library Association*, last modified January 22, 2008, http://www.ala.org/advocacy/proethics/codeofethics/codeethics.

107. "Bill of Rights," *American Library Association*.

108. "Policy Concerning Confidentiality of Personally Identifiable Information about Library Users," *American Library Association*.

109. Association of Specialized and Cooperative Library Agencies, *Library Standards*, 2.

110. American Correctional Association, *Standards for Adult Correctional Institutions*, 4th ed., 76.

111. Katherine Skolnick, ed., *A Jailhouse Lawyer's Manual*, 8th ed. (New York: Columbia Human Rights Law Review, 2009), 32–33.

112. U.S. Department of Justice, *Federal Standards for Prisons and Jails*, 1.05.

113. ABA Standards for Criminal Justice, *Treatment of Prisoners*, 315–316.

114. Bosworth, *The U.S. Federal Prison System*, 70.

## *Chapter 2*

1. "Directory of State Prison Libraries," *Washington Office of the Secretary of State*, last modified July 10, 2014, http://wiki.sos.wa.gov/ils/.

2. *Ibid.*

3. "Inmate Library Services," *State of Connecticut Department of Correction*, last modified September 1, 2011, http://www.ct.gov/doc/LIB/doc/PDF/AD/ad1016.pdf, 1.

4. "Library Service," *Department of Public Safety Corrections Administration Policy and Procedures*, last modified February 23, 2010, http://dps.hawaii.gov/wp-content/uploads/2012/10/COR.14.16.pdf, 1.

5. This policy was subsequently revised in 2015 after research for this chapter was completed. "Education Resource Center Services," *New Mexico Corrections Department*, last modified May 31, 2012, http://corrections.state.nm.us/policies/docs/CD-120200.pdf, 1.

6. "Inmate Programs," *Arkansas Department of Correction*, last modified 2011, http://adc.arkansas.gov/inmates/Pages/InmatePrograms3.aspx.

7. "Education Services," *Florida Department of Corrections*, last modified 2012, http://www.dc.state.fl.us/orginfo/education/index.html (page discontinued).

8. "Library Service," *Department of Public Safety*, 2.

9. "Library," *Minnesota Department of Corrections*, last modified July 6, 2010, http://www.doc.state.mn.us/DOcpolicy2/html/DPW_Display.asp?Opt=204.045.htm. A newer version of this policy was posted in 2015 after research for this chapter was completed.

10. "Library Services (Inmate)," *Oregon Department of Corrections*, last modified 2012, http://arcweb.sos.state.or.us/pages/rules/oars_200/oar_291/291_141.html.

11. "103 CMR 478.00: Library Services," *Massachusetts Department of Correction*, last accessed September

27, 2013, http://www.lawlib.state.ma.us/source/mass/cmr/cmrtext/103CMR478.pdf, 3 (page discontinued).

12. "Library Services," *Department of Correctional Services State of Nebraska*, last modified March 15, 2011, http://www.corrections.state.ne.us/pdf/ar/rights/AR%20107.01.pdf, 2 (page discontinued).

13. "Library Services: General Library," *State of Alaska Department of Corrections Policies and Procedures*, last modified 2002, http://www.correct.state.ak.us/pnp/pdf/814.01.pdf, 2. This policy has been subsequently updated since research for this book was completed.

14. "Education Services," *Florida Department of Corrections*.

15. "Library Service," *Department of Public Safety*, 1.

16. "Section 430.20 Library Services and Legal Materials," *Joint Committee on Administrative Rules*, last modified 1984, http://ilga.gov/commission/jcar/admincode/020/020004300000200R.html.

17. "Selection and Acquisition of Library Materials," *State of Ohio Department of Rehabilitation and Correction*, last modified October 26, 2011, http://www.drc.ohio.gov/web/drc_policies/documents/58-LIB-03.pdf, 3; "The Development and Delivery of Education and Recreation Library Services," *Indiana Department of Correction*, last modified May 1, 2008, http://www.in.gov/idoc/files/01-01-102_Library_Services__5-01-08.pdf, 4. Ohio's policy was updated in 2014 after research for this chapter was completed.

18. "103 CMR 478.00: Library Services," *Massachusetts Department of Correction*, 5.

19. "Library Services," *State of Montana Department of Corrections*, last modified April 20, 2011, http://www.cor.mt.gov/content/Resources/Policy/Chapter5/5-3-2.pdf, 1 (page discontinued).

20. "Inmate Library Services," *State of Connecticut Department of Correction*; "Institutional Library Services," *Michigan Department of Corrections*, last modified November 1, 2010, https://www.michigan.gov/documents/corrections/05_03_110_337354_7.pdf, 2; "Education Resource Center Services," *New Mexico Corrections Department*, 5.

21. "Institutional Library Services," *Michigan Department of Corrections*, 2; "Library," *Minnesota Department of Corrections*.

22. "Library and Law Library," *State of California Department of Corrections and Rehabilitation*, last modified April 8, 2010, http://www.cdcr.ca.gov/regulations/adult_operations/docs/DOM/NCDOM/2010NCDOM/10-06/DOM%20Text%20Chp10%20Art12%20clean.pdf, 4 (page discontinued).

23. "Library Services," *Colorado Department of Corrections*, last modified November 1, 2011, http://www.doc.state.co.us/sites/default/files/ar/0500_02_110111_0.pdf, 10.

24. "Institutional Library Services," *Rhode Island Department of Corrections*, last modified August 11, 2008, http://www.doc.ri.gov/documents/rehabilitative/library%20english.pdf, 3–4.

25. "Library Services," *Wyoming Department of Corrections*, last modified May 15, 2013, http://corrections.wy.gov/Media.aspx?mediaId=396, 7–8. This policy was updated in 2015 after research for this chapter was completed.

26. "Library Services," *State of Washington Department of Corrections*, last modified April 23, 2012, http://www.doc.wa.gov/policies/showFile.aspx?name=510010, 3.

27. "Offender Libraries," *Oklahoma Department of Corrections*, last modified June 7, 2012, http://www.ok.gov/doc/documents/op030115.pdf, 2. This policy was updated in 2015 after research for this chapter was completed.

28. "Education Resource Center Services," *New Mexico Corrections Department*, 2. The abbreviation ERC stands for Education Resource Center.

29. "Library Facilities, Holdings, and Services," *Kansas Department of Corrections*, last modified January 7, 2011, http://www.doc.ks.gov/kdoc-policies/AdultIMPP/chapter-10/10107.pdf, 1.

30. "Inmate Education and Resource Center Services," *Arizona Department of Corrections*, last modified March 14, 2006, http://www.azcorrections.gov/Policies/900/0910.pdf, 13 (page discontinued).

31. "Library Services," *State of Washington Department of Corrections*, 3.

32. "Inmate Programs," *Arkansas Department of Correction*; "Library and Law Library," *State of California Department of Corrections and Rehabilitation*.

33. "Library Services," *State of North Carolina Department of Correction Division of Prisons*, last modified September 24, 2007, http://www.doc.state.nc.us/dop/policy_procedure_manual/D1100.pdf.

34. "Library Services: General Library," *State of Alaska Department of Corrections Policies and Procedures*.

35. "Library Facilities, Holdings, and Services," *Kansas Department of Corrections*, 1; "103 CMR 478.00: Library Services," *Massachusetts Department of Correction*, 5; "Library Services," *Nevada Department of Corrections*, last modified April 8, 2011, http://www.doc.nv.gov/sites/doc/files/pdf/AR840.pdf, 1 (page discontinued); "Education Resource Center Services," *New Mexico Corrections Department*, 2; "Library Services," *State of North Carolina Department of Correction Division of Prisons*, 2.

36. "Library Services," *Department of Correctional Services State of Nebraska*, 3; "The Development and Delivery," *Indiana Department of Correction*.

37. "Library Services," *State of Montana Department of Corrections*, 1.

38. "Library Services: General Library," *State of Alaska Department of Corrections*, 2.

39. "Library Services," *State of Washington Department of Corrections*, 2.

40. "Library Services (Inmate)," *Oregon Department of Corrections*.

41. "Comprehensive Library Services," *State of Ohio Department of Rehabilitation and Correction*, last modified December 11, 2012, http://www.drc.ohio.gov/web/drc_policies/documents/58-LIB-01.pdf, 2. This policy was updated in 2014 after research for this chapter was completed.

42. "Inmate Library Services," *State of Connecticut Department of Correction*.

43. "Library Service," *Department of Public Safety*, 2.

44. "Institutional Library Services," *Rhode Island Department of Corrections*, 2.

45. "Institutional Library Services," *Michigan Department of Corrections*, 2.

46. "Library Services," *Wyoming Department of Corrections*, 6.

47. "Library and Law Library," *State of California Department of Corrections and Rehabilitation*, 2.

48. "Library Services," *Colorado Department of Corrections.*

49. "Library," *Minnesota Department of Corrections.*

50. "Library Service," *Department of Public Safety*, 3.

51. "Inmate Library Services," *State of Connecticut Department of Correction*, 4.

52. "Connecticut Department of Correction Annual Report 2010," *Connecticut Department of Correction*, last modified July 1, 2010, http://www.ct.gov/doc/lib/doc/PDF/PDFReport/annualreport2010.pdf.

53. "Library Services," *Colorado Department of Corrections*, 9.

54. "The Development and Delivery," *Indiana Department of Correction*, 5.

55. *Ibid.*, 3.

56. "103 CMR 478.00: Library Services," *Massachusetts Department of Correction*, 2.

57. *Ibid.*, 2.

58. "Education Resource Center Services," *New Mexico Corrections Department*, 4.

59. "California Code of Regulations: Title 15. Crime Prevention and Corrections," *State of California Department of Corrections and Rehabilitation*, last modified January 2013, http://www.cdcr.ca.gov/Regulations/Adult_Operations/docs/Title15–2013.pdf (page discontinued).

60. "Library Services," *Colorado Department of Corrections.*

61. "Access to Courts/Law Library," *Oklahoma Department of Corrections*, last modified October 12, 2012, http://www.ok.gov/doc/documents/op030115.pdf. This policy was updated in 2015 after the research for this chapter was completed.

62. "Inmate Access to Courts," *State of Vermont Agency of Human Services Department of Corrections*, last modified January 11, 1999, http://www.doc.state.vt.us/about/policies/rpd/correctional-services-301–550/385–389-programs-education-services/385.01%20Inmate%20Access%20To%20Courts%20Template.pdf.

63. "Library Services: Law Library," *State of Alaska Department of Corrections Policies and Procedures*, 2.

64. "California Code of Regulations," *State of California Department of Corrections and Rehabilitation*, 79.

65. "Offender Legal Services," *Colorado Department of Corrections*, last modified February 1, 2013, http://www.doc.state.co.us/sites/default/files/ar/0750_01_020113.pdf, 5.

66. "Education Services," *Florida Department of Corrections.*

67. "Inmate Legal Access," *Nevada Department of Corrections*, last modified June 17, 2012, http://www.doc.nv.gov/sites/doc/files/pdf/ar/AR722.pdf (page discontinued).

68. "Legal Affairs (Inmate)," *Oregon Department of Corrections*, last modified 2012, http://arcweb.sos.state.or.us/pages/rules/oars_200/oar_291/291_139.html.

69. "Access to Courts/Law Library," *Oklahoma Department of Corrections.*

70. "Inmate Access to Courts," *Wyoming Department of Corrections*, last modified October 22, 2012, http://corrections.wy.gov/Media.aspx?mediaId=33. This policy was updated in 2015 after research for this chapter was completed.

71. "Offender Legal Access," *Virginia Department of Corrections*, last modified March 1, 2012, http://vadoc.

virginia.gov/about/procedures/documents/800/866–3.pdf. This policy was updated in 2015 after research for this chapter was completed.

72. "Inmate Legal Access to the Courts," *Arizona Department of Corrections*, last modified July 6, 2013, http://www.azcorrections.gov/policysearch/900/0902.pdf (page discontinued).

73. "Library Facilities, Holdings, and Services," *Kansas Department of Corrections.*

74. Ben Branstetter, "The Case for Internet Access in Prisons," *Intersect*, February 9, 2015, https://www.washingtonpost.com/news/the-intersect/wp/2015/02/09/the-case-for-internet-access-in-prisons/.

75. "Education Resource Center Services," *New Mexico Corrections Department*, 2.

76. "Library Services: Law Library," *State of Alaska Department of Corrections Policies and Procedures*, last modified May 16, 2013, http://www.correct.state.ak.us/pnp/pdf/814.02.pdf; "Offender Legal Services," *Colorado Department of Corrections.*

77. "California Code of Regulations," *State of California Department of Corrections and Rehabilitation*, 29.

78. "Offender Legal Access," *Virginia Department of Corrections*, 3.

79. "Inmate Access to Courts," *Wyoming Department of Corrections.*

80. "Inmate Legal Access," *Nevada Department of Corrections.*

81. "Section 430.20 Library Services and Legal Materials," *Joint Committee on Administrative Rules.*

82. "103 CMR 478.00: Library Services," *Massachusetts Department of Correction*, 4.

83. "Law Libraries," *Michigan Department of Corrections*, last modified November 1, 2010, http://www.michigan.gov/documents/corrections/0503115_409693_7.pdf, 2.

## *Chapter 3*

1. Larry E. Sullivan and Brenda Vogel, "Reachin' Behind Bars: Library Outreach to Prisoners 1798–2000," in *Libraries to the People: Histories of Outreach*, ed. Robert S. Freeman and David M. Hovde (Jefferson, NC: McFarland, 2003), 121.

2. Larry E. Sullivan, "Between Empty Covers: Prison Libraries in Historical Perspective," *Wilson Library Bulletin* 64, October 1989, 26.

3. Rudolf Engelbarts, *Books in Stir: A Bibliographic Essay about Prison Libraries and about Books Written by Prisoners and Prison Employees* (Metuchen, NJ: Scarecrow Press, 1972), 19.

4. Kathleen de la Peña McCook, "Public Libraries and People in Jail," *Reference and User Services Quarterly* 44, no. 1 (2004): 28.

5. Robert Stearns, "The Prison Library: An Issue for Corrections, or a Correct Solution for its Issues?," *Behavioral and Social Sciences Librarian* 23, no. 1 (2004): 50.

6. Larry E. Sullivan, "Reading in American Prisons: Structures and Strictures," *Libraries and Culture* 33, no. 1 (1998): 113.

7. Robert Stearns, "The Prison Library," 62; David W. Wilhelmus, "A New Emphasis for Correctional Facil-

ities' Libraries," *The Journal of Academic Librarianship* 25, no. 2 (1999): 114.

8. Sheila Clark and Erica MacCreaigh, *Library Services to the Incarcerated: Applying the Public Library Model in Correctional Facility Libraries* (Westport, CT: Libraries Unlimited, 2006), 2.

9. Daniel Suvak, "'Throw the Book at 'Em': The Change-Based Model for Prison Library," *Wilson Library Bulletin* 64, October 1989, 33; Sullivan and Vogel, "Reachin' Behind Bars," 123.

10. William J. Coyle, *Libraries in Prison: A Blending of Institutions*, New Directions in Information Management 15 (New York: Greenwood Press, 1987), 2.

11. Sullivan, "Between Empty Covers," 26.

12. Vibeke Lehmann, "The Prison Library: A Vital Link to Education, Rehabilitation, and Recreation," *Education Libraries* 24, no. 1 (2000): 7.

13. Avi Steinberg, *Running the Books: The Adventures of an Accidental Prison Librarian* (New York: Anchor Books, 2010).

14. Virgil Gulker, *Books Behind Bars* (Metuchen, NJ: Scarecrow Press, 1973), viii.

15. *Ibid.*, 55.

16. *Ibid.*, 59.

17. Susan McDonald, ed., "Acquisitions for Prison Libraries," *Library Acquisitions: Practice & Theory* 7, no. 1 (1983): 33.

18. *Ibid.*, 33.

19. Fred R. Hartz, Michael B. Krimmel, and Emilie K. Hartz, *Prison Librarianship: A Selective, Annotated, Classified Bibliography, 1945–1985* (Jefferson, NC: McFarland & Company, Inc., 1987), 6–8.

20. Brenda Vogel, "Bailing Out Prison Libraries," *Library Journal* 122, no. 19, November 15, 1997, 36.

21. Brenda Vogel, *Prison Library Primer* (Lanham, MD: Scarecrow Press, 2009), 181–188.

22. Rhea Joyce Rubin, "U.S. Prison Library Services and their Theoretical Base" (occasional paper no. 110, Graduate School of Library and Information Science, University of Illinois, 1973), 2.

23. Sullivan, "Reading in American Prisons," 113–114.

24. Vibeke Lehmann, "Challenges and Accomplishments in U.S. Prison Libraries," *Library Trends* 59, no. 3 (2011): 494.

25. Sandra A. Greenway, "Library Services Behind Bars," *Bookmobiles and Outreach Services* 10, no. 2 (2007): 49.

26. Diane K. Campbell, "The Context of the Information Behavior of Prison Inmates," *Progressive Librarian* 26 (Winter 2005): 18.

27. Vogel, *Prison Library Primer*, 19.

28. Judith Jordet, "Part I: The Prison Library as Pro-Social Institution," *Corrections.com*, April 11, 2011, http://www.corrections.com/news/article/27732.

29. Vogel, "Bailing Out Prison Libraries," 37.

30. Sullivan and Vogel, "Reachin' Behind Bars," 125.

31. Coyle, *Libraries in Prisons*, 66; Sullivan and Vogel, "Reachin' Behind Bars," 125.

32. Vibeke Lehmann, "Introduction," *Library Trends* 59, no. 3 (2011): 385.

33. Vogel, *Prison Library Primer*, 20–21.

34. Engelbarts, *Books in Stir*, 35.

35. Vogel, *Prison Library Primer*, 176.

36. Linda Lucas, "Educating Prison Librarians,"

*Journal of Education for Library and Information Science* 30, no. 3 (Winter 1990).

37. Harris C. McClaskey, "Training and Research in Correctional Librarianship," *Library Trends* 26, no. 1 (Summer 1977): 47.

38. Vogel, *Prison Library Primer*, 146.

39. *Ibid.*, 148.

40. Brenda Vogel, "In Preparation for a Visit to a Smaller Planet," *Wilson Library Bulletin* 64, October 1989.

41. Glen Singer, "Prison Libraries Inside Out," *Education Libraries* 24, no. 1 (2000): 13.

42. Clark and MacCreaigh, *Library Services to the Incarcerated*, 46.

43. Campbell, "The Context of Information Behavior," n.p.

44. Hartz et al., *Prison Librarianship*, 3.

45. *Ibid.*, vi.

46. *Ibid.*, xvi.

47. Gulker, *Books Behind Bars*, 46.

48. Larry E. Sullivan, "The Least of Our Brethern: Library Service to Prisoners," *American Libraries* 31, no. 5, May 2000, 56–57.

49. Megan Sweeney, *Reading is My Window: Books and the Art of Reading in Women's Prisons* (Chapel Hill: University of North Carolina Press, 2010), 41.

50. Stearns, "The Prison Library," 63.

51. Gulker, *Books Behind Bars*, 46.

52. Diana Reese, "Collection Development," in *Libraries Inside: A Practical Guide for Prison Libraries*, ed. Rhea J. Rubin and Daniel Suvak (Jefferson, NC: McFarland & Co., 1995), 78.

53. Clark and MacCreaigh, *Library Services to the Incarcerated*, 46.

54. *Ibid.*, 101.

55. Hartz et al., *Prison Librarianship*, 5.

56. Stearns, "The Prison Library," 70.

57. *Ibid.*, 73.

58. Clark and MacCreaigh, *Library Services to the Incarcerated*, 6.

59. Gerald Bramley, *Outreach: Library Services for the Institutionalized, the Elderly, and the Physically Handicapped* (Hamden, CT: Linnet, 1978), 58.

60. Wilhelmus, "A New Emphasis for Correctional Facilities' Libraries," 114.

61. Lehmann, "Challenges and Accomplishments in U.S. Prison Libraries," 503.

62. Coyle, *Libraries in Prisons*, 3.

63. Glennor Shirley, "Correctional Libraries, Library Standards, and Diversity," *JCE* 54, no. 2 (June 2003): 73.

64. *Ibid.*, 73.

65. Engelbarts, *Books in Stir*, 51–52.

66. Rhea Joyce Rubin, "The Planning Process," in *Libraries Inside: A Practical Guide for Prison Libraries*, ed. Rhea J. Rubin and Daniel Suvak (Jefferson, NC: McFarland & Co., 1995), 34–35.

67. *Ibid.*, 36.

68. Stearns, "The Prison Library," 73.

69. Bramley, *Outreach: Library Services for the Institutionalized*, 57.

70. Greenway, "Library Services Behind Bars," 53.

71. *Ibid.*, 49.

72. Marjorie LeDonne, *Survey of Library and Information Problems in Correctional Institutions*, vol. 1, *Findings and Recommendations, ILR-73-008, Final Report,*

special report prepared at the request of the Office of Education, Washington, D.C. (Berkeley: University of California, Berkeley Institute of Library Research, 1974), 70–71.

73. *Ibid.*, 71.

74. McDonald, "Acquisitions for Prison Libraries," 33.

75. Gulker, *Books Behind Bars*, 20.

76. Vogel, *Prison Library Primer*, 43.

77. Sweeney, *Reading is My Window*, 7.

78. Reese, "Collection Development," 69.

79. *Ibid.*, 70–71.

80. Vogel, *Prison Library Primer*, 43.

81. *Ibid.*, 54–55.

82. "Prisoners' Right to Read," *American Library Association*, last modified July 1, 2014, http://www.ala.org/advocacy/prisoners-right-read.

83. Bramley, *Outreach: Library Services for the Institutionalized*, 91–92.

84. *Ibid.*, 93.

85. Hartz et al., *Prison Librarianship*, 7–8.

86. Reese, "Collection Development," 78.

87. Michael Bemis, "Prison Librarian—An Inside Job with Outsize Benefits: 'You Work Where?,'" *Library Journal* 136, no. 17, October 15, 2011, 108.

88. Vogel, "Bailing Out Prison Libraries," 36.

89. *Ibid.*, 36.

90. Vogel, *Prison Library Primer*, 170.

91. Steinberg, *Running the Books*, 66.

92. Gulker, *Books Behind Bars*, 19.

93. Gulker, *Books Behind Bars*, 36, 47.

94. Greenway, "Library Services Behind Bars," 53–54.

95. Amy Mark, "Libraries Without Walls: An Internship at Oshkosh Correctional Institution Library," *Behavioral and Social Sciences Librarian* 23, no. 2 (2005): 103.

96. *Ibid.*, 104.

97. Teresa S. Bowden, "A Snapshot of State Prison Libraries with a Focus on Technology," *Behavioral and Social Sciences Librarian* 21, no. 2 (December 2002): 5.

98. Singer, "Prison Libraries Inside Out," 14.

99. Steinberg, *Running the Books*, 218.

100. Larry E. Sullivan, "Prison is Dull Today: Prison Libraries and the Ironies of Pious Reading," *PMLA: Publications of the Modern Language Association of America* 123, no. 3 (2008).

101. *Ibid.*, 703.

102. Greenway, "Library Services Behind Bars," 49–50.

103. Mark, "Libraries without Walls: An Internship at Oshkosh Correctional Institution Library," 103.

104. McDonald, "Acquisitions for Prison Libraries, 31.

105. Vogel, *Prison Library Primer*, 48.

106. LeDonne, *Survey of Library and Information Problems*, 45–46.

107. *Ibid.*, 53.

108. Hartz et al., *Prison Librarianship*, 8.

109. Brenna Doyle, "Incarceration and the 'Freedom to Read': How Prison Libraries Function as Instruments of State Power," *Genders Journal* 58 (2013), http://www.genders.org/g58/g58_doyle.html (page discontinued).

110. Clark and MacCreaigh, *Library Services to the Incarcerated*, 102.

111. Daniel Suvak, "'Throw the Book at 'Em': The

Change-Based Model for Prison Library," *Wilson Library Bulletin* 64, October 1989, 31.

112. Vogel, "Bailing Out Prison Libraries," 35.

113. *Ibid.*, 37.

114. Sullivan, "The Least of Our Brethern," 58.

115. Bowden, "A Snapshot of State Prison Libraries," 9.

116. Some of these policies may have been updated since the research in Chapter 2 was completed, however, as of the dates of research in 2013, very few mentioned technology.

117. Lehmann, "Introduction," 385.

118. Lehmann, "Challenges and Accomplishments in U.S. Prison Libraries," 499.

119. *Ibid.*, 501–502.

120. Vogel, *Prison Library Primer*, 68.

121. William Payne and Michael J. Sabath, "Trends in the Use of Information Management Technology in Prison Libraries," *Behavioral and Social Sciences Librarian* 26, no. 2 (2007).

122. Shirley, "Correctional Libraries, Library Standards, and Diversity."

123. Vogel, *Prison Library Primer*, 154.

124. *Ibid.*, 153.

125. *Ibid.*, 157–162.

126. *Ibid.*, 164–165.

127. *Ibid.*, 181–182.

128. Brenda Vogel, "Two Million on the Wrong Side of the Digital Divide," *Interface* 30, no. 1 (2008).

129. *Ibid.*, n.p.

130. Lehmann, "Challenges and Accomplishments in U.S. Prison Libraries," 500.

131. *Ibid.*, 504.

132. Kimberley Railey, "Some Prisons Let Inmates Connect with Tablets," *USA Today*, last modified August 18, 2013, http://www.usatoday.com/story/news/nation/2013/08/17/tabletsforinmates/2651727/.

133. "From Prisoners to Programmers—San Quentin Inmates Are Learning to Code," *CBS SF Bay Area*, November 13, 2014, http://sanfrancisco.cbslocal.com/2014/11/13/from-prisoners-to-programmers-san-quentin-inmates-are-learning-how-to-code-the-last-mile/.

134. Engelbarts, *Books in Stir*, 36.

135. Brenda Vogel, "Inmate Informational Needs Survey: Final Report," special report prepared at the request of the Maryland Department of Public Safety, February 1976, 4. https://www.ncjrs.gov/pdffiles1/Digitization/74789NCJRS.pdf.

136. *Ibid.*, 8.

137. *Ibid.*, 8.

138. Gulker, *Books Behind Bars*, 10.

139. *Ibid.*, 21–22, 42.

140. *Ibid.*, 35.

141. LeDonne, *Survey of Library and Information Problems*, 70.

142. Sullivan, "The Least of Our Brethren," 57.

143. Clark and MacCreaigh, *Library Services to the Incarcerated*, 83.

144. Stearns, "The Prison Library," 65.

145. Lehmann, "Challenges and Accomplishments in U.S. Prison Libraries," 503.

146. Gulker, *Books Behind Bars*, 21.

147. Wilhelmus, "A New Emphasis," 115.

148. Judith Jordet, "Part II: The Prison Library as Cul-

tural Connection," Corrections.com, April 25, 2011, http://www.corrections.com/news/article/28421-part-ii-the-prison-library-as-cultural-connection.

149. Judith Jordet, "Part III: The Prison Library: Promoting Reading & Pro-Social Connection," Corrections.com, May 2, 2011, http://www.corrections.com/news/article/28433-part-iii-the-prison-library-promoting-reading-pro-social-connection.

150. Rubin, "The Planning Process," 31–33.

151. Reese, "Collection Development," 79.

152. Campbell, "The Context of Information Behavior," 18.

153. Clark and MacCreaigh, *Library Services to the Incarcerated*, 61.

154. Gulker, *Books Behind Bars*, 3.

155. *Ibid.*, 12.

156. Doyle, "Incarceration and the 'Freedom to Read.'"

157. Reese, "Collection Development," 77–79.

158. Greenway, "Library Services Behind Bars," 49.

159. Elizabeth Jahnke and Laura Sherbo, "Prison Libraries Guard Intellectual Freedom," *Alki* 23, no. 3 (December 2007): 23.

160. Singer, "Prison Libraries Inside Out," 12.

161. LeDonne, *Survey of Library and Information Problems*, i.

162. Lehmann, "Challenges and Accomplishments in U.S. Prison Libraries," 501.

163. Clark and MacCreaigh, *Library Services to the Incarcerated*, 13.

164. Vogel, *Prison Library Primer*, 60.

165. *Ibid.*, v.

166. *Ibid.*, 77.

167. Doyle, "Incarceration and the 'Freedom to Read.'"

168. LeDonne, *Survey of Library and Information Problems*, 69.

169. Coyle, *Libraries in Prisons*, 2.

170. Suzanna Conrad, "Collection Development and Circulation Policies in Prison Libraries: An Exploratory Survey of Librarians in U.S. Correctional Institutions," *The Library Quarterly* 82, no. 4 (October 2012): 407–427.

171. Clark and MacCreaigh, *Library Services to the Incarcerated*, 17.

172. *Ibid.*, 18.

173. *Ibid.*, 102.

174. Herman K. Spector, *The Library Program of the State Department of Correction* (Sacramento: Department of Correction, 1959), 14.

175. Eric Cummins, *The Rise and Fall of California's Radical Prison Movement* (Stanford: Stanford University Press, 1994), 27.

176. Sullivan and Vogel, "Reachin' Behind Bars," 124.

177. Vogel, "Bailing Out Prison Libraries," 37.

178. Vogel, *Prison Library Primer*, 66.

179. Campbell, "The Context of Information Behavior," 18.

180. Vogel, *Prison Library Primer*, 71–72.

181. Clark and MacCreaigh, *Library Services to the Incarcerated*, 193–194.

182. Vogel, *Prison Library Primer*, 68.

## Chapter 4

1. Norval Morris and David J. Rothman, eds., *The Oxford History of the Prison: The Practice of Punishment in Western Society* (New York: Oxford University Press, 1995), 171.

2. Michael B. Mushlin, *Rights of Prisoners*, 4th ed. ([United States?]: Thomson/West, 2009), 1:9.

3. *Ibid.*, 15.

4. William Mark Roth, "Turner v. Safley: The Supreme Court Further Confuses Prisoners' Constitutional Rights," *Loyola of Los Angeles Law Review* 22, no. 2 (January 1, 1989): 667, accessed January 6, 2014, http://digitalcommons.lmu.edu/llr/vol22/iss2/6.

5. "Postcard only" policies only allow prisoners to receive correspondence in short form such as a postcard.

6. "Legal Action," *Prison Legal News*, accessed December 30, 2015, https://www.prisonlegalnews.org/legal-action-map/.

## Chapter 5

1. Michael B. Mushlin, *Rights of Prisoners*, 4th ed. ([United States?]: Thomson/West, 2009).

2. Norval Morris and David J. Rothman, eds., *The Oxford History of the Prison: The Practice of Punishment in Western Society* (New York: Oxford University Press, 1995), 171.

3. Mushlin, *Rights of Prisoners*, 3:136.

4. Rebecca S. Trammell, *Werner's Manual for Prison Law Libraries*, 3rd ed. (Buffalo, NY: William S. Hein & Co., Inc., 2004), 11.

5. Lynn S. Branham, *The Law of Sentencing, Corrections, and Prisoners' Rights in a Nutshell*, 6th ed. (St. Paul, MN: West Group, 2002).

6. Mushlin, *Rights of Prisoners*, 3:140.

7. Joseph L. Gerken, "Does Lewis v. Casey Spell the End to Court-Ordered Improvement of Prison Law Libraries?," *Law Library Journal* 95, no. 4 (Fall 2003).

8. Branham, *The Law of Sentencing*, 170–171.

9. *Ibid.*

10. *Ibid.*, 199.

11. Wayne Ryan, "Access to the Courts: Prisoners' Right to a Law Library," *Howard Law Journal* 26, no. 91 (1983), 91.

12. Steven D. Hinckley, "Bounds and Beyond: A Need to Reevaluate the Right of Prison Access to the Courts," *University of Richmond Law Review* 22, no. 19 (1987).

13. *Ibid.*, 19–20.

14. Arturo A. Flores, "Bounds and Reality: Lawbooks Alone Do Not a Lawyer Make," *Law Library Journal* 77, no. 275 (1984–1985).

15. Christopher E. Smith, "Examining the Boundaries of Bounds: Prison Law Libraries and Access to the Courts," *Howard Law Journal* 30, no. 27 (1987): 31.

16. *Ibid.*

17. American Association of Law Libraries, Standing Committee on Law Library Service to Institution Residents, Contemporary Social Problems Special Section, *Correctional Facility Law Libraries: An A to Z Resource Guide* (Laurel, Maryland: American Correctional Association, 1991), xi.

18. Jonathan Abel, "Ineffective Assistance of Library: The Failings and the Future of Prison Law Libraries," *Georgetown Law Journal* 101, no. 5 (2013, June): 1175.

19. *Ibid.*, 1193.

20. Marjorie LeDonne, "The Problem Explained, Ad-

dress Before the 'Prison Legal Libraries: Idea into Reality,'" in *Prison Legal Libraries, Idea into Reality* (Berkeley, CA, April 22, 1972); O. James Werner, "Law Libraries for Correctional Facilities," *Library Trends* 26, no. 1 (Summer 1997): 92.

21. Linda Martz, "Inmate Sues Over Access to Law Books," *Mansfield News*, September 6, 2011.

22. Werner, "Law Libraries for Correctional Facilities," 93.

23. Trammell, *Werner's Manual for Prison Law Libraries*, 3.

24. David Steinberger, "Lewis v. Casey: Tightening the Boundaries of Prisoner Access to the Courts?," *Pace Law Review* 18, no. 2 (1998): 378.

25. Mushlin, *Rights of Prisoners*, 3:150.

26. Gerken, "Does *Lewis v. Casey* Spell the End," 502.

27. Joseph A. Schouten, "Not So Meaningful Anymore: Why a Law Library is Required to Make a Prisoner's Access to the Courts Meaningful," *William and Mary Law Review* 45, no. 1195 (2004): 1227.

28. Karen Westwood, "'Meaningful Access to the Courts' and Law Libraries: Where Are We Now?," *Law Library Journal* 90, no. 2 (1998).

29. Trammell, *Werner's Manual for Prison Law Libraries*, 5.

30. David W. Wilhemus, "Where Have All the Law Libraries Gone?," *Corrections Today,* December 1999, 122.

31. Michael J. Sabath and William Payne, "Providing Inmate Access to the Courts: U.S. Prison Strategies for Complying with Constitutional Rights," *The Prison Journal* 92, no. 1 (2012).

32. Abel, "Ineffective Assistance of Library," 1212.

33. Mushlin, *Rights of Prisoners*, 3:567.

34. Trammell, *Werner's Manual for Prison Law Libraries*.

35. Mushlin, *Rights of Prisoners,* 3:597.

36. *Ibid.,* 662.

37. *Private Prison Information Act of 2007, and Review of the Prison Litigation Reform Act: a Decade of Reform or an Increase in Prison and Abuses?: Hearings on H.R. 1889, Before the Subcommittee on Crime, Terrorism, and Homeland Security of the Committee on the Judiciary, House of Representatives,* 107th Cong. 149 (2007).

38. *Ibid.,* 99.

39. The Minnesota State Law Library maintains a comprehensive bibliography on "Meaningful Access to the Courts" and Law Libraries available here: https://mn.gov/law-library-stat/prisbi.html. This resource includes articles and court decisions related to *Bounds* and *Lewis* and was extremely helpful in kick-starting the list compiled for this book.

40. This case was the basis for the book *Inspecting a Prison Law Library* written by Gene Teitelbaum detailing his inspection of this library for this specific case.

41. Abel, "Ineffective Assistance of Library," 1174.

42. Mushlin, *Rights of Prisoners,* 3:572.

43. *Ibid.,* 150.

## *Chapter 6*

1. Fred R. Hartz, Michael B. Krimmel, and Emilie K. Hartz, *Prison Librarianship: A Selective, Annotated, Classified Bibliography, 1945–1985* (Jefferson, NC: McFarland & Company, Inc., 1987), 1.

2. Harris C. McClaskey, "Training and Research in Correctional Librarianship," *Library Trends* 26, no. 1 (Summer 1977): 45.

3. "List of IFLA Standards," *International Federation of Library Associations and Institutions*, last modified May 2014, http://www.ifla.org/files/assets/standards-committee/documents/ifla-standards-version_6.pdf.

4. This average was calculated on the assumption that IFLA policies without edition numbers or versions had only been published once. It is possible that this number is higher if any of the published editions were actually subsequent editions.

5. Vibeke Lehmann and Joanne Locke, "Guidelines for Library Services to Prisoners," 3rd ed., in *IFLA Professional Reports*, no. 92 (The Hague: International Federation of Library Associations and Institutions, 2005). In general, the requirements in the ASCLA policy tend to be more specific: the ASCLA discusses the importance of the library within the organizational structure, defines who must be involved in the administration, includes more details about providing access for segregated prisoners, and defines exact staffing requirements. These staffing requirements from ASCLA are not realistic when reviewing actual practice in prisons; IFLA's standards are more in line with U.S. practice in this regard. IFLA's policy is more specific in terms of library materials collection with examples of what materials should be selected and what kinds of selection procedures should be used. An automated catalog is also recommended within those standards. The ASCLA policy includes more references to external policies such as ALA policies and results of a 1990 national prison library survey.

6. Hartz et al., 2–3.

7. David M. Gillespie, "A Citation-Entry Analysis of the Literature on Prison Libraries," *AHIL Quarterly* 8 (Spring 1968): 65–72.

8. Hartz et al., 3.

9. The Online Computer Library Center (OCLC) is a nonprofit company that develops systems for library usage. WorldCat is an online worldwide library catalog, which is one of the systems that OCLC develops and maintains.

10. "A Global Library Resource," *OCLC*, accessed January 2, 2015, http://www.oclc.org/worldcat/catalog.en.html.

11. Laura Manzari, "Library and Information Science Journal Prestige as Assessed by Library and Information Science Faculty," *Library Quarterly* 83, no. 1 (January 2013): 42–60.

12. RefWorks is an online bibliographic management system.

13. Robert Stearns, "The Prison Library: An Issue for Corrections, or a Correct Solution for its Issues?," *Behavioral and Social Sciences Librarian* 23, no. 1 (2004): 49–80; Amy Mark, "Libraries without Walls: An Internship at Oshkosh Correctional Institution Library," *Behavioral and Social Sciences Librarian* 23, no. 2 (2005): 97–112.

14. Hartz et al., 3.

15. *Ibid.*, 3; William J. Coyle, *Libraries in Prisons: A Blending of Institutions*, New Directions in Information Management, 15 (New York: Greenwood Press, 1987), 57.

16. Works authored by organizations were not included in the count of 57.

## Chapter 7

1. American Correctional Association, *Standards for Adult Correctional Institutions*, 2nd ed. (College Park, MD: American Correctional Association, 1981), 113.

2. "Library Services," *Department of Correctional Services State of Nebraska*, last modified March 15, 2011, http://www.corrections.state.ne.us/pdf/ar/rights/AR%20107.01.pdf (page discontinued), 2.

3. Sheila Clark and Erica MacCreaigh, *Library Services to the Incarcerated: Applying the Public Library Model in Correctional Facility Libraries* (Westport, CT: Libraries Unlimited, 2006), 13.

4. *Ibid.*, 14.

5. Glen Singer, "Prison Libraries Inside Out," *Education Libraries* 24, no. 1 (2000): 12.

6. Marjorie LeDonne, *Survey of Library and Information Problems in Correctional Institutions*, vol. 1, *Findings and Recommendations, ILR-73-008, Final Report*, special report prepared at the request of the Office of Education, Washington, D.C. (Berkeley: University of California, Berkeley Institute of Library Research, 1974), 70–71.

7. *Ibid.*, 65.

8. William J. Coyle, *Libraries in Prisons: A Blending of Institutions*, New Directions in Information Management 15 (New York: Greenwood Press, 1987), 2.

9. *Ibid.*, 86.

10. *Ibid.*, 81.

11. *Ibid.*, 73–74.

12. *Ibid.*, 80.

13. Brenda Vogel, *Prison Library Primer* (Lanham, MD: Scarecrow Press, 2009), 148.

14. *Ibid.*, 150–151.

15. Glennor Shirley, "Correctional Libraries, Library Standards, and Diversity," *JCE* 54, no. 2 (June 2003): 74.

16. Stephen Lilienthal, "Prison and Public," *Library Journal* 138, no. 2, February 1, 2013, 31.

17. Clark and MacCreaigh, *Library Services to the Incarcerated*, 7.

18. *Ibid.*, 51.

19. *Ibid.*, 70.

20. *Ibid.*, 181.

21. Association of Specialized and Cooperative Library Agencies, *Library Standards for Adult Correctional Institutions* (Chicago: American Library Association, 1992), 11.

22. "Strategic Plan 2014–2017," *Public Library Association*, last modified June 2014, http://www.ala.org/pla/sites/ala.org.pla/files/content/about/strategicplan/PLA_strategic_plan_approved_june_2014_withappB.pdf.

23. Association of Specialized and Cooperative Library Agencies, *Library Standards*, 10.

24. Kathleen de la Peña McCook, "Public Libraries and People in Jail," *Reference & User Services Quarterly* 44, no. 1 (2004): 27.

25. *Ibid.*, 28.

26. Vogel, *Prison Library Primer*, 148.

27. "Chapter 26, Public Library Outreach," last modified August 4, 2008, http://www.in.gov/library/files/Chapter_26_Rev08.pdf.

28. Barbara Huntington, "Early Initiative for Wisconsin Public Libraries," *Wisconsin Department of Public Instruction*, last modified 2005, http://pld.dpi.wi.gov/sites/default/files/imce/pld/pdf/earlylearning.pdf.

29. "Correctional Services," *New York Public Library*, accessed January 25, 2015, http://www.nypl.org/help/community-outreach/correctional-services.

30. The "Test Assessing Secondary Completion" workbooks are test-taking books published by McGraw Hill.

31. "What to Donate to Correctional Services," *New York Public Library*, accessed January 25, 2015, http://www.nypl.org/help/community-outreach/correctional-services/donate.

32. "Jail Libraries: BPL Jail, Prison and Transitional Services," *Brooklyn Public Library*, accessed January 25, 2015, http://www.bklynlibrary.org/outreach-services/jail-libraries.

33. "Institutional Services," *Buffalo and Erie County Public Library*, accessed January 25, 2015, http://www.buffalolib.org/content/institutional-services.

34. "Outreach Services," *Arapahoe Library District*, accessed January 25, 2015, http://old.arapahoelibraries.org/locations.cfm?lid=OS.

35. "Outreach Services," *Hennepin County Library*, accessed January 25, 2015, http://www.hclib.org/about/outreach. Librarian Daniel Marcou has given frequent presentations about the services offered between Hennepin County Library and Hennepin County Jail where he is employed, which are available on his website: http://www.danielmarcou.com/presentations.

36. "Community Outreach," Monroe County Public Library, accessed January 25, 2015, http://www.monroe.lib.in.us/outreach.

37. *Ibid.*

38. "Library Program," *Concord Prison Outreach*, accessed January 25, 2015, http://www.concordprisonoutreach.org/program-description-library-program/.

39. "Jail Services," *Multnomah County*, accessed January 25, 2015, https://multcolib.org/jail-services.

40. "Outreach Services," *Coastline Coos County Libraries*, accessed January 25, 2015, https://www.cooslibraries.org/content/outreach-services.

41. "Jail Tutoring and Literacy Services," *Alameda County Library*, accessed January 25, 2015, http://guides.aclibrary.org/content.php?pid=121671&sid=3341989.

42. "Annual Report 2012," *Lompoc Public Library System*, accessed January 25, 2015, http://www1.cityoflompoc.com/library/pdf/Annual_Report_2012.pdf.

43. "Innovative Programming: 'Books in Jails' in Western NC," *State Library of North Carolina*, last modified July 11, 2014, http://statelibrarync.org/ldblog/2014/07/11/innovative-programming-books-jails-western-nc/.

44. Margarita Rhoden and Molly Crumbley, "An Evaluation of Current Outreach Services at Calvert Library and Its Future Outlook," *Qualitative and Quantitative Methods in Libraries (QQML)* 4 (2013): 382, http://www.qqml.net/papers/December_2013_Issue/244QQML_Journal_2013_Rhoden_Crumbley_4_379_386.pdf.

45. *Ibid.*, 383.

46. Jennifer Burek Pierce, "Service Learning Sustains Hope," *American Libraries* 37, no. 10, November, 2006, 45.

47. "Arts on the Inside," *Library Journal* 138, no. 2, February 2013, 30–31.

48. Vogel, *Prison Library Primer*, 149.

49. "Prison Librarianship in a SLIS Context," *The University of Iowa, School of Library and Information Science*, accessed January 25, 2015, http://slis.grad.uiowa.edu/

news-and-events/2013–2–27/prison-librarianship-slis-context.

50. Farhan Nuruzzaman, "Durland Alternatives Library Promotes Social Justice," *Cornell Chronicle*, April 3, 2012, http://www.news.cornell.edu/stories/2012/04/alternatives-library-helps-promote-social-justice.

51. "Other Books to Prisoners Programs," *Prison Book Program*, accessed January 25, 2015, http://www.prisonbookprogram.org/resources/other-books-to-prisoners-programs/.

52. "University of Iowa Prison Projects Symposium," *Incarcerated in Iowa*, accessed May 9, 2015, http://www.incarceratediniowa.com/.

53. Renea Arnold and Nell Colburn, "From a Distance," *School Library Journal* 52, no. 9 (2006): 32.

54. Jennifer Burek Pierce, "Service Learning Sustains Hope," 45.

55. "Outreach Services," *Hennepin County Library*; Megan Cottrell, "Programs Help Incarcerated Parents Connect with Their Children through Books," *American Libraries*, December 8, 2014, https://americanlibraries-magazine.org/2014/12/08/reading-on-the-inside/.

56. "Correctional Services," *New York Public Library*.

57. "Little Children, Big Challenges: Incarceration," *Sesame Street*, accessed January 25, 2015, http://www.sesamestreet.org/parents/topicsandactivities/toolkits/incarceration.

58. Glennor Shirley, "Reflections on Family Literacy @ a Prison Library," last modified April 2, 2004, http://olos.ala.org/columns/?p=121.

59. Glennor Shirley, "Has Your Public Librarian Been to Prison?," in *Librarians as Community Partners*, ed. Carol Smallwood (Chicago: Americana Library Association, 2010), 69–71.

60. "Jail Libraries: BPL Jail, Prison and Transitional Services," *Brooklyn Public Library*.

61. Bill Zlatos, "Carnegie Library Teams with Allegheny County Jail Inmates for Unique Programs," *Trib Live*, May 31, 2014, http://triblive.com/news/allegheny/5702870–74/inmates-library-jail#axzz3PJZ5JxiF.

62. Lilienthal, "Prison and Public," 28–29.

63. "Outreach Services," *Hennepin County Library*.

64. "Pathways from Prison," *Library Journal* 140, no. 5, March 16, 2015, 48.

65. Zlatos, "Carnegie Library Teams with Allegheny County Jail."

66. Lilienthal, "Prison and Public," 30–31.

67. Joseph Bouchard and Linda Kunze, "Teaching Diverse Students in a Corrections Setting with Assistance from the Library," *JCE* 54, no. 2 (2003): 67.

68. Felicia A. Smith, "Freedom Readers in a Juvenile Correctional Facility," in *Librarians as Community Partners*, ed. Carol Smallwood (Chicago: American Library Association, 2010), 68.

69. Sheila Clark and Bobbie Patrick, "Choose Freedom Read: Book Talks Behind Bars," *American Libraries* 30, no. 7, August 1999, 63–64.

70. "Outreach Services," *Hennepin County Library*.

71. "Jail Services," *Multnomah County*.

72. "Correctional Services," *New York Public Library*.

73. Kenny Walter, "Library Program Offers Some a Second Chance," *Atlanticville*, January 6, 2011, http://atl.gmnews.com/news/2011–01–06/Front_Page/Library_program_offers_some_a_second_chance.html.

74. "Free to Learn: Denver Public Library Resources for People Who Have Served Time in Prison or Jail," *Denver Public Library*, accessed January 25, 2015, http://denverlibrary.org/free-to-learn.

75. Amy DelPo, Melanie Colletti, Eva Hallock, and Nicole Lewis, "Free to Learn: Best Practices for Serving Former Prisoners in Public Libraries," *Colorado Libraries* 36, no. 1 (2011), http://coloradolibrariesjournal.org/content/free-learn-best-practices-serving-former-prisoners-public-libraries (site discontinued).

76. Lilienthal, "Prison and Public," 29.

77. "Prisoner Re-entry—General," *Newark Public Library*, last modified November 17, 2014, http://nplwebguides.pbworks.com/w/page/5673574/Prisoner%20Re-entry%20-%20General.

78. "Institutional Services," *Buffalo and Erie County Public Library*.

## Chapter 8

1. "Directory of State Prison Libraries," *Washington Office of the Secretary of State*, last modified July 10, 2014, http://wiki.sos.wa.gov/ils/.

2. American Correctional Association, *2013 Directory Adult and Juvenile Correctional Departments, Institutions, Agencies, and Probation and Parole Authorities*, 74th ed. (Alexandria, VA: American Correctional Association, 2013), 28–29.

3. Marjorie LeDonne, *Survey of Library and Information Problems in Correctional Institutions*, vol. 1, *Findings and Recommendations*, ILR-73–008, Final Report, special report prepared at the request of the Office of Education, Washington, D.C. (Berkeley: University of California, Berkeley Institute of Library Research, 1974).

4. American Correctional Association, *2013 Directory*, 28–29.

5. American Correctional Association, *2013 Directory*, 48–53.

6. "Census Regions and Divisions of the United States," *U.S. Census Bureau*, accessed October 19, 2014, http://www.census.gov/geo/maps-data/maps/pdfs/reference/us_regdiv.pdf (page discontinued).

7. "Census Regions and Divisions of the United States," *U.S. Census Bureau*.

8. American Correctional Association, *2013 Directory*, 28–29; "Our Locations," *Federal Bureau of Prisons*, accessed October 1, 2014, http://www.bop.gov/locations/list.jsp.

9. American Correctional Association, *2013 Directory*, 48–49.

10. "Prisoners in 2013," *Bureau of Justice Statistics*, last modified December 31, 2013, http://www.bjs.gov/content/pub/pdf/p13.pdf, 13.

11. Association of Specialized and Cooperative Library Agencies, *Library Standards for Adult Correctional Institutions* (Chicago: American Library Association, 1992), 14.

12. Jacquelyn Smith, "The Best and Worst Master's Degrees for Jobs," *Forbes*, June 8, 2012, http://www.forbes.com/sites/jacquelynsmith/2012/06/08/the-best-and-worst-masters-degrees-for-jobs-2/.

13. Association of Specialized and Cooperative Library Agencies, *Library Standards*, 12.

14. Association of Specialized and Cooperative Library Agencies, *Library Standards*, 17; Vibeke Lehmann and Joanne Locke, "Guidelines for Library Services to Prisoners," 3rd ed., in *IFLA Professional Reports,* no. 92 (The Hague: International Federation of Library Associations and Institutions, 2005), 11.

15. Association of Specialized and Cooperative Library Agencies, *Library Standards*, 11.

16. Association of Specialized and Cooperative Library Agencies, *Library Standards,* 21.

17. Association of Specialized and Cooperative Library Agencies, *Library Standards,* 23.

18. Marjorie LeDonne, *Survey of Library and Information Problems in Correctional Institutions*, vol. 2, *Access to Legal Reference Materials in Correctional Institutions, ILR-73–009, Final Report,* special report prepared at the request of the Office of Education, Washington, D.C. (Berkeley: University of California, Berkeley Institute of Library Research, 1974).

19. Brenda Vogel, "Two Million on the Wrong Side of the Digital Divide," *Interface* 30, no. 1 (2008).

20. Suzanna Conrad, "Collection Development and Circulation Policies in Prison Libraries: An Exploratory Survey of Librarians in U.S. Correctional Institutions," *The Library Quarterly* 82, no. 4 (October 2012): 419.

21. "Policy on Confidentiality of Library Records," *American Library Association,* last modified July 2, 1986, http://www.ala.org/advocacy/intfreedom/statementspols/otherpolicies/policyconfidentiality.

22. "Fact Sheet: Trends in U.S. Corrections," *The Sentencing Project,* accessed December 31, 2015, http://sentencingproject.org/doc/publications/inc_Trends_in_Corrections_Fact_sheet.pdf.

23. "Time Served: The High Cost, Low Return of Longer Prison Terms," *The Pew Center on the States,* last modified June 6, 2012, http://www.pewtrusts.org/en/research-and-analysis/reports/2012/06/06/time-served-the-high-cost-low-return-of-longer-prison-terms, 2.

## *Chapter 9*

1. Steiner Kvale, *Interviews: An Introduction to Qualitative Research Interviewing* (Thousand Oaks, CA: Sage Publications, 1996).

2. Mario Luis Small, "'How Many Cases Do I Need?' On Science and the Logic of Case Selection in Field-Based Research," *Ethnography* 10, no. 1 (2006): 28.

3. Sarah Elsie Baker and Rosalind Edwards, "How Many Qualitative Interviews is Enough? Expert Voices and Early Career Reflections on Sampling and Cases in Qualitative Research" (discussion paper, ERSC National Centre for Research Methods, University of Southampton, 2012), 42.

4. Greg Guest, Arwen Bunce, and Laura Johnson, "How Many Interviews are Enough? An Experiment with Data Saturation and Variability," *Field Methods* 18, no. 1 (February 2006): 59–82.

5. "Online Courses and Webinars," *ASCLA,* accessed May 9, 2015, http://www.ala.org/ascla/asclaevents/online learning/onlinelearning.

6. "Successful Initiatives in Library Services for People who are Incarcerated," *ASCLA,* accessed May 9, 2015, http://www.ala.org/ascla/successful-initiatives.

7. "From Prisoners to Programmers—San Quentin Inmates Are Learning to Code," *CBS SF Bay Area,* November 13, 2014, http://sanfrancisco.cbslocal.com/2014/11/13/from-prisoners-to-programmers-san-quentin-inmates-are-learning-how-to-code-the-last-mile/; Kimberley Railey, "Some Prisons Let Inmates Connect with Tablets," *USA Today,* last modified August 18, 2013, http://www.usatoday.com/story/news/nation/2013/08/17/tabletsforinmates/2651727/.

## *Conclusion*

1. Larry E. Sullivan and Brenda Vogel, "Reachin' Behind Bars: Library Outreach to Prisoners 1798–2000," in *Libraries to the People: Histories of Outreach*, ed. Robert S. Freeman and David M. Hovde (Jefferson, NC: McFarland, 2003), 121.

2. Association of Specialized and Cooperative Library Agencies, *Library Standards for Adult Correctional Institutions* (Chicago: American Library Association, 1992), 35.

# References

ABA Standards for Criminal Justice. *Treatment of Prisoners*. 3rd ed. United States of America: American Bar Association, 2011.

Abel, Jonathan. "Ineffective Assistance of Library: The Failings and the Future of Prison Law Libraries." *Georgetown Law Journal* 101, no. 5 (June 2013): 1175–1215.

"Access to Courts/Law Library." *Oklahoma Department of Corrections*. Last modified October 12, 2012. http://www.ok.gov/doc/documents/op030115.pdf.

Altimari, Daniela. "Prison Book Policies under Review." *Hartford Courant,* August 28, 2013. http://articles.courant.com/2013–08-28/news/hc-prison-reading-0829–20130828_1_books-library-shelves-new-yorker.

*An Act to Deter and Punish Terrorist Acts in the United States and Around the World, to Enhance Law Enforcement Investigatory Tools, and for Other Purposes*, H.R. 3162, 107th Cong. (2001).

"Annual Report 2012." *Lompoc Public Library System*. Accessed January 25, 2015. http://www1.cityoflompoc.com/library/pdf/Annual_Report_2012.pdf.

American Association of Law Libraries. Standing Committee on Law Library Service to Institution Residents, Contemporary Social Problems Special Section. *Correctional Facility Law Libraries: An A to Z Resource Guide*. Laurel, Maryland: American Correctional Association, 1991.

American Correctional Association. *2013 Directory Adult and Juvenile Correctional Departments, Institutions, Agencies, and Probation and Parole Authorities*. 74th ed. Alexandria, VA: American Correctional Association, 2013.

American Correctional Association. *Standards for Adult Correctional Institutions*. 2nd ed. College Park, MD: American Correctional Association, 1981.

American Correctional Association. *Standards for Adult Correctional Institutions*. 4th ed. College Park, MD: American Correctional Association, 2003.

American Library Association. "Resolution on Guantanamo and the Rights of Prisoners to Read." *SRRT Newsletter* 11, January 2009.

"Arts on the Inside." *Library Journal* 138, no. 2, February 2013, 30–31.

Association of Specialized and Cooperative Library Agencies. *Library Standards for Adult Correctional Institutions*. Chicago: American Library Association, 1992.

Baker, Sarah Elsie, and Rosalind Edwards. "How Many Qualitative Interviews is Enough? Expert Voices and Early Career Reflections on Sampling and Cases in Qualitative Research." Discussion Paper, ESRC National Centre for Research Methods, University of Southampton, 2012.

Bayley, Linda, Leni Greenfield, and Flynn Nogueira. *Jail Library Service: a Guide for Librarians and Jail Administrators*. Chicago: American Library Association, 1981.

Bemis, Michael. "Prison Librarian—An Inside Job with Outsize Benefits: 'You Work Where?'" *Library Journal* 136, no. 17, October 15, 2011, 108.

Berman, Matt. "What You Can and Can't Read in Connecticut State Prisons." *National Journal,* August 30, 2013. http://www.nationaljournal.com/s/71586/what-you-can-cant-read-connecticut-state-prisons.

"Bill of Rights." *American Library Association*. Last modified January 23, 1996. http://www.ala.org/advocacy/intfreedom/librarybill.

Bosworth, Mary. *The U.S. Federal Prison System*. Thousand Oaks, CA: Sage Publications, 2002.

Bouchard, Joseph, and Linda Kunze. "Teaching Diverse Students in a Corrections Setting with Assistance from the Library." *JCE* 54, no. 2 (2003): 66–69.

Bowden, Teresa S. "A Snapshot of State Prison Libraries with a Focus on Technology." *Behavioral and Social Sciences Librarian* 21, no. 2 (December 2002): 1–12.

Bramley, Gerald. *Outreach: Library Services for the Institutionalized, the Elderly and the Physically Handicapped*. Hamden, CT: Linnet, 1978.

Branham, Lynn S. *The Law of Sentencing, Corrections, and Prisoners' Rights in a Nutshell*. 6th ed. St. Paul, MN: West Group, 2002.

Branstetter, Ben. "The Case for Internet Access in Prisons." *Intersect,* February 9, 2015. https://www.washingtonpost.com/news/the-intersect/wp/2015/02/09/the-case-for-internet-access-in-prisons/.

Brinkman, Gervase. "Correctional Libraries and LSCA Title IV-A." *American Libraries* 7, no. 4, April 1970, 380–383.

"California Code of Regulations: Title 15. Crime Prevention and Corrections." *State of California Department of Corrections and Rehabilitation*. Last modified January 2013. http://www.cdcr.ca.gov/Regulations/Adult_Operations/docs/Title15–2013.pdf (pdf discontinued).

Campbell, Diane K. "The Context of the Information Behavior of Prison Inmates." *Progressive Librarian* 26 (Winter 2005): 18.

"Census Regions and Divisions of the United States." *U.S. Census Bureau*. Accessed October 19, 2014. http://www.census.gov/geo/maps-data/maps/pdfs/reference/us_regdiv.pdf (page discontinued).

"Chapter 26, Public Library Outreach." Last modified August 4, 2008. http://www.in.gov/library/files/Chapter_26_Rev08.pdf.

Chepesiuk, Ron. "S.C. Scraps Innovative Prison Library System." *American Libraries* 26, no. 6, June 1995, 501–503.

Clark, Sheila, and Bobbie Patrick. "Choose Freedom Read: Book Talks Behind Bars." *American Libraries* 30, no. 7, August 1999, 63–64.

Clark, Sheila, and Erica MacCreaigh. *Library Services to the Incarcerated: Applying the Public Library Model in Correctional Facility Libraries*. Westport, CT: Libraries Unlimited, 2006.

"Code of Ethics of the American Library Association." *American Library Association*. Last modified January 22, 2008. http://www.ala.org/advocacy/proethics/codeofethics/codeethics.

"Community Outreach." *Monroe County Public Library*. Accessed January 25, 2015. http://www.monroe.lib.in.us/outreach.

"Comprehensive Library Services." *State of Ohio Department of Rehabilitation and Correction*. Last modified December 11, 2012. http://www.drc.ohio.gov/web/drc_policies/documents/58-LIB-01.pdf.

"Connecticut Department of Correction Annual Report 2007." *Connecticut Department of Correction*. Last modified July 1, 2007. http://www.ct.gov/doc/lib/doc/PDF/PDFReport/annualreport2007.pdf.

"Connecticut Department of Correction Annual Report 2008." *Connecticut Department of Correction*. Last modified July 1, 2008. http://www.ct.gov/doc/lib/doc/PDF/PDFReport/annualreport2008.pdf.

"Connecticut Department of Correction Annual Report 2009." *Connecticut Department of Correction*. Last modified July 1, 2009. http://www.ct.gov/doc/lib/doc/PDF/PDFReport/annualreport2009.pdf.

"Connecticut Department of Correction Annual Report 2010." *Connecticut Department of Correction*. Last modified July 1, 2010. http://www.ct.gov/doc/lib/doc/PDF/PDFReport/annualreport2010.pdf.

"Connecticut Department of Correction Annual Report 2011." *Connecticut Department of Correction*. Last modified July 1, 2011. http://www.ct.gov/doc/lib/doc/PDF/PDFReport/annualreport2011.pdf.

"Connecticut Department of Correction Annual Report 2012." *Connecticut Department of Correction*. Last modified July 1, 2012. http://www.ct.gov/doc/lib/doc/PDF/PDFReport/annualreport2012.pdf.

"Connecticut Department of Correction Annual Report 2013." *Connecticut Department of Correction*. Last modified July 1, 2013. http://www.ct.gov/doc/lib/doc/PDF/PDFReport/annualreport2013.pdf.

"Connecticut Department of Correction Annual Report 2014." *Connecticut Department of Correction*. Last modified July 1, 2014. http://www.ct.gov/doc/lib/doc/PDF/PDFReport/annualreport2014.pdf.

Conrad, Suzanna. "Collection Development and Circulation Policies in Prison Libraries: An Exploratory Survey of Librarians in US Correctional Institutions." *The Library Quarterly* 82, no. 4 (October 2012): 407–427.

"Correctional Services." *New York Public Library*. Accessed January 25, 2015. http://www.nypl.org/help/community-outreach/correctional-services.

Cottrell, Megan. "Programs Help Incarcerated Parents Connect with their Children through Books." *American Libraries*. Last modified December 8, 2014. https://americanlibrariesmagazine.org/2014/12/08/reading-on-the-inside/.

Coyle, William J. *Libraries in Prisons: A Blending of Institutions*, New Directions in Information Management 15. New York: Greenwood Press, 1987.

Cummins, Eric. *The Rise and Fall of California's Radical Prison Movement*. Stanford: Stanford University Press, 1994.

Dayan, Colin. "Words Behind Bars: Do Prisoners Have a Right to Read What They Want?" *Boston Review*, November 1, 2007. http://www.bostonreview.net/colin-dayan-words-behind-bars.

DelPo, Amy, Melanie Colletti, Eva Hallock and Nicole Lewis. "Free to Learn: Best Practices for Serving Former Prisoners in Public Libraries." *Colorado Libraries* 36, no. 1 (2011). http://coloradolibrariesjournal.org/content/free-learn-best-practices-serving-former-prisoners-public-libraries (page discontinued).

"The Development and Delivery of Education and Recreation Library Services." *Indiana Department of Correction*. Last modified May 1, 2008. http://www.in.gov/idoc/files/01–01-102_Library_Services_–5-01-08.pdf.

"Directory of State Prison Libraries." *Washington Office of the Secretary of State*. Last modified July 10, 2014. http://wiki.sos.wa.gov/ils/.

Doyle, Brenna. "Incarceration and the 'Freedom to Read': How Prison Libraries Function as Instruments of State Power." *Genders Journal* 58 (2013). http://www.genders.org/g58/g58_doyle.html (page discontinued).

Eaton-Robb, Pat. "Conn. Prison Inmates Have Choice of Violent Books." *Associated Press*, October 3, 2010. http://www.washingtonpost.com/wp-dyn/content/article/2010/10/03/AR2010100301715.html.

"Education Resource Center Services." *New Mexico Corrections Department*. Last modified May 31, 2012. http://corrections.state.nm.us/policies/docs/CD-120200.pdf.

"Education Services." *Florida Department of Corrections*. Last modified 2012. http://www.dc.state.fl.us/orginfo/education/index.html (page discontinued).

Engelbarts, Rudolf. *Books in Stir: A Bibliographic Essay about Prison Libraries and About Books Written by Prisoners and Prison Employees.* Metuchen, NJ: Scarecrow Press, 1972.

"Fact Sheet: Trends in U.S. Corrections." *The Sentencing Project.* Accessed December 31, 2015. http://sentencingproject.org/doc/publications/inc_Trends_in_Corrections_Fact_sheet.pdf.

"Fair Information Practice Principles." *Federal Trade Commission.* Last modified 2012. http://www.ftc.gov/reports/privacy3/fairinfo.shtm (page discontinued).

Flores, Arturo. A. "Bounds and Reality: Lawbooks Alone Do Not a Lawyer Make." *Law Library Journal* 77, no. 275 (1984–1985): 275–287.

Floyd, Janet. "Dislocations of the Self: Eliza Farnham at Sing Sing Prison." *Journal of American Studies* 40, no. 2 (August 2006): 311–325.

"Free to Learn: Denver Public Library Resources for People Who Have Served Time in Prison or Jail." *Denver Public Library.* Accessed January 25, 2015. http://denverlibrary.org/free-to-learn.

"From Prisoners to Programmers—San Quentin Inmates Are Learning to Code." *CBS SF Bay Area.* November 13, 2014. http://sanfrancisco.cbslocal.com/2014/11/13/from-prisoners-to-programmers-san-quentin-inmates-are-learning-how-to-code-the-last-mile/.

Gaes, Gerald G. "The Impact of Prison Education Programs on Post-Release Outcomes." Paper presented at the Reentry Roundtable on Education, John Jay College of Criminal Justice, New York City, March 31 and April 2008.

Gendreau, Leanne. "Lawmaker Wants Answers on Prison Library Policy." *NBC Connecticut,* July 22, 2010. http://www.nbcconnecticut.com/news/local/Lawmaker-Wants-Prison-Book-Policy-in-Light-of-Cheshire-Case-99007644.html.

Gerken, Joseph L. "Does *Lewis v. Casey* spell the end to court-ordered improvement of prison law libraries?" *Law Library Journal* 95, no. 4 (Fall 2003): 491–513.

Gillespie, David M. "A Citation-Entry Analysis of the Literature on Prison Libraries." *AHIL Quarterly* 8 (Spring 1968): 65–72.

Glaberson, William. "Prison Books Bring Plot Twist to Cheshire Killings." *New York Times,* July 10, 2010. http://www.nytimes.com/2010/07/22/nyregion/22cheshire.html.

"A Global Library Resource." *OCLC.* Accessed January 2, 2015. http://www.oclc.org/worldcat/catalog.en.html.

Goldberg, Beverly. "Ban Violent Books from Prison Libraries, Urges Connecticut State Senator." *American Libraries,* October 12, 2010. http://www.americanlibrariesmagazine.org/article/ban-violent-books-prison-libraries-urges-connecticut-state-senator.

Greenway, Sandra A. "Library Services Behind Bars." *Bookmobiles and Outreach Services* 10, no. 2 (2007): 43–63.

Guest, Greg, Arwen Bunce, and Laura Johnson. "How Many Interviews are Enough? An Experiment with Data Saturation and Variability." *Field Methods* 18, no. 1 (February 2006): 59–82.

Gulker, Virgil. *Books Behind Bars.* Metuchen, NJ: Scarecrow Press, 1973.

Harlow, Caroline Wolf. "Education and Correctional Populations." Special report prepared at the request of the Bureau of Justice Statistics, January 2003: 1–12.

Hartz, Fred R., Michael B. Krimmel, and Emilie K. Hartz. *Prison Librarianship: A Selective, Annotated, Classified Bibliography, 1945–1985.* Jefferson, NC: McFarland, 1987.

Hinckley, Steven D. "Bounds and Beyond: A Need to Reevaluate the Right of Prisoner Access to the Courts." *University of Richmond Law Review* 22, no. 19 (1987): 19–49.

Hirsch, Adam Jay. *The Rise of the Penitentiary: Prisons and Punishment in Early America.* New Haven: Yale University Press, 1992.

"History of Eastern State Penitentiary, Philadelphia." Accessed January 10, 2016. *Eastern State Penitentiary.* http://www.easternstate.org/sites/default/files/pdf/ESP-history6.pdf.

Huntington, Barbara. "Early Initiative for Wisconsin Public Libraries." *Wisconsin Department of Public Instruction.* Last modified 2005. http://pld.dpi.wi.gov/sites/default/files/imce/pld/pdf/earlylearning.pdf.

"Incarceration." *Sentencing Project.* Accessed March 3, 2014. http://www.sentencingproject.org/template/page.cfm?id=107.

"Inmate Access to Court and Counsel." *State of Ohio Department of Rehabilitation and Correction.* Last modified February 14, 2013. http://www.drc.ohio.gov/web/drc_policies/documents/59-LEG-01.pdf.

"Inmate Access to Courts." *State of Vermont Agency of Human Services Department of Corrections.* Last modified January 11, 1999. http://www.doc.state.vt.us/about/policies/rpd/correctional-services-301–550/385–389-programs-education-services/385.01%20Inmate%20Access%20To%20Courts%20Template.pdf.

"Inmate Access to Courts." *Wyoming Department of Corrections.* Last modified October 22, 2012. http://corrections.wy.gov/Media.aspx?mediaId=33.

"Inmate Communications." *State of Connecticut Department of Correction.* Last modified June 19, 2012. http://www.ct.gov/doc/LIB/doc/PDF/AD/ad1007.pdf.

"Inmate Education and Resource Center Services." *Arizona Department of Corrections.* Last modified March 14, 2006. http://www.azcorrections.gov/Policies/900/0910.pdf (page discontinued).

"Inmate Handbook." *Rhode Island Department of Corrections.* Last modified May 2007. http://www.doc.ri.gov/documents/Inmate%20Handbook%20507.pdf.

"Inmate Legal Access." *Nevada Department of Corrections.* Last modified June 17, 2012. http://www.doc.nv.gov/sites/doc/files/pdf/ar/AR722.pdf.

"Inmate Legal Access to the Courts." *Arizona Department of Corrections*. Last modified July 6, 2013. http://www.azcorrections.gov/policysearch/900/0902.pdf (page discontinued).

"Inmate Library Services." *State of Connecticut Department of Correction*. Last modified September 1, 2011. http://www.ct.gov/doc/LIB/doc/PDF/AD/ad1016.pdf.

"Inmate Programs." *Arkansas Department of Correction*. Last modified 2011. http://adc.arkansas.gov/inmates/Pages/InmatePrograms3.aspx.

"Inmate Rights." *Department of Correctional Services State of Nebraska*. Last modified October 31, 2011. http://www.corrections.state.ne.us/pdf/ar/rights/AR%20116.01.pdf (page discontinued).

"Innovative Programming: 'Books in Jails' in Western NC." *State Library of North Carolina*. Last modified July 11, 2014. http://statelibrarync.org/ldblog/2014/07/11/innovative-programming-books-jails-western-nc/.

"Institutional Library Services." *Michigan Department of Corrections*. Last modified November 1, 2010. https://www.michigan.gov/documents/corrections/05_03_110_337354_7.pdf.

"Institutional Library Services." *Rhode Island Department of Corrections*. Last modified August 11, 2008. http://www.doc.ri.gov/documents/rehabilitative/library%20english.pdf.

"Institutional Services." *Buffalo and Erie County Public Library*. Accessed January 25, 2015. http://www.buffalolib.org/content/institutional-services.

Jahnke, Elizabeth, and Laura Sherbo. "Prison Libraries Guard Intellectual Freedom." *Alki* 23, no. 3 (December 2007): 15–23.

"Jail Libraries: BPL Jail, Prison and Transitional Services." *Brooklyn Public Library*. Accessed January 25, 2015. http://www.bklynlibrary.org/outreach-services/jail-libraries.

"Jail Services." *Multnomah County*. Accessed January 25, 2015. https://multcolib.org/jail-services.

"Jail Tutoring and Literacy Services." *Alameda County Library*. Accessed January 25, 2015. http://guides.aclibrary.org/content.php?pid=121671&sid=3341989.

Jordet, Judith. "Part I: The Prison Library as Pro-Social Institution." *Corrections.com*, April 11, 2011. http://www.corrections.com/news/article/27732.

Jordet, Judith. "Part II: The Prison Library as Cultural Connection." *Corrections.com*, April 25, 2011. http://www.corrections.com/news/article/28421-part-ii-the-prison-library-as-cultural-connection.

Jordet, Judith. "Part III: The Prison Library: Promoting Reading & Pro-Social Connection." *Corrections.com*, May 2, 2011. http://www.corrections.com/news/article/28433-part-iii-the-prison-library-promoting-reading-pro-social-connection.

Kvale, Steinar. *Interviews: An Introduction to Qualitative Research Interviewing*. Thousand Oaks, CA: Sage Publications, 1996.

"Law Libraries." *Michigan Department of Corrections*. Last modified November 1, 2010. http://www.michigan.gov/documents/corrections/0503115_409693_7.pdf.

"Law Library Operations." *The City of New York Department of Correction*. Last modified May 19, 1986. http://www.nyc.gov/html/doc/downloads/pdf/3501.pdf.

"Law Library Supervisors." *Alabama Department of Corrections*. Last modified June 29, 2004. http://www.doc.state.al.us/docs/AdminRegs/AR214.pdf.

"Legal Action." *Prison Legal News*. Accessed December 30, 2015. https://www.prisonlegalnews.org/legal-action-map/.

"Legal Affairs (Inmate)." *Oregon Department of Corrections*. Last modified 2012. http://arcweb.sos.state.or.us/pages/rules/oars_200/oar_291/291_139.html.

LeDonne, Marjorie. "The Problem Explained, Address Before the 'Prison Legal Libraries: Idea into Reality.'" In *Prison Legal Libraries, Idea into Reality*, 15–21. Berkeley, CA, April 22, 1972.

LeDonne, Marjorie. *Survey of Library and Information Problems in Correctional Institutions*. Vol. 1, *Findings and Recommendations, ILR-73–008, Final Report*. Special report prepared at the request of the Office of Education, Washington, D.C. Berkeley: University of California, Berkeley Institute of Library Research, 1974.

LeDonne, Marjorie. *Survey of Library and Information Problems in Correctional Institutions*. Vol. 2, *Access to Legal Reference Materials in Correctional Institutions, ILR-73–009, Final Report*. Special report prepared at the request of the Office of Education, Washington, D.C. Berkeley: University of California, Berkeley Institute of Library Research, 1974.

Lehmann, Vibeke. "Challenges and Accomplishments in U.S. Prison Libraries." *Library Trends* 59, no. 3 (2011): 490–508.

———. "Introduction." *Library Trends* 59, no. 3 (2011): 383–385.

———. "The Prison Library: A Vital Link to Education, Rehabilitation, and Recreation." *Education Libraries* 24, no. 1 (2000): 5–10.

Lehmann, Vibeke. and Joanne Locke. "Guidelines for Library Services to Prisoners." 3rd ed. In *IFLA Professional Reports*, no. 92. The Hague: International Federation of Library Associations and Institutions, 2005.

"Library." *Minnesota Department of Corrections*. Last modified July 6, 2010. http://www.doc.state.mn.us/DOcpolicy2/html/DPW_Display.asp?Opt=204.045.htm.

"Library and Law Library." *State of California Department of Corrections and Rehabilitation*. Last modified April 8, 2010. http://www.cdcr.ca.gov/regulations/adult_operations/docs/DOM/NCDOM/2010NCDOM/10-06/DOM%20Text%20Chp10%20Art12%20clean.pdf (page discontinued).

"Library Facilities, Holdings, and Services." *Kansas Department of Corrections*. Last modified January 7, 2011. http://www.doc.ks.gov/kdoc-policies/AdultIMPP/chapter-10/10107.pdf.

"Library Personnel and Development." *State of Ohio*

*Department of Rehabilitation and Correction.* Last modified October 26, 2011. http://www.drc.ohio.gov/web/drc_policies/documents/58-LIB-02.pdf.

"Library Program." *Concord Prison Outreach.* Accessed January 25, 2015. http://www.concordprisonoutreach.org/program-description-library-program/.

"Library Service." *Department of Public Safety Corrections Administration Policy and Procedures.* Last modified February 23, 2010. http://dps.hawaii.gov/wp-content/uploads/2012/10/COR.14.16.pdf.

"Library Services." *Colorado Department of Corrections.* Last modified November 1, 2011. http://www.doc.state.co.us/sites/default/files/ar/0500_02_110111_0.pdf.

"Library Services." *Department of Correctional Services State of Nebraska.* Last modified March 15, 2011. http://www.corrections.state.ne.us/pdf/ar/rights/AR%20107.01.pdf (page discontinued).

"Library Services." *Nevada Department of Corrections.* Last modified April 8, 2011. http://www.doc.nv.gov/sites/doc/files/pdf/AR840.pdf.

"Library Services." *State of Montana Department of Corrections.* Last modified April 20, 2011. http://www.cor.mt.gov/content/Resources/Policy/Chapter5/5-3-2.pdf (page discontinued).

"Library Services." *State of North Carolina Department of Correction Division of Prisons.* Last modified September 24, 2007. http://www.doc.state.nc.us/dop/policy_procedure_manual/D1100.pdf.

"Library Services." *State of Washington Department of Corrections.* Last modified April 23, 2012. http://www.doc.wa.gov/policies/showFile.aspx?name=510010.

"Library Services." *Wyoming Department of Corrections.* Last modified May 15, 2013. http://corrections.wy.gov/Media.aspx?mediaId=396.

"Library Services: General Library." *State of Alaska Department of Corrections Policies and Procedures.* Last modified 2002. http://www.correct.state.ak.us/pnp/pdf/814.01.pdf.

"Library Services (Inmate)." *Oregon Department of Corrections.* Last modified 2012. http://arcweb.sos.state.or.us/pages/rules/oars_200/oar_291/291_141.html.

"Library Services: Law Library." *State of Alaska Department of Corrections Policies and Procedures.* Last modified May 16, 2013. http://www.correct.state.ak.us/pnp/pdf/814.02.pdf.

Lilienthal, Stephen. "Prison and Public." *Library Journal* 138, no. 2, February 1, 2013, 27–32.

"List of IFLA Standards." *International Federation of Library Associations and Institutions.* Last modified May 2014. http://www.ifla.org/files/assets/standards-committee/documents/ifla-standards-version_6.pdf.

Litchfield, Kathrina. "A Critical Impasse: Literacy Practice in American Prisons and the Future of Transformative Reading." Master's thesis, University of Iowa, 2014. http://ir.uiowa.edu/cgi/viewcontent.cgi?article=5194&context=etd.

"Little Children, Big Challenges: Incarceration." *Sesame Street.* Accessed January 25, 2015. http://www.sesamestreet.org/parents/topicsandactivities/toolkits/incarceration.

Lucas, Linda. "Educating Prison Librarians." *Journal of Education for Library and Information Science* 30, no. 3 (Winter 1990): 218–225.

Manzari, Laura. "Library and Information Science Journal Prestige as Assessed by Library and Information Science Faculty." *Library Quarterly* 83, no. 1 (January 2013): 42–60.

Mark, Amy. "Libraries without Walls: An Internship at Oshkosh Correctional Institution Library." *Behavioral and Social Sciences Librarian* 23, no. 2 (2005): 97–112.

Martz, Linda. "Inmate Sues over Access to Law Books." *Mansfield News,* September 6, 2011.

McClaskey, Harris C. "Training and Research in Correctional Librarianship." *Library Trends* 26, no. 1 (Summer 1977): 39–52.

McCook, Kathleen de la Peña. "Public Libraries and People in Jail." *Reference and User Services Quarterly* 44, no. 1 (2004): 26–30.

McDonald, Susan, ed. "Acquisitions for Prison Libraries." *Library Acquisitions: Practice & Theory* 7, no. 1 (1983): 29–33.

McFarland, Sheena. "Inmates See Prison Libraries as Tools to Making a Better Life." *Salt Lake Tribute,* May 11, 2010.

Morris, Norval, and David J., Rothman, eds. *The Oxford History of the Prison: The Practice of Punishment in Western Society.* New York: Oxford University Press, 1995.

Mushlin, Michael B. *Rights of Prisoners,* 4th ed. [United States?]: Thomson/West, 2009.

New York Prison Association. *Catalogue and Rules for Prison Libraries to aid in the Suitable Selection and Economical Maintenance of Reading Matter in the Prisons and Jails.* Albany: The Argus Company, 1877.

Nuruzzaman, Farhan. "Durland Alternatives Library Promotes Social Justice." *Cornell Chronicle,* April 3, 2012. http://www.news.cornell.edu/stories/2012/04/alternatives-library-helps-promote-social-justice.

"Offender Access to the Courts." *Indiana Department of Correction.* Last modified November 15, 2004. http://www.in.gov/idoc/dys/files/00–01-102_AP_11-15-04.pdf.

"Offender Legal Access." *Virginia Department of Corrections.* Last modified March 1, 2012. http://vadoc.virginia.gov/about/procedures/documents/800/866–3.pdf.

"Offender Legal Services." *Colorado Department of Corrections.* Last modified February 1, 2013. http://www.doc.state.co.us/sites/default/files/ar/0750_01_020113.pdf.

"Offender Libraries." *Oklahoma Department of Corrections.* Last modified June 7, 2012. http://www.ok.gov/doc/documents/op030115.pdf.

"103 CMR 478.00: Library Services." *Massachusetts Department of Correction.* Accessed September 27, 2013. http://www.lawlib.state.ma.us/source/mass/cmr/cmrtext/103CMR478.pdf (page discontinued).

"Online Courses and Webinars." *ASCLA*. Accessed May 9, 2015. http://www.ala.org/ascla/asclaevents/onlinelearning/onlinelearning.

"Other Books to Prisoners Programs." *Prison Book Program*. Accessed January 25, 2015. http://www.prisonbookprogram.org/resources/other-books-to-prisoners-programs/.

"Our Locations." *Federal Bureau of Prisons*. Accessed October 1, 2014. http://www.bop.gov/locations/list.jsp.

"Outreach Services." *Arapahoe Library District*. Accessed January 25, 2015. http://old.arapahoelibraries.org/locations.cfm?lid=OS.

"Outreach Services." *Coastline Coos County Libraries*. Accessed January 25, 2015. https://www.cooslibraries.org/content/outreach-services.

"Outreach Services." *Hennepin County Library*. Accessed January 25, 2015. http://www.hclib.org/about/outreach.

Palmer, John W. *Constitutional Rights of Prisoners*. 8th ed. Newark, NJ: LexisNexis, 2006.

"Pathways from Prison." *Library Journal* 140, no. 5, March 16, 2015, 48.

Payne, William, and Michael J. Sabath. "Trends in the Use of Information Management Technology in Prison Libraries." *Behavioral and Social Sciences Librarian* 26, no. 2 (2007): 1–10.

Pierce, Jennifer Burek. "Service Learning Sustains Hope." *American Libraries* 37, no. 10, November 2006, 45.

"Policy Concerning Confidentiality of Personally Identifiable Information about Library Users." *American Library Association*. Last modified June 30, 2004. http://www.ifmanual.org/piipolicy.

"Policy on Confidentiality of Library Records." *American Library Association*. Last modified July 2, 1986. http://www.ala.org/advocacy/intfreedom/statementspols/otherpolicies/policyconfidentiality.

"Prison Librarianship in a SLIS Context." *The University of Iowa, School of Library and Information Science*. Accessed January 25, 2015. http://slis.grad.uiowa.edu/news-and-events/2013-2-27/prison-librarianship-slis-context.

"The Prison Litigation Reform Act: Know Your Rights." *American Civil Liberties Union*. Last modified August 1, 2011. https://www.aclu.org/prisoners-rights/know-your-rights-prison-litigation-reform-act.

"Prisoner Re-entry—General." *Newark Public Library*. Last modified November 17, 2014. http://nplwebguides.pbworks.com/w/page/5673574/Prisoner%20Re-entry%20-%20General.

"Prisoners in 2013." *Bureau of Justice Statistics*. Last modified December 31, 2013. http://www.bjs.gov/content/pub/pdf/p13.pdf.

"Prisoners' Right to Read." *American Library Association*. Last modified July 1, 2014. http://www.ala.org/advocacy/prisoners-right-read.

"Privacy: An Interpretation of the Library Bill of Rights." *American Library Association*. Last modified June 19, 2002. http://www.ala.org/advocacy/intfreedom/librarybill/interpretations/privacy.

*Private Prison Information Act of 2007, and review of the Prison Litigation Reform Act: a decade of reform or an increase in prison and abuses?: Hearings on H.R. 1889, Before the Subcommittee on Crime, Terrorism, and Homeland Security of the Committee on the Judiciary, House of Representatives*, 107th Cong. 149 (2007).

Railey, Kimberley. "Some Prisons Let Inmates Connect with Tablets." *USA Today*. Last modified August 18, 2013. http://www.usatoday.com/story/news/nation/2013/08/17/tabletsforinmates/2651727/.

Raphael, Steven, and Michael Stoll. *Do Prisons Make Us Safer?* New York: Russell Sage Foundation, 2009.

Raphael, Steven, and Michael Stoll. *Why Are So Many Americans in Prison?* New York: Russell Sage Foundation, 2013.

"Raunchy 'Prison Classics' Pulled from Prison Libraries." *American Libraries* 26, no. 2, February 1995, 126–127.

Renea, Arnold and Nell Colburn. "From a Distance." *School Library Journal* 52, no. 9 (2006): 32.

"Resolution on the Retention of Library Usage Records." *American Library Association*. Last modified June 28, 2006. http://www.ifmanual.org/resolutionretention.

"Resolution on the USA Patriot Act and Libraries." *American Library Association*. Last modified June 29, 2005. http://www.ala.org/offices/sites/ala.org.offices/files/content/wo/reference/colresolutions/PDFs/062905-CD20.6.pdf.

Rhoden, Margarita and Molly Crumbley. "An Evaluation of Current Outreach Services at Calvert Library and its Future Outlook." *Qualitative and Quantitative Methods in Libraries (QQML)* 4 (2013): 379–386. http://www.qqml.net/papers/December_2013_Issue/244QQML_Journal_2013_Rhoden_Crumbley_4_379_386.pdf.

Roth, William Mark. "Turner v. Safley: The Supreme Court Further Confuses Prisoners' Constitutional Rights." *Loyola of Los Angeles Law Review* 22, no. 2 (January 1989): 667–716. Accessed January 6, 2014. http://digitalcommons.lmu.edu/llr/vol22/iss2/6.

Rubin, Rhea Joyce. "U.S. Prison Library Services and their Theoretical Base." Occasional Paper no. 110, Graduate School of Library and Information Science, University of Illinois, 1973.

Rubin, Rhea Joyce, and Daniel Suvak, eds. *Libraries Inside: A Practical Guide for Prison Libraries*. Jefferson, NC: McFarland & Co., 1995.

Ryan, Wayne. "Access to the Courts: Prisoners' Right to a Law Library." *Howard Law Journal* 26, no. 91 (1983): 91–117.

Sabath, Michael J., and William Payne. "Providing Inmate Access to the Courts: U.S. Prison Strategies for Complying with Constitutional Rights." *The Prison Journal* 92, no. 1 (2012): 45–62.

Sanders, Rabun. C., Jr., Hazel B. Kerper, George G. Killinger, and John C. Watkins. *Prisoners' First Amendment Rights within the Institution*. In *Criminal Justice Monograph* 3 no. 3. Huntsville, TX: Institute of Contemporary Corrections and the Behavioral Sciences, Sam Houston State University, 1971.

Scafuri, Jenna. "Best in Business: Prison Libraries Make a Difference in Colorado." *Corrections Today,* June/July 2012: 30.

Schexnaydre, Linda, and Kaylyn Robbins. *Workshops for Jail Library Service: a Planning Manual.* Chicago: American Library Association, 1981.

Schneider, Julia, and Ron Chepesiuk. "Prison Libraries Change Lives." *American Libraries,* 27, no. 10, November 1996, 46–48.

Schouten, Joseph A. "Not So Meaningful Anymore: Why a Law Library is Required to Make a Prisoner's Access to the Courts Meaningful." *William and Mary Law Review* 45, no. 1195 (2004): 1195–1227.

"Section 430.20 Library Services and Legal Materials." *Joint Committee on Administrative Rules.* Last modified 1984. http://ilga.gov/commission/jcar/admin code/020/020004300000200R.html.

"Selection and Acquisition of Library Materials." *State of Ohio Department of Rehabilitation and Correction.* Last modified October 26, 2011. http://www.drc.ohio. gov/web/drc_policies/documents/58-LIB-03.pdf.

Shirley, Glennor. "Correctional Libraries, Library Standards, and Diversity." *JCE* 54, no. 2 (June 2003): 70–74.

_____. "Has Your Public Librarian Been to Prison?" In *Librarians as Community Partners,* edited by Carol Smallwood, 69–71. Chicago: American Library Association, 2010.

_____. "Reflections on Family Literacy @ a Prison Library." Last modified April 2, 2004. http://olos.ala. org/columns/?p=121.

Singer, Glen. "Prison Libraries Inside Out." *Education Libraries* 24, no. 1 (2000): 11–16.

Skolnick, Katherine, ed. *A Jailhouse Lawyer's Manual.* 8th ed. New York: Columbia Human Rights Law Review, 2009.

Small, Mario Luis. "'How Many Cases Do I Need?' On Science and the Logic of Case Selection in Field-Based Research." *Ethnography* 10, no. 1 (2006): 5–38.

Smith, Christopher E. "Examining the Boundaries of Bounds: Prison Law Libraries and Access to the Courts." *Howard Law Journal* 30, no. 27 (1987): 27–44.

Smith, Felicia A. "Freedom Readers in a Juvenile Correctional Facility." In *Librarians as Community Partners,* edited by Carol Smallwood, 65–68. Chicago: American Library Association, 2010.

Smith, Jacquelyn. "The Best and Worst Master's Degrees for Jobs." *Forbes.* June 8, 2012. http://www. forbes.com/sites/jacquelynsmith/2012/06/08/the-best-and-worst-masters-degrees-for-jobs-2/.

Spector, Herman, K. *The Library Program of the State Department of Correction.* Sacramento: Department of Correction, 1959.

Stearns, Robert. "The Prison Library: An Issue for Corrections, or a Correct Solution for Its Issues?" *Behavioral and Social Sciences Librarian* 23, no. 1 (2004): 49–80.

Steinberg, Avi. *Running the Books: The Adventures of an Accidental Prison Librarian.* New York: Anchor Books, 2010.

Steinberger, David. "Lewis v. Casey: Tightening the Boundaries of Prisoner Access to the Courts?" *Pace Law Review* 18, no. 2 (1998): 377–417.

"Strategic Plan 2014–2017." *Public Library Association.* Last modified June 2014. http://www.ala.org/pla/ sites/ala.org.pla/files/content/about/strategicplan/ PLA_strategic_plan_approved_june_2014_ withappB.pdf.

"Successful Initiatives in Library Services for People who are Incarcerated." *ASCLA.* Accessed May 9, 2015. http://www.ala.org/ascla/successful-initiatives.

Sullivan, Larry E. "Between Empty Covers: Prison Libraries in Historical Perspective." *Wilson Library Bulletin* 64, October 1989: 26–28.

_____. "The Least of Our Brethern: Library Service to Prisoners." *American Libraries* 31, no. 5, May 2000, 56–58.

_____. "Prison Is Dull Today: Prison Libraries and the Ironies of Pious Reading." *PMLA: Publications of the Modern Language Association of America* 123, no. 3 (2008): 702–706.

_____. "Reading in American Prisons: Structures and Strictures." *Libraries and Culture* 33, no. 1 (1998): 113–119.

Sullivan, Larry E., and Brenda Vogel. "Reachin' Behind Bars: Library Outreach to Prisoners 1798–2000." In *Libraries to the People: Histories of Outreach,* edited by Robert S. Freeman and David M. Hovde, 113–127. Jefferson, NC: McFarland, 2003.

Suvak, Daniel. "'Throw the Book at 'Em': The Change-Based Model for Prison Libraries," *Wilson Library Bulletin* 64, October 1989, 31–33.

Sweeney, Megan. "Living to Read True Crime: Theorizations from Prison." Pts. 1 and 2. *Discourse 25,* no. 1 (Winter 2003); 25 no. 2 (Spring 2003): 55–80.

_____. *Reading Is My Window: Books and the Art of Reading in Women's Prisons.* Chapel Hill: University of North Carolina Press, 2010.

"Time Served: The High Cost, Low Return of Longer Prison Terms." *The Pew Center on the States.* Last modified June 2012. http://www.pewtrusts.org/en/ research-and-analysis/reports/2012/06/06/time-served-the-high-cost-low-return-of-longer-prison-terms.

"Title 18—Correctional Institutions and Department of Correction." *Department of Correction.* Last modified March 7, 2015. https://eregulations.ct.gov/ eRegsPortal/Browse/RCSA/%7B4EED71A5–398E-4A4F-A487-ABECF98318C4%7D.

Trammell, Rebecca S. *Werner's Manual for Prison Law Libraries.* 3rd ed. Buffalo, NY: William S. Hein & Co., Inc., 2004.

"The Universal Declaration of Human Rights." *United Nations.* Last modified 1948. http://www.un.org/ en/documents/udhr/index.shtml.

"University of Iowa Prison Projects Symposium." Incarcerated in Iowa. Accessed May 9, 2015. http:// www.incarcerediniowa.com/.

US Department of Justice. *Federal Standards for Prisons and Jails*. US Department of Justice, 1980.

Vogel, Brenda. "Bailing Out Prison Libraries." *Library Journal* 122, no. 19, November 15, 1997, 35–37.

———. "In Preparation for a Visit to a Smaller Planet." *Wilson Library Bulletin* 64, October 1989, 34–36.

———. "Inmate Informational Needs Survey: Final Report." Special report prepared at the request of the Maryland Department of Public Safety. February 1976, 4. https://www.ncjrs.gov/pdffiles1/Digitization/74789NCJRS.pdf.

———. *Prison Library Primer*. Lanham, MD: Scarecrow Press, 2009.

———. "Two Million on the Wrong Side of the Digital Divide." *Interface* 30, no. 1 (2008). http://www.ala.org/ascla/archives/contentlistingby/volume30/digdivide.

Walter, Kenny. "Library Program Offers Some a Second Chance." *Atlanticville,* January 6, 2011. http://atl.gmnews.com/news/2011-01-06/Front_Page/Library_program_offers_some_a_second_chance.html.

Werner, O. James. "Law Libraries for Correctional Facilities." *Library Trends* 26, no. 1 (Summer 1997): 71–96.

Westwood, Karen. "'Meaningful Access to the Courts' and Law Libraries: Where Are We Now?" *Law Library Journal* 90, no. 2 (1998): 193–207.

"What to Donate to Correctional Services." *New York Public Library*. Accessed January 25, 2015. http://www.nypl.org/help/community-outreach/correctional-services/donate.

Wilhelmus. David W. "A New Emphasis for Correctional Facilities' Libraries." *The Journal of Academic Librarianship* 25, no. 2 (1999): 114–120.

Wilhemus, David W. "Where Have All the Law Libraries Gone?" *Corrections Today*, December 1999, 122–153.

Winterfield, Laura, Mark Coggeshall, Michelle Burke-Storer, Vanessa Correa, and Simon Tidd. "The Effects of Postsecondary Correctional Education: Final Report." Washington, D.C.: Urban Institution, Justice Policy Center, 2009, 1–42.

Zlatos, Bill. "Carnegie Library Teams with Allegheny County Jail Inmates for Unique Programs." *Trib Live,* May 31, 2014. http://triblive.com/news/allegheny/5702870-74/inmates-library-jail#axzz3PJZ5JxiF.

# Index